Sexualised Crimes, Armed Conflict and the Law

From ancient to modern times, sexualised war violence against women was tolerated if not encouraged as a means of reward, propaganda, humiliation and terror. This was and is in defiance of international laws that have criminalised acts of sexualised war violence since the 18th century. *Ad hoc* international tribunals have addressed especially war rape since the 15th century. The International Criminal Court (ICC), however, is the first independent, permanent, international criminal court that recognises not only war rape but also sexual slavery and other sexualised crimes as crimes against humanity, war crimes and acts of genocide in its statute and supporting documents.

This book explores how the ICC definitions of rape and forced marriage came about, and addresses the ongoing challenge of how to define war rape and forced marriage in times of armed conflict in a way that adequately reflects women's experiences, as well as the nature of the crimes. In addition to deepening the understanding of the ICC negotiations of war rape and forced marriage, and of the crimes themselves, this volume highlights relevant factors that need to be considered when criminalising acts of sexualised war violence under international law.

Sexualised Crimes, Armed Conflict and the Law draws on feminist and constructivist theories and offers a comprehensive theoretical and empirical examination of the definition of rape and forced marriage. It presents the latest state of knowledge on the topic and will be of interest to researchers, academics, policymakers, officials and intergovernmental organisations, and students in the fields of post-conflict law and justice, international law, human rights law, international relations, gender studies, politics, and criminology.

Hannah Baumeister is a Lecturer in Law at Middlesex University Mauritius.

Post-Conflict Law and Justice
Series Editors: James A. Sweeney
Lancaster University, and Matthew Saul, University of Oslo

International law has great relevance in post-conflict contexts, but the complexity of its role, both as a supporting and restraining factor, can be underestimated. This series explores the role of law, and in particular international law, in securing 'justice' in post-conflict contexts. The remit of the series extends to matters of law connected to, for example: post-conflict legal reforms and the development of constitutions; the establishment of the rule of law; the place of international organisations in post-conflict; peace-keeping; transitional justice mechanisms (including criminal justice); and discussion of jus post bellum. It also seeks self-reflexive works on notions of post-conflict justice, transitional justice, and similar.

Available titles in this series include

Sexualised Crimes, Armed Conflict and the Law
The International Criminal Court and the Definitions of Rape and Forced Marriage
Hannah Baumeister

International Law and Post-Conflict Reconstruction Policy
Matthew Saul and James A. Sweeney

Silenced Victims of Wartime Sexual Violence
Olivera Simic

Sexualised Crimes, Armed Conflict and the Law

The International Criminal Court and the Definitions of Rape and Forced Marriage

Hannah Baumeister

Routledge
Taylor & Francis Group
LONDON AND NEW YORK

First published 2018 by Routledge
2 Park Square, Milton Park, Abingdon, Oxon OX14 4RN
605 Third Avenue, New York, NY 10017

First issued in paperback 2021

Routledge is an imprint of the Taylor & Francis Group, an informa business

British Library Cataloguing-in-Publication Data
A catalogue record for this book is available from the British Library

Library of Congress Cataloging-in-Publication Data
Names: Baumeister, Hannah, author.
Title: Sexualized crimes, armed conflict and the law : the International Criminal Court and the definitions of rape and forced marriage / by Hannah Baumeister.
Description: Abingdon, Oxon ; New York, NY : Routledge, 2018. | Series: Post conflict law and justice
Identifiers: LCCN 2018002276 | ISBN 9781138085121 (hbk) | ISBN 9781315111490 (ebk)
Subjects: LCSH: Rape as a weapon of war. | Forced marriage. | International criminal law. | International Criminal Court.
Classification: LCC KZ7162 .B38 2018 | DDC 345/.02532—dc23
LC record available at https://lccn.loc.gov/2018002276

ISBN 13: 978-0-367-90026-7 (pbk)
ISBN 13: 978-1-138-08512-1 (hbk)

Typeset in Galliard
by Apex CoVantage, LLC

Contents

Acknowledgments

Thank you very much:

Aberystwyth University, Christine Chinkin, Chris Harding, the interviewees, Bianca Maier, Anèl Marais, Middlesex University, Ryszard Piotrowicz, Marcel van der Stroom and Janna Wolff.

Table of cases

International Criminal Tribunal for Rwanda

International Military Tribunal

International Military Tribunal for the Far East

Special Court for Sierra Leone

United States Military Commission

Table of conventions and statutes

Table of United Nations documents

Commission on Human Rights

General Assembly

Preparatory Committee on the Establishment of an International Criminal Court

Preparatory Commission for the International Criminal Court

Preparatory Commission for the International Criminal Court

UN Doc PCINCC/1999/DP.4/Add.2 <http://www.legal-tools.org/doc/d6dfdc/> accessed 10 August 2017 .... 133n87

PrepCom2 'Report of the Preparatory Commission for the International Criminal Court, Addendum: Part II, Finalized draft text of the Elements of Crimes' (02 November 2000) PCNICC/2000/1/Add.2 <http://www.legal-tools.org/doc/843931/> accessed 10 August 2017 .... 144n153

PrepCom2 'Report of the Working Group on Elements of Crimes: Crimes against Humanity (Article 7): Addendum' UN Doc PCNICC/2000/WGEC/L.1/Add.1 <http://www.legal-tools.org/doc/2be303/> accessed 10 August 2017 .... 142n144

PrepCom2 'Request from the Governments of Belgium, Costa Rica, Finland, Hungary, the Republic of Korea and South Africa and the Permanent Observer Mission of Switzerland Regarding the Text Prepared by the International Committee of the Red Cross on Article 8, Paragraph 2 (b), (c) and (e) of the Rome Statute of the International Criminal Court' (17 July 1999) UN Doc PCNICC/1999/WGEC/INF.2 <http://www.legal-tools.org/doc/d8ff04/> accessed 10 August 2017 .... 136n107

Security Council

UNSC Resolution 827 (25 May 1993) UN Doc S/RES/827 <http://www.legal-tools.org/doc/dc079b/> accessed 18 August 2017...4n8, 59n44

UNSC Resolution 955 (08 November 1994) UN Doc S/RES/955 <http://www.legal-tools.org/doc/f5ef47/> accessed 18 August 2017 ....148n171

Other

Ad Hoc Committee on the Establishment of an International Criminal Court 'Report of the Ad Hoc Committee on the Establishment of an International Criminal Court' (06 September 1995) UN Doc A/50/22 <http://www.legal-tools.org/doc/b50da8/> accessed 08 August 2017...7n25, 119n2

Assembly of States Parties to the Rome Statute of the International Criminal Court 'Official Records of the Assembly of States Parties to the Rome Statute of the International Criminal Court, First session, New York, 3-10 September 2002' (09 September 2002) ICC-ASP/1/3 (Part II.B) <http://www.legal-tools.org/doc/3c0e2d/> accessed 09 August 2017..9n31, 157n229

Committee on the Elimination of Discrimination against Women 'General Recommendation No. 19' (29 July 1994) UN Doc HRI/GEN/1/Rev.1 <https://www.legal-tools.org/en/browse/record/f8d998/> accessed 18 August 2017..........................58n42

Diplomatic Conference for the Establishment of International Conventions for the Protection of Victims of War, 'Final Record of the

Table of other legal documents

Abbreviations

Additional Protocol I	Protocol Additional to the Geneva Conventions of 12 August 1949, and relating to the Protection of Victims of International Armed Conflicts
Additional Protocol II	Protocol Additional to the Geneva Conventions of 12 August 1949, and relating to the Protection of Victims of Non-International Armed Conflicts
AFRC	Armed Forces Revolutionary Council
Banjul Charter	African Charter on Human Rights and Peoples' Rights
Beijing Conference	Fourth World Conference on Women
Cairo Conference	International Conference on Population and Development
CEDAW	Convention on the Elimination of Discrimination against Women
CICC	Coalition for the International Criminal Court
Convention	Slavery, the Slave Trade, and Institutions and Practices Similar to Slavery
DEVAW	Declaration on the Elimination of Violence against Women
ECCC	Extraordinary Chambers in the Courts of Cambodia
ECHR	Convention for the Protection of Human Rights and Fundamental Freedoms
Forced Labour Convention	Convention Concerning Forced or Compulsory Labour
Genocide Convention	Convention on the Prevention and Punishment of the Crime of Genocide
ICC	International Criminal Court
ICCPR	International Covenant on Civil and Political Rights
ICESCR	International Covenant on Economic, Social and Cultural Rights
ICJ	International Court of Justice

ICRC	International Committee of the Red Cross
ICTR	International Criminal Tribunal for Rwanda
ICTY	International Criminal Tribunal for the former Yugoslavia
ILC	United Nations International Law Commission
IMT, Nuremberg Tribunal	International Military Tribunal
IMTFE, Tokyo Tribunal	International Military Tribunal for the Far East
Lieber Code	Instructions for the Government of Armies of the United States in the Field, General Order No 100
LMG	Like-Minded Group
London Agreement	Charter of the International Military Tribunal
LRA	Lord's Resistance Army
NAM	Non-Aligned Movement
NGO	Non-governmental organisation
PrepCom	Preparatory Committee on the Establishment of an International Criminal Court
PrepCom2	Preparatory Commission for the International Criminal Court
RUF	Revolutionary United Front
SADC	Southern African Development Community
SCSL	Special Court for Sierra Leone
Slavery Convention	Convention to Suppress the Slave Trade and Slavery
Supplementary Slavery	Supplementary Convention on the Abolition of
TRC	Truth and Reconciliation Commission
UDHR	Universal Declaration of Human Rights
UK	United Kingdom of Great Britain and Northern Ireland
UN	United Nations
UNGA	United Nations General Assembly
UNSC	United Nations Security Council
USA, US	United States of America
Vienna Conference	World Conference on Human Rights

1 Introduction

Introduction

This book analyses the international criminalisation of war rape and forced marriage in times of armed conflict under the statute of the International Criminal Court (ICC). It addresses the ongoing challenge of how to define the two crimes in a way that adequately reflects women's experiences, as well as the nature of the crimes.

The ICC definition of war rape is considered one of the most progressive and broad definitions of rape under international and national law.[1] This, however, overlooks the awkward, limiting and partly regressive wording of the first element, defining rape as an invasion resulting in penetration.[2] This formulation is puzzling considering that actors in the ICC negotiations could have relied on a more progressive precedent in defining rape. Contrastingly, the crime of forced marriage was understood as a form of sexual slavery and was not discussed in any depth.[3] This neglect is perplexing considering the widespread use of

1 Interview 13 (15 May 2014). For the purpose of this book, progressive definitions of war rape and forced marriage are understood to adequately reflect women's experiences as well as the nature of the crimes.

2 Rome Statute of the International Criminal Court (17 July 1998) 2187 UNTS 3 art 7(1)(g), art 8(b)(xxii), art 8(e)(vi) <www.legal-tools.org/doc/7b9af9/> accessed 9 August 2017; United Nations Commission on Human Rights, 'Final Report of the Special Rapporteur on the Situation of Systematic Rape, Sexual Slavery and Slavery-Like Practices during Armed Conflict' (22 June 1998) UN Doc E/CN.4/Sub.2/1998/13 <www.ohchr.org> accessed 28 August 2017 ©1998 United Nations. Reprinted with the Permission of the United Nations; Christopher Keith Hall, 'The First Five Sessions of the UN Preparatory Commission for the International Criminal Court' (2000) 94 *American Journal of International Law* 773, 778; Human Rights Watch, 'Commentary on the Second Preparatory Commission on Rules of Procedure and Elements of Crime' (July 1999) <www.iccnow.org/documents/HRWComment2ndPrepComJuly99.pdf> accessed 9 February 2012.

3 Interview 17 (17 June 2014); Interview 18 (25 June 2014).

forced marriage in conflicts that were ongoing while the ICC instruments were negotiated[4] and would likely be considered by the court.[5]

Based on this critique of the ICC's definition of war rape and forced marriage, the book analyses the process of how those definitions came about. Using a feminist and constructivist lens, it focuses on the driving actors, what influenced them, how they understood the crimes of war rape and forced marriage, and how they shaped the ICC negotiations. It is argued that, in addition to state delegations, non-governmental organisations (NGOs) in general and women's organisations in particular played a role in developing the definitions of war rape and forced marriage. Actors represented all parts of the world and included survivors of sexualised war violence.[6] Opposition to progressive definitions of rape and forced marriage came mainly from states with strong patriarchal structures where religion plays a leading role in legal and social matters. Influenced by national and international norms, rape and forced marriage were interpreted as honour crimes as well as acts

4 Khristopher Carlson and Dyan Mazurana, 'Forced Marriage within the Lord's Resistance Army, Uganda' (2008) Tufts University Feinstein International Center <https://wikis.uit.tufts.edu/confluence/download/attachments/14553676/Forced+Marriage+within+the+LRA.pdf?version=1> accessed 8 July 2013; Women Under Siege, 'Liberia' <www.womenundersiegeproject.org/conflicts/profile/Liberia> accessed 23 January 2015; Women Under Siege, 'Sierra Leone' <www.womenundersiegeproject.org/conflicts/profile/sierra-leone> accessed 23 January 2015.

5 International Criminal Court, 'Situations and Cases: Uganda' <www.icc-cpi.int/en_menus/icc/situations%20and%20cases/situations/situation%20icc%200204/Pages/situation%20index.aspx> 23 January 2015.

6 Susan Brownmiller, 'Making Female Bodies the Battlefield' in Ronald J. Berger and Patricia Searles (eds), *Rape and Society: Readings on the Problem of Sexual Assault* (Westview Press 1995); Slavenka Drakulić, 'The Rape of Women in Bosnia' in Miranda Davies (ed), *Women and Violence: Realities and Responses World Wide* (Zed Books 1994) 180; Christine Eifler, 'Krieg – Gewalt – Geschlecht' in medica mondiale, Marlies W. Fröse and Ina Volpp-Teuscher (eds), *Krieg, Geschlecht und Traumatisierung: Erfahrungen und Reflexionen in der Arbeit mit traumatisierten Frauen in Kriegs- und Krisengebieten* (IKO-Verlag für Interkulturelle Kommunikation 1999) 91; Joshua S. Goldstein, *War and Gender: How Gender Shapes the War System and Vice Versa* (Cambridge University Press 2001) 359; Gabriela Mischkowski, 'Sexualisierte Gewalt im Krieg: Eine Chronik' in medica mondiale and Karin Griese (eds), *Sexualisierte Kriegsgewalt und ihre Folgen: Handbuch zur Unterstützung traumatisierter Frauen in verschiedenen Arbeitsfeldern* (2nd edn, Mabuse-Verlag 2006); Ruth Seifert, 'Krieg und Vergewaltigung: Ansätze zu einer Analyse' in Alexandra Stiglemayer (ed), *Massenvergewaltigungen: Krieg gegen die Frauen* (Fischer Taschenbuchverlag 1993) 88: This book uses the term 'sexualised' rather than 'sexual' violence. The term 'sexual' violence emphasises sexuality in the context of violence and can lead to a confusion of sexuality, and violence using sexual means. 'Sexualised' violence, in contrast, highlights the act of violence itself. It describes a form of violence which is deliberately directed against the most intimate part of a person's body. An act of sexualised violence demonstrates power and domination by debasing, subordinating and humiliating another person. The term 'sexualised' violence is broader than 'sexual' violence. It includes rape but also acts such as forced undressing, touching without permission, forced shaving of pubic hair, inflicting deliberate harm to breasts and genitals, purposefully infecting someone with sexually transmitted diseases, and forced pregnancy. Sexualised violence includes gender-based violence. Therefore, in this book, the term 'sexualised' violence is used.

of structural violence. Actors shaped the ICC definitions of the two crimes by conducting research and policy analysis, producing and distributing reports and proposals, organising briefings, and lobbying. Non-state actors also influenced the negotiations as civil society members of state delegations.

The aim and potential contribution of this book is to deepen the understanding of the ICC negotiations of war rape and forced marriage. By comparing the criminalisation of war rape and forced marriage, this book highlights relevant factors that need to be considered when criminalising acts of sexualised war violence under international law. This way it contributes to debates about the nature of international law-making. By considering forced marriage in the context of the ICC negotiations, the book also aims at raising awareness of the crime and intends to contribute towards a better understanding of it.

Context

Legislative histories of war rape and forced marriage

From ancient to modern times, sexualised war violence against women was viewed as a socially acceptable practice in war, as collateral damage. Women were spoils of war, a reward to which the victors had a right. Sexualised violence was tolerated, if not encouraged, as a means of propaganda, humiliation and terror. The criminalisation of sexualised war violence has been attempted at the international level at least since the 18th century when bilateral and multilateral conventions criminalised sexualised war violence in the form of rape as an honour crime. This understanding was maintained in international agreements of the early and mid-20th century as well as by the Nuremberg and Tokyo tribunals established after the Second World War. International instruments of the second half of the 20th century moved away from an honour-based interpretation of sexualised war violence towards an understanding of it as a gender-based violation of women's integrity. Sexualised war violence was framed as an issue of discrimination against as well as of protecting women and their fundamental rights. A connection was established between the vulnerability of women in wartime and the discrimination and disadvantages they experience in everyday life. Despite this growing recognition of sexualised war violence as a wrong, acts of sexualised war violence were perpetrated systematically on a massive scale during the conflicts in the former Yugoslavia and Rwanda in the 1990s. War rape was used as a strategic method to destroy culture and life as well as a method of ethnic cleansing and genocide. This was a known fact, condoned, encouraged and even ordered.[7] In response, the statutes of the International Criminal

7 Anne-Marie L.M. de Brouwer, *Supranational Criminal Prosecution of Sexual Violence: The ICC and the Practice of the ICTY and the ICTR* (Insertia 2005); Mischkowski, 'Sexualisierte Gewalt im Krieg' (n 6); Seifert (n 6); Alexandra Stiglemayer (ed), *Massenvergewaltigungen: Krieg gegen die Frauen* (Fischer Taschenbuchverlag 1993).

Tribunal for the former Yugoslavia (ICTY) and the International Criminal Tribunal for Rwanda (ICTR) explicitly included war rape as a crime against humanity. The ICTR statute also explicitly listed rape as an outrage upon personal dignity which constitutes a violation of Article 3 common to the Geneva Conventions and to Additional Protocol II.[8] In the tribunals' jurisprudence, war rape was defined as a crime against humanity,[9] a war crime,[10] as constituting torture,[11] an act of genocide[12] and a grave breach of the Geneva Conventions.[13] Before the ICC negotiations had been completed, the Yugoslavia and Rwanda tribunals developed different definitions of the crime of rape as such. In *Prosecutor v Jean-Paul Akayesu*, the ICTR introduced a definition using the term 'invasion'.[14] The term 'penetration' was used in definitions developed in *Prosecutor v Anto Furundžija*[15] and in *Prosecutor v Dragoljub Kunarac, Radomir Kovač and Zoran Vuković* (*Foča* case).[16] The latter can also be found in most national definitions.[17]

8 UNSC Resolution 827 (25 May 1993) UN Doc S/RES/827 <www.legal-tools.org/doc/dc079b/> accessed 18 August 2017; UNSC Resolution 955 (8 November 1994) UN Doc S/RES/955 <www.legal-tools.org/doc/f5ef47/> accessed 18 August 2017.

9 *Prosecutor v Jean-Paul Akayesu* (Amended Indictment) ICTR-96-4-I (16 February 1996), Mechanism for International Criminal Tribunals, Count 13; *Prosecutor v Jean-Paul Akayesu* (Trial Judgment) ICTR-96-4-T (2 September 1998) <www.legal-tools.org/doc/b8d7bd/> accessed 9 August 2017, Mechanism for International Criminal Tribunals; *Prosecutor v Dragoljub Kunarac, Radomir Kovač and Zoran Vuković* (Indictment) IT-96-23-T 'Foča Case' (19 June 1996) para 4.8 <www.legal-tools.org/doc/3a081b/> accessed 18 August 2017, Mechanism for International Criminal Tribunals.

10 *Foča* Indictment (n 9) para 4.8; *Prosecutor v Anto Furundžija* (Trial Judgment) ICTY IT-95-17/1-T (10 December 1998) Section IX <www.legal-tools.org/doc/e6081b/> accessed 9 August 2017, Mechanism for International Criminal Tribunals.

11 *Foča* Indictment (n 9) para 4.8.

12 *Akayesu* Trial Judgment (n 9) para 507–508.

13 *Foča* Indictment (n 9) para 4.8 and counts 56–59.

14 *Akayesu* Trial Judgment (n 9) para 598.

15 *Furundžija* Trial Judgment (n 10) para 185.

16 *Foča* Indictment (n 9) para 4.8; *Prosecutor v Dragoljub Kunarac, Radomir Kovač and Zoran Vuković* (Trial Judgment) ICTY IT-96-23-T and IT-96-23/1-T 'Foča Case' (22 February 2001) para 460 <www.legal-tools.org/doc/fd881d/> accessed 9 August 2017, Mechanism for International Criminal Tribunals.

17 For example see Bahrain Penal Code (1976) art 344, art 346 <www.bahrainrights.org/sites/default/files/Bahrain-Penal-Code.doc> accessed 17 March 2014; The Criminal Act of 1991 (Sudan) art 149(1) <www.icrc.org/applic/ihl/ihl-nat.nsf/xsp/.ibmmodres/domino/OpenAttachment/applic/ihl/ihl-nat.nsf/B9EEBA1CA8F54121C1256DC9005573F2/TEXT/Criminal%20Act%20-%20Sudan%20-%20EN.pdf> accessed 1 April 2014; Iraqi Penal Code No 111 (1969) art 21(1)(f), art 393(1) <www.iraq-lg-law.org/en/webfm_send/1350> accessed 18 March 2014; Ley No 599 de 2000 Por la cual se expide el Código Penal (24 July 2000) (Colombia) art 205 <www.alcaldiabogota.gov.co/sisjur/normas/Norma1.jsp?i=6388> accessed 8 May 2015; The Libyan Penal Code (1953) art 407 <https://ia600704.us.archive.org/25/items/LibyanPenalCodeenglish/LibyanPenalCode.pdf> accessed 24 March 2014; Omani Penal Code (1974) art 218(1) <www.fiu.gov.om/forms.html> accessed 24 March 2014; Qatari Penal Code (2004)

While the *ad hoc* tribunals largely focused on war rape, some, especially women's rights advocates, began to criticise the overemphasis on war rape in the discussion of sexualised war violence. They stressed that women also experience other acts and forms of violence in wartime. The United Nations (UN) Special Rapporteur on Violence against Women, its Causes and Consequences, for example, directly mentioned forced marriage in times of armed conflict in her reports from 1995 on.[18] The first definition of forced marriage, however, was put forward by the UN Special Rapporteur on the Situation of Systematic Rape, Sexual Slavery and Slavery-Like Practices during Armed Conflict. At a time when the ICC's Rome Statute had been passed and the discussion of the Elements of Crimes had begun, she found the constituting elements of forced marriage to include being forced into a conjugal relationship, forced labour and acts of sexualised violence.[19] After the ICC Elements of Crimes were passed, the Special Court for Sierra Leone (SCSL) addressed the issue as a form of sexual slavery and an inhumane act in *Prosecutor v Alex Tamba Brima, Brima Bazzy Kamara and Santigie Borbor Kanu* (*AFRC* case),[20] *Prosecutor v Issa*

art 279 <http://portal.www.gov.qa/wps/wcm/connect/8abaea8046be1deaae97ef70b3652ad8/Penal+Code.pdf?MOD=AJPERES&useDefaultText=0&useDefaultDesc=0> accessed 24 March 2014; Federal Bureau of Investigation, 'Frequently Asked Questions about the Change in the UCR Definition of Rape' (11 December 2014) <www.fbi.gov/about-us/cjis/ucr/recent-program-updates/new-rape-definition-frequently-asked-questions> accessed 19 January 2015; Mona Chemali Khalaf, 'Lebanon' in Julia Breslin and Sanja Kelly (eds), *Women's Rights in the Middle East and North Africa: Progress Amid Resistance* (Freedom House/Rowman & Littlefield Publishers 2010) 6 <www.freedomhouse.org/sites/default/files/inline_images/Lebanon.pdf> accessed 21 March 2014; US Department of State: Bureau of Democracy, Human Rights, and Labor, '2009 Human Rights Report: Saudi Arabia' (2010) <www.state.gov/j/drl/rls/hrrpt/2009/nea/136079.htm> accessed 1 April 2014; US Department of State: Bureau of Democracy, Human Rights, and Labor, '2009 Human Rights Report: Syria' (2010) <www.state.gov/j/drl/rls/hrrpt/2009/nea/136080.htm> accessed 1 April 2014.

18 United Nations Commission on Human Rights, 'Preliminary Report Submitted by the Special Rapporteur on Violence against Women, Its Causes and Consequences, Ms. Radhika Coomaraswamy, in Accordance with Commission on Human Rights Resolution 1994/45' (22 November 1994) UN Doc E/CN.4/1995/42 fn 228 <www.ohchr.org> accessed 28 August 2017; United Nations Commission on Human Rights, 'Report on the Mission of the Special Rapporteur to Poland on the Issue of Trafficking and Forced Prostitution of Women (24 May to 1 June 1996)' (10 December 1996) UN Doc E/CN.4/1997/47/Add.1 para 77–78, para 84 <www.ohchr.org> accessed 28 August 2017; United Nations Commission on Human Rights, 'Report of the Special Rapporteur on Violence against Women, Its Causes and Consequences, Ms. Radhika Coomaraswamy, Submitted in Accordance with Commission Resolution 1997/44' (26 January 1998) UN Doc E/CN.4/1998/54 para 17, para 23, para 27, para 36 <www.ohchr.org> accessed 28 August 2017.

19 United Nations Commission on Human Rights, 'Final Report of the Special Rapporteur on the Situation of Systematic Rape, Sexual Slavery and Slavery-Like Practices during Armed Conflict' (n 2) para 30.

20 *Prosecutor v Alex Tamba Brima, Brima Bazzy Kamara and Santigie Borbor Kanu* (Appeals Chamber Judgment) SCSL SLS-2004-16-A 'AFRC Case' (22 February 2008)

Hassan Sesay, Morris Kallon and Augustine Gbao (*RUF* case)[21] and *Prosecutor v Charles Taylor*.[22] In these cases, the Special Court also developed different ways of referring to the crime.

War rape, forced marriage and the ICC

The ICC, based in The Hague in the Netherlands, is the first independent, permanent international criminal court established to try persons accused of the most serious crimes of international concern: genocide, crimes against humanity, war crimes and the crime of aggression.[23]

The ICC is a treaty-based court, governed by the Rome Statute that is binding only on those states which formally express their consent to be bound by its provisions. The Rome Statute was negotiated between 1994 and 1998.[24]

<www.legal-tools.org/doc/4420ef/> accessed 9 August 2017; *Prosecutor v Alex Tamba Brima, Brima Bazzy Kamara and Santigie Borbor Kanu* (Trial Judgment) SCSL-04-16-T 'AFRC Case' (20 June 2007) <www.legal-tools.org/doc/87ef08/> accessed 9 August 2017.

The AFRC (Armed Forces Revolutionary Council) was a Sierra Leone fighting group that participated in the conflict in the 1990s and early 2000s. For further information see for example Davidson S.H.W. Nicol, 'Sierra Leone' (13 May 2014) *Encyclopaedia Britannica* <www.britannica.com/place/Sierra-Leone/Civil-war#ref978722> accessed 2 July 2015.

21 *Prosecutor v Issa Hassan Sesay, Morris Kallon and Augustine Gbao* (Trial Judgment) SCSL-04-15-PT 'RUF Case' (2 March 2009) <www.legal-tools.org/doc/4420ef/> accessed 9 August 2017.

The RUF (Revolutionary United Front) was a Sierra Leonean fighting group that participated in the conflict in the 1990s and early 2000s. For further information see for example Richard McHugh, 'RUF' (23 November 2015) *Encyclopaedia Britannica* <www.britannica.com/topic/Revolutionary-United-Front> accessed 20 February 2016.

22 *Prosecutor v Charles Taylor* (Trial Judgment) SCSL-03-01-T (18 May 2012) <www.legal-tools.org/doc/3e7be5/> accessed 9 August 2017.

23 International Criminal Court, 'About the Court' <www.icc-cpi.int/en_menus/icc/about%20the%20court/Pages/about%20the%20court.aspx> accessed 28 January 2015; International Criminal Court, 'At a Glance' <www.icc-cpi.int/en_menus/icc/about%20the%20court/icc%20at%20a%20glance/Pages/icc%20at%20a%20glance.aspx> accessed 28 January 2015; International Criminal Court, 'Factsheet' <www.icc-cpi.int/en_menus/icc/about%20the%20court/icc%20at%20a%20glance/factsheets/Pages/fact%20sheets.aspx> accessed 28 January 2015.

24 Code of Offences against the Peace and Security of Mankind (28 July 1954) 9 UN GAOR Supp. (No. 9) at 11, UN Doc A/2693 (1954), 45 AJIL 123 (1951) <www.legal-tools.org/doc/80a02d/> accessed 18 August 2017; Convention on the Prevention and Punishment of the Crime of Genocide (9 December 1948) 78 UNTS 277 (Genocide Convention) <www.legal-tools.org/doc/498c38/> accessed 18 August 2017; M. Cherif Bassiouni, *The Legislative History of the International Criminal Court* (Transnational Publishers 2005) 31–34, 54–64; Fanny Benedetti, Karine Bonneau and John Washburn, *Negotiating the International Criminal Court: New York to Rome, 1994–1998* (Brill 2013) 15–16; Antonio Cassese, Paola Gaeta and John R.W.D. Jones (eds), *The Rome Statute of the International Criminal Court: A Commentary* (Oxford University Press 2002); Coalition for the International Criminal Court, 'History of the ICC' <www.iccnow.org/?mod=icchistory> accessed 3 December 2013; Roy S. Lee, *The International*

A draft statute for an international criminal court was submitted to the United Nations General Assembly (UNGA) by the United Nations International Law Commission (ILC) in 1994. The ILC recommended convening a conference of plenipotentiaries to negotiate a treaty and enact the draft statute. The UNGA, however, decided to establish the Ad Hoc Committee on the Establishment of an International Criminal Court to review the draft statute and to work towards an international conference to finalise and adopt it. After meeting twice, the Ad Hoc Committee submitted its report to the UNGA in 1995.[25] After considering the report, the UNGA created the Preparatory Committee on the Establishment of an International Criminal Court (PrepCom) to prepare a consolidated draft text. Between March 1996 and April 1998, the PrepCom met six times at the UN headquarters in New York. In January 1998, the intersessional meeting in Zutphen, the Netherlands, took place to technically consolidate and restructure the draft articles into a draft statute. Based on the PrepCom's draft, the UNGA convened the United Nations Conference of Plenipotentiaries on the Establishment of an International Criminal Court (Rome

---

Criminal Court: The Making of the Rome Statute: Issues, Negotiations, Results (Kluwer Law International 1999); William A. Schabas, *An Introduction to the International Criminal Court* (Cambridge University Press 2007): The history of the establishment of an international criminal court goes back further than 1994 though. Efforts to create a global criminal court can be traced back to the 19th century when Gustav Moynier proposed a permanent court in response to the crimes perpetrated in the context of the Franco-Prussian War. After the First World War, the drafters of the Treaty of Versailles envisaged an *ad hoc* international court to try the German Kaiser and other war criminals. International military tribunals were established by the Allies in Nuremberg and Tokyo after the Second World War to try Axis war criminals. Article 6 of the Genocide Convention calls for violations to be dealt with by international criminal tribunals. In the early 1950s, the International Law Commission (ILC) drafted a Code of Offences against the Peace and Security of Mankind. A United Nations (UN) Committee established by the United Nations General Assembly (UNGA) prepared two drafts of a statute for an international criminal court. Disagreement over the definition of the crime of aggression as well as the Cold War, however, got in the way of these efforts and the UNGA effectively abandoned the project without an agreement on how to define the crime of aggression and on an international Code of Crimes having been reached. Motivated partly by the desire to combat drug trafficking, Trinidad and Tobago revived a pre-existing proposal for the establishment of an international criminal court in June 1989. The UNGA asked the ILC to resume its work on drafting a statute. After the conflicts in the former Yugoslavia and Rwanda in the early 1990s, the United Nations Security Council (UNSC) established two *ad hoc* tribunals to hold individuals accountable for crimes committed during these conflicts.

25 Ad Hoc Committee on the Establishment of an International Criminal Court, 'Report of the Ad Hoc Committee on the Establishment of an International Criminal Court' (6 September 1995) UN Doc A/50/22 para 255 <www.legal-tools.org/doc/b50da8/> accessed 8 August 2017.

The Ad Hoc Committee discussed issues related to the establishment and composition of the ICC, the principle of complementarity, applicable law and jurisdiction of the court, exercise of jurisdiction, methods of proceedings, the relationship between states parties, non-states parties and the ICC as well as budget and administration.

Conference) to finalise and adopt a convention on the establishment of an international criminal court. The Rome Conference took place from 15 June to 17 July 1998 in Rome, Italy. The Rome Statute was adopted on 17 July 1998 with 120 state delegations voting in favour, seven against and 21 states abstaining.[26] After the Rome Conference, the Preparatory Commission for the International Criminal Court (PrepCom2) was charged with completing the establishment and enabling smooth functioning of the ICC by negotiating complementary documents[27] setting out the court's structure, jurisdiction and functions. Of particular relevance to this research project are the Elements of Crimes that were negotiated between February 1999 and July 2000.[28]

State and non-state delegations participated in the ICC negotiations. States were the main actors in the sense that they made the final decisions. They acted individually as well as in groups. NGOs attended the negotiations under the umbrella of the international NGO Coalition for the International Criminal Court (CICC). This facilitated networking and cooperation between NGOs at multiple levels, as well as between NGOs and states. NGOs closely monitored the discussions and produced and distributed information on developments. They also produced, distributed and promoted new research, expert documents and news articles. Additionally, they briefed and lobbied state delegations. This way, they facilitated exchange and provided input into the discussions. NGOs provided more detailed and specific contexts for the decisions that were to be made by states. However, members of NGOs also influenced states' decisions by becoming members of state delegations. Furthermore, NGOs had an impact on the ICC negotiations by undertaking preliminary drafting work. NGOs engaged in capacity building, provided orientation and guidance and mobilised other NGOs. NGOs also facilitated parallel activities, raising awareness of the ICC.[29]

The Rome Statute's provisions on sexualised violence are considered to be great achievements. They build on existing international laws, especially the

26 International Criminal Court, 'About the Court' (n 23): By 11 April 2002, the Rome Statute had been ratified by 60 states and entered into force on 1 July 2002.

27 Those include the Rules of Procedure and Evidence, the Elements of Crimes, the Relationship Agreement between the Court and the United Nations, the Financial Regulations and the Agreement on the Privileges and Immunities of the Court. According to art 9(1) of the Rome Statute (n 2), the Elements of Crimes help the ICC judges to interpret and apply the articles covering genocide, crimes against humanity, war crimes and crimes of aggression.

28 Bassiouni, *The Legislative History of the International Criminal Court* (n 24) 36; Benedetti, Bonneau and Washburn (n 24); Cassese, Gaeta and Jones (n 24); Coalition for the International Criminal Court, 'History of the ICC' (n 24); International Criminal Court, 'Establishment of the Court' <www.icc-cpi.int/en_menus/icc/about%20the%20court/icc%20at%20a%20glance/Pages/establishment%20of%20the%20court.aspx> accessed 28 January 2015; International Criminal Court, 'Factsheet' (n 23); Lee, *The International Criminal Court: The Making of the Rome Statute* (n 24); Schabas (n 24).

29 Benedetti, Bonneau and Washburn (n 24) 1428; Cassese, Gaeta and Jones (n 24); Coalition for the International Criminal Court, 'History of the ICC' (n 24); Roy S. Lee (ed), *The International Criminal Court: Elements of Crimes and Rules of Procedure and Evidence* (Transnational Publishers 2001); Schabas (n 24).

experience and expertise of the ICTY and ICTR, and recognise rape as a war crime and a crime against humanity.[30] Going further than the *ad hoc* tribunals, the ICC Elements of Crimes also specify that rape can cause serious bodily or mental harm and therefore constitute an act of genocide if the qualifying elements of genocide are met.[31] In addition to rape, the Rome Statute also explicitly recognises 'sexual slavery, enforced prostitution, forced pregnancy, enforced sterilization, [and] any other form of sexual violence of comparable gravity'[32] as well as gender-based persecution.[33]

Previous research on the evolution of the ICC and its instruments considered the process of including rape as a war crime and crime against humanity in the Rome Statute and the outcome of the process of defining the crime.[34] The final definition of war rape is generally considered one of the most progressive and broad definitions of rape under international and national law.[35] However, from a feminist perspective, the formulation 'invasion resulting in penetration' in the first element of the ICC definition[36] is puzzling. While the actors in the ICC

30 Rome Statute (n 2) art 7(1)(g), art 8(b)(xxii), art 8(e)(vi).

31 Assembly of States Parties to the Rome Statute of the International Criminal Court, 'Official Records of the Assembly of States Parties to the Rome Statute of the International Criminal Court, First Session, New York, 3–10 September 2002' (9 September 2002) ICC-ASP/1/3 (Part II.B) art 6(b)(2)-(4), fn 3 <www.legal-tools.org/doc/3c0e2d/> accessed 9 August 2017.

32 Rome Statute (n 2) art 7(1)(g), art 8(b)(xxii), art 8(e)(vi).

33 Rome Statute (n 2) art 7(1)(h).

34 Benedetti, Bonneau and Washburn (n 24); Machteld Boot, 'Article 7 Crimes against Humanity para. 1 (g) Rape ... or Any Other Form of Sexual Violence of Comparable Gravity' in Otto Triffterer (ed), *Commentary on the Rome Statute of the International Criminal Court: Observers' Notes, Article by Article* (2nd edn, CH Beck 2008); Brouwer, *Supranational Criminal Prosecution of Sexual Violence* (n 7); Nichole Eva Erb, 'Gender-Based Crimes under the Draft Statute of the Permanent International Criminal Court' (1998) 29 *Columbia Human Rights Law Review* 401; Brook Sari Moshan, 'Women, War, and Words: The Gender Component in the Permanent International Criminal Court's Definition of Crimes against Humanity' (1998) 22 *Fordham International Law Journal* 154.

35 Interview 13 (n 1); Michael Cottier, 'Article 8 War Crimes para. 2 (b) (xxii) Rape and Other Forms of Sexual Violence' in Otto Triffterer (ed), *Commentary on the Rome Statute of the International Criminal Court: Observers' Notes, Article by Article* (2nd edn, CH Beck 2008).

36 Assembly of States Parties to the Rome Statute of the International Criminal Court (n 31) art 7(1)(g)(1), art 8(2)(b)(xxii)(1), art 8(2)(e)(vi)(1): The first element of the ICC rape definition reads: 'The perpetrator invaded the body of a person by conduct resulting in penetration, however slight, of any part of the body of the victim or of the perpetrator with a sexual organ, or of the anal or genital opening of the victim with any object or any other part of the body.' The second element to the definition of rape as a crime against humanity and as a war crime reads: 'The invasion was committed by force, or by threat of force or coercion, such as that caused by fear of violence, duress, detention, psychological oppression or abuse of power, against such person or another person, or by taking advantage of a coercive environment, or the invasion was committed against a person incapable of giving genuine consent.' The third and fourth element of the rape definition is related to the qualifying elements of crimes against humanity and war crimes.

negotiations could have relied solely on the broad and gender-neutral *Akayesu* precedent,[37] they combined it with the rape definition developed by the ICTY in the *Furundžija* case[38] that reflects many national laws. This can be interpreted as regressive and limiting.[39] By using the term 'penetration', the ICC reverted to a male definition of rape that invokes concerns regarding women's chastity, paternity and honour.[40] It represents the perpetrator's point of view and focuses on the physical aspect of rape. 'Invasion', in contrast, illustrates the survivor's point of view.[41] This term is broader than 'penetration' as it connotes not only a physical, but also a psychological invasion of a person's autonomy, self-determination and integrity. Moreover, the ICC rape definition includes a limiting reference to body parts, which potentially makes it more difficult for survivors to build a case because they have to go into great detail about the physical aspects of the rape. Not only can this be difficult for survivors, it may also infringe upon cultural sensitivities.[42]

While research on the evolution of the ICC and its instruments analyses and assesses the court's rape definition, it seldom examines the process of defining rape itself, which took place after the Rome Conference in the PrepCom2. When the process of defining rape is considered, it is merely noted that the *ad hoc* tribunals' definitions influenced the ICC definition.[43]

37 *Akayesu* Trial Judgment (n 9) para 598.

38 *Furundžija* Trial Judgment (n 10) para 185.

39 Hall, 'The First Five Sessions of the UN Preparatory Commission for the International Criminal Court' (n 2) 778; Human Rights Watch, 'Commentary on the Second Preparatory Commission on Rules of Procedure and Elements of Crime' (n 2); United Nations Commission on Human Rights, 'Final Report of the Special Rapporteur on the Situation of Systematic Rape, Sexual Slavery and Slavery-Like Practices during Armed Conflict' (n 2).

40 Human Rights Watch, 'Commentary on the Second Preparatory Commission on Rules of Procedure and Elements of Crime' (n 2); United Nations Commission on Human Rights, 'Final Report of the Special Rapporteur on the Situation of Systematic Rape, Sexual Slavery and Slavery-Like Practices during Armed Conflict' (n 2) para 24.

41 Kristen Boon, 'Rape and Forced Pregnancy under the ICC Statute: Human Dignity, Autonomy, and Consent' (2001) 32 Columbia Human Rights Law Review 625; Brouwer, *Supranational Criminal Prosecution of Sexual Violence* (n 7) 107.

42 Brouwer, *Supranational Criminal Prosecution of Sexual Violence* (n 7) 115.

43 Publications that comment on the making of the ICC rape definition include Boon (n 41); Cottier (n 35); Knut Dörmann, *Elements of War Crimes under the Rome Statute of the International Criminal Court: Sources and Commentary* (Cambridge University Press 2003); Knut Dörmann, 'War Crimes under the Rome Statute of the International Criminal Court, with a Special Focus on the Negotiations on the Elements of Crimes' in Armin von Bogdandy and Rüdiger Wolfrum (eds), *Max Planck Yearbook of United Nations Law* (Volume 7, Martinus Nijhoff Publishers 2003); Eve La Haye, 'Article 8(2)(b)(xii): Rape, Sexual Slavery, Enforced Prostitution, Forced Pregnancy, Enforced Sterilization, and Sexual Violence' in Roy S. Lee (ed), *The International Criminal Court: Elements of Crimes and Rules of Procedure and Evidence* (Transnational Publishers 2001).

Eve La Haye (n 43) is an exception. She provides a more detailed analysis, also including relevant state proposals and reasons for supporting certain wordings.

While war rape was extensively discussed in the ICC negotiations, forced marriage in times of armed conflict was mentioned as a form of sexual slavery but not discussed further.[44] This disregard is puzzling, considering the widespread use of forced marriage in, for example, the conflicts in Liberia,[45] Sierra Leone[46] and Uganda[47] that were ongoing while the ICC instruments were negotiated and could have been considered by the court.[48] It is a lost opportunity to raise awareness of and directly acknowledge forced marriage not only as a harmful experience, but also as a wrong requiring legal redress. Explicitly including forced marriage in the Rome Statute would have legitimised women's experiences during and after armed conflicts and enabled the court to fully address them.[49]

Research questions

Against this background, it is of interest and importance to analyse how the ICC definitions of war rape and forced marriage in times of armed conflict came about. Secondary research questions are:

1 Who were the driving actors in the process of defining war rape and seeking to define forced marriage?
2 What influenced them?
3 What was their understanding of war rape and forced marriage?
4 How did the driving actors influence the ICC negotiations of war rape and forced marriage?

It is expected to find that:

1 NGOs in general and women's organisations in particular played a role in the development of the ICC definitions of war rape and forced marriage;
2 States with strong patriarchal structures, where religion plays a leading role in legal and social matters, opposed the development of progressive definitions of war rape and forced marriage;

44 Women's Caucus for Gender Justice, 'Recommendations and Commentary for December 1997 PrepCom on the Establishment of an International Criminal Court' (December 1997) <www.iccnow.org/documents/5PrepComRecommWomensC.pdf> accessed 4 December 2013.
45 Women Under Siege, 'Liberia' (n 4).
46 Chris Coulter, *Bush Wives and Girl Soldiers: Women's Lives through War and Peace in Sierra Leone* (Cornell University Press 2009); Women Under Siege, 'Sierra Leone' (n 4).
47 Carlson and Mazurana (n 4).
48 International Criminal Court, 'Situations and Cases: Uganda' (n 5).
49 Valerie Oosterveld, 'Forced Marriage and the Special Court for Sierra Leone: Legal Advances and Conceptual Difficulties' (2011) 2 *Journal of International Humanitarian Legal Studies* 127.

3 Domestic norms explain the resistance towards more progressive definitions of war rape and forced marriage;
4 Survivors of war rape and forced marriage and actors from the global South were not involved;
5 War rape and forced marriage were interpreted as honour crimes;
6 Structural causes of the perpetration of war rape and forced marriage were not addressed.

From a feminist and constructivist perspective, it is necessary to consider the actors as well as the normative structures that shape actors' understandings of war rape and forced marriage and, consequently, law-making. International law is made by women and men, state and non-state actors. Their interests and actions are shaped by personal, national and international values, norms and rules and influence law-making processes and outcomes. Therefore, law(-making) is biased. Arguably, this bias can be decreased through the intervention of outside actors.

Supported by preliminary research, a combined feminist and constructivist analysis of the actors in the ICC negotiations suggested that NGOs in general and women's organisations in particular played a role in the development of the ICC definitions of war rape and forced marriage. Preliminary research also suggested that states with strong patriarchal structures, where religion plays a leading role in legal and social matters, opposed the development of more progressive laws. This claim supports the constructivist theory that domestic norms matter in international relations and law-making, here in the sense of opposing progressive definitions of rape and forced marriage. A feminist analysis of the ICC negotiations raises the question whether survivors of sexualised war violence were involved as their participation would give a voice to those unheard and contribute to women's empowerment. Considering that the ICC is an international court with jurisdiction over all states that ratified the Rome Statute, it is of interest and relevance to examine whether that was reflected in the ICC negotiations or whether actors from the global South were not involved. Tracing progress in the understanding of sexualised crimes, it has to be analysed whether sexualised crimes were understood as honour crimes or forms of structural violence. This way, continuities and/or discontinuities in international law-making processes can be highlighted and state-centric notions as well as the priority of international norms and rules in international treaty negotiations can be challenged.

Chapter outline

This book addresses the research questions in three steps. First, Chapter 2 sets out the theoretical and methods framework of this research project. Chapter 3 then examines theoretical considerations about the causes and meanings of the perpetration of war rape and forced marriage as well as their legislative histories. Chapters 4–7 form the main part of this book and directly address the ICC negotiations and how the court's definitions of war rape and forced marriage came about.

Chapter 2 outlines feminism and constructivism as the main theories underpinning and applied in this research project. According to feminist and constructivist theorists, reality is socially constructed. Therefore, it can change. Constructivists such as Martha Finnemore and Peter Katzenstein emphasise the role of domestic and international normative structures in this process of change as well as impetuses that are internal as well as external to actors. Both shape and are being shaped by actors (constructivist circle).[50] Feminists, in contrast, are interested in the gender aspects of this process of change and their gendered outcomes. Feminist legal theories expose and draw attention to the sex/gender issues that patriarchal structures such as legal rules, institutions and processes hide.[51] Feminist theories shape the author's understanding of the research topic and its relevance. They are useful for this research project because its subject is a gender issue. Constructivist theories, however, allow for a more detailed analysis of the process of criminalising rape and forced marriage. In contrast to rationalist theories that understand actors as atomistic egoists and their identities and interests as autogenous, constructivism establishes actors, their identities and interests as socially constructed and shaped by normative rather than material structures. Therefore, they see society as a constitutive realm whereas for rationalists, society is a strategic sphere where actors come together to pursue and maximise their predefined interests. This indicates that rationalism focuses on interest satisfaction while constructivism is interested in interest formation.[52] Since these key rationalist assumptions are irreconcilable with the focus of this project, law-making is analysed from a constructivist and feminist perspective, rather than a constructivist and rationalist one.

The research questions are addressed using qualitative research methods as they are more suitable than quantitative methods to develop a better understanding of the ICC negotiations and how the definitions of war rape and forced marriage came about. Consistent with the theoretical basis of this research project, feminist research methods are employed. More specifically, the research project used a critical analysis of existing literature and relevant documents as

50 Milja Kurki and Andriana Sinclair, 'Hidden in Plain Sight: Constructivist Treatment of Social Context and Its Limitations' (2010) 47 *International Politics* 1, 3–4; see also Martha Finnemore, *National Interests in International Society* (Cornell University Press 1996) 1–33; Peter Katzenstein, *Cultural Norms and National Security: Police and Military in Postwar Japan* (Cornell University Press 1996) 1–32.

51 Emily Jackson and Nicola Lacey, 'Introducing Feminist Legal Theory' in Richard Nobles, James Penner and David Schiff (eds), *Introduction to Jurisprudence and Legal Theory: Commentary and Materials* (Oxford University Press 2002); Carol Smart, *Law, Crime and Sexuality: Essays in Feminism* (Sage Publications 1995) 189–190.

52 Christian Reus-Smit, 'Constructivism' in Scott Burchill and others (eds), *Theory of International Relations* (3rd edn, Palgrave Macmillan 2005).

well as semi-structured interviews with people who participated in the ICC negotiations to address the research question.

Chapter 3 provides the thematic context for the analysis of the ICC negotiations of war rape and forced marriage. It retraces theoretical considerations regarding the causes and meanings of the perpetration of the two crimes as well as their legislative histories. War rape and forced marriage are understood to be weapons of war that are grounded in patriarchy, attributable to peacetime gender norms and stereotypes, and ways to regulate gender relationships. Forced marriages are also formed in wartime to create dependency structures within fighting groups. War rape is also used as a theme in propaganda. War rape was first defined as an honour crime before it was more adequately understood as a breach of a person's fundamental rights and established as a crime in its own right as well as potentially constituting other crimes such as torture and an act of genocide. Regarding the definition of rape itself, it developed from a conceptual coercion-based definition towards a mechanical coercion- and consent-based definition. In regard to forced marriage, a similar pattern can be noticed. First forced marriage was defined as a form of sexual slavery before it was considered whether it would be more adequate to see it as another inhumane act. As such, forced marriage was understood to include a forced conjugal association, acts of sexualised violence and forced labour. Comparing the legislative histories of war rape and forced marriage highlights that a conduct is established as a serious problem first and then discussed in the context of existing crimes before it is criminalised in its own right.

Chapter 4 focuses on the identity of actors involved in the ICC negotiations in general and on what generally influenced them. It argues that individuals, states and NGOs played an important role in the ICC negotiations. They represented all parts of the world and included survivors of sexualised war violence. They shaped and were shaped by personal, national and international values, norms and rules. However, practical and strategic considerations also came into play. Moreover, Chapter 4 argues that while participation of, and equality between, actors was furthered through their work in coalitions and caucuses, it was impeded by perpetuated traditional power dynamics. In addition, actors' ability to influence the ICC negotiations was limited by the need for consensus in all decisions. Despite this, actors influenced the ICC negotiations by conducting research and policy analysis, producing and distributing reports and proposals, organising briefings, and lobbying. Non-state actors' ability to influence the ICC negotiations was increased by being perceived as strategic partners of state actors. This enabled them to become members of state delegations or to teach their views to states.[53]

53 Martha Finnemore (n 50) claims that NGOs are 'active teachers' of states in the sense that NGOs as outside actors present problems and solutions to state governments. They teach their views to states by setting agendas, defining tasks and shaping interests of states.

While Chapter 4 demonstrates how NGOs taught their views to states, Chapter 5 shows that they succeeded. It contains a detailed analysis of the developments in the ICC negotiations regarding the definitions of war rape and forced marriage, outlining who the main state and non-state actors were, why they got involved in the ICC negotiations of the crimes of war rape and forced marriage specifically and what influenced their positions as well as how they interpreted the crimes.

Chapter 5 demonstrates that the international Women's Caucus, an umbrella organisation of women's organisations and advocates, was a driving actor regarding the process of defining war rape and especially forced marriage in times of armed conflict. The Arab block[54] raised concerns regarding the definition of rape and sexual slavery. In addition to the Women's Caucus and the Arab block, the International Committee of the Red Cross (ICRC) and the delegations of Colombia and the United States of America (USA, US) drove the ICC negotiations of the crimes of war rape and forced marriage.

The Women's Caucus became active in the ICC negotiations of war rape and forced marriage to ensure that sexualised crimes were appropriately addressed, keeping women's concerns in mind. The ICRC's participation was motivated by its role as the guardian and expert of international humanitarian law. The Arab block engaged in this particular aspect of the ICC negotiations to protect national marriage laws and practices from international interference and from falling within the reach of crimes against humanity. Colombia was aware that it might fall to be investigated by the ICC. Therefore, it had an interest in shaping the definitions of crimes its citizens might be accused of. The US insisted on defining the crimes under the jurisdiction of the ICC as it was concerned about its national sovereignty and the prosecution of its own citizens.

The Women's Caucus understood war rape to be a form of structural violence that is rooted in discrimination against women in peacetime. Based on the *Akayesu* definition, the Women's Caucus proposed an inclusive coercion-based rape definition that uses the term 'invasion'. The ICRC, in contrast, built its definition of rape on the *Furundžija* case and suggested to use the term 'penetration'. Contrary to the Women's Caucus and the ICRC, the US initially was influenced by its national laws and advanced a consent-based rape definition using the term 'penetration'. Eventually, however, it followed the Women's Caucus and suggested a coercion-based definition. Like the US, Colombia initially developed a definition of rape based on its national laws and suggested using the phrase 'to have sexual access to' before following the ICRC and

54 PrepCom2, 'Proposal Submitted by Bahrain, Iraq, Kuwait, Lebanon, the Libyan Arab Jamahiriya, Oman, Qatar, Saudi Arabia, the Sudan, the Syrian Arab Republic and United Arab Emirates Concerning the Elements of Crimes against Humanity (9 December 1999)' UN Doc PCNICC/1999/WGEC/DP.39 <www.legal-tools.org/doc/33d070/> accessed 10 August 2017. The Arab block included the delegations of Bahrain, Iraq, Kuwait, Lebanon, Libya, Oman, Qatar, Saudi Arabia, Sudan, Syria and the United Arab Emirates.

suggesting a definition using the term 'penetration'. National normative structures also influenced the Arab block's understanding of rape as an honour crime which excludes marital sexual intercourse. Chapter 5 argues that the final definition of rape as 'invasion resulting in penetration' was a compromise based on international and national rules.

Regarding forced marriage, the Women's Caucus was the first actor to introduce the issue in the ICC negotiations. Later, it was also explicitly mentioned by the ICRC. Following the understanding of the international community as well as the Final Report of the UN Special Rapporteur on the Situation of Systematic Rape, Sexual Slavery and Slavery-Like Practices during Armed Conflict, the Women's Caucus and the ICRC understood forced marriage as a form of sexual slavery. Therefore, it was seen as an exercise of powers attaching to the right of ownership and an emphasis was placed on the sexual elements of a forced marriage. Contrary to establishing a link between forced marriage and sexual slavery like the Women's Caucus and the ICRC, the Arab block explicitly suggested disconnecting sexual slavery from marital rights and duties. In a proposal submitted by the Holy See, the crime of sexual slavery was replaced by enslavement and involuntary servitude, which could still include forced marriage. Like the crime of rape, forced marriage was understood as a question of honour by some and as a form of structural violence by others. Chapter 5 argues that the definition of forced marriage as a form of sexual slavery was guided by international normative structures in which it had only ever been discussed in that context. The outline of actors' understandings of forced marriage indicates that, in the negotiations of the crime of sexual slavery, the Women's Caucus and the ICRC as well as the Arab block and the Holy See played a role. In addition, the US, Colombia and Canada were also involved. Eventually, actors agreed that sexual slavery includes direct and indirect threats but not necessarily a pecuniary element. It was also recognised that the crime can be perpetrated by more than one person. The discussions confirmed the distinction between traditional and contemporary forms of slavery and established sexual slavery, enslavement and human trafficking as separate crimes despite overlaps.

Building on Chapters 4 and especially 5, Chapters 6 and 7 present a more detailed snapshot of specific parts of the ICC negotiations. Chapter 6 analyses how the Women's Caucus came to understand forced marriage as a form of sexual slavery. It explores if the Caucus incorrectly viewed forced marriage as essentially a sexual crime or if the sexual elements of a forced marriage were overemphasised. This could explain the group's interpretation of forced marriage as a form of sexual slavery. As mentioned in relation to Chapter 5, accounts of the discussions in the ICC negotiations also suggest that the Women's Caucus followed the opinion of the international community, interpreting forced marriage as a form of sexual slavery. Interpretations of the written recommendations and comments submitted by the Caucus at different stages of the negotiation process, however, suggest the group might have followed the UN Special Rapporteur on the Situation of Systematic Rape, Sexual Slavery and Slavery-Like Practices during Armed Conflict and strategically framed forced marriage as a form of slavery to benefit from the connotations of the *jus cogens* nature of the norm.

Chapter 7 focuses on a proposal submitted by the Arab block,[55] dissenting from developments in international criminal law regarding the crimes of war rape and sexual slavery. This was motivated by the Arab block's wish to protect national marriage laws and practices from amounting to rape or sexual slavery, constituting crimes against humanity. Chapter 7 explores which national norms and rules exactly the Arab block might have wanted to protect. It argues that domestic non-criminalisation of marital rape could explain the Arab block's suggestions regarding the ICC definition of rape. Two explanations are advanced for the non-criminalisation of marital rape under the Arab block's national laws: the religiously grounded and legally reinforced ideal of an obedient wife and the patriarchal understanding of rape as an honour crime. Chapter 7 furthermore argues that the Arab block sought to exclude marriage rights, duties and obligations such as the ideal of an obedient wife, the accepted language of a marriage offer, understandings of dowry and maintenance as well as irregular and temporary marriages from powers attaching to the right of ownership because they allow for husbands to subjugate their wives. Fundamental to the Arab block's dissent towards developments in national and international law in regard to sexualised crimes is the wish to maintain existing patriarchal power structures.

Finally, the Conclusion summarises the main findings, drawing together the discussion of war rape and forced marriage respectively, the theories behind their perpetration, their legislative histories, the critique of the ICC definitions of war rape and forced marriage, and the analysis of the process of defining the two crimes. Based on this, the Conclusion considers whether the ICC definitions of war rape and forced marriage could have been different. It argues that actors' incompatible mandates, divergent or non-existent precedents, the policy of unanimity, differences in standing between state and non-state actors and the work in coalitions made different outcomes of the ICC negotiations in this regard unlikely. Comparing the criminalisation of war rape and forced marriage highlights that the unequal standing of the two crimes at the time of the ICC negotiation influenced the actors' approach to them.

How war rape and forced marriage are criminalised can have significance for the characteristics of post-conflict justice in a particular context. Therefore, the Conclusion discusses the significance of the analysis presented in this book for post-conflict justice and recommends steps to ensure that it is better heard in the development of broader post-conflict strategies. In this context, it is important to consider what conduct should be criminalised, who should deal with allegations and what consequences should follow if they are upheld. It is argued

55 PrepCom2, 'Proposal Submitted by Bahrain, Iraq, Kuwait, Lebanon, the Libyan Arab Jamahiriya, Oman, Qatar, Saudi Arabia, the Sudan, the Syrian Arab Republic and United Arab Emirates Concerning the Elements of Crimes against Humanity (9 December 1999)' (n 54).

that a culture-sensitive approach is desirable. However, it has to be scrutinised whose interests are really served when criminalising, hearing or responding to certain acts. The definitions of war rape and forced marriage advocated in this book are survivor-oriented and better reflect their experiences as well as the nature of the crimes. They indicate the importance of a holistic post-conflict approach to sexualised war violence. NGOs are well-placed to teach progressive views on sexualised war violence and how to holistically address it to a variety of stakeholders.

In addition to advocating progressive definitions of war rape and forced marriage, the Conclusion addresses the book's other potential contributions of deepening the understanding of the ICC negotiations of war rape and forced marriage, narrowing gaps in the existing literature, contributing a different view on the ICC rape definition, raising awareness of forced marriage in times of armed conflict and highlighting relevant factors that need to be considered in the process of internationally criminalising yet unrecognised acts of sexualised war violence.

The Conclusion also draws attention to problems encountered in the course of this research such as the state-centric focus of the official record of the ICC negotiations. Following on from this, it introduces areas for future research emerging from this project, including a different theoretical approach to the ICC negotiations and the relevance and role of national normative structures as well as an analysis of the application, influence and impact of the ICC definitions of war rape and forced marriage on national and international jurisprudence.

Aims and potential contributions

Based on the above-mentioned critique of the ICC's approach to war rape and forced marriage, the aim of this research project is to narrow the two aforementioned gaps in the existing literature regarding the process of defining war rape in itself and the neglect of forced marriage in the ICC negotiations.

By addressing forced marriage in the context of the ICC negotiations, the aim of this research project is to raise awareness of the crime and to contribute towards its theorisation.

By comparing war rape, a well-theorised and well-established crime, and forced marriage in times of armed conflict, which is still undergoing definition and theorisation, relevant factors that need to be considered in the process of criminalising yet unrecognised acts of sexualised war violence under international law are highlighted. This way, as well as by giving a detailed account of the dynamics of the ICC negotiations, this book contributes to debates about the nature of international law-making.

Identifying shortcomings of the ICC definitions of war rape and forced marriage and how they came about can be a lesson for the future. Law-makers can learn from past mistakes and develop more adequate definitions of sexualised crimes committed in wartime in the future. More adequate definitions that better match survivors' experiences will facilitate obtaining legal redress.[56] Therefore, analysing the process of defining war rape and forced marriage in the ICC negotiations cannot only help law-makers to make better laws, but it can also help survivors. It serves the outcome of the law and therefore the survivors rather than the political fictions that are being protected.

Scope

While national and regional norms and laws covering acts of sexualised war violence are referred to, this project places a clear focus on international law as these are supposedly universal standards that all consenting parties should adhere to.

While men also become targets for acts of sexualised war violence, this research project focuses on women as the majority of survivors. However, the book makes clear that this is not the only way in which women experience war. Their roles as survivors, witnesses and perpetrators of acts of war violence are touched upon but an in-depth analysis and discussion of all of them is too comprehensive and therefore beyond the scope of this book.

While acts of war rape are implicitly covered by other crimes such as genocide by imposing measures intended to prevent births,[57] this research focuses on provisions that explicitly mention war rape. While definitions of war rape, for example as an outrage upon personal dignity, are relevant for an analysis of the legislative history of the crime, this project focuses on the definition of rape as a crime in and of itself. This is motivated by the view that it is crucial to directly name crimes for what they are in order to advance women's rights. However, since no definition of the crime of forced marriage itself existed at the time of the ICC negotiations, this research also analyses forced marriage defined as a form of sexual slavery. This decision is further informed by the fact that the SCSL also discussed forced marriage in that context. However, even though the book discusses sexual slavery in relation to forced marriage, it is not examined independently.

Even though crimes like forced prostitution, trafficking in human beings and the recruitment of child soldiers can also become relevant when discussing forced marriage, this book does not place a particular emphasis on them or their relationship to forced marriage.

While forced marriage in times of armed conflict is also discussed by the Extraordinary Chambers in the Courts of Cambodia (ECCC), little discussion has taken place at the time of writing. Therefore, the research project focuses on jurisprudence of the *ad hoc* tribunals and the SCSL. While the Cambodian type of forced marriage is mentioned, this book focuses on the Sierra Leonean type.

56 Oosterveld, 'Forced Marriage and the Special Court for Sierra Leone' (n 49); Seifert (n 6).

57 *Akayesu* Trial Judgment (n 9) para 507–508.

The analysis of the ICC definition of rape is clearly focused on the first element of the definition which, as explained above, raises questions especially in light of the initial progress made by the ICTR in defining rape.

As highlighted above, this book analyses and assesses the ICC definition of war rape and forced marriage. This serves as the starting point and motivation for the exploration of the process of how these definitions came about. It is not the aim of the research to analyse and assess the ICC definitions of the two crimes in detail as this has been done elsewhere.[58]

Since the focus of this research is on definitions of crimes and how they came about, it does not consider the ICC's rules and procedures, staffing requirements, structures or special measures for survivors of sexualised war violence. It also does not examine how the definitions are used in the court's jurisprudence as this project focuses on the legislative process.

While this research project uses feminist and constructivist theories to guide the analysis of the ICC negotiations of war rape and forced marriage, it does not intend to analyse the theories themselves but to apply them to practice.

In accord with feminist and constructivist scepticism of generalisability, only a limited generalisability is aimed for in this project in relation to its potential contribution mentioned above.

Bibliography

Conventions and statutes

Code of Offences against the Peace and Security of Mankind (28 July 1954) 9 UN GAOR Supp. (No. 9) at 11, UN Doc A/2693 (1954), 45 AJIL 123 (1951) <www.legal-tools.org/doc/80a02d/> accessed 18 August 2017.

Convention on the Prevention and Punishment of the Crime of Genocide (09 December 1948) 78 UNTS 277 (Genocide Convention) <www.legal-tools.org/doc/498c38/> accessed 18 August 2017.

Rome Statute of the International Criminal Court (17 July 1998) 2187 UNTS 3 <www.legal-tools.org/doc/7b9af9/> accessed 9 August 2017.

United Nations documents

Commission on Human Rights

Commission on Human Rights, 'Final Report of the Special Rapporteur on the Situation of Systematic Rape, Sexual Slavery and Slavery-Like Practices during Armed Conflict' (22 June 1998) UN Doc E/CN.4/Sub.2/1998/13 <www.ohchr.

58 For an analysis and assessment of the ICC definitions of war rape and forced marriage see supra 42–43 as well as for example Brouwer, *Supranational Criminal Prosecution of Sexual Violence* (n 7) 137–141; Valerie Oosterveld, 'Sexual Slavery and the International Criminal Court: Advancing International Law' (2004) 25 *Michigan Journal of International Law* 605.

org> accessed 28 August 2017 ©1998 United Nations. Reprinted with the Permission of the United Nations.

———, 'Preliminary Report Submitted by the Special Rapporteur on Violence against Women, Its Causes and Consequences, Ms. Radhika Coomaraswamy, in Accordance with Commission on Human Rights Resolution 1994/45' (22 November 1994) UN Doc E/CN.4/1995/42 <www.ohchr.org> accessed 28 August 2017.

———, 'Report on the Mission of the Special Rapporteur to Poland on the Issue of Trafficking and Forced Prostitution of Women (24 May to 1 June 1996)' (10 December 1996) UN Doc E/CN.4/1997/47/Add.1 <www.ohchr.org> accessed 28 August 2017.

———, 'Report of the Special Rapporteur on Violence against Women, Its Causes and Consequences, Ms. Radhika Coomaraswamy, Submitted in Accordance with Commission Resolution 1997/44' (26 January 1998) UN Doc E/CN.4/1998/54 <www.ohchr.org> accessed 28 August 2017.

Preparatory Commission for the International Criminal Court

PrepCom2, 'Proposal Submitted by Bahrain, Iraq, Kuwait, Lebanon, the Libyan Arab Jamahiriya, Oman, Qatar, Saudi Arabia, the Sudan, the Syrian Arab Republic and United Arab Emirates Concerning the Elements of Crimes against Humanity (09 December 1999)' UN Doc PCNICC/1999/WGEC/DP.39 <www.legal-tools.org/doc/33d070/> accessed 10 August 2017.

Security Council

UNSC Resolution 827 (25 May 1993) UN Doc S/RES/827 <www.legal-tools.org/doc/dc079b/> accessed 18 August 2017.

UNSC Resolution 955 (8 November 1994) UN Doc S/RES/955 <www.legal-tools.org/doc/f5ef47/> accessed 18 August 2017.

Other

Ad Hoc Committee on the Establishment of an International Criminal Court, 'Report of the Ad Hoc Committee on the Establishment of an International Criminal Court' (6 September 1995) UN Doc A/50/22 <www.legal-tools.org/doc/b50da8/> accessed 8 August 2017.

Assembly of States Parties to the Rome Statute of the International Criminal Court, 'Official Records of the Assembly of States Parties to the Rome Statute of the International Criminal Court, First session, New York, 3–10 September 2002' (9 September 2002) ICC-ASP/1/3 (Part II.B) <www.legal-tools.org/doc/3c0e2d/> accessed 9 August 2017.

Other legal documents

Bahrain Penal Code (1976) <www.bahrainrights.org/sites/default/files/Bahrain-Penal-Code.doc> accessed 17 March 2014.

The Criminal Act of 1991 (Sudan) <www.icrc.org/applic/ihl/ihl-nat.nsf/xsp/.ibmmodres/domino/OpenAttachment/applic/ihl/ihl-nat.nsf/B9EEBA1CA8F54121

C1256DC9005573F2/TEXT/Criminal%20Act%20-%20Sudan%20-%20EN.pdf> accessed 1 April 2014.

Iraqi Penal Code No 111 (1969) <www.iraq-lg-law.org/en/webfm_send/1350> accessed 18 March 2014.

Ley No 599 de 2000 Por la cual se expide el Código Penal (24 July 2000) (Colombia) <www.alcaldiabogota.gov.co/sisjur/normas/Norma1.jsp?i=6388> accessed 8 May 2015.

The Libyan Penal Code (1953) <https://ia600704.us.archive.org/25/items/LibyanPenalCodeenglish/LibyanPenalCode.pdf> accessed 24 March 2014.

Omani Penal Code (1974) <www.fiu.gov.om/forms.html> accessed 24 March 2014.

Qatari Penal Code (2004) <http://portal.www.gov.qa/wps/wcm/connect/8abaea8046be1deaae97ef70b3652ad8/Penal+Code.pdf?MOD=AJPERES&useDefaultText=0&useDefaultDesc=0> accessed 24 March 2014.

Cases

International Criminal Tribunal for the former Yugoslavia

Prosecutor v Anto Furundžija (Trial Judgment) ICTY IT-95-17/1-T (10 December 1998) <www.legal-tools.org/doc/e6081b/> accessed 9 August 2017, Mechanism for International Criminal Tribunals.

Prosecutor v Dragoljub Kunarac, Radomir Kovač and Zoran Vuković (Indictment) IT-96-23-T "Foča Case" (19 June 1996) <www.legal-tools.org/doc/3a081b/> accessed 18 August 2017, Mechanism for International Criminal Tribunals.

Prosecutor v Dragoljub Kunarac, Radomir Kovač and Zoran Vuković (Trial Judgment) ICTY IT-96-23-T and IT-96-23/1-T "Foča Case" (22 February 2001) <www.legal-tools.org/doc/fd881d/> accessed 9 August 2017, Mechanism for International Criminal Tribunals.

International Criminal Tribunal for Rwanda

Prosecutor v Jean-Paul Akayesu (Amended Indictment) ICTR-96-4-I (16 February 1996), Mechanism for International Criminal Tribunals.

Prosecutor v Jean-Paul Akayesu (Trial Judgment) ICTR-96-4-T (02 September 1998) <www.legal-tools.org/doc/b8d7bd/> accessed 9 August 2017, Mechanism for International Criminal Tribunals.

Special Court for Sierra Leone

Prosecutor v Alex Tamba Brima, Brima Bazzy Kamara and Santigie Borbor Kanu (Trial Judgment) SCSL-04-16-T 'AFRC Case' (20 June 2007) <www.legal-tools.org/doc/87ef08/> accessed 9 August 2017.

Prosecutor v Alex Tamba Brima, Brima Bazzy Kamara and Santigie Borbor Kanu (Appeals Chamber Judgment) SCSL SLS-2004-16-A 'AFRC Case' (22 February 2008) <www.legal-tools.org/doc/4420ef/> accessed 9 August 2017.

Prosecutor v Issa Hassan Sesay, Morris Kallon and Augustine Gbao (Trial Judgment) SCSL-04-15-PT 'RUF Case' (02 March 2009) <www.legal-tools.org/doc/4420ef/> accessed 9 August 2017.

Prosecutor v Charles Taylor (Trial Judgment) SCSL-03-01-T (18 May 2012) <www.legal-tools.org/doc/3e7be5/> accessed 9 August 2017.

Interviews

Interview 13 (15 May 2014).
Interview 17 (17 June 2014).
Interview 18 (25 June 2014).

Books

Bassiouni, M.C., *The Legislative History of the International Criminal Court* (Transnational Publishers 2005).

Benedetti, F., Bonneau, K. and Washburn, J., *Negotiating the International Criminal Court: New York to Rome, 1994–1998* (Brill 2013).

Brouwer, A.M.L.M. de, *Supranational Criminal Prosecution of Sexual Violence: The ICC and the Practice of the ICTY and the ICTR* (Insertia 2005).

Cassese, A., Gaeta, P. and Jones, J.R.W.D. (eds), *The Rome Statute of the International Criminal Court: A Commentary* (Oxford University Press 2002).

Coulter, C., *Bush Wives and Girl Soldiers: Women's Lives through War and Peace in Sierra Leone* (Cornell University Press 2009).

Dörmann, K., *Elements of War Crimes under the Rome Statute of the International Criminal Court: Sources and Commentary* (Cambridge University Press 2003).

Finnemore, M., *National Interests in International Society* (Cornell University Press 1996).

Goldstein, J.S., *War and Gender: How Gender Shapes the War System and Vice Versa* (Cambridge University Press 2001).

Katzenstein, P., *Cultural Norms and National Security: Police and Military in Postwar Japan* (Cornell University Press 1996).

Lee, R.S. (ed), *The International Criminal Court: Elements of Crimes and Rules of Procedure and Evidence* (Transnational Publishers 2001).

———, *The International Criminal Court: The Making of the Rome Statute: Issues, Negotiations, Results* (Kluwer Law International 1999).

Schabas, W.A., *An Introduction to the International Criminal Court* (Cambridge University Press 2007).

Smart, C., *Law, Crime and Sexuality: Essays in Feminism* (Sage Publications 1995).

Stiglemayer, A. (ed), *Massenvergewaltigungen: Krieg gegen die Frauen* (Fischer Taschenbuchverlag 1993).

Chapters in edited books

Boot, M., 'Article 7 Crimes against Humanity Para. 1 (g) Rape … or Any Other Form of Sexual Violence of Comparable Gravity' in Otto Triffterer (ed), *Commentary on the Rome Statute of the International Criminal Court: Observers' Notes, Article by Article* (2nd edn, CH Beck 2008).

Brownmiller, S., 'Making Female Bodies the Battlefield' in Ronald J. Berger and Patricia Searles (eds), *Rape and Society: Readings on the Problem of Sexual Assault* (Westview Press 1995).

Cottier, M., 'Article 8 War Crimes Para. 2 (b) (xxii) Rape and Other Forms of Sexual Violence' in Otto Triffterer (ed), *Commentary on the Rome Statute of the International Criminal Court: Observers' Notes, Article by Article* (2nd edn, CH Beck 2008).

Dörmann, K., 'War Crimes under the Rome Statute of the International Criminal Court, with a Special Focus on the Negotiations on the Elements of Crimes' in Armin von Bogdandy and Rüdiger Wolfrum (eds), *Max Planck Yearbook of United Nations Law* (Volume 7, Martinus Nijhoff Publishers 2003).

Drakulić, S., 'The Rape of Women in Bosnia' in Miranda Davies (ed), *Women and Violence: Realities and Responses World Wide* (Zed Books 1994).

Eifler, C., 'Krieg – Gewalt – Geschlecht' in Medica Mondiale, Marlies W. Fröse and Ina Volpp-Teuscher (eds), *Krieg, Geschlecht und Traumatisierung: Erfahrungen und Reflexionen in der Arbeit mit traumatisierten Frauen in Kriegs- und Krisengebieten* (IKO-Verlag für Interkulturelle Kommunikation 1999).

Jackson, E. and Lacey, N., 'Introducing Feminist Legal Theory' in Richard Nobles, James Penner and David Schiff (eds), *Introduction to Jurisprudence and Legal Theory: Commentary and Materials* (Oxford University Press 2002).

Khalaf, M.C., 'Lebanon' in Julia Breslin and Sanja Kelly (eds), *Women's Rights in the Middle East and North Africa: Progress Amid Resistance* (Freedom House/Rowman & Littlefield Publishers 2010) <www.freedomhouse.org/sites/default/files/inline_images/Lebanon.pdf> accessed 21 March 2014.

La Haye, E., 'Article 8(2)(b)(xii): Rape, Sexual Slavery, Enforced Prostitution, Forced Pregnancy, Enforced Sterilization, and Sexual Violence' in Roy S. Lee (ed), *The International Criminal Court: Elements of Crimes and Rules of Procedure and Evidence* (Transnational Publishers 2001).

Mischkowski, G., 'Sexualisierte Gewalt im Krieg: Eine Chronik' in Medica Mondiale and Karin Griese (eds), *Sexualisierte Kriegsgewalt und ihre Folgen: Handbuch zur Unterstützung traumatisierter Frauen in verschiedenen Arbeitsfeldern* (2nd edn, Mabuse-Verlag 2006).

Reus-Smit, C., 'Constructivism' in Scott Burchill and others (eds), *Theory of International Relations* (3rd edn, Palgrave Macmillan 2005).

Seifert, R., 'Krieg und Vergewaltigung: Ansätze zu einer Analyse' in Alexandra Stiglemayer (ed), *Massenvergewaltigungen: Krieg gegen die Frauen* (Fischer Taschenbuchverlag 1993).

Journal articles

Erb, N.E., 'Gender-Based Crimes under the Draft Statute of the Permanent International Criminal Court' (1998) 29 *Columbia Human Rights Law Review* 401.

Hall, C.K., 'The First Five Sessions of the UN Preparatory Commission for the International Criminal Court' (2000) 94 *American Journal of International Law* 773.

Kurki, M. and Sinclair, A., 'Hidden in Plain Sight: Constructivist Treatment of Social Context and its Limitations' (2010) 47 *International Politics* 1.

Moshan, B.S., 'Women, War, and Words: The Gender Component in the Permanent International Criminal Court's Definition of Crimes against Humanity' (1998) 22 *Fordham International Law Journal* 154.

Oosterveld, V., 'Forced Marriage and the Special Court for Sierra Leone: Legal Advances and Conceptual Difficulties' (2011) 2 *Journal of International Humanitarian Legal Studies* 127.

———, 'Sexual Slavery and the International Criminal Court: Advancing International Law' (2004) 25 *Michigan Journal of International Law* 605.

(Research) reports and working papers

Carlson, K. and Mazurana, D., 'Forced Marriage within the Lord's Resistance Army, Uganda' (2008) Tufts University Feinstein International Center <https://wikis.uit.tufts.edu/confluence/download/attachments/14553676/Forced+Marriage+within+the+LRA.pdf?version=1> accessed 8 July 2013.

U.S. Department of State, Bureau of Democracy, Human Rights, and Labor, '2009 Human Rights Report: Saudi Arabia' (2010) <www.state.gov/j/drl/rls/hrrpt/2009/nea/136079.htm> accessed 1 April 2014.

———, '2009 Human Rights Report: Syria' (2010) <www.state.gov/j/drl/rls/hrrpt/2009/nea/136080.htm> accessed 1 April 2014.

Women Under Siege, 'Liberia' <www.womenundersiegeproject.org/conflicts/profile/Liberia> accessed 23 January 2015.

———, 'Sierra Leone' <www.womenundersiegeproject.org/conflicts/profile/sierra-leone> accessed 23 January 2015.

ICC advocacy papers, commentaries, recommendations, reports and working papers

Human Rights Watch, 'Commentary on the Second Preparatory Commission on Rules of Procedure and Elements of Crime' (July 1999) <www.iccnow.org/documents/HRWComment2ndPrepComJuly99.pdf> accessed 9 February 2012.

Women's Caucus for Gender Justice, 'Recommendations and Commentary for December 1997 PrepCom on the Establishment of an International Criminal Court' (December 1997) <www.iccnow.org/documents/5PrepComRecommWomensC.pdf> accessed 4 December 2013.

Other

Coalition for the International Criminal Court, 'History of the ICC' <www.iccnow.org/?mod=icchistory> accessed 3 December 2013.

Federal Bureau of Investigation, 'Frequently Asked Questions about the Change in the UCR Definition of Rape' (11 December 2014) <www.fbi.gov/about-us/cjis/ucr/recent-program-updates/new-rape-definition-frequently-asked-questions> accessed 19 January 2015.

International Criminal Court, 'About the Court' <www.icc-cpi.int/en_menus/icc/about%20the%20court/Pages/about%20the%20court.aspx> accessed 28 January 2015.

———, 'At a Glance' <www.icc-cpi.int/en_menus/icc/about%20the%20court/icc%20at%20a%20glance/Pages/icc%20at%20a%20glance.aspx> accessed 28 January 2015.

———, 'Establishment of the Court' <www.icc-cpi.int/en_menus/icc/about%20the%20court/icc%20at%20a%20glance/Pages/establishment%20of%20the%20court.aspx> accessed 28 January 2015.

———, 'Factsheet' <www.icc-cpi.int/en_menus/icc/about%20the%20court/icc%20at%20a%20glance/factsheets/Pages/fact%20sheets.aspx> accessed 28 January 2015.

———, 'Situations and Cases: Uganda' <www.icc-cpi.int/en_menus/icc/situations%20and%20cases/situations/situation%20icc%200204/Pages/situation%20index.aspx> 23 January 2015.

McHugh, R., 'RUF' (23 November 2015) Encyclopaedia Britannica <www.britannica.com/topic/Revolutionary-United-Front> accessed 20 February 2016.

Nicol, D.S.H.W., 'Sierra Leone' (13 May 2014) Encyclopaedia Britannica <www.britannica.com/place/Sierra-Leone/Civil-war#ref978722> accessed 2 July 2015.

2 Theories and methods

Introduction

Feminism and constructivism are the two main theories underpinning this research project. Chapter 2 explains first feminist theories, then constructivist theories, and their respective value for this research project. Within the brief description of feminist theories, Chapter 2 highlights the male subject, substance, and methods of law that are a product of, and produce, realities. Within the field of constructivist theories, a focus is placed on Martha Finnemore's and Peter Katzenstein's claims regarding the relevance of state and non-state actors as well as international and national normative structures respectively in international relations. The shortcomings of feminism and constructivism as well as the advantages of a combined theoretical approach are considered.

After Chapter 2 outlined the theoretical underpinnings of this research project, it discusses the methods used. It elaborates on the main preoccupations and limitations of qualitative research methods. Establishing a link to the theoretical basis of this project, the feminist research method of asking 'the woman question' is explained and illustrated. The foundational literature and document analysis, and the semi-structured interviews conducted for this research project are discussed. Before summing up, the chapter covers the methods of analysis and synthesis of research findings.

Theories

'Feminism is a varied and evolving philosophy and those who consider themselves to be "feminist" are a diverse group with a broad range of perspectives.'[1] Nevertheless, feminists are considered to share the view that sex/gender is one important social structure or axis of social organisation and differentiation. In

1 Dianne L. Martin, 'Retribution Revisited: A Reconsideration of Feminist Criminal Law Reform Strategies' (1998) 36 *Osgoode Hall Law Journal* 151, 152.

While the author is aware of the multitude of feminist theories, the singular 'feminism' is used throughout this book for reasons of readability.

addition, feminist theories come together in taking a critical stance in their analysis of patriarchy.[2]

Feminist legal theories aim to show how, where and why the law, legal institutions and legal processes fail women. Their project is to uncover and claim as valid the experiences of women.[3] 'Feminist legal theories offer a thoroughgoing critique of law's claim to be [rational, abstract,] impartial and objective.'[4] As law is made by men and based on their norms, knowledge and experiences, feminist legal theories understand legal reasoning to be male, the legal subject to implicitly be a man, and the substance of law to reflect a male point of view.[5] '[I]ssues traditionally of concern to men become seen [and legitimised] as general human concerns, while 'women's concerns' are relegated to a special, limited category.'[6] The male method, subject and substance of law is furthered by the public/private dichotomy law rests on.[7] In consequence, women's voices in law are silenced. Gender hierarchies are created and gender stereotypes reinforced.

Like feminism, constructivism is not a single, unified approach.[8] '[T]here is vibrant debate within constructivism, with competing understandings [amongst others] of logics of interaction.'[9] Nevertheless, it is possible to define certain

2 Hilary Charlesworth, 'Feminists Critiques of International Law and Their Critics' (1995) *Third World Legal Studies* 1; Emily Jackson and Nicola Lacey, 'Introducing Feminist Legal Theory' in Richard Nobles, James Penner and David Schiff (eds), *Introduction to Jurisprudence and Legal Theory: Commentary and Materials* (Oxford University Press 2002) 784; Martin (n 1) 152.

3 Hilaire Barnett, *Introduction to Feminist Jurisprudence* (Cavendish Publishing 1998) 93–119; Catharine MacKinnon, 'Feminism, Marxism, Method and the State: Towards a Feminist Jurisprudence' (1983) 8 *Signs* 635, 638; Ngaire Naffine, 'In Praise of Legal Feminism' (2002) 22 *Legal Studies* 71, 73.

4 Jackson and Lacey (n 2) 779.

Carol Gilligan, *In a Different Voice: Psychological Theory and Women's Development* (2nd edn, Harvard University Press 1993): Rationality, abstraction, impartiality and objectivity are associated with a male type of reasoning, focused on ethics of individual rights and justice. Feminine reasoning, in contrast, emphasises ethics of care, including relationships, contexts and communication.

5 Jackson and Lacey (n 2) 814–815; Carol Smart, *Law, Crime and Sexuality: Essays in Feminism* (Sage Publications 1995) 189–190.

6 Hilary Charlesworth, Christine Chinkin and Shelly Wright, 'Feminist Approaches to International Law' (1991) 85 *American Journal of International Law* 613, 625.

7 For further reading see Gayle Binion, 'Human Rights: A Feminist Perspective' (1995) 17 *Human Rights Quarterly* 509; Hilary Charlesworth, 'Feminist Methods in International Law' (1999) 93 *American Journal of International Law* 379; Hilary Charlesworth and Christine Chinkin, *The Boundaries of International Law: A Feminist Analysis* (Manchester University Press 2000) 30–31, 43–44, 56–59; Charlesworth, Chinkin and Wright (n 6); Christine Chinkin, 'A Critique of the Public/Private Dimension' (1999) 10 *European Journal of International Law* 387.

8 While the present researcher is aware of the multitude of constructivist theories, the singular 'constructivism' is used in this book for reasons of readability.

9 Jutta Brunnée and Stephen J. Toope, 'Constructivism and International Law' in Jeffrey L. Dunoff and Mark A. Pollack (eds), *Interdisciplinary Perspectives on International Law and International Relations: The State of the art* (Cambridge University Press 2012) 9 <http://papers.ssrn.com/sol3/papers.cfm?abstract_id=2088132> accessed 14 January 2015.

key assumptions and ideas that are held in common by most constructivist scholars. Constructivists assume that the world is socially constructed by people. Therefore, it can change and constructivists seek to explain these changes. They understand people's backgrounds to influence their identities and interests, and to be largely made up of normative structures. Constructivists also recognise material structures but understand their content and significance to be directed by normative structures. Actors' identities and interests influence their actions which can lead to change in normative structures (constructivist circle).[10]

The relevant actors for this research project are state and non-state delegations and their members that participated in the International Criminal Court (ICC) negotiations. For the purpose of this book, a state is an entity with 'a) a permanent population; b) a defined territory; c) government; and d) capacity to enter into relations with other states.'[11] Non-governmental organisations (NGOs) are defined as local, national or international non-profit groups that are independent from government.[12]

Structures that will be considered are relevant personal, national and international values, norms and rules. For the purpose of this project, a value is one's judgment of what is important in life. Norms are 'standards of behaviour created through mutual expectation in a social setting'.[13] They are understood as emanating from shared values and as the basis of legally enforceable rules.[14] Rules are legal norms, sets of regulations governing conduct.

This book will draw particularly on the constructivist theories advanced by Martha Finnemore and Peter Katzenstein. Katzenstein offers domestic normative structures as explanations of variations in actors' identities, interests and actions.[15] Finnemore, in contrast, focuses on the international domain. In addition, she claims that NGOs are 'active teachers' of states. NGOs as outside actors present problems and solutions to state governments. They teach their views to states

10 Brunnée and Toope (n 9) 7; Milja Kurki and Andriana Sinclair, 'Hidden in Plain Sight: Constructivist Treatment of Social Context and Its Limitations' (2010) 47 *International Politics* 1, 1, 3–4; see also Martha Finnemore, *National Interests in International Society* (Cornell University Press 1996) 1–33; Peter Katzenstein, *Cultural Norms and National Security: Police and Military in Postwar Japan* (Cornell University Press 1996) 1–32.

11 Montevideo Convention on Rights and Duties of States (26 December 1933) 165 INTS 19 art 1.

12 United Nations Rule of Law, 'Non-governmental Organizations' <www.unrol.org/article.aspx?article_id=23> accessed 10 April 2015.

Although some organisations have government officials as their members, they are still considered non-governmental organisations (NGOs) here. Even though the International Committee of the Red Cross (ICRC) has a hybrid nature, including characteristics of an NGO and an international organisation, for the purpose of this book, it is included in the category of NGOs as this is the role of interest for this research. The terms 'NGO', 'civil society' and 'non-state actors' are used synonymously.

13 Brunnée and Toope (n 9) 1.

14 See Alan Boyle and Christine Chinkin, *The Making of International Law* (Oxford University Press 2007).

15 Katzenstein (n 10).

by setting agendas, defining tasks and shaping interests of states.[16] This way, NGOs not only influence states' actions but also their identities. Therefore, Finnemore's theory allows for examining shifts in states' actions and for tracing the causes of these shifts back to normative claims made by NGOs.[17] By focusing on structures and actors, Finnemore's theory also allows for exploring how NGOs came to hold certain normative views and the mechanisms enabling NGOs to teach their views to states.[18] Taken together, Martha Finnemore's and Peter Katzenstein's theories create a holistic constructivist explanation of the factors influencing the process of defining war rape and forced marriage in times of armed conflict under the ICC. They bridge the dichotomy between the international and the domestic domain and enable explanations of the development of normative structures of the present international system.[19]

Various criticisms are raised against feminist and constructivist theories. One of them claims that, even though feminism is committed to gender equality, it is biased towards women and to elevate women's interests above men's. Feminism is pre-committed to making distinctions between *m* and *f* – men and women, male and female, masculine and feminine – where *f* is subordinate or disadvantaged to *m*. Feminism is pre-committed to side with *f*. This priority for *m/f* and of siding with *f* results in a neglect to examine *m* and *f* without assuming a domination–subordination relationship that necessarily takes the form of *m>f*. Not every issue and every challenge can be attributed to *m/f* in the first place.[20]

Regarding constructivism, it is suggested that it ignores power structures like gender and patriarchy that prevent change. This leads to hierarchies and inequalities not being adequately addressed. Linked to this, the criticism is raised that

16 Finnemore (n 10) 12: Finnemore contrasted this teaching with learning processes where states learn from each other or from NGOs. The difference is that in this learning process, 'the impetus for learning […] lies inside the state. What is causal lies at the state or sub-state level. There are no active teachers in this process. To the extent that states are taught, they are self-taught.' It can be argued that the term 'teach' downplays states' understanding of an issue and overrates the effect NGOs have on states. It indicates bias for NGOs. Against this background, 'influence' may be a more appropriate, if more cautious term to use. However, if 'teaching' is understood as introducing someone to (a different angle on) a topic, as imparting information rather than as instructing someone what to do or how to do something, the term reflects the role NGOs played in the International Criminal Court (ICC) negotiations. Therefore, it is maintained in this book.

17 Finnemore (n 10) 1–33.

18 ibid.

19 Christian Reus-Smit, 'Constructivism' in Scott Burchill and others (eds), *Theory of International Relations* (3rd edn, Palgrave Macmillan 2005) 201.

20 Barnett (n 3) 19–23; Janet Halley, 'Take a Break from Feminism?' in Karen Knop (ed), *Gender and Human Rights* (Oxford University Press 2004) 61, 65–68, 166, 197; Smart (n 5) 162–185.

the constructivist idea that actors and structures mutually constitute each other assumes equality of actors.[21]

Taken together, feminism and constructivism resolve their respective limitations mentioned above. Feminism emphasises power structures in a constructivist analysis. Constructivism goes beyond feminism's focus on *m/f* and *m>f* and enables a gender-neutral approach.

Feminism and constructivism share the desire to challenge and rethink what is treated as given, including traditional power structures. Both theories recognise that realities are socially constructed. Constructivism focuses on the fact that realities are constructed and the process of how a particular reality came about through the interaction of normative structures and actors. For feminism, in contrast, the outcome, the way realities are made to be, is more important than the fact that they are constructed. Feminism highlights that normative structures are not neutral but gendered and therefore influence actors in different ways. In addition, both, feminism and constructivism stress the importance of diversity which highlights the importance of contexts and makes communication necessary. Both theories are also interested in change, raising scepticism about absolutes and objective grand theories. While constructivism focuses on the process of change, feminism focuses on substance. As mentioned above, it adds politics to a constructivist analysis. By not taking a political position, however, constructivism establishes itself as a flexible theory that moves beyond specific sets of domination and subordination. Therefore, the outcome of a constructivist analysis of the development of normative structures is more complex and less predictable than that of a feminist analysis.

Feminist theories are useful to address the gender issues this book deals with. War rape and forced marriage in times of armed conflict are gendered crimes as they target women and men to different extents, in different ways and for different purposes. Acts of gender-based violence include violations that are based on, and perpetuate, socially constructed or stereotyped gender roles, and the power differences between women and men. In addition to the crimes discussed in this book, the nature of law-making is gendered. More men than women are involved in law-making processes. Consequently, law-making reflects male reasoning. In a rational, abstract, impartial and objective way, issues are defined, precedents analysed and concussions recommended. The resulting laws are based on, and reflect, male norms, knowledge and experiences.

Constructivist theories allow for a detailed analysis of the process of criminalising rape and forced marriage in times of armed conflict under the statute of the ICC. By placing a focus on actors as well as normative structures and their interactions, they support the focus of this research project. Constructivists understand the nature of law-making to be a process of social construction.

21 Brunnée and Toope (n 9); Kurki and Sinclair (n 10); Birgit Lochner and Elisabeth Prügl, 'Feminism and Constructivism: Worlds Apart or Sharing the Middle Ground?' (2001) 45 *International Studies Quarterly* 111.

Actors involved are state and non-state actors. They are influenced by normative structures such as personal, national and international values, norms and rules. Actors exchange their ideas and interests and their shared understandings of normative structures build the foundation of legal rules.

Building on a feminist and constructivist understanding of the nature of law-making, it is argued in this book that yet unrecognised acts of sexualised war violence against women have to be recognised as a serious issue first before they are considered under existing legal categories and eventually defined as crimes in their own right. Based on shared normative understandings, state and non-state actors define a conduct as serious. It is then categorised abstractly based on existing male legal rules. This provides an opportunity for further deliberation. Existing normative structures are then adapted to make 'room for new insights and perspectives generated by new contexts'[22] and the conduct is defined as a crime in and of itself.

Methods

To develop a better understanding of the process of the ICC negotiations and the actors' identities, interests and actions, qualitative research methods were used. In addition to being influenced by the project's objectives and questions, the choice of research methods was guided by feminist and constructivist theories. To generate a better contextual understanding of events such as the ICC negotiations, qualitative research methods probe beneath surface appearances. This is in accord with feminist and constructivist theories that aim to deconstruct what is taken for granted. Since feminist and constructivist theories understand experiences to be socially constructed and to vary over time and space, the flexible, context- and process-sensitive research approach that qualitative research methods offer was fitting. Linked to this is feminism's and constructivism's scepticism of absolutes, generalisations and objectivity. Consequently, feminists make cautious claims about the data constructed.[23]

22 Katharine Bartlett, 'Feminist Legal Methods' (1990) 103 *Harvard Law Review* 829, 852–853.

23 Bartlett (n 22) 852–863; Alan Bryman, *Social Research Methods* (4th edn, Oxford University Press 2012) 380, 399–404; Charlesworth, 'Feminist Methods in International Law' (n 7); Charlesworth, Chinkin and Wright (n 6) 613–645; Sandra Harding, 'Is There a Feminist Method?' in Sandra Harding (ed), *Feminism and Methodology* (Indiana University Press 1987); Sharlene Nagy Hesse-Biber, 'Feminist Research: Exploring the Interconnections of Epistemology, Methodology, and Method' in Sharlene Nagy Hesse-Biber (ed), *Handbook of Feminist Research* (Sage Publications 2007); Jackson and Lacey (n 2) 789; Celia Kitzinger, 'Feminist Approaches' in Giampietro Gobo and others (eds), *Qualitative Research Practice* (Sage Publications 2007) 114–118; Debbie Kralik and Antonia van Loon, 'Feminist Research' in Seamus Cowman and others (eds), *Nursing Research: Designs and Methods* (Churchill Livingstone Elsevier 2008) 36; Kurki and Sinclair (n 10); Steinar Kvale and Svend Brinkmann, *Interviews: Learning the Craft of Qualitative Research Interviewing* (2nd edn, Sage Publications 2009) 1–20, 53–56;

While qualitative research methods are appropriate for this research project, their limitations have to be taken into account. Critics often assert that qualitative research is too subjective and consequently difficult to replicate and verify. Within the feminist and constructivist framework of this research project, however, subjectivity and even biases are generally considered unavoidable and acceptable as long as the researcher reflects on them and communicates them to the research participants. However, it has to be noted that the researcher's self-disclosure creates the risk of being stereotyped and vulnerable to criticism. The researcher's values might also challenge research participants who might second-guess their answers in an interview. The subjective construction, selection and interpretation of information means that any findings are tentative.[24]

While it is criticised that findings resulting from qualitative research rely upon personal relationships between the researcher and the research participants, this is unproblematic according to feminist values that emphasise trusting relationships, mutual understanding and true dialogues.[25]

In addition to difficulties in replicating qualitative studies, qualitative findings are difficult to generalise due to the small number of research participants or cases (small n). A degree of generalisability is nevertheless achieved in this research project through links established to, and comparisons drawn with, other researchers' work or other cases. In addition to questions of generalisability, the validity of small n studies is problematised as they arguably are not representative and therefore misleading. This criticism, however, ignores that qualitative research involving a small number of participants often provides more intense accounts, considerable detail and more insights into a situation or event than studies involving larger samples. Particularly relevant for this research project, small n studies allow for acquiring a better sense of an experience at an individual and subjective level.[26]

Maeve Landmann, 'Getting Quality in Qualitative Research: A Short Introduction to Feminist Methodology and Methods' (2006) 65 *Proceedings of Nutrition Society* 429, 430–431.

24 Bartlett (n 22) 857; Kvale and Brinkmann (n 23) 85; Bryman (n 23) 382–383, 404–406, 492; Christopher Harding, 'Anecdote, Vignette and Quantification: A Biographical Dilemma' Aberystwyth University, Department of Law and Criminology, Cartel Biographies Project <www.aber.ac.uk/en/law-criminology/research/researchclusters/global-commerce/cartel-collusion/anecdote/> accessed 24 September 2014; Harding, 'Is There a Feminist Method?' (n 23); Kralik and van Loon (n 23) 37; Landmann (n 23) 431; Shulamit Reinhartz, *Feminist Methods in Social Research* (Oxford University Press 1992) 33.

25 Marjorie L. DeVault and Glenda Gross, 'Feminist Qualitative Interviewing: Experience, Talk, and Knowledge' in Sharlene Nagy Hesse-Biber (ed), *Handbook of Feminist Research* (Sage Publications 2007); Sharlene Nagy Hesse-Biber, 'The Practice of Feminist In-Depth Interviewing' in Sharlene Nagy Hesse-Biber and Patricia Leavy (eds), *Feminist Research Practice* (Sage Publications 2007); Reinhartz (n 24) 18–45; Sotirios Sarantakos, *Social Research* (4th edn, Palgrave Macmillan 2013).

26 Bryman (n 23) 405–406; Harding, 'Anecdote, Vignette and Quantification' (n 24).

Feminist research methods: Asking 'the woman question'

As mentioned above, feminist legal theories claim that women's realities are shaped by male law, legal institutions and legal processes.[27] This assumption is linked to asking 'the woman question' which examines the gender implications of rules and social practices which may otherwise appear to be objective or neutral. It includes questions such as the following: Have women been considered? If not, in what way have they been left out? How could that be corrected? What difference would a correction make? Asking 'the woman question' in law means

- asking how, where and why the law, legal institutions and legal processes fail women;
- analysing the production of a system of rules;
- challenging assumptions, power structures and stereotypes;
- questioning who examines an issue, who makes a law and whom particular rules serve;
- scrutinising the definition of, and explanation for, an issue, the focus of an inquiry and which social conditions are reflected and impacted;
- uncovering silences; and
- examining possibilities for an empowering transformation of the law.[28]

In addition to asking 'the woman question' as a method to analyse the criminalisation of war rape and forced marriage under the ICC instruments, it can be argued that the substance of this book itself is asking 'the woman question'. After all, the research project focuses on issues of gender within the making of international law. However, from a constructivist perspective, this is unavoidable as methods do not only shape the substance of research, but substance also shapes the research methods that are used.[29]

As a general word of caution, when asking 'the woman question' it is crucial to keep in mind that women are not a homogenous group. Patriarchal culture, however, essentialises women and establishes hierarchies based on the degree to which women adhere to their patriarchal definition.[30]

27 Jackson and Lacey (n 2); Smart (n 5) 189–190.

28 Barnett (n 3) 93–119; Bartlett (n 22) 837–849; Binion (n 7) 510–513; Kvale and Brinkmann (n 23) 1–20, 53–56; Charlesworth, 'Feminists Critiques of International Law and Their Critics' (n 2); Charlesworth, 'Feminist Methods in International Law' (n 7); Charlesworth, Chinkin and Wright (n 6); Harding, 'Is There a Feminist Method?' (n 23); Hesse-Biber, 'Feminist Research' (n 23); Jackson and Lacey (n 2) 826; Kitzinger (n 23) 114–118; Kralik and van Loon (n 23) 36; Landmann (n 23) 430–431; Julie Mertus and Pamela Goldberg, 'A Perspective on Women and International Human Rights after the Vienna Declaration: The Inside/Outside Construct' (1994) 26 *New York University Journal of International Law and Politics* 201, 220; Naffine (n 3) 73.

29 Bartlett (n 22) 844.

30 ibid 843–835; Charlesworth and Chinkin (n 7) 40–42; Harding, 'Is There a Feminist Method?' (n 23).

Critical analysis of existing literature and relevant documents

This research employed a critical analysis of existing literature and relevant documents related to the ICC negotiations of war rape and forced marriage as the foundational research method. The aim was to draw conclusions about the factors that influenced the ICC definition of war rape and forced marriage. A document analysis is a necessary part of every research project and invaluable for most triangulation. It was of special significance for this research project as primary sources were studied.

The documents analysed included secondary literature as well as primary sources such as conventions and statutes, United Nations (UN) documents, other legal documents as well as case reports of national and international courts. ICC advocacy papers, commentaries, recommendations, reports and working papers were also analysed. Together, these sources are considered to establish a comprehensive record of the ICC negotiations.

Most documents analysed for this research project were publicly available in libraries, archives and online. The research project profited from the existence and easy availability of documents. It has to be kept in mind, however, that library and online searches provide only partial and limited access to information in the sense that not every source may be available.[31] To access as many documents as possible, various libraries, archives and databases were used.

In general, the documents used were deemed authentic, reliable and meaningful.[32] A large majority of documents is of unquestioned authorship. Comparisons were established between information constructed from different documents as well as between information constructed from documents and in interviews to ensure their credibility. This way, erroneous or distorted information was balanced.

Interviews

When the document analysis reached theoretical saturation, many research questions could still not be answered satisfactorily. Therefore the critical document analysis was supplemented with interviews aimed at gaining a better understanding of the dynamics of the ICC negotiations, the main actors, their positions on sexualised violence, particularly war rape and forced marriage, and how these developed.

Research participants were sampled applying a generic purpose sampling approach to increase the prospect that research participants would have something of relevance to say about the research questions central to this project. The state and non-state delegations included in the sample were determined based on preliminary research on the main actors in the ICC negotiations,

31 Bryman (n 23) 655.
32 ibid 544.

especially in relation to sexualised violence, particularly war rape and forced marriage. In sampling members of various state and non-state delegations that participated in the ICC negotiations, a great deal of variety in the resulting sample was ensured. Consequently, different points of view were heard and considered. Despite the fact that the criteria for selecting participants were established at the outset of this project, the sample itself grew as research participants proposed other participants who could contribute to the research project. This limited the negative effects of the availability of only incomplete information about the actors who participated in the ICC negotiations. It also ensured the necessary flexibility to add to the initial sample as benefited the research questions and expected answers.[33]

Modern technology greatly facilitated access to the eventually 16 research participants who were involved in the ICC negotiations. Based on the purpose of this research project, this number was judged big enough to ensure meaningful contributions to the understanding of the ICC negotiations, especially of the main actors and their positions in relation to the crimes of war rape and forced marriage in times of armed conflict. At the same time, it was small enough to undertake a deep, case-orientated analysis.[34]

In the initial email sent to potential interviewees, they were informed about the purpose of the interview and the research project as well as the way in which the interview would be conducted. A list of general themes that would be discussed was included to give further information about the topic of the interviews. Including a list of general themes rather than of questions aimed at preventing the research participants from fully preparing and adjusting their answers beforehand. After the researcher received initial agreement of research participants to take part in an interview, informed consent forms were emailed to them. These included information on confidentiality, anonymity, the right to withdraw and the researcher's right to publish data constructed in the interviews.

For reasons of access as well as efficiency and effectiveness regarding time and costs, the interviews were carried out via Skype or telephone. Following feminist research methods, the fact that both the researcher and the research participants remained in familiar environments facilitated equality and context naturalness. The critique raised against Skype or telephone interviews that responses in face-to-face interviews are more accurate because the researcher and research participant have a 'normal' conversation was deemed outdated since video and telephone calls are a frequently used part of modern communication. Additionally, evidence suggests that little difference exists in the kinds of responses researchers get when asking questions in person or on the phone.[35]

33 ibid 418, 422–424.

34 ibid 424.

35 Kvale and Brinkmann (n 23) 147; Hesse-Biber, 'The Practice of Feminist In-Depth Interviewing' (n 25) 128; Roger W. Shuy, 'In-Person Versus Telephone Interviewing'

The critique that it is not possible to observe participants' body language in telephone interviews was addressed through Skype's video call function.

The interviews themselves were semi-structured. This open-ended and discursive format was chosen to allow flexibility to add questions spontaneously to the prepared interview guide. The questions asked in the interviews were based on the research questions, existing literature and initial document-based research. If relevant, lines of thought identified by earlier research participants were taken up and presented to later ones. The prepared interview questions mainly asked about values, behaviours, opinions, formal and informal roles, and relationships. Interviewees were also invited to raise additional or complementary issues to those brought up by the interviewer. This balanced the forms of engagement and facilitated an appreciation of what interviewees saw as relevant for the research area, conveying an additional sense of interviewee-orientation. More practically, it also aimed at preventing misunderstandings and ensuring the research participants did not feel that any relevant points remained unsaid. To prevent interviewees from avoiding unfamiliar or sensitive topics that were important for the research, follow-up questions, probing questions, specifying questions, direct questions and interpreting questions were asked.[36]

With the consent of the research participants, every interview was digitally recorded and notes were taken in the course of every interview. These were completed extensively when reviewing the interview recordings. As the notes were considered to serve the same purpose as transcriptions in terms of becoming familiar with what was said and conducting an initial analysis of the interviews, the interviews were not transcribed.

The constructed data was judged to be reliable. Following feminist research methods, the researcher relied on the authority of the interviewees' experiences. This is not to say that they were taken at face value without critically triangulating them with other data from different sources of information. Judged by the trustworthiness of the interviewees' reports and their credibility based on triangulation and a thorough data analysis, the constructed data was considered to be valid, sound and worth depending on.[37]

---

in Jaber F. Gubrium and James A. Holstein (eds), *Handbook of Interview Research: Context and Method* (Sage Publications 2001) 541; see also Paul Drew, Annie Irvine and Roy Sainsbury, 'Mode Effects in Qualitative Interviews: A Comparison of Semi-Structured Face-to-Face and Telephone Interviews Using Conversation Analysis' (2010) Social Policy Research Unit, University of York <www.york.ac.uk/inst/spru/research/pdf/modeEffects.pdf> accessed 6 May 2015; Judith E. Sturges and Kathleen J. Hanrahan, 'Comparing Face-to-Face Qualitative Interviewing: A Research Note' (2004) 4 *Qualitative Research* 107, 107–118.

36 Kvale and Brinkmann (n 23) 135–137; Bryman (n 23) 471–473; Beth L. Leech, 'Asking Questions: Techniques for Semistructured Interviews' (2002) 35 *PS Online* 665, 667–668.

37 Kvale and Brinkmann (n 23) 249, 304–305; Bryman (n 23) 390–391; Hesse-Biber, 'The Practice of Feminist In-Depth Interviewing' (n 25) 119; Reinhartz (n 24) 21.

In terms of a thematic evaluation of the interviews, it can be stated that they provided first-hand accounts and information that was not on record before. This way, the interviews helped to understand the context and established the atmosphere of the negotiations. They also contributed towards a better understanding of what drove the actors who participated in the negotiations. Speaking to some of the authors of crucial proposals facilitated a more thorough interpretation thereof. Therefore, the results of the interviews were considered worthwhile, valuable, insightful and beneficial.[38]

In terms of a dynamic evaluation, interviewees replied to the questions posed in an expansive, detailed and considered fashion. Indicated by the use of the personal pronoun 'we' or phrases like 'in my opinion', they gave private and/or public accounts of the ICC negotiations. The researcher was aware that the interviewees' accounts of the ICC negotiations were snapshots rather than the full story. They were accounts drawn from individual and personal experience and might have been presented in a way to impress. This meant they had to be interpreted with care. It also meant, however, that the accounts provided strong impressions of characters, ideas and objects, and allowed themes to be drawn from their telling. In most interviews, the conversation between the researcher and research participant was on equal footing. The conversation was regarded by the researcher as a reciprocal co-construction of meaning in the sense that both interviewer and interviewees shared relevant knowledge and influenced each other in what information was shared and where a focus was placed. Most interviewees appeared to be used to giving interviews which contributed to the clearness of articulation as well as to the consistency of their accounts. Some research participants asked for a list of questions to be sent prior to the interview. Therefore, they had and used the opportunity to prepare their responses. This occasionally limited the spontaneity of the interviewer and reduced interaction between the interviewee and the interviewer. Overall, however, the interviews where questions were sent to the research participant beforehand were not viewed as less informative as the ones where only general topics were shared with the interviewee prior to the interview.[39]

Reflecting on possible points of critique of interviews as a method of research, feminist and constructivist theories and methods render many of them irrelevant. As with qualitative research methods in general, it could be argued that interview-based findings are difficult to replicate as the whole interview process is subjective rather than objective. Following feminist and constructivist understandings, however, this is inevitable, even desirable. Subjectivity is balanced by a theory-led interpretation of research findings. These are generalisable to a certain extent

38 Kvale and Brinkmann (n 23) 304–305; Bryman (n 23) 395.

39 Michael Bloor and Fiona Wood, *Keywords in Qualitative Methods: A Vocabulary of Research Concepts* (Sage Publications 2006) 139–142; Harding, 'Anecdote, Vignette and Quantification' (n 24); Kitzinger (n 23) 114, 116; Kralik and van Loon (n 23) 38; Landmann (n 23) 430–431; Reinhartz (n 24) 18–21.

as they are compared with, and linked to, other researchers' work or other cases.[40]

Analysis and synthesis of research findings

Research findings were analysed and synthesised thematically as well as theoretically. The themes employed for the thematic analysis and synthesis related to the research questions and hypotheses. Examples are 'the role of NGOs' or 'the relevance of national norms and rules'. Feminist and constructivist theories formed the base of the theoretical analysis and synthesis of research findings. The risk of noticing only those aspects that can be seen through these theoretical lenses was countered by staying open to alternative interpretations. Research findings were summarised both under thematic and theoretical headings. This allowed for the identification of prominent sub-themes as well as comparing and contrasting research findings and establishing connections between them. This way, it was determined how research findings from different sources of information related to each other. Narratives which went beyond individual accounts were identified and used to produce new interpretations of the process of defining war rape and forced marriage under the ICC. Moreover, the importance of a context-sensitive analysis became apparent especially in relation to documents related to the legislative histories of war rape and forced marriage and their relationship to, and impact on, the ICC negotiations.[41]

Summary

Chapter 2 outlined feminism and constructivism as the main theories underpinning and applied in this thesis. Feminist and constructivist theorists understand reality to be constructed and are interested in its change. However, constructivists such as Martha Finnemore and Peter Katzenstein are interested in the fact that reality is constructed and the process of how it is constructed and how it changes. They emphasise the role of normative structures in international relations and law-making, shaping and being shaped by actors (constructivist circle). In their analysis of change, constructivist theorists focus on the role of domestic as well as international normative structures and on impetuses that are internal as well as external to actors. Feminists, in contrast, are interested in the outcome of construction processes and their gendered implications. They are interested

40 Bartlett (n 22) 863–867; Bloor and Wood (n 39) 79; Kvale and Brinkmann (n 23) 168–171; Harding, 'Anecdote, Vignette and Quantification' (n 24); Harding, 'Is There a Feminist Method?' (n 23); Kitzinger (n 23); Landmann (n 23); Reinhartz (n 24) 18–45; Sarantakos (n 25).

41 Kvale and Brinkmann (n 23) 234–239; Centre for Reviews and Dissemination, 'Incorporating Qualitative Evidence in or Alongside Effectiveness Reviews' in Centre for Reviews and Dissemination (eds), Systematic Reviews: CRD's Guidance for Undertaking Reviews in Health Care (January 2009) <www.york.ac.uk/crd/SysRev/!SSL!/WebHelp/6_5_SYNTHESIS_OF_QUALITATIVE_RESEARCH.htm> accessed 2 June 2015.

in the substance of reality and change. Feminist legal theories unmask and highlight sex/gender issues that are hidden by patriarchal structures such as legal rules, institutions and processes.

After Chapter 2 discussed the theoretical underpinnings of this thesis, it outlined the methods used. Qualitative research methods are used in this project as they are more appropriate than quantitative methods to create a better understanding of the ICC negotiations and how the definitions of war rape and forced marriage came about. Consistent with the theoretical basis of this thesis, feminist research methods are employed. They ask about gender implications of rules and social practices which may otherwise appear neutral. In addition, this research project employed a critical analysis of existing literature and relevant primary documents as a foundational research method to examine the factors that influenced the ICC definitions of war rape and forced marriage. To complement the critical document analysis, semi-structured interviews were conducted with state and non-state actors who participated in the ICC negotiations. The interviews aimed at gaining a better understanding of the dynamics of the ICC negotiations, the main actors, their positions on sexualised violence, particularly war rape and forced marriage, and how these developed.

Bibliography

Conventions and statutes

Montevideo Convention on Rights and Duties of States (26 December 1933) 165 INTS 19.

Books

Barnett, H., *Introduction to Feminist Jurisprudence* (Cavendish Publishing 1998).

Bloor, M. and Wood, F., *Keywords in Qualitative Methods: A Vocabulary of Research Concepts* (Sage Publications 2006).

Boyle, A. and Chinkin, C., *The Making of International Law* (Oxford University Press 2007).

Bryman, A., *Social Research Methods* (4th edn, Oxford University Press 2012).

Charlesworth, H. and Chinkin, C., *The Boundaries of International Law: A Feminist Analysis* (Manchester University Press 2000).

Finnemore, M., *National Interests in International Society* (Cornell University Press 1996).

Gilligan, C., *In a Different Voice: Psychological Theory and Women's Development* (2nd edn, Harvard University Press 1993).

Katzenstein, P., *Cultural Norms and National Security: Police and Military in Postwar Japan* (Cornell University Press 1996).

Kvale, S. and Brinkmann, S., *Interviews: Learning the Craft of Qualitative Research Interviewing* (2nd edn, Sage Publications 2009).

Reinhartz, S., *Feminist Methods in Social Research* (Oxford University Press 1992).

Sarantakos, S., *Social Research* (4th edn, Palgrave Macmillan 2013).

Smart, C., *Law, Crime and Sexuality: Essays in Feminism* (Sage Publications 1995).

Chapters in edited books

Brunnée, J. and Toope, S.J., 'Constructivism and International Law' in Jeffrey L. Dunoff and Mark A. Pollack (eds), *Interdisciplinary Perspectives on International Law and International Relations: The State of the Art* (Cambridge University Press 2012) 9 <http://papers.ssrn.com/sol3/papers.cfm?abstract_id=2088132> accessed 14 January 2015.

Centre for Reviews and Dissemination, 'Incorporating Qualitative Evidence in or Alongside Effectiveness Reviews' in Centre for Reviews and Dissemination (ed), *Systematic Reviews: CRD's Guidance for Undertaking Reviews in Health Care* (January 2009) <www.york.ac.uk/crd/SysRev/!SSL!/WebHelp/6_5_SYNTHESIS_OF_QUALITATIVE_RESEARCH.htm> accessed 2 June 2015.

DeVault, M.L. and Gross, G., 'Feminist Qualitative Interviewing: Experience, Talk, and Knowledge' in Sharlene Nagy Hesse-Biber (ed), *Handbook of Feminist Research* (Sage Publications 2007).

Halley, J., 'Take a Break from Feminism?' in Karen Knop (ed), *Gender and Human Rights* (Oxford University Press 2004).

Harding, S., 'Is There a Feminist Method?' in Sandra Harding (ed), *Feminism and Methodology* (Indiana University Press 1987).

Hesse-Biber, S.N., 'Feminist Research: Exploring the Interconnections of Epistemology, Methodology, and Method' in Sharlene Nagy Hesse-Biber (ed), *Handbook of Feminist Research* (Sage Publications 2007).

———, 'The Practice of Feminist In-Depth Interviewing' in Sharlene Nagy Hesse-Biber and Patricia Leavy (eds), *Feminist Research Practice* (Sage Publications 2007).

Jackson, E. and Lacey, N., 'Introducing Feminist Legal Theory' in Richard Nobles, James Penner and David Schiff (eds), *Introduction to Jurisprudence and Legal Theory: Commentary and Materials* (Oxford University Press 2002).

Kitzinger, C., 'Feminist Approaches' in Giampietro Gobo and others (eds), *Qualitative Research Practice* (Sage Publications 2007).

Kralik, D. and van Loon, A.M., 'Feminist Research' in Seamus Cowman and others (eds), *Nursing Research: Designs and Methods* (Churchill Livingstone Elsevier 2008).

Reus-Smit, C., 'Constructivism' in Scott Burchill and others (eds), *Theory of International Relations* (3rd edn, Palgrave Macmillan 2005).

Shuy, R.W., 'In-Person Versus Telephone Interviewing' in Jaber F. Gubrium and James A. Holstein (eds), *Handbook of Interview Research: Context and Method* (Sage Publications 2001).

Journal articles

Bartlett, K., 'Feminist Legal Methods' (1990) 103 *Harvard Law Review* 829.

Binion, G., 'Human Rights: A Feminist Perspective' (1995) 17 *Human Rights Quarterly* 509.

Charlesworth, H., 'Feminists Critiques of International Law and Their Critics' (1995) *Third World Legal Studies* 1.

———, 'Feminist Methods in International Law' (1999) 93 *American Journal of International Law* 379.

———, Chinkin, C. and Wright, S., 'Feminist Approaches to International Law' (1991) 85 *American Journal of International Law* 613.

Chinkin, C., 'A Critique of the Public/Private Dimension' (1999) 10 *European Journal of International Law* 387.

Kurki, M. and Sinclair, A., 'Hidden in Plain Sight: Constructivist Treatment of Social Context and Its Limitations' (2010) 47 *International Politics* 1.

Landmann, M., 'Getting Quality in Qualitative Research: A Short Introduction to Feminist Methodology and Methods' (2006) 65 *Proceedings of Nutrition Society* 429.

Leech, B.L., 'Asking Questions: Techniques for Semistructured Interviews' (2002) 35 *PS Online* 665.

Lochner, B. and Prügl, E., 'Feminism and Constructivism: Worlds Apart or Sharing the Middle Ground?' (2001) 45 *International Studies Quarterly* 111.

MacKinnon, C., 'Feminism, Marxism, Method and the State: Towards a Feminist Jurisprudence' (1983) 8 *Signs* 635.

Martin, D.L., 'Retribution Revisited: A Reconsideration of Feminist Criminal Law Reform Strategies' (1998) 36 *Osgoode Hall Law Journal* 151.

Mertus, J. and Goldberg, P., 'A Perspective on Women and International Human Rights after the Vienna Declaration: The Inside/Outside Construct' (1994) 26 *New York University Journal of International Law and Politics* 201.

Naffine, N., 'In Praise of Legal Feminism' (2002) 22 *Legal Studies* 71.

Sturges, J.E. and Hanrahan, K.J., 'Comparing Face-to-Face Qualitative Interviewing: A Research Note' (2004) 4 *Qualitative Research* 107.

(Research) reports and working papers

Drew, P., Irvine, A. and Sainsbury, R., 'Mode Effects in Qualitative Interviews: A Comparison of Semi-Structured Face-to-Face and Telephone Interviews Using Conversation Analysis' (2010) Social Policy Research Unit, University of York <www.york.ac.uk/inst/spru/research/pdf/modeEffects.pdf> accessed 6 May 2015.

Harding, C., 'Anecdote, Vignette and Quantification: A Biographical Dilemma' Aberystwyth University, Department of Law and Criminology, Cartel Biographies Project <www.aber.ac.uk/en/law-criminology/research/researchclusters/global-commerce/cartel-collusion/anecdote/> accessed 24 September 2014.

Other

United Nations Rule of Law, 'Non-Governmental Organizations' <www.unrol.org/article.aspx?article_id=23> accessed 10 April 2015.

3 Theories and legislative histories of war rape and forced marriage

Introduction

After Chapter 2 set out the theoretical and methods framework of this research project, Chapter 3 provides the thematic context for the analysis of the International Criminal Court (ICC) negotiations of the definitions of war rape and forced marriage in times of armed conflict. It situates the ICC negotiations within the broader context of theoretical and legal discussions and developments regarding war rape and forced marriage, retracing their legislative histories and including some of the key discussions that inform the current understanding of the two crimes. In doing so, Chapter 3 discusses the background against which the actors in the ICC negotiations debated the definitions of war rape and forced marriage. Chapter 3 also forms the background against which the present researcher assesses these definitions. The aim of Chapter 3 is to generate a common understanding of the nature and definitions as well as the causes and meanings of war rape and forced marriage in times of armed conflict for the purpose of this book.

Chapter 3 first outlines theoretical considerations regarding the causes and meanings of war rape and forced marriage. It also advances a new understanding of forced marriage based on the theory of hegemonic masculinity. The chapter then analyses and assesses the legislative histories and current understandings of war rape and forced marriage. In relation to war rape, it analyses early bilateral and multilateral conventions, the fourth Geneva Convention, international military tribunals established after the Second World War, international agreements and documents from the period of the mid-1970s until mid-1990s, and the jurisprudence of the International Criminal Tribunal for the former Yugoslavia (ICTY) and the International Criminal Tribunal for Rwanda (ICTR). In the absence of a similarly extensive legislative history of forced marriage, its increasing recognition as a crime in the second half of the 20th century is discussed before the jurisprudence of the Special Court for Sierra Leone (SCSL) is analysed. The conclusion of Chapter 3 draws together the understanding of war rape and forced marriage for the purpose of this book.

Theoretical considerations regarding the causes and meanings of war rape and forced marriage

Parallels can be drawn between explanations of the causes and meanings of war rape and forced marriage. The perpetration of forced marriages and war rapes can be ascribed to essentialist understandings of men as aggressive hunters and women as submissive gatherers. Forced marriages and war rapes are seen as forms of compensation or reward for successful fighters. The perpetration of both crimes can be ascribed to unequal power relationships where men are seen as powerful and women as powerless. These exist in peacetime and are exacerbated in times of war, indicating a continuum of sexualised violence perpetrated against women in peace and war. Forced marriages and war rapes target women because of their membership in a particular social category as well as for economic reasons. Forced marriages and war rapes are also aimed at the destruction of the opponent. Within one's own group, peer pressure can explain the perpetration of war rapes and forced marriage. The perpetration of both crimes can also be ascribed to different ideals of masculinity. A notable difference is found in the fact that forced marriages, in contrast to war rapes, are perpetrated to create lasting interpersonal bonds.

War rape

When discussing the causes and meanings of war rape, it needs to be kept in mind that war rapes are perpetrated in the context of other acts of war violence committed by soldiers and civilians against civilians. Moreover, it is important to stress that the causes and meanings of war rape are context-dependent, complex and interconnected. No single cause determines acts of war rape.[1]

Historically, the perpetration of sexualised violence against women[2] in peace and wartime was ascribed to a natural male aggression, the physical superiority of men to women and an uncontrollable male sexual desire. Contrasting these

1 Ruth Seifert, 'Krieg und Vergewaltigung: Ansätze zu einer Analyse' in Alexandra Stiglemayer (ed), *Massenvergewaltigungen: Krieg gegen die Frauen* (Fischer Taschenbuchverlag 1993); Elisabeth Jean Wood, 'Conflict-Related Sexual Violence and the Policy Implications of Recent Research' (2015) *International Review of the Red Cross/First View Article* 1 <http://journals.cambridge.org/action/displayAbstract?fromPage=online&aid=9579578&fileId=S1816383115000077> accessed 6 May 2015.

2 Joanna Bourke, *Rape: A History from 1860 to the Present Day* (Virago 2007) 361–362; Susan Brownmiller, *Against our Will: Men, Women and Rape* (Penguin Books 1977) 48–49; Janie L. Leatherman, *Sexual Violence and Armed Conflict* (Polity Press 2011) 1, 157; Inger Skjelsbeak, 'Sexual Violence and War: Mapping Out a Complex Relationship' (2001) 7 *European Journal of International Relations* 211, 215, 225–226: Women are readily seen as victims of sexualised war violence and men as perpetrators. However, it has to be stressed that this is not always the case. The rape of men by other men in times of war and peace is an exertion of power and control by feminising the victim and masculinising the perpetrator. Considering that war rapes do not only target one individual but also the group he belongs to, groups of people are feminised or masculinised. Gendering groups becomes a way of ascribing power to warring parties. Masculinised identities are ascribed power while feminised identities are not, situating both in a hierarchical power relationship.

supposedly natural male dispositions with constructivist arguments, rape can be explained as a means to regulate unequal power relationships between men and women in peace and wartime. In times of crisis, the underlying hostility against women is actualised as the threshold for direct acts of sexualised violence is lower than in times of peace (continuum thesis). Focusing on times of war, a different but connected line of argument emphasises that sexualised war violence can be the product of social interactions in fighting groups and military masculinity. They foster the construction and exercise of a monopoly of power and heterosexuality, the suppression of feelings of insecurity, gentleness and other 'feminine' characteristics. Furthermore, war rapes are used as a weapon of war[3] and a propaganda tool. This indicates individual, interpersonal, institutional and structural causes for the perpetration of the crime, framing war rape as a form of interpersonal, social, political and economic violence. The explanations of the causes and meanings of war rape focus on male to female rape. They understand rape as an act of aggression and force, perpetrated under coercive circumstances. Different explanations of the causes and meanings of war rape advance different views on whether war rape is an act of violence between two individuals, or a form of social violence targeting a particular group of people. Consequently, different theories locate the causes of war rape within the perpetrator and in unequal power structures respectively.[4]

Forced marriage

Explanations for the causes and meanings of the perpetration of forced marriage centre on the wish to control someone's sexuality without resorting to rape. It is also suggested that forced marriages build on peacetime conventions

3 Paul Kirby, 'How Is Rape a Weapon of War? Feminist International Relations, Modes of Critical Explanation and the Study of Wartime Sexual Violence' (2012) 9 *European Journal of International Relations* 797: The rape of men in war, in contrast, arguably is peripheral to military strategy.

4 See for example Bourke (n 2); Brownmiller, *Against our Will* (n 2); Doris E. Buss, 'Rethinking "Rape as a Weapon of War"' (2009) 17 *Feminist Legal Studies* 145; Cynthia Cockburn, 'The Gendered Dynamics of Armed Conflict and Political Violence' in Fiona Clark and Caroline N.O. Moser (eds), *Victims, Perpetrators or Actors? Gender, Armed Conflict and Political Violence* (Zed 2001); Barbara Ehrenreich, *Blood Rites: Origins and History of the Passions of War* (Virago 1997); Stevi Jackson, 'The Social Context of Rape: Sexual Scripts and Motivations' in Ronald J. Berger and Patricia Searles (eds), *Rape and Society: Readings on the Problem of Sexual Assault* (Westview Press 1995); Kirby (n 3); Leatherman (n 2); Caroline O.N. Moser, 'The Gendered Continuum of Violence and Conflict: An Operational Framework' in Fiona Clark and Caroline N.O. Moser (eds), *Victims, Perpetrators or Actors? Gender, Armed Conflict and Political Violence* (Zed 2001); Donna Pankhurst, 'Sexual Violence in War' in Laura J. Shepherd (ed), *Gender Matters in Global Politics: A Feminist Introduction to International Relations* (Routledge 2010); Seifert (n 1); Skjelsbeak (n 2); Meredeth Turshen, 'The Political Economy of Rape: An Analysis of Systematic Rape and Sexual Abuse of Women during Armed Conflict in Africa' in Fiona Clark and Caroline N.O. Moser (eds), *Victims, Perpetrators or Actors? Gender, Armed Conflict and Political Violence* (Zed 2001); Wood (n 1).

of marriage by capture that are pushed into the context of conflict. Furthermore, it is argued that forced marriages are perpetrated to demoralise and disable the opponent by dissolving traditional bonds between families and within society while at the same time creating bonds within the fighting group that strengthen cohesion and reduce the likelihood of escape of forced wives. Fighting groups also need women to perform women's work. Against the background of the lack of material wealth of fighting groups, forced wives also serve as a substitute payment system and a reward for fighters' bravery. Moreover, forced wives and children born out of forced marriage increase a fighter's social status.[5]

5 See for example *Prosecutor v Alex Tamba Brima, Brima Bazzy Kamara and Santigie Borbor Kanu* (Prosecution Filing of Expert Report Pursuant to Rule 94(bis) and Decision of Prosecution Request for Leave to Call an Additional Expert Witness) SCSL-04-16-T 'AFRC Case' (8 August 2005) <www.rscsl.org/Documents/Decisions/AFRC/365/SCSL-04-16-T-369.pdf> accessed 28 September 2017; Tim Allen and Mareike Schomerus, 'A Hard Homecoming: Lessons Learned from the Reception Center Process in Northern Uganda: An Independent Study' (2006) <http://pdf.usaid.gov/pdf_docs/PNADI241.pdf> accessed 8 July 2013; Lynn L. Amowitz and others, 'Prevalence of War-Related Sexual Violence and Other Human Rights Abuses among Internally Displaced Persons in Sierra Leone' (2002) 287 *Journal of the American Medical Association* 513; Jeannie Annan and Christopher Blattman, 'On the Nature and Causes of LRA Abduction: What the Abductees Say' in Bernd Allen and Koen Vlassenroot (eds), *The Lord's Resistance Army: Myth and Reality* (Zed Books 2010); Jeannie Annan and others, 'Civil War, Reintegration, and Gender in Northern Uganda' (2011) 55 *Journal of Conflict Resolution* 877; Erin Baines, 'Forced Marriage as a Political Project: Sexual Rules and Relations in the Lord's Resistance Army' (2014) 51 *Journal of Peace Research* 405; Bernd Beber and Christopher Blattman, 'The Logic of Child Soldiering and Coercion' (2011) <http://chrisblattman.com/documents/research/2011.LogicOfChildSoldiering.pdf> accessed 23 December 2012; Khristopher Carlson and Dyan Mazurana, 'Forced Marriage within the Lord's Resistance Army, Uganda' (2008) Tufts University Feinstein International Center <https://wikis.uit.tufts.edu/confluence/download/attachments/14553676/Forced+Marriage+within+the+LRA.pdf?version=1> accessed 8 July 2013; Khatidja Chantler, 'Recognition of and Intervention in Forced Marriage as a Form of Violence and Abuse' (2012) 13 *Trauma, Violence and Abuse* 176; Chris Coulter, *Bush Wives and Girl Soldiers: Women's Lives through War and Peace in Sierra Leone* (Cornell University Press 2009); Catherine Dauvergne and Jenni Millbank, 'Forced Marriage as a Harm in Domestic and International Law' (2010) 73 *Modern Law Review* 57; Barbara E. Harrell-Bond, *Modern Marriage in Sierra Leone: A Study of the Professional Group* (Mouton 1975); The Justice and Reconciliation Project, 'Young Mothers, Marriage, and Reintegration in Northern Uganda: Considerations for the Juba Peace Talks' (2006) Liu Institute for Global Issues and the Gulu District NGO Forum, the Justice and Reconciliation Project Field Notes, No 2 <www.ligi.ubc.ca/sites/liu/files/Publications/23Oct2006_YoungMothers_JRP.pdf> accessed 8 July 2013; Sophie Kramer, 'Forced Marriage and the Absence of Gang Rape: Explaining Sexual Violence by the Lord's Resistance Army in Northern Uganda' (2012) 23 (1) *Columbia University Journal of Politics and Society* 11; Leatherman (n 2); Zoe Marks, 'Sexual Violence in Sierra Leone's Civil War: "Virgination", Rape, and Marriage' (2013) 112 *African Affairs* 67; Refugee Law Project, 'Behind the Violence: Causes, Consequences and the Search for Solutions to the War in Northern Uganda' (2004) Refugee Law Project Working Paper No 11 <www.refugeelawproject.org/files/working_papers/RLP.WP11.pdf> accessed 8 July 2013.

Iris Haenen, *Force & Marriage: The Criminalisation of Forced Marriage in Dutch, English and International Criminal Law* (Intersentia 2014) 88–99: Haenen puts forward

Hegemonic masculinity and forced marriage

The above-mentioned understanding of forced marriages can be developed further when applying R.W. Connell's theory of hegemonic masculinity[6] to Uganda.

Hegemonic masculinity is the context-dependent ideal of a man that is enacted only by a minority of men.[7] Hegemonic masculinity maintains and reinforces the link between men and power as it provides a pattern for the continuing subordination of women and marginalisation of other versions of masculinity. Therefore, hegemonic masculinity is relational. It may incorporate elements of marginalised masculinities if they are of use, and requires all other men to position themselves in relation to it. Recognising a plurality and hierarchy of masculinities, those men who benefit from patriarchy without enacting its hegemonic version show a complicit masculinity. They sustain, honour, desire and support the hegemonic version of masculinity.[8]

Any analysis of hegemonic masculinity in practice must take into account the plurality of masculinities in any country. Versions of masculinity are socio-culturally constructed and therefore context- and time-dependent. Since there are as many exceptions as there are assumptions about proper gender roles in Uganda as anywhere else in the world, it is difficult to present a unified and

---

similar explanations for the perpetration of forced marriages in Cambodia under the Khmer Rouge. Men and women were forced into marriage for the reproductive capacities. This way, the Khmer Rouge aimed to increase Cambodia's population and replace traditional family ties with absolute loyalty to the organisation and to transform society. Comparable to the Lord's Resistance Army (LRA) and the Revolutionary United Front (RUF), extramarital sexual relations were considered a crime against morality and as counterrevolutionary. This indicates that forced marriage was a means to control people's sexuality and to destabilise family structures. Forced marriage was also used as a means of reward and compensation for Khmer Rouge soldiers. Loyal soldiers were allowed to choose their spouse.

6 R.W. Connell, *Gender and Power: Society, the Person and Sexual Politics* (Polity Press 1987); R.W. Connell and James W. Messerschmidt, 'Hegemonic Masculinity: Rethinking the Concept' (2005) 19 *Gender and Society* 829.

7 Connell, *Gender and Power* (n 6) 183–184; R.W. Connell, 'The Social Organization of Masculinity' in Frank J. Barrett and Stephen M. Whitehead (eds), *The Masculinities Reader* (Polity Press 2001) 39; Connell and Messerschmidt (n 6) 832: Hegemony in this context means dominance achieved through culture, institutions and persuasion. It is a successful claim to authority. Although hegemony here does not mean violence, it could be underpinned or supported by force. According to Connell it is '[i]ndeed [...] common for the two to go together. Physical [...] violence backs up a dominant cultural pattern [...], or ideologies justify the holders of power [...]. The connection between hegemonic masculinity and patriarchal violence is close, though not simple.'

8 Connell, *Gender and Power* (n 6) 183–184; Connell and Messerschmidt (n 6) 832, 347; Demetrakis Z. Demetriou, 'Connell's Concept of Hegemonic Masculinity: A Critique' (2001) 30 *Theory and Society* 337, 342; Jane L. Parpart and Marysia Zalewski, 'Introduction' in Jane L. Parpart and Marysia Zalewski (eds), *Rethinking the Man Question: Sex, Gender and Violence in International Relations* (Zed Books 2008) 11.

generalised picture of the normative version of masculinity in Uganda. In any case, it is necessary to distinguish between men's lived experiences and expectations of masculinity. Taking marriage and fatherhood as an example, the lived experience is that not all men want to or can become husbands and fathers. However, lived expectations dictate it. Breaking out of these expectations is not considered an option. In Uganda's patrilocal, patrilineal society, a man pays a bride price for the woman he wishes to marry. After marriage, the wife is considered subordinate to, and property of, her husband. Seen as unfit for formal education, women are regarded as there to help, to perform domestic work and to produce children. They are seen as exploitable bodies and tools, and their voices are often ignored. Violence against women is an internalised norm. For some men, it is a means to get a woman to love him. In a relationship, violence against women is considered a sign that the man emotionally invests into the connection. On a different note, violence against women is also viewed as a socially sanctioned extension of male authority; a way to achieve and maintain power and authority over women. As a means of discipline, it is socially acceptable to beat a woman if she does not show respect to men or because of actual or suspected infidelity, allegedly evidenced, for example, by the refusal to engage in sexual activities with their partner. This indicates that men hold a power position in regard to their and their partner's sexuality. Sexualised violence and coercion as well as more general aggressiveness in regard to sexuality are common. Being sexually active demonstrates masculine prowess, competence and achievement rather than intimacy. It is a way for men to gain respect and social status.[9]

Men, in contrast to women, take priority. They are more educated, richer and own other assets in addition to their wives.[10] 'To be recognised as an "adult" and a "man" [, however,] men are expected to become husbands and fathers [...] and to exercise considerable control over wife and children.'[11] Financial independence and subsequently marriage and fatherhood are preconditions to be socially and politically accepted; they are preconditions to be taken seriously and to be listened to, to be perceived as responsible and able to participate in political life. Adult men have access to important resources like information, contacts and solidarity.[12] Unmarried young men, in contrast, are

9 Gary Barker and Christine Ricardo, 'Young Men and the Construction of Masculinity in Sub-Saharan Africa: Implications for HIV/AIDS, Conflict, and Violence' (2005) The World Bank, Social Development Papers, Conflict Prevention and Reconstruction, Paper Number 26 <www-wds.worldbank.org/external/default/WDSContentServer/WDSP/IB/2005/06/23/000012009_20050623134235/Rendered/PDF/327120rev0PAPER0AFR0young0men0WP26.pdf> accessed 16 October 2014; Chris Dolan, 'Collapsing Masculinities and Weak States: A Case Study of Northern Uganda' in Frances Cleaver (ed), *Masculinity Matters: Men, Masculinities and Gender Relations in Development* (Zed Books 2003).

10 Dolan (n 9) 4–5.

11 ibid 5.

12 Barker and Ricardo (n 9) 6; Dolan (n 9) 5.

viewed with suspicion and seen as idle troublemakers.[13] To increase their status as adult men, some men have multiple wives and many children. They use their wealth in people for material and political advancement. In addition to marriage and fatherhood, being able to provide for the material needs of wife and children as well as to physically protect a family are two more key markers of Ugandan hegemonic masculinity. This indicates that the achievement of manhood and masculinity is judged by other men and women rather than by the individual man himself.[14]

However, the context of ongoing conflict, heavy militarisation and internal displacement make it very difficult or even impossible for the majority of men to fulfil these expectations and to become a husband and father, and then the provider for and protector of their family. In the absence of cattle or cash as the basis for bride-wealth payments, many men cannot get married and therefore cannot fulfil their roles as husbands and fathers. Continuing rebel and military activities compromise men's roles as protectors. Consequently, men experience an inability to take up, or sustain, roles and positions defined as the masculine norm. This leads to a crisis of identity and/or social presentation. Their fear of being seen as less than a man leads to and/or strengthens feelings of humiliation, intimidation, resentment, oppression, frustration and anger that are expressed in violent acts justified in terms of self-preservation and revenge. Men actively join the war to achieve what they feel they have been denied and to avail themselves of economic opportunities the conflict offers.[15] The use of violence is seen as a 'potential means to achieve an end, namely masculinity, rather than an integral component of that masculinity'.[16]

Explaining the causes and meanings of forced marriage on the basis of hegemonic masculinity theory is a novel approach that contributes to a more comprehensive understanding of the crime by adding to existing explanations. Applying the theory of hegemonic masculinity to Uganda also highlights that forced marriages are not perpetrated in times of armed conflict simply because men have the power to do it. Forced marriages are perpetrated in times of armed conflict because men cannot otherwise fulfil a certain masculine ideal which would leave them socially disadvantaged. Consequently, an analysis of the crime through the lens of hegemonic masculinity offers an explanation as to why forced marriages are only perpetrated in certain regions of the world. Rather than being an extension of a highly patriarchal society in general where men hold a power position and exercise control over women, forced marriage in times of armed conflict is an expression of a thwarted hegemonic masculinity based on men's roles as husbands, fathers, providers and protectors. In regions

13 Dolan (n 9) 5.
14 Barker and Ricardo (n 9) 4, 6–7; Dolan (n 9) 4, 16–17.
15 Barker and Ricardo (n 9) v-9; Dolan (n 9).
16 Dolan (n 9) 16–17.

where masculinity is based on different norms, the crime would be meaningless. Consequently, it is unlikely to be committed.

As outlined above, the precarious economic situation in Uganda makes it difficult for men to become financially independent. Therefore, their chances to pay bride-wealth to get married and consequently to start a family are diminished. This thwarts their pursuit of hegemonic masculinity. Men's economic responsibilities and diminished chances to fulfil these motivate them to join the war.[17] However, even though becoming a fighter might put men into an economic position to get married and to start a family and therefore to meet key elements of Ugandan hegemonic masculinity, forced marriage in times of armed conflict offers them the same opportunity without having to pay a bride price. Fighters abduct women, take them to their camp (patrilocality) and label them their wives. No official marriage ceremony takes place and neither the women's nor their parents' consent is sought. The women are subjected to rape and forced pregnancy.[18] They reproduce their traditional feminine roles as wives and mothers, enabling their forced husband[19] to fulfil his role as husband and father.

17 Barker and Ricardo (n 9); Dolan (n 9).

18 Carlson and Mazurana (n 5); Coulter (n 5); *AFRC* Prosecution Filing of Expert Report (n 5).

19 *AFRC* Prosecution Filing of Expert Report (n 5); Carlson and Mazurana (n 5) 5; Coulter (n 5) 99; GBV under the Khmer Rouge, 'Forced Marriage' <http://gbvkr.org/gender-based-violence-under-khmer-rouge/facts-and-figures/forced-marriage/> accessed 8 April 2015; Kramer (n 5) 24; Lynn Lawry, 'Panel Six: Methodological Challenges and Opportunities' (The Missing Peace Symposium 2013, Washington, DC, 14–16 February 2013); Katerina Novotna and Ryszard Piotrowicz, 'Forced Marriage in the Jungle: Time to Stop Beating about the Bush' (2007) 81 *Australian Law Journal* 302, 304; Bridgette A. Toy-Cronin, 'What Is Forced Marriage? Towards a Definition of Forced Marriage as a Crime against Humanity' (2010) 19 *Columbia Journal of Gender and Law* 539, 543, 558: It could be argued that the term 'enforced husband' would be a more appropriate name for the male party to a forced marriage as he makes the choice to marry; the woman does not. However, as discussed below, it is crucial to emphasise that men are also coerced or forced into forced marriages. In a number of African conflicts, fighters who do not conform and engage in forced marriages are excluded from, and punished by, the fighting group. This suggests that forced husbands gain the acceptance of the group by choosing forced marriage. Therefore, to be accepted into the fighting group, men who actually reject forced marriage are forced or coerced into them. They have to desire, support and sustain forced marriage and cooperate against their will. In Khmer Rouge-ruled Cambodia, men and women were equally forced into marriage. According to GBV under the Khmer Rouge, 'couples were arbitrarily married without […] consent and pressured to consummate their marriage [to ensure the emergence of the next generation of workers in a union that would naturally provide less family loyalty, and as a corollary decreased opposition to State practices which could be considered a threat to family members]'. In addition to men being coerced or forced into marriage, it is important to stress women's agency. Some women strategically chose to join a fighting group and to become a fighter's wife in hope for protection, to limit the abuses they face, to benefit from looted goods or to escape parental control. Therefore, forced marriage can be understood as a means of survival. However, it has to be considered whether cases where women made a self-determined, strategic choice to join a fighting group

Patrilineal norms are reproduced if a couple splits up after the conflict. If the woman returns to her community, she is often not allowed to keep her children as they are understood to belong to their father's clan.[20] In addition to playing on culturally accepted peacetime gender norms, this indicates the subordination of forced wives by their forced husbands. In a highly patriarchal, misogynist environment, forced wives are seen as exploitable bodies and tools. In addition to rape and forced pregnancy, they are subjected to enslavement, torture, forced labour, and forced participation in direct combat. Forced husbands exercise control over their sexuality, movements and work.[21] This is supported by the internalised norm that violence against women is an extension of men's authority and power over women. Members of fighting groups also use violence against women as a means of discipline for disobedience, resistance, not conceiving, talking together unsupervised, having blank expressions on their faces, looking miserable, allegedly planning an escape, or breaking rules or taboos of the fighting group. The means of punishment range from severe beating to rape, torture or death.[22] Women are also punished for actual or suspected infidelity, based on the expectation that forced wives should have an exclusive relationship only with their forced husband. Forced husbands, in contrast, often have more than one wife. This again is supported by cultural norms. A fighter's status in the group depends on his wealth in people (wives and dependants).[23] He supports

and consequently were made a fighter's wife are still examples of forced marriage or rather of marriage of convenience, of choosing the lesser evil rather than making an independent decision. Leaving this question aside, as women and men exercise degrees of choice in regard to entering into a forced marriage, and as coercion and/or force are used against both parties to a forced marriage, both, the use of the term 'forced wife/husband' and 'enforced wife/husband' would be justifiable. Due to the understudied nature of forced husbands as victims, and the tendency to negate forced wives' agency, the present researcher wants to refrain from establishing a hierarchy in terms of which spouse exercised more choice and which spouse was subjected to a higher degree of coercion and/or force. Therefore, the same adjective should be used for both parties to a forced marriage. Emphasising the degree of coercion and/or force exercised against both spouses, and therefore the context in which forced marriages are formed, the terms 'forced wife' and 'forced husband' are used throughout this book.

20 Carlson and Mazurana (n 5) 29; Coulter (n 5) 232.

21 *AFRC* Prosecution Filing of Expert Report (n 5); Carlson and Mazurana (n 5) 7; Coulter (n 5); Valerie Oosterveld and Andrea Marlowe, 'Prosecutor v Alex Tamba Brima, Brima Bazzy Kamara & Santigie Borbor Kanu. Case No SCSL-04-16-T. at <www.sc-sl.org/AFRC.html>. Special Court for Sierra Leone, Trial Chamber II, June 20, 2007 and Prosecutor v Moinina Fofana & Allieu Kondewa. Case No SCSL-04-14-T. at <www.sc-sl.org/CDF.html>. Special Court for Sierra Leone, Trial Chamber I, August 2, 2007' (2007) 101 *American Journal of International Law* 848.

22 Allen and Schomerus (n 5) vi; Annan and others (n 5) 883; Carlson and Mazurana (n 5) 17–28; Kramer (n 5) 24–25.

23 *Prosecutor v Alex Tamba Brima, Brima Bazzy Kamara and Santigie Borbor Kanu* (Appeals Chamber Judgment) SCSL SLS-2004-16-A 'AFRC Case' (22 February 2008) para 195 <www.legal-tools.org/doc/4420ef/> accessed 9 August 2017; Barker and Ricardo (n 9); Carlson and Mazurana (n 5) 28; Dolan (n 9); Kramer (n 5).

them materially and protects them from acts of violence perpetrated by other men.[24] Therefore, forced husbands fulfil their role as providers and protectors. As a result, he keeps his forced wives in a situation of dependency upon him, coercing them into staying with him.[25] While forced husbands can rid themselves of forced wives by abandoning or killing them, forced wives have to escape the fighting group if they want to leave their forced husband. Escape, however, is almost impossible.[26] It becomes clear that forced marriage provides fighters with access to different internal and external resources like a 'proper' household, support, wealth in people, status and respect as well as solidarity and social participation in terms of bonding with other members of the fighting group. The reverse example of the exclusion and punishment of fighters who do not conform and engage in forced marriages[27] suggests that forced husbands gain the acceptance of the group for choosing forced marriage as a way of achieving hegemonic masculinity.

To be accepted into the fighting group, men who actually reject forced marriage are forced or coerced into complicit masculinity. They have to honour, desire, support and sustain forced marriage. In addition to complicit men, forced wives themselves support and sustain the perpetration of forced marriage. Older wives turn on younger women who are considered a shame to the household in which they live. For this reason, older wives influence their forced husbands to marry younger women.[28]

Unmarried young men and lower level fighters who are given fewer wives than higher ranks and commanders constitute the group of marginalised men in fighting groups.[29] This indicates that hegemonic masculinity in fighting groups in Uganda is established through differentiation from marginalised men rather than through incorporation of certain elements of their version of masculinity. Like men who meet the norms of hegemonic masculinity, marginalised men benefit from the domestic and support work forced wives perform. Forced wives also provide the advantage of additional combatants. The fighting group as a whole benefits from the bonds and dependency structures forced wives create.[30]

24 Carlson and Mazurana (n 5) 24; Kramer (n 5) 29–30.

25 ibid.

26 *Prosecutor v Issa Hassan Sesay, Morris Kallon and Augustine Gbao* (Trial Judgment) SCSL-04-15-PT 'RUF Case' (2 March 2009) para 1293 <www.legal-tools.org/doc/7f05b7/> accessed 9 August 2017.

27 Carlson and Mazurana (n 5) 5; Kramer (n 5) 24.

28 Erin Baines and Beth Stewart, '"I Cannot Accept What I Have Not Done": Storytelling, Gender and Transitional Justice' (2001) 3 *Journal of Human Rights Practice* 245, 251–252: Paradoxically, however, older wives who influence their forced husbands to marry younger women know that they would have to compete against the new wife for their husband's favour which is crucial for survival.

29 Kramer (n 5) 25.

30 Carlson and Mazurana (n 5) 14, 21–23; Coulter (n 5) 79–80, 102–103, 112–117; Kramer (n 5) 25, 29–30.

The existence of marginalised but complicit masculinities constitutes a continuous test for, and increases the need to, demonstrate one's masculinity. This creates an environment of vulnerability and potential failure, resulting in constant competition between the fighters. Increased by the atmosphere of violent conflict, this environment of humiliation, intimidation, frustration and anger as well as personal uncertainty, insecurity and fear of failure creates a desire to be in control. Associated with sexuality, the fear to lose control is implied by intimacy in the sense that physical intimacy involves giving up control and letting go. For a person who is afraid to lose control, this can be an uneasy situation. Against this background, in addition to a strategy of bonding, forced marriage, which includes a very violent form of sexuality, can be interpreted as a means to disguise feelings of inadequacy and weakness, and as a means for empowerment. (Sexual) aggressiveness can also be seen as a way to negotiate the latent tensions and aggressiveness between the fighters. If these tensions are based on the aforementioned competition between male fighters, killing another man's forced wives can be understood as a way to subordinate him. Violence in war, as in peace, becomes a means of self-preservation as a man as well as of revenge for not being able to achieve manhood and masculinity otherwise.[31]

In addition to providing a new explanation of the causes and meanings of forced marriage in times of armed conflict, analysing the crime based on the theory of hegemonic masculinity also highlights inconsistencies of some of the existing explanations outlined above.

When thinking about forced marriage through a hegemonic masculinity lens, the substitution argument that forced marriages were engaged in to reduce the number of war rapes of civilians appears to be based on the false assumption that both crimes would serve the same purpose. While forced marriage provides fighters with the opportunity to become husbands, fathers, and providers for, and protectors of, a family, war rapes do not. War rapes confirm a different kind of hegemonic masculinity which includes, for example, sexual prowess. While forced marriages provide fighting groups with additional and necessary manpower, war rapes do not. In most cases, women who were raped by male fighters do not become part of a fighting group to support its operation.

31 Frank J. Barrett, 'The Organizational Construction of Hegemonic Masculinity: The Case of the US Navy' in Frank J. Barrett and Stephen M. Whitehead (eds), *The Masculinities Reader* (Polity Press 2001) 96–97; Frank J. Barrett and Stephen M. Whitehead (eds), *The Masculinities Reader* (Polity Press 2001) 73–76, 219–222; Deborah Kerfoot, 'The Organization of Intimacy: Managerialism, Masculinity and the Masculine Subject' in Frank J. Barrett and Stephen M. Whitehead (eds), *The Masculinities Reader* (Polity Press 2001) 237; Michael A. Messner, 'Friendship, Intimacy, and Sexuality' in Frank J. Barrett and Stephen M. Whitehead (eds), *The Masculinities Reader* (Polity Press 2001) 259; Sandra Whitworth, 'Militarized Masculinity and Post-Traumatic Stress Disorder' in Jane L. Parpart and Marysia Zalewski (eds), *Rethinking the Man Question: Sex, Gender and Violence in International Relations* (Zed Books 2008) 121.

The understanding of forced wives as status symbols is another explanation that can be developed further on the basis of an understanding of forced marriage informed by the theory of hegemonic masculinity. Following this, the question arises why highly ranked fighters and leaders of fighting groups would give any women to their men instead of keeping them all for themselves to increase their status. It has to be noted here that the perpetration of forced marriages does not only benefit a fighter personally as in achieving hegemonic masculinity. It also confirms the fighter's man- and adulthood and makes him a full member of society. Therefore, for the benefit of the whole fighting group, its effectiveness and efficiency, fighting group leaders and high ranks have to give women to their fighters to make them men.

Seeing forced marriage through a hegemonic masculinity lens also offers an opportunity to adapt the argument that forced marriages in times of armed conflict are based on socio-culturally accepted peacetime marriage practices that are simply pushed into wartime. The analysis of hegemonic masculinity in Uganda and the parallels that can be drawn to forced marriages in times of armed conflict indicate that it is not a socio-culturally accepted peacetime marriage practice that is pushed into wartime, but rather socio-culturally accepted peacetime gender norms. Men strive to be financially independent, husbands, fathers, providers and protectors, and in the context of Uganda's precarious economic situation and the conflict, they see forced marriage as a way to fulfil this socially accepted ideal. However, while forced marriage in times of armed conflict may be based on socio-culturally accepted masculine ideals and men may use it as an opportunity to fulfil these, forced marriage violates women's gender norms. While marriage and motherhood are expected of women and achieved through forced marriage, forced wives transgress women's gender roles by participating in combat. This resonates with their stigmatisation as collaborators, rebels and killers.

Even though the theory of hegemonic masculinity holds great explanatory power in regard to forced marriage in times of armed conflict, its shortcomings have to be mentioned as well. Since the theory is based on essentialist concepts of gender, it negates the prospect of ascribing women with masculine characteristics. It negates the prospect of women forcing men into forced marriage.[32] If the Ugandan ideal of masculinity is applied to women, forced wives' improved access to food and looted goods through engaging in combat roles, for example, can be interpreted as a means to gain economic, and consequently more general, independence from their forced husbands and the fighting group.

A focus on hegemonic masculinity also easily overlooks how men who meet the ideal of masculinity simultaneously can be seen as deviating from it. Taking the example of fighters, they meet the masculine requirement of physical strength,

32 Lawry (n 19).

Forced same-sex marriages also fall outside the explanatory powers of hegemonic masculinity.

toughness, activeness and capacity for violence. However, at the same time they are required to be obedient, to submit to authority and to endure humiliation, which are generally seen as feminine traits.[33]

Since hegemonic masculinity theory assumes that all men aspire to conform to a certain ideal of masculinity or benefit from it, it cannot explain why some male fighters never marry.[34]

A legislative history of war rape and forced marriage

Bilateral, multilateral and international conventions, agreements and documents as well as cases dealt with by the international military tribunals after the Second World War, the ICTR and ICTY reflect various theoretical considerations of the causes and meanings of war rape. They indicate that, motivated by patriarchal power structures, war rapes are used as a weapon of war.

The Final Report of the Special Rapporteur on the Situation of Systematic Rape, Sexual Slavery and Slavery-Like Practices during Armed Conflict as well as the SCSL cases reflect theoretical considerations regarding the causes and meanings of the crime of forced marriage. They highlight that forced marriages are formed in times of armed conflict because women are needed to perform women's work such as cooking and cleaning while also recognising that forced marriages are a means to exercise control over women beyond their household duties. The SCSL indicated that forced marriages create dependency structures within a fighting group while at the same time destroying traditional family and community ties. Expert evidence submitted to the SCSL in the *AFRC* case furthermore discredits the theory that forced marriages are an extension of peacetime marriage practices into times of conflict.

War rape

Bilateral, multilateral and international conventions and agreements concluded in the 19th and early and mid-20th century were early attempts at the criminalisation of war rape. They saw it as an honour crime.[35] The international

33 Charlotte Hooper, *Manly States: Masculinities, International Relations, and Gender Politics* (Columbia University Press 2001) 47.

34 Baines (n 5) 411.

35 Geneva Convention (IV) Relative to the Protection of Civilian Persons in Time of War (12 August 1949) 75 UNTS 287, 6 UST 3516, TIAS 3365 art 27(2) <www.legal-tools.org/doc/d5e260/> accessed 18 August 2017; Hague Convention (IV) Respecting the Laws and Customs of War on Land and Its Annex: Regulation Concerning the Laws and Customs of War on Land (18 October 1907) 36 Stat 2277, 187 CTS 2271, Bevans 631, 205 Consol TS 277, 3 Martens Nouveau Recueil (ser 3) 461 art 46 <www.legal-tools.org/doc/fa0161/> accessed 18 August 2017; Institute of International Law, 'Manual of the Laws and Customs of War' (9 September 1880) (Oxford Manual) art 49 <www1.umn.edu/humanrts/instree/1880a.htm> accessed 9 August 2013; Project of an International Declaration Concerning the Laws and Customs of War (27 August

military tribunals established after the Second World War retained this understanding.[36] It has to be noted, however, that evidence of rape was also submitted to the International Military Tribunal (IMT, Nuremberg Tribunal) to support charges of torture and of having conceived, willed, ordained or tolerated a systematic policy of terror and extermination of civilians.[37] The International

1874) (Declaration of Brussels) art 38 <www.icrc.org/ihl/INTRO/135> accessed 9 August 2013.

These bilateral and multilateral conventions were preceded by national military codes that prohibited war rapes. Examples are the Instructions for the Government of Armies of the United States in the Field, General Order No 100 (24 April 1863) (Lieber Code) and the Rules and Articles of War, Order No 20 (1847) (United States of America). Article 44 of the Lieber Code, for example, explicitly prohibits war rape as an act of wanton – not systematic – violence punishable as a capital crime. It places war rapes in context with the destruction and unlawful taking of property, as well as with other acts of violence like 'wounding, maiming, or killing'. It also has to be noted that, in the 18th century, bilateral and multilateral conventions such as the Treaty of Amity and Commerce (10 September 1785) differed from the Declaration of Brussels, the Oxford Manual and the fourth Hague convention as they frame sexual war violence against women as molestation which 'shall not' happen. It is put into context with the destruction of property like homes, goods and fields.

36 *The United States of America and others v Hermann Wilhelm Göring and Others* in International Military Tribunal Nuremberg, *Trial of the Major War Criminals before the International Military Tribunal, Vol. 1* (Nuremberg 1947) 232 <www.legal-tools.org/doc/388b07/> accessed 18 August 2017; *The United States of America and Others v Sadao Araki and Others* (Indictment) No 1 (3 May 1946) in Neil Boister and Robert Cryer (eds), *Documents on the Tokyo International Military Tribunal: Charter, Indictment and Judgments* (Oxford University Press 2008) 62.

Allied Control Council Law No 10 Punishment of Persons Guilty of War Crimes, Crimes against Peace and Against Humanity (20 December 1945) 3 Official Gazette Control Council for Germany 50–55 (1946) <www.legal-tools.org/doc/ffda62/> accessed 18 August 2017; *Trial of General Tomoyuki Yamashita*, Case No 21, IV Law Reports of Trials of War Criminals 1, United States Military Commission, Manila (8 October–7 December 1945) <www.legal-tools.org/doc/c6673f/> accessed 18 August 2017; Kelly Dawn Askin, 'Prosecuting Wartime Rape and Other Gender-Related Crimes under International Law: Extraordinary Advances, Enduring Obstacles' (2003) 21 *Berkeley Journal of International Law* 288; Kelly Dawn Askin, *War Crimes against Women: Prosecution in International War Crimes Tribunals* (Kluwer International Law 1997) 122–125, 192–201; M. Cherif Bassiouni, *The Legislative History of the International Criminal Court* (Transnational Publishers 2005) 39: Control Council Law No 10 gave authority to 12 subsequent trials conducted by the United States of lesser German war criminals. Article 2(1)(c) explicitly includes rape as a crime against humanity. However, there was little jurisprudence on rape. Therefore, the significance of Control Council Law No 10 regarding war rape lies not in straightforward jurisprudence on the subject but rather in its explicit acknowledgement of rape as a crime against humanity. Similarly, based on the Pacific Regulations of 24 September 1945 Governing the Trial of War Criminals, General Yamashita was tried by the Allied powers before a United States (US) military commission in Manila. He was accused, and found guilty, of having failed to control his troops and permitting them to perpetrate war crimes such as rapes.

37 Charter of the International Military Tribunal (8 August 1945) 82 UNTS 279, 59 Stat 1544, 3 Bevans 1238, 39 AJIL 258 (London Agreement) art 6(c) <www.legal-tools.

Military Tribunal for the Far East (IMTFE, Tokyo Tribunal) also addressed war rape as inhumane treatment and mistreatment.[38] Eventually, the IMTFE found Iwande Matsui and Koki Hirota guilty on the basis of command responsibility for war crimes and crimes against humanity including rape.[39]

The understanding of war rape as an honour crime established rape as particularly harmful and therefore necessary to be legally addressed. It highlights that war rape causes intense suffering of the survivor as well as the disintegration of communities. The understanding of rape as an honour crime reflects the purpose of war rape as targeting a whole community rather than 'just' the individual survivors. Nevertheless, survivors are often stigmatised and excluded from their communities. Therefore, even if the understanding of rape as an honour crime that inflicts collective harm is in line with the purpose of war rape, it is detrimental to survivors. Their individual violation is subsumed under the violation of the community. The understanding of war rape as an honour crime denies the complex physical and psychological harm rape causes survivors and overlooks considerations of sexual autonomy.[40] It 'legitimise[s] and

---

org/doc/64ffdd/> accessed 18 August 2017; *The United States of America and others v Hermann Wilhelm Göring and Others, Vol. 1* (n 36) 254–255; *The United States of America and Others v Hermann Wilhelm Göring and Others* in International Military Tribunal Nuremberg, *Trial of the Major War Criminals before the International Military Tribunal, Vol. 6* (Nuremberg 1947) 178, 419, 422 <www.legal-tools.org/doc/18bdcd/> accessed 18 August 2017; *The United States of America and Others v Hermann Wilhelm Göring and Others in International Military Tribunal Nuremberg, Trial of the Major War Criminals before the International Military Tribunal, Vol. 7* (Nuremberg 1947) 442 <www.legal-tools.org/doc/6cefff/> accessed 18 August 2017.

38 *The United States of America and Others v Sadao Araki and Others* Indictment (n 36) 59–60.

39 *The United States of America and Others v Sadao Araki and Others* (Judgment) No 1 (November 1948) in Neil Boister and Robert Cryer (eds), *Documents on the Tokyo International Military Tribunal: Charter, Indictment and Judgments* (Oxford University Press 2008) 538, 604, 612. See Askin, *War Crimes against Women* (n 36) 28–29; Bassiouni, *The Legislative History of the International Criminal Court* (n 36) 17–19; M. Cherif Bassiouni, 'The Perennial Conflict Between International Criminal Justice and Realpolitik' (2006) 22 *Georgia State University Law Review* 541; Patricia Viseur Sellers, 'The Context of Sexual Violence: Sexual Violence as Violations of International Humanitarian Law' in Gabrielle Kirk McDonald and Olivia Swaak (eds), *Substantive and Procedural Aspects of International Criminal Law: The Experience of International and National Courts, Volume 1, Commentary* (Kluwer Law International 2000) 267–268: Earlier (attempted) prosecutions of war rape by international tribunals included holding Kaiser Wilhelm II responsible for rapes committed by the troops of the German Reich and the Axis Powers during the First World War, the van Hagenbach trial, and the trial of Napoleon.

40 Judith Gardam, 'Women and the Law of Armed Conflict: Why the Silence?' (1997) 46 *International and Comparative Law Quarterly* 55; Janet Halley, 'Rape at Rome: Feminist Interventions in the Criminalization of Sex-Related Violence in Positive International Criminal Law' (2009) 30 *Michigan Journal of International Law* 1, 56–58; Valerie Oosterveld, 'Sexual Slavery and the International Criminal Court: Advancing International Law' (2004) 25 *Michigan Journal of International Law* 605, 612; Noelle N.R. Quénivet,

entrench[es] the idea that the rape […] harmed a wife, daughter, or sister because it impugned a husband's, father's, or brother's honor'.[41] Therefore, the understanding of war rape as an honour crime results in a relational view of women.

In the period from the mid-1970s to the mid-1990s, international agreements and documents moved away from an honour-based view of rape and towards an understanding that it is a gender-based violation of women's integrity. A link was established between everyday discrimination against and disadvantages of women, and the general vulnerability of women in wartime. War rape was framed as an issue of protecting women and their fundamental rights as well as an issue of discrimination.[42]

Moving away from categorising war rape in various way, the United Nations (UN) Special Rapporteur on the Situation of Systematic Rape, Sexual Slavery and Slavery-Like Practices during Armed Conflict, Gay J McDougall, defined rape in her Final Report as:

> the insertion, under conditions of force, coercion or duress, of any object, including but not limited to a penis, into a victim's vagina or anus; or the

---

Sexual Offenses in Armed Conflict and International Law (Transnational Publishers 2005) 94–95; United Nations Division for the Advancement of Women, 'Sexual Violence and Armed Conflict: United Nations Response' (April 1998) <www.un.org/womenwatch/daw/public/cover.htm> accessed 20 November 2014; Women's Caucus for Gender Justice, 'Recommendations and Commentary for December 1997 PrepCom on the Establishment of an International Criminal Court' (December 1997) <www.iccnow.org/documents/5PrepComRecommWomensC.pdf> accessed 4 December 2013; see also Rhonda Copelon, 'Surfacing Gender: Re-Engraving Crimes Against Women in Humanitarian Law' (1994) 5 *Hastings Women's Law Journal* 243, 243; Judith Gardam, 'Law of Armed Conflict: A Gendered Regime?' in Dorinda G. Dallmeyer (ed), *Reconceiving Reality: Women and International Law* (American Society of International Law 1993) 171.

41 Halley, 'Rape at Rome' (n 40) 57.

42 Committee on the Elimination of Discrimination against Women, 'General Recommendation No 19' (29 July 1994) UN Doc HRI/GEN/1/Rev.1 <www.legal-tools.org/en/browse/record/f8d998/> accessed 18 August 2017; International Conference on Population and Development 'Report' (13 September 1994) UN Doc A/CONF.171/13/Rev.1; Protocol Additional to the Geneva Conventions of 12 August 1949, and Relating to the Protection of Victims of International Armed Conflicts (Additional Protocol I) (08 June 1977) 1125 UNTS 3 art 76 <www.legal-tools.org//d9328a/> accessed 18 August 2017; Protocol Additional to the Geneva Conventions of 12 August 1949, and Relating to the Protection of Victims of Non-International Armed Conflicts (Additional Protocol II) (8 June 1977) 1125 UNTS 609 art 4 <www.legal-tools.org/doc/fd14c4/> accessed 18 August 2017; United Nations Commission on Human Rights, 'Preliminary Report Submitted by the Special Rapporteur on Violence against Women, Its Causes and Consequences, Ms. Radhika Coomaraswamy, in Accordance with Commission on Human Rights Resolution 1994/45' (22 November 1994) UN Doc E/CN.4/1995/42 fn 228 <www.ohchr.org> accessed 28 August 2017; UNGA, 'Declaration on the Elimination of Violence against Women' (20 December 1993) UN Doc A/RES/48/104 (DEVAW); The World Conference on Human Rights, 'Vienna Declaration and Programme of Action' (12 July 1993) UN Doc A/CONF.157/23 <www.legal-tools.org/doc/65dc31/> accessed 18 August 2017.

> insertion, under conditions of force, coercion or duress, of a penis into the mouth of the victim. Rape is defined in gender-neutral terms, as both men and women are victims of rape.[43]

This definition is reflected in elaborations and applications of domestic and international law, including definitions of rape that have been developed by the ICTY and ICTR. It was developed when the negotiations of the ICC had already begun.

At a time when the Rome Statute had been passed and the discussion of the Elements of Crimes was underway, the statutes of the ICTR and ICTY explicitly included war rape as a crime against humanity.[44] In addition, the ICTR statute explicitly mentioned rape as an outrage upon personal dignity, constituting a violation of Article 3 common to the Geneva Conventions and of Additional Protocol II.[45] The tribunals' jurisprudence defined war rape as a crime against humanity,[46] a war crime,[47] as constituting torture,[48] an act of genocide[49] and a grave breach of the Geneva Conventions.[50] Examining the definitions of rape as such, the ICTR's and ICTY's jurisprudence reveals different perspectives on the element of invasion/penetration as well as coercion/consent.

Taking national rape definitions and the context of conflict as well as the definition of the crime of torture into consideration,[51] the Trial Chamber in the *Akayesu* case arrived at a conceptual definition where rape was understood as 'a physical invasion of a sexual nature, committed on a person under

43 Commission on Human Rights, 'Final Report of the Special Rapporteur on the Situation of Systematic Rape, Sexual Slavery and Slavery-Like Practices during Armed Conflict' (22 June 1998) UN Doc E/CN.4/Sub.2/1998/13 para 24 <www.ohchr.org> accessed 28 August 2017 ©1998 United Nations. Reprinted with the Permission of the United Nations.

44 UNSC Resolution 827 (25 May 1993) UN Doc S/RES/827 art 5(g) <www.legal-tools.org/doc/dc079b/> accessed 18 August 2017; UNSC Resolution 955 (8 November 1994) UN Doc S/RES/955 art 3(g) <www.legal-tools.org/doc/f5ef47/> accessed 18 August 2017.

45 UNSC Resolution 955 (n 44) art 4(e).

46 *Prosecutor v Jean-Paul Akayesu* (Amended Indictment) ICTR-96-4-I (16 February 1996) Count 13, Mechanism for International Criminal Tribunals; *Prosecutor v Jean-Paul Akayesu* (Trial Judgment) ICTR-96-4-T (02 September 1998) <www.legal-tools.org/doc/b8d7bd/> accessed 9 August 2017, Mechanism for International Criminal Tribunals; *Prosecutor v Dragoljub Kunarac, Radomir Kovač and Zoran Vuković* (Indictment) IT-96-23-T 'Foča Case' (19 June 1996) para 4.8 <www.legal-tools.org/doc/3a081b/> accessed 18 August 2017, Mechanism for International Criminal Tribunals.

47 *Foča* Indictment (n 46) para 4.8; *Prosecutor v Anto Furundžija* (Trial Judgment) ICTY IT-95-17/1-T (10 December 1998) Section IX <www.legal-tools.org/doc/e6081b/> accessed 9 August 2017, Mechanism for International Criminal Tribunals.

48 *Foča* Indictment (n 46) para 4.8.

49 *Akayesu* Trial Judgment (n 46) para 507–508.

50 *Foča* Indictment (n 46) para 4.8 and counts 56–59.

51 *Akayesu* Trial Judgment (n 46) para 596–597.

circumstances which are coercive'.[52] This broad and gender-neutral definition[53] supports the understanding that no genuine consent to sexual contact is possible under coercive circumstances. Emphasising the element of coercion, the nature of the crime is understood as a crime of inequality of force, physical power, status or relationship. Consequently, the focus lies on power, domination and violence. The physical acts, surrounding contexts and the exploitation of a situation are emphasised. The relevant events are framed in a social, contextual and collective way.[54] Therefore, coercion-based definitions of rape highlight that rape is a crime of violence for which the survivor is not responsible. In addition to disconnecting rape and consent, the *Akayesu* definition detaches rape and honour by overcoming the male and perpetrator-centred notion of penetration. Traditionally, the concept of penetration relates to the insertion of the man's penis into an orifice of the victim's body. Therefore, it focuses on the physical aspect of rape.[55] A rape definition that uses the term 'invasion', in contrast, provides a gender-neutral definition that illustrates the survivor's point of view. It is more comprehensive than a rape definition that uses the term 'penetration' as it encompasses a wider range of acts of sexualised violence. Therefore, 'invasion' keeps the definition open so as to be inclusive. A rape definition using the term 'invasion' emphasises violence and subordination rather than sexual arousal. It indicates that war rape does not only cause physical, but also psychological harm. Rape is an invasion into a person's autonomy, self-determination and integrity. Consequently, a rape definition using the term 'invasion' captures the nature of the crime more adequately. It also enables survivors and witnesses to speak about rape without having to use words that may be culturally forbidden.[56]

52 ibid para 598.

53 Quénivet (n 40) 14: While a gender-neutral definition of rape is widely supported, it also can be considered to obscure 'the reality that an overwhelming majority of rape victims are women [and that] it dismisses the gender power relations expressed through men's sexual violence towards women'.

54 Centre on Law and Globalization, 'What Counts as Rape in International Crimes?' <http://clg.portalxm.com/library/keytext.cfm?keytext_id=182> accessed 27 October 2012.

55 Interview 9 (11 April 2014); Human Rights Watch, 'Commentary on the Second Preparatory Commission on Rules of Procedure and Elements of Crime' (July 1999) <www.iccnow.org/documents/HRWComment2ndPrepComJuly99.pdf> accessed 9 February 2012; United Nations Commission on Human Rights, 'Final Report of the Special Rapporteur on the Situation of Systematic Rape, Sexual Slavery and Slavery-Like Practices during Armed Conflict' (n 43) para 24; Women's Caucus for Gender Justice, 'Priority Concerns Related to the Elements Annex' (February 1999) <www.iccwomen.org/wigjdraft1/Archives/oldWCGJ/icc/iccpc/021999pc/pcconcerns.htm> accessed 22 January 2014; For further discussion of using the term 'penetration' in defining rape see Chapters 1 and 2.

56 Interview 10 (22 April 2014); PrepCom2, 'Proposal Submitted by Costa Rica on Elements of Crimes' (24 February 1999) UN Doc PCNICC/1999/WGEC/DP.6 <www.legal-tools.org/doc/318088/> accessed 18 August 2017; Kristen Boon, 'Rape and Forced Pregnancy under the ICC Statute: Human Dignity, Autonomy, and Consent'

Based on a review of criminal law principles shared by major legal systems,[57] the Trial Chamber in *Furundžija* arrived at a more specific, mechanical and male definition of the objective elements of rape, describing the crime as

> (i) the sexual penetration, however slight:
>
> > (a) of the vagina or anus of the victim by the penis of the perpetrator or any other object used by the perpetrator; or
> > (b) of the mouth of the victim by the penis of the perpetrator;
>
> (ii) by coercion or force or threat of force against the victim or a third person.[58]

Regressing from the gender-neutral, inclusive, victim-centred definition that emphasises rape as an act of violence advanced in *Akayesu*, a definition of war rape using the term 'penetration' can be seen as male as it invokes concerns regarding women's chastity, paternity and honour.[59] This advances a male understanding of women as reproducers, preservers of civil society and the property of men. The categorisation of rape as an honour crime leads to women being seen only in relation to another (male) person instead of as an individual.[60]

While the definition of rape developed in the *Foča* case is comparable to the *Furundžija* definition in that they both use the term 'penetration', they differ in the element of coercion/consent.[61] While the *Foča* indictments indicates

(2001) 32 *Columbia Human Rights Law Review* 625; Anne-Marie L.M. de Brouwer, *Supranational Criminal Prosecution of Sexual Violence: The ICC and the Practice of the ICTY and the ICTR* (Insertia 2005) 107; Christopher Keith Hall, 'The First Five Sessions of the UN Preparatory Commission for the International Criminal Court' (2000) 94 *American Journal of International Law* 773, 778; Women's Caucus for Gender Justice, 'Recommendations and Commentary for the Elements Annex' (July 1999) <www.iccwomen.org/wigjdraft1/Archives/oldWCGJ/icc/iccpc/071999pc/elements.htm> accessed 22 January 2014.

57 *Furundžija* Trial Judgment (n 47) para 177.

58 ibid para 185.

59 Human Rights Watch, 'Commentary on the Second Preparatory Commission on Rules of Procedure and Elements of Crime' (n 55); United Nations Commission on Human Rights, 'Final Report of the Special Rapporteur on the Situation of Systematic Rape, Sexual Slavery and Slavery-Like Practices during Armed Conflict' (n 43) para 24.

60 Halley, 'Rape at Rome' (n 40) 56–58; Quénivet (n 40) 94–95.

61 Megan Lutz-Priefert, 'A Call for a More Permanent International Definition of Rape' (2015) 6 *Creighton International Law and Comparative Law Journal* 85: Lutz-Priefert stresses that despite the progress made by the *ad hoc* tribunals in defining rape, their jurisdiction and duration is limited. Before the establishment of the ICC, no rape definition existed in international instruments.

For more information on the discussion of a coercion- or consent-based rape definition see for example Anne-Marie de Brouwer, 'Gacumbitsi Judgement' in Goran Sluiter and André Klip (eds), *Annotated Leading Cases of International Criminal Tribunals: The*

that the sexualised crimes dealt with in the case were committed under coercive circumstances,[62] the Trial Chamber moved away from a purely coercion-base definition and understood rape as

> sexual penetration, however slight: (a) of the vagina or anus of the victim by the penis of the perpetrator or any other object used by the perpetrator; or (b) of the mouth of the victim by the penis of the perpetrator; where such sexual penetration occurs without the consent of the victim. Consent for this purpose must be consent given voluntarily, as a result of the victim's free will, assessed in the context of the surrounding circumstances.[63]

Contrary to the understanding of coercion as being the central element of the crime of rape, in a consent-based definition the nature of the crime of rape is understood along the lines of deprivation of sexual freedom and self-determination.[64] The focus lies on 'passion gone wrong'.[65] An emphasis is placed on the psyche of the victim and perpetrator. The relevant events are framed as individuals engaged in single interactions.[66] It can be argued that a consent-based rape definition is victim-centred and stresses the survivor's agency. This establishes rape survivors as active subjects, empowering them. Consequently, a consent-based definition would serve rape survivors. However, it would be detrimental for them if their lack of consent would need to be proven as this can be very problematic and may lead to unsuccessful claims. Therefore, the ICTY Trial Chamber's acknowledgement that coercion or (threat of) force establish lack of consent is crucial.

International Criminal Tribunal for Rwanda 2005–2006 (Volume 24, Intersentia 2009); Phillip Weiner, 'The Evolving Jurisprudence of the Crime of Rape in International Criminal Law' (2013) 54 *Boston College Law Review* 1207. See also Haenen, *Force & Marriage* (n 5) 27–29.

62 *Foča* Indictment (n 46) para 1.2, para 1.4, para 6.4, para 6.11, para 7.5, para 10.7; *Prosecutor v Dragoljub Kunarac, Radomir Kovač and Zoran Vuković* (Third Amended Indictment (Kunarac and Kovač)) IT-96-23-PT 'Foča Case' (8 November 1999) para 4.8, Mechanism for International Criminal Tribunals.

63 *Prosecutor v Dragoljub Kunarac, Radomir Kovač and Zoran Vuković* (Trial Judgment) ICTY IT-96-23-T and IT-96-23/1-T 'Foča Case' (22 February 2001) para 460 <www.legal-tools.org/doc/fd881d/> accessed 9 August 2017, Mechanism for International Criminal Tribunals; *Prosecutor v Mikaeli Muhimana* (Trial Judgment) ICTR-95-1B-T (28 April 2005) para 550 <www.legal-tools.org/doc/87fe83/> accessed 9 August 2017, Mechanism for International Criminal Tribunals: The Trial Chamber in the Muhimana case '[took] the view that the Akayesu definition and the Kunarac elements are not incompatible or substantially different in their application. Whereas Akayesu referred broadly to a "physical invasion of a sexual nature", Kunarac went on to articulate the parameters of what would constitute a physical invasion of a sexual nature amounting to rape.'

64 Centre on Law and Globalization (n 54).

65 ibid.

66 ibid.

Forced marriage

While the ICC negotiations could draw on a fairly extensive legislative history in defining war rape, forced marriage in times of armed conflict was less well-theorised and well-established at that time. Bilateral and multilateral conventions form early attempts at the criminalisation of war rape. However, similar steps were not taken regarding forced marriage in times of armed conflict. While international agreements mentioned war rape from the early 20th century on, forced marriage in general only began to be referred to in the second half of the century.[67]

From the mid-1950s on, international human rights instruments highlight that consent of both intending spouses is crucial for a marriage.[68] The Supplementary Convention on the Abolition of Slavery, the Slave Trade, and Institutions and Practices Similar to Slavery of 1956 condemns slavery-like practices, including bride sale and wife inheritance which include elements of coercion.[69]

67 See for example Convention on Consent to Marriage, Minimum Age for Marriage and Registration of Marriages (7 November 1962) 521 UNTS 231 art 1(1).

68 Convention on the Elimination of Discrimination against Women (18 December 1979)1279 UNTS 13 (CEDAW) art 16 <www.legal-tools.org/doc/6dc4e4/> accessed 18 August 2017; International Covenant on Civil and Political Rights (16 December 1966) 999 UNTS 171 (ICCPR) art 23(3) <www.legal-tools.org/doc/2838f3/> accessed 18 August 2017; International Covenant on Economic, Social and Cultural Rights (16 December 1966) 993 UNTS 3 (ICESCR) art 10(1) <www.legal-tools.org/doc/06b87e/> accessed 18 August 2017.

69 Supplementary Convention on the Abolition of Slavery, the Slave Trade, and Institutions and Practices Similar to Slavery (7 September 1956) 266 UNTS 3 (Supplementary Slavery Convention) art 1(c) <www.legal-tools.org/doc/d038c8/> accessed 18 August 2017; 'The Woman's Rights Movement' <http://utc.iath.virginia.edu/abolitn/wmhp.html> accessed 3 April 2015; Ehrenreich (n 4); Judy Groves and Cathia Jenainati, *Feminism: A Graphic Guide* (2nd edn, Icon Books 2013); National Women's History Museum, 'The Abolition Movement and Woman Suffrage' (2007) <www.nwhm.org/online-exhibits/rightsforwomen/abolitionandsuffrage.html> accessed 3 April 2015: In the Anglo-speaking world of the 17th and 18th century, slavery was linked to women's status and marriage and the fight for women's rights was equated with the abolitionist cause. This is demonstrated, for example, in Lady Mary Chudleigh's poem *To the Ladies* (1703) and in Elizabeth Cady Stanton's 1860 speech before the New York Legislature where she said: 'The negro's skin and the woman's sex are both prima facie evidence that they were intended to be in subjection to the white Saxon man.' By being actively involved in the abolitionist movement, the early leaders of the women's movement learned how to organise, publicise and articulate a political protest. Women wrote articles for papers; circulated pamphlets; circulated, signed and delivered petitions; and made speeches to mixed male and female audiences. However, their male fellow campaigners did not always welcome women playing active roles or taking speaking parts. Efforts to silence women at anti-slavery conventions in the US and the United Kingdom of Great Britain and Northern Ireland (UK) influenced Elizabeth Cady Stanton and Lucretia Mott to hold the first women's rights convention at Seneca Falls, New York, in June 1848. One of the tenets declared at the first and subsequent women's rights conventions was that, in

From 1995 onwards, the UN Special Rapporteur on Violence against Women, its Causes and Consequences directly addressed forced marriage in the context of persecution,[70] trafficking and forced prostitution[71] as well as in the context of armed conflict.[72] However, a detailed discussion and definition remained missing. Similar to the developments of a definition of war rape, the first definition of forced marriage in times of armed conflict was put forward at a time when the Rome Statute had been passed and the discussion of the Elements of Crimes had begun. The UN Special Rapporteur on the Situation of Systematic Rape, Sexual Slavery and Slavery-Like Practices during Armed Conflict recognised forced marriage as 'situations where women and girls are forced into "marriage", domestic servitude or other forced labour that ultimately involves forced sexual activity, including rape by their captors'.[73] Despite this recognition and awareness of both the sexual and non-sexual elements of forced marriage, however, the Special Rapporteur defined forced marriage as a form of sexual slavery.[74]

In 2001, the ICTY recognised forced marriage during armed conflict as an act of sexual violence without defining it further.[75] While this explicit

a way, women were slaves too. Women active in the abolitionist movement began to see some legal similarities between their situation and that of slaves. Taking the historic link between slavery and women's rights and their status into consideration, the categorisation of forced marriage as a form of (sexual) slavery may have deeper historical roots. Barbara Ehrenreich suggested that they go even further back than the 17th century. She argued that in the Ancient Middle East, war made men predators and women slaves.

70 United Nations Commission on Human Rights 'Preliminary Report Submitted by the Special Rapporteur on Violence against Women, Its Causes and Consequences' (n 42) fn 228.

71 United Nations Commission on Human Rights 'Report on the Mission of the Special Rapporteur to Poland on the Issue of Trafficking and Forced Prostitution of Women (24 May to 1 June 1996)' (10 December 1996) UN Doc E/CN.4/1997/47/Add.1 para 77–78, para 84 <www.ohchr.org> accessed 28 August 2017.

72 United Nations Commission on Human Rights, 'Report of the Mission to Rwanda on the Issues of Violence against Women in Situations of Armed Conflict, Ms. Radhika Coomaraswamy, Submitted in Accordance with Commission Resolution 1997/44' (4 February 1998) UN Doc E/CN.4/1998/54/Add.1 <www.ohchr.org> accessed 28 August 2017; Commission on Human Rights, 'Report of the Special Rapporteur on Violence against Women, Its Causes and Consequences, Ms. Radhika Coomaraswamy, Submitted in Accordance with Commission Resolution 1997/44' (26 January 1998) UN Doc E/CN.4/1998/54 para 17, 23, 27, 36 <www.ohchr.org> accessed 28 August 2017.

73 United Nations Commission on Human Rights, 'Final Report of the Special Rapporteur on the Situation of Systematic Rape, Sexual Slavery and Slavery-Like Practices during Armed Conflict' (n 43) para 30.

74 United Nations Commission on Human Rights, 'Final Report of the Special Rapporteur on the Situation of Systematic Rape, Sexual Slavery and Slavery-Like Practices during Armed Conflict' (n 43) para 30; see Chapter 6 for further discussion of the Final Report.

75 *Prosecutor v Miroslav Kvočka and Others* (Trial Judgment) IT-98-30/1-T 'Omarska, Keraterm & Trnopolje Camps' (2 November 2001) fn 343 <www.legal-tools.org/doc/34428a/> accessed 18 August 2017, Mechanism for International Criminal Tribunals.

recognition of forced marriage as a crime serves survivors,[76] it overemphasises the sexual elements of forced marriage, neglecting the non-sexual but gendered ones. Consequently, it acknowledges only a part of survivors' realities.

The SCSL build on the Final Report of the Special Rapporteur on the Situation of Systematic Rape, Sexual Slavery and Slavery-Like Practices during Armed Conflict as well as the ICTY's work. It categorised forced marriage as a form of sexual slavery and as an inhumane act. Evidence of forced marriage was also heard in relation to charges of acts of terror[77] and outrages upon personal dignity.[78] Reflecting these different categorisations, the Special Court referred to the crime as 'forced marriage' and 'conjugal slavery'.

Drawing on the ICTY's elaborations on the crime of enslavement in the *Foča* case,[79] the Trial Chamber in the *AFRC* case conveyed an understanding of forced marriage as a form of sexual slavery. It found that the use of the term 'wife' was one element of a forced marital relationship that was one of ownership and one-sided exclusivity where the forced husband exercised control over the forced wife's sexuality, movements and labour.[80] The Appeals Chamber, in

76 See Chapters 1 and 3 for further discussion.

77 *RUF* Trial Judgment (n 26) para 1352.

78 *Prosecutor v Alex Tamba Brima, Brima Bazzy Kamara and Santigie Borbor Kanu* (Trial Judgment) SCSL-04-16-T 'AFRC Case' (20 June 2007) para 93–95, para 713–714, para 719, para 2113, para 2117, para 2121 <www.legal-tools.org/doc/87ef08/> accessed 9 August 2017; *RUF* Trial Judgment (n 26) para 1474–1475.

79 *AFRC* Trial Judgment (n 78) para 708*; Foča* Trial Judgment (n 63): The judges in the *Foča* case held that the detention of Bosnian Muslim women in various centres, private apartments and houses where they had to cook and clean for, and (sexually) serve, the Bosnian Serb soldiers living there falls under the crime of enslavement. Considering and reviewing the relevant provisions on enslavement under a number of international humanitarian law and international human rights instruments as well as case law of the US Military Tribunal, the European Commission and Court of Human Rights, and the 1976 Criminal Code of the Socialist Federal Republic of Yugoslavia, the ICTY defined enslavement in a broad, gender-neutral and non-exhaustive way as a situation where '(1) [t]he perpetrator exercised any or all of the powers attaching to the right of ownership over one or more persons, such as by purchasing, selling, lending or bartering such a person or persons, or by imposing on them a similar deprivation of liberty [and when] (2) [t]he perpetrator caused such person or persons to engage in one or more acts of a sexual nature' (para 539). The tribunal determined that the factors taken into consideration in determining whether or not the crime of enslavement was committed include 'control of someone's movement, control of physical environment, psychological control, measures taken to prevent or deter escape, force, threat of force or coercion, duration, assertion of exclusivity, subjection to cruel treatment and abuse, control of sexuality and forced labour' (para 543). Moreover, the ICTY stressed that enslavement includes situations where, even if the survivor would attempt to flee, she has nowhere to go and is aware of the risks involved if recaptured.

80 *AFRC* Trial Judgment (n 78) para 704–705. See also *AFRC* Trial Judgment (n 78) para 713; *Prosecutor v Alex Tamba Brima, Brima Bazzy Kamara and Santigie Borbor Kanu* (Decision on Prosecution Request for Leave to Amend the Indictment) SCSL SLS-2004-16-PT 'AFRC Case' (06 May 2004) para 51–52 <www.sierralii.org/sl/judgment/special-court/2004/84> accessed 28 September 2017; *Prosecutor v Alex Tamba Brima, Brima*

contrast, concluded that forced marriage is of similar gravity to the crimes against humanity listed under the SCSL's statute and to be sufficiently serious to qualify as an inhumane act.[81] It found that

> [w]hile forced marriage shares certain elements with sexual slavery such as non-consensual sex and deprivation of liberty, there are also distinguishing factors. First, forced marriage involves a perpetrator compelling a person by force or threat of force, through the words or conduct of the perpetrator or those associated with him, into a forced conjugal association with another person resulting in great suffering, or serious physical or mental injury on the part of the victim. Second, unlike sexual slavery, forced marriage implies a relationship of exclusivity between the 'husband' and 'wife', which could lead to disciplinary consequences for breach of this exclusive arrangement. These distinctions imply that forced marriage is not predominantly a sexual crime.[82]

Even though the Appeals Chamber declined to enter a further conviction,[83] the categorisation of forced marriage as an inhumane act adequately reflects the conduct's distinctive and multifaceted nature. It avoids a too narrow categorisation that misrepresents the nature of the offence. Forced marriage is understood as including sexual and non-sexual elements. Therefore, charging forced marriage as an inhumane act can be seen as a success for the feminist goal to challenge gender stereotypes. It is recognition that, in times of armed conflict, women are not only affected by sexual, but also by other forms of violence. For these reasons, the understanding of forced marriage as an inhumane act serves survivors. However, classifying forced marriage as an inhumane act arguably conceals

Bazzy Kamara and Santigie Borbor Kanu (Separate Concurring Opinion on the Trial Chamber's Decision on Defence Motions for Judgement of Acquittal Pursuant to Rule 98) SCSL-04-16-T 'AFRC Case' (31 March 2006) para 19(iii); *AFRC* Prosecution Filing of Expert Report (n 5); *AFRC* Trial Judgment (n 78) para 701; *AFRC* Trial Judgment (n 78) Judge Doherty's Partly Dissenting Opinion para 51–53: This view is contrary to that advanced by expert witness Zainab H Bangura, the prosecution, and Judge Teresa Doherty's Partly Dissenting Opinion. They understood forced marriage to amount to another inhumane act. The prosecution emphasised that forced marriage and sexual slavery are different as a sex slave does not necessarily have to pretend to be her captor's wife and perform 'wifely duties'. It defined the crime of forced marriage gender-neutrally as a fairly clear-cut act that 'consists of words or other conduct intended to confer a status of marriage by force or threat of force or coercion, such as that caused by fear of violence, duress, detention, psychological oppression or abuse of power against the victim, or by taking advantage of a coercive environment, with the intention of conferring the status of marriage'. Judge Doherty emphasised the psychological suffering, stigmatisation and difficult reintegration process for survivors that indicate that forced marriage is of similar gravity and nature as other crimes against humanity.

81 *AFRC* Appeals Chamber Judgment (n 23) para 200.

82 ibid para 195.

83 ibid para 105.

the serious violations it encompasses. Despite this downside, naming 'forced marriage' as a crime is recognition of the reality of women during and after armed conflicts as they experience and understand it. It legitimises women's experiences and consequently empowers them. Beyond that, by naming 'forced marriage' as a crime, it was acknowledged as a wrong that needs to be legally addressed. The term 'forced marriage' makes it easier to identify and stress the interrelatedness of its parts and distinctive harms associated with it that are not adequately or fully captured by other crimes. This conveys an understanding of forced marriage as more than the sum of its parts. The totality makes it a distinct crime that cannot be adequately captured in a collection of separate charges.[84] In contrast to these advantages of naming the conduct 'forced marriage', it can be argued, that the use of the noun 'marriage' hides the degree of violence, coercion and control as well as the exploitation of gender roles that is characteristic of a forced marriage. Since mutual consent is seen as crucial to a marriage, the use of the noun 'marriage' suggests a degree of voluntarism, stigmatising the woman and downplaying the responsibility of the perpetrator. It suggests that the services a forced wife renders to her forced husband are offered as part of a marriage arrangement rather than forced. However, the adjective 'forced' can be interpreted to show that the noun 'marriage' is a perversion of what marriage really means.

The Trial Chamber in the *RUF* case confirmed the Appeals Chamber's finding in the *AFRC* case that forced marriage is not fully captured by the crime of sexual slavery and rather constitutes another inhumane act.[85] The Trial Chamber took a gender-neutral approach and determined the objective element of forced marriage to be the 'imposition of a forced conjugal association'.[86] This imposition of a forced conjugal status was understood as a distinct act including being married against the woman's will and forced to engage in sexual intercourse and to perform domestic tasks,[87] rather than the diffuse process that was indicated by the *AFRC* Appeals Chamber in its judgment.[88]

84 Annie Bunting, '"Forced Marriage" in Conflict Situations: Researching and Prosecuting Old Harms and New Crimes' (2012) *Canadian Journal of Human Rights* 165, 179; Kristastout, 'What's in a Name? The Feasibility and Desirability of Naming Forced Marriage as a Separate Crime under International Humanitarian Law' (8 May 2012) <http://de.scribd.com/doc/94709906/3/III-The-Constituent-Crimes-that-Underpin-the-Crime-of-Forced-Marriage> accessed 6 December 2012; Valerie Oosterveld, 'Forced Marriage and the Special Court for Sierra Leone: Legal Advances and Conceptual Difficulties' (2011) 2 *Journal of International Humanitarian Legal Studies* 127; Toy-Cronin (n 19) 565.

85 *RUF* Trial Judgment (n 26) para 1297, 2307.

86 ibid para 1295.

87 ibid para 1293. See also Iris Haenen, 'The Parameters of Enslavement and the Act of Forced Marriage' (2013) 13 *International Criminal Law Review* 895.

88 *AFRC* Appeals Chamber Judgment (n 23) para 199.

Haenen, *Force & Marriage* (n 5); Melanie O'Brien, '"Don't Kill Them, Let's Choose Them as Wives": The Development of the Crime of Forced Marriage, Sexual Slavery

While the judges in the *RUF* case followed the *AFRC* Appeals Chamber's approach to forced marriage, the Trial Chamber in *Taylor* reverted to the *AFRC* Trial Chamber's judgment and found that the evidence related to forced marriage satisfied the elements of sexual slavery.[89] Fighters exercised rights of ownership over their forced wives by depriving them of their liberty, forcing them to work for the fighters' and group's benefit. Additionally, forced wives were subjected to various acts of sexualised violence.[90] The Trial Chamber, however, stressed that the term 'forced marriage' is a misnomer because there is no actual marriage 'in the universally understood sense of a consensual and sacrosanct union, and [what has been termed "forced marriage"] should rather [...] be considered a conjugal form of enslavement'.[91]

The categorisation of forced marriage as a form of sexual slavery serves conservative forces within international law that prefer relying on legal precedents to potentially developing new law. It neglects that forced marriage is not (only) an exercise of powers attaching to the right of ownership. The categorisation of forced marriage as a form of sexual slavery also perpetuates stereotypes that

---

and Enforced Prostitution in International Criminal Law' (2016) 20 *The International Journal of Human Rights* 386: Considering whether forced marriage is framed as a distinct act or a complex and diffuse process becomes interesting when comparing forced marriage to rape. It can be claimed that rape can be more easily translated into a narrow criminal act that is defined, for example, by coerced physical invasion. However, the argument can be made that this is the current, well-established, legal understanding of rape. Survivors, however, can struggle to fit their experiences into these narrow confines. Someone who experienced forced undressing, forced nudity or forced bodily contact may 'feel raped' even though these acts fall outside any legal definition of the crime. Moreover, similar to forced marriage, rape has various serious long-term consequences for the survivor as well as for her social environment that cannot be disconnected from the coerced physical invasion. Consequently, it can be argued that if the crime of rape would have been defined differently, more broadly, it may be perceived as a process comparable to the understanding of forced marriage advanced by the *AFRC* Appeals Chamber and the *Taylor* Trial Chamber. Following on from this, forced marriage may only be perceived as a complex and diffuse process now because it is still undergoing legal definition. Would it be as well-theorised and would its definition be as well-established as that of rape, it may be seen differently. Haenen, for example, argues that forced marriage should purely be defined as the 'forced conferral of marital status on a person against that person's will'. The crimes committed in a forced marriage should be prosecuted separately as existing crimes against humanity to put proper emphasis on them. This approach, however, would disconnect the interrelated whole that is forced marriage and may distort the understanding of the crime. A disjunctive and conjunctive definition of forced marriage as the act of conferring the status of marriage and/or, for example, forced labour and sexual crimes as suggested by O'Brien might capture a broader range of situations.

89 *Prosecutor v Charles Taylor* (Trial Judgment) SCSL-03-01-T (18 May 2012) para 426 <www.legal-tools.org/doc/3e7be5/> accessed 9 August 2017.

90 *Taylor* Trial Judgment (n 89) para 1102, para 1144.

91 ibid para 427.

women primarily experience war as victims of sexual violence. It creates the false impression that forced marriage would predominantly be a sexualised crime. The categorisation of forced marriage as a form of sexual slavery ignores the gendered elements of forced marriage. Women are targeted because of their ascribed social roles as domestic workers, caretakers and sexual beings.[92] The categorisation of forced marriage as a form of sexual slavery does not capture the forced exclusivity and intimacy of a forced marriage. It disregards the psychological force of acts of violence being disguised within the legitimate situation of marriage. Forced marriages cause different forms of suffering than sexual slavery and cause survivors to be discriminated against in unique ways. The woman is forced into marriage with a person who often committed terrible atrocities against her family. They are forced into exclusivity and intimacy while at the same time they experience on-going abuse from the same person. The label 'marriage' attached to this relationship is deliberate and strategic. It demonstrates a fighter's control over a woman, manipulating forced wives into loyalty towards their forced husbands. It renders them unable to deny their forced husband's wishes and makes them feel saved from more abuse by other fighters. Children born into forced marriages make forced wives dependent on their forced husbands even after the conflict has ended. This is aggravated by the social stigmatisation and exclusion the women experience from their families and communities as they are seen as collaborators, rebels and killers. This perception is based on the fact that forced wives often participated in direct combat. They are victims, witnesses and perpetrators of war violence.

The *Taylor* judgment makes clear that the Trial Chamber analysed the evidence of forced marriage under two categories. The evidence of sexual violence including rape was considered under the charge of sexual slavery. The evidence of forced labour, in contrast, was considered under the enslavement charge.[93] This approach better reflects the acts intended to be captured by the term 'forced marriage'. The construction of the constituting elements of forced marriage as two forms of enslavement highlights that the crime consists of sexual and non-sexual aspects. It confirms the acts of violence perpetrated against forced wives as serious crimes while avoiding the drawbacks of classifying forced marriage as a form of sexual slavery. A disadvantage, however, would be that enslavement does not immediately highlight the gendered dimension of the crime. Moreover, the experiences of forced wives would be fragmented into different forms of enslavement. Additionally, (ex-)forced wives are unlikely to self-identify with the label of enslavement.[94]

92 Kristastout (n 84) 23.

93 *Prosecutor v Charles Taylor* (Second Amended Indictment) SCSL-03-01-PT (29 May 2007) para 23–27; *Taylor* Trial Judgment (n 89) para 447–448, para 1698–1699.

94 Oosterveld, 'Forced Marriage and the Special Court for Sierra Leone' (n 84); Haenen, *The Parameters of Enslavement* (n 87) 913; O'Brien (n 88): While it is argued here that forced marriage should not be defined as a form of enslavement or sexual slavery, Haenen (913–914) acknowledges that 'customary law in some countries recognizes the practice of wife ownership, which means a husband has complete control over his wife. If

In addition to contributing to the categorisation of forced marriage by solidifying the international legal definition of sexual slavery and helping to define its contours, the judges in the *Taylor* case also contributed to the discussion on how to name the crime. While the above discussion emphasised that labelling the conduct 'forced marriage' serves survivors, 'conjugal slavery' serves patriarchal structures as marriage is considered too important and fundamental to be interfered with, preserving men's traditional power position in the private sphere. Regardless of whether the crime is termed forced marriage or conjugal slavery, however, there is a risk that forced marriage is defined based on the context-dependent and highly gendered roles wives and husbands perform in a forced marriage. It is crucial to keep the meaning of the term 'marriage' or 'conjugality' flexible and wide so as to adapt to the context and to capture different scenarios. In doing so, courts would also address concerns regarding the female victim/male perpetrator focus that shapes current understandings of the crime of forced marriage. This understanding neglects situations where both spouses are forced into the marriage, where a man is forced into marriage by a woman and forced same-sex marriage. In addition to interpreting forced marriage as gender-neutral, this broader view of the identity of a survivor of forced marriage would contribute to the growing recognition of sexualised war violence perpetrated against men.[95] In addition to keeping the meaning of the term 'marriage' or 'conjugality' flexible and broad so as to capture different victim/perpetrator constellations, context-sensitivity is crucial regarding the roles wives and husbands perform in a forced marriage as they may vary in different contexts. Care should also be taken that patriarchal stereotypes of a wife's position in the private sphere are not enshrined into international law that aims to empower women. The inclusion of such gender stereotypes would constitute a step backwards rather than a success for the feminist project of gender-sensitive recognition of crimes. If the terms 'marriage' or 'conjugality' prevail in the criminalisation of this conduct, it would be crucial for courts to explicitly state that definitions of forced marriage that include forced wives' domestic duties do not legitimise those duties to counter the incorporation of patriarchal gender stereotypes into international law.[96]

---

marriage results in wife ownership, a marriage is the necessary act to enslave someone. The "ownership" over a woman or girl is transferred from her father to her husband by the act of marriage. In these cases, marriage, forced or not, is used as a means to enslave someone.' However, it has to be stressed that the marriage is not entered into to establish ownership over another person. Moreover, defining forced marriage as an exercise of powers attaching to the right of ownership is context dependent and arguably excludes for example forced marriages as perpetrated in Cambodia under the Khmer Rouge.

95 *AFRC* Appeals Chamber Judgment (n 23) para 199; Prosecution Final Brief para 1009–1012 as cited in *AFRC* Trial Judgment (n 78) para 701; *RUF* Trial Judgment (n 26) para 1293, para 1295; Lawry (n 19); Oosterveld, 'Forced Marriage and the Special Court for Sierra Leone' (n 84); Toy-Cronin (n 19).

96 Binaifer Nowrojee, 'Making the Invisible War Crime Visible: Post-Conflict Justice for Sierra Leone's Rape Victims' (2005) *Harvard Human Rights Journal* 85; Oosterveld, 'Forced Marriage and the Special Court for Sierra Leone' (n 84); Toy-Cronin (n 19).

Conclusion

Taking together the above elaborations on war rape, for the purpose of this book, war rape is understood as 'a physical invasion of a sexual nature',[97] a sexual expression of violence and aggression. It is an act of force that exploits power inequalities. Consequently, war rapes are committed under (possibly especially created) coercive circumstances expressed through, for example, threats or deceit, rendering the victim incapable of giving genuine consent. However, it has to be stressed that not all sexual interactions in times of armed conflict are rapes. Moreover, women's agency has to be emphasised. Therefore, an element of lack of consent remains important in defining war rape. However, consent has to be interpreted as genuine agreement. Silence or the lack of resistance does not necessarily amount to consent. Moreover, an element of absence of consent has to be included in a definition of rape in a way that it can be established by proving coercive circumstances without having to introduce evidence of the survivor's lack of consent. Downsides of a (partly) consent-based definition such as a focus on the behaviour of the survivor have to be considered. War rapes are an extreme continuation of structural peacetime violence. They target a person's autonomy, self-determination, bodily integrity and identity. War rapes cause physical, psychological and social harm. They humiliate, intimidate, stigmatise and punish the individual survivor as well as their families, communities and society as a whole. War rape is a crime in and of itself and it can also constitute, for example, an act of genocide, ethnic cleansing and torture.

Forced marriage in times of armed conflict means that, in the coercive context of armed conflict, the status of marriage is conferred on someone by words or deeds.[98] Forced marriage includes acts of physical and psychological violence such as abduction, manipulation, enslavement, deprivation of liberty, sexualised violence, forced pregnancy, forced labour, corporal punishment and forced recruitment. Nevertheless, some see it as a way to survive; to protect themselves from what they consider worse acts of violence and to gain economic benefits. Forced marriages are formed in times of armed conflict to exercise control over someone, targeting a person's self-determination. Forced wives also are a reward and status symbol. Forced marriages create dependency structures in fighting groups and destroy traditional interpersonal bonds because forced wives are stigmatised by, and excluded from, their families and communities. Forced marriage is a way to fulfil a certain masculine ideal that cannot be achieved otherwise. This indicates that forced marriage is a form of structural gender-based violence that is a continuation from peacetime norms and practices. Legally, forced marriage has been categorised as a form of sexual slavery, which highlights the seriousness of the crime. However, it overemphasises the sexual elements of

97 *Akayesu* Trial Judgment (n 46) para 598.
98 Prosecution Final Brief para 1009–1012 as cited in *AFRC* Trial Judgment (n 78) para 701.

forced marriages. An inhumane act of forced marriage instead reflects the conduct's distinctive and multifaceted nature, although it arguably conceals the seriousness of the crime. In addition to these different categorisations, different terms for the conduct have been developed: forced marriage and conjugal slavery. The SCSL argued that since no actual marriage takes place between the spouses, 'forced marriage' is a misnomer for what would better be called 'conjugal slavery'. As mentioned above, even though the label 'slavery' highlights the seriousness of the conduct, it creates a fragmentation of the elements of forced marriage into different forms of slavery. Moreover, (ex-)forced wives are unlikely to self-identify with that label. The term 'forced marriage' has the advantage that it recognises an 'interrelated, whole conduct'.[99] Naming forced marriage 'provid[es] a single name for the larger overarching harm associated with a particular collection of offences and therefore capturing, in one definition, harm that other international criminal law terms do not adequately or fully capture'.[100] Therefore, the term 'forced marriage' is used throughout the book.[101]

Bibliography

Conventions and statutes

Charter of the International Military Tribunal (8 August 1945) 82 UNTS 279, 59 Stat 1544, 3 Bevans 1238, 39 AJIL 258 (London Agreement) <www.legal-tools.org/doc/64ffdd/> accessed 18 August 2017.

Convention on Consent to Marriage, Minimum Age for Marriage and Registration of Marriages (7 November 1962) 521 UNTS 231.

Convention on the Elimination of Discrimination against Women (18 December 1979) 1279 UNTS 13 (CEDAW) <www.legal-tools.org/doc/6dc4e4/> accessed 18 August 2017.

Geneva Convention (IV) Relative to the Protection of Civilian Persons in Time of War (12 August 1949) 75 UNTS 287, 6 UST 3516, TIAS 3365 <www.legal-tools.org/doc/d5e260/> accessed 18 August 2017.

Hague Convention (IV) Respecting the Laws and Customs of War on Land and Its Annex: Regulation Concerning the Laws and Customs of War on Land (18 October 1907) 36 Stat 2277, 187 CTS 2271, Bevans 631, 205 Consol TS 277, 3 Martens Nouveau Recueil (ser 3) 461 <www.legal-tools.org/doc/fa0161/> accessed 18 August 2017.

International Covenant on Civil and Political Rights (16 December 1966) 999 UNTS 171 (ICCPR) <www.legal-tools.org/doc/2838f3/> accessed 18 August 2017.

99 Oosterveld, 'Forced Marriage and the Special Court for Sierra Leone' (n 84) 142.

100 Oosterveld, 'Forced Marriage and the Special Court for Sierra Leone' (n 84) 144.

101 O'Brien (n 88): O'Brien, however, raises the point that the term 'conjugal' may carry fewer challenges for the survivor and her community than the term 'marriage'.

International Covenant on Economic, Social and Cultural Rights (16 December 1966) 993 UNTS 3 (ICESCR) <www.legal-tools.org/doc/06b87e/> accessed 18 August 2017.

Protocol Additional to the Geneva Conventions of 12 August 1949, and Relating to the Protection of Victims of International Armed Conflicts (8 June 1977) 1125 UNTS 3 (Additional Protocol I) <www.legal-tools.org//d9328a/> accessed 18 August 2017.

Protocol Additional to the Geneva Conventions of 12 August 1949, and Relating to the Protection of Victims of Non-International Armed Conflicts (8 June 1977) 1125 UNTS 609 (Additional Protocol II) <www.legal-tools.org/doc/fd14c4/> accessed 18 August 2017.

Supplementary Convention on the Abolition of Slavery, the Slave Trade, and Institutions and Practices Similar to Slavery (7 September 1956) 266 UNTS 3 (Supplementary Slavery Convention) <www.legal-tools.org/doc/d038c8/> accessed 18 August 2017.

Treaty of Amity and Commerce (10 September 1785).

United Nations documents

Commission on Human Rights

Commission on Human Rights, 'Final Report of the Special Rapporteur on the Situation of Systematic Rape, Sexual Slavery and Slavery-Like Practices during Armed Conflict' (22 June 1998) UN Doc E/CN.4/Sub.2/1998/13 <www.ohchr.org> accessed 28 August 2017 ©1998 United Nations. Reprinted with the Permission of the United Nations.

———, 'Preliminary Report Submitted by the Special Rapporteur on Violence against Women, Its Causes and Consequences, Ms. Radhika Coomaraswamy, in Accordance with Commission on Human Rights Resolution 1994/45' (22 November 1994) UN Doc E/CN.4/1995/42 <www.ohchr.org> accessed 28 August 2017.

———, 'Report of the Mission to Rwanda on the Issues of Violence against Women in Situations of Armed Conflict, Ms. Radhika Coomaraswamy, Submitted in Accordance with Commission Resolution 1997/44' (04 February 1998) UN Doc E/CN.4/1998/54/Add.1 <www.ohchr.org> accessed 28 August 2017.

———, 'Report on the Mission of the Special Rapporteur to Poland on the Issue of Trafficking and Forced Prostitution of Women (24 May to 1 June 1996)' (10 December 1996) UN Doc E/CN.4/1997/47/Add.1 <www.ohchr.org> accessed 28 August 2017.

———, 'Report of the Special Rapporteur on Violence against Women, Its Causes and Consequences, Ms. Radhika Coomaraswamy, Submitted in Accordance with Commission Resolution 1997/44' (26 January 1998) UN Doc E/CN.4/1998/54 <www.ohchr.org> accessed 28 August 2017.

General Assembly

UNGA, 'Declaration on the Elimination of Violence against Women' (20 December 1993) UN Doc A/RES/48/104 (DEVAW).

Preparatory Commission for the International Criminal Court

PrepCom2, 'Proposal Submitted by Costa Rica on Elements of Crimes' (24 February 1999) UN Doc PCNICC/1999/WGEC/DP.6 <www.legal-tools.org/doc/318088/> accessed 18 August 2017.

Security Council

UNSC Resolution 827 (25 May 1993) UN Doc S/RES/827 <www.legal-tools.org/doc/dc079b/> accessed 18 August 2017.

UNSC Resolution 955 (08 November 1994) UN Doc S/RES/955 <www.legal-tools.org/doc/f5ef47/> accessed 18 August 2017.

Other

Committee on the Elimination of Discrimination against Women, 'General Recommendation No 19' (29 July 1994) UN Doc HRI/GEN/1/Rev.1 <www.legal-tools.org/en/browse/record/f8d998/> accessed 18 August 2017.

International Conference on Population and Development, 'Report' (13 September 1994) UN Doc A/CONF.171/13/Rev.1.

The World Conference on Human Rights, 'Vienna Declaration and Programme of Action' (12 July 1993) UN Doc A/CONF.157/23 <www.legal-tools.org/doc/65dc31/> accessed 18 August 2017.

Other legal instruments

Allied Control Council Law No 10 Punishment of Persons Guilty of War Crimes, Crimes against Peace and against Humanity (20 December 1945) 3 Official Gazette Control Council for Germany 50–55 (1946) <www.legal-tools.org/doc/ffda62/> accessed 18 August 2017.

Institute of International Law, 'Manual of the Laws and Customs of War' (9 September 1880) (Oxford Manual) <www1.umn.edu/humanrts/instree/1880a.htm> accessed 9 August 2013.

Instructions for the Government of Armies of the United States in the Field, General Order No 100 (24 April 1863) (Lieber Code).

Project of an International Declaration Concerning the Laws and Customs of War (27 August 1874) (Declaration of Brussels) <www.icrc.org/ihl/INTRO/135> accessed 9 August 2013.

Rules and Articles of War, Order No 20 (1847) (United States of America).

Cases

International Criminal Tribunal for the former Yugoslavia

Prosecutor v Anto Furundžija (Trial Judgment) ICTY IT-95-17/1-T (10 December 1998) <www.legal-tools.org/doc/e6081b/> accessed 9 August 2017, Mechanism for International Criminal Tribunals.

Prosecutor v Dragoljub Kunarac, Radomir Kovač and Zoran Vuković (Indictment) IT-96-23-T 'Foča Case' (19 June 1996) <www.legal-tools.org/doc/3a081b/> accessed 18 August 2017, Mechanism for International Criminal Tribunals.

Prosecutor v Dragoljub Kunarac, Radomir Kovač and Zoran Vuković (Third Amended Indictment (Kunarac and Kovač)) IT-96-23-PT 'Foča Case' (8 November 1999), Mechanism for International Criminal Tribunals.

Prosecutor v Dragoljub Kunarac, Radomir Kovač and Zoran Vuković (Trial Judgment) ICTY IT-96-23-T and IT-96-23/1-T 'Foča Case' (22 February 2001) <www.legal-tools.org/doc/fd881d/> accessed 9 August 2017, Mechanism for International Criminal Tribunals.

Prosecutor v Miroslav Kvočka and Others (Trial Judgment) IT-98-30/1-T 'Omarska, Keraterm & Trnopolje Camps' (02 November 2001) <www.legal-tools.org/doc/34428a/> accessed 18 August 2017, Mechanism for International Criminal Tribunals.

International Criminal Tribunal for Rwanda

Prosecutor v Jean-Paul Akayesu (Amended Indictment) ICTR-96-4-I (16 February 1996), Mechanism for International Criminal Tribunals.

Prosecutor v Jean-Paul Akayesu (Trial Judgment) ICTR-96-4-T (2 September 1998) <www.legal-tools.org/doc/b8d7bd/> accessed 9 August 2017, Mechanism for International Criminal Tribunals.

Prosecutor v Mikaeli Muhimana (Trial Judgment) ICTR-95-1B-T (28 April 2005) <www.legal-tools.org/doc/87fe83/> accessed 9 August 2017, Mechanism for International Criminal Tribunals.

International Military Tribunal

The United States of America and Others v Hermann Wilhelm Göring and Others in International Military Tribunal Nuremberg, *Trial of the Major War Criminals before the International Military Tribunal, Vol. 1* (Nuremberg 1947) <www.legal-tools.org/doc/388b07/> accessed 18 August 2017.

The United States of America and Others v Hermann Wilhelm Göring and Others in International Military Tribunal Nuremberg, *Trial of the Major War Criminals before the International Military Tribunal, Vol. 6* (Nuremberg 1947) <www.legal-tools.org/doc/18bdcd/> accessed 18 August 2017.

The United States of America and Others v Hermann Wilhelm Göring and Others in International Military Tribunal Nuremberg, *Trial of the Major War Criminals before the International Military Tribunal, Vol. 7* (Nuremberg 1947) <www.legal-tools.org/doc/6cefff/> accessed 18 August 2017.

International Military Tribunal for the Far East

The United States of America and Others v Sadao Araki and Others (Indictment) No 1 (3 May 1946) in Neil Boister and Robert Cryer (eds), *Documents on the Tokyo International Military Tribunal: Charter, Indictment and Judgments* (Oxford University Press 2008).

The United States of America and Others v Sadao Araki and Others (Judgment) No 1 (November 1948) in Neil Boister and Robert Cryer (eds), *Documents on the Tokyo International Military Tribunal: Charter, Indictment and Judgments* (Oxford University Press 2008).

Special Court for Sierra Leone

Prosecutor v Alex Tamba Brima, Brima Bazzy Kamara and Santigie Borbor Kanu (Appeals Chamber Judgment) SCSL SLS-2004-16-A 'AFRC Case' (22 February 2008) <www.legal-tools.org/doc/4420ef/> accessed 9 August 2017.

Prosecutor v Alex Tamba Brima, Brima Bazzy Kamara and Santigie Borbor Kanu (Decision on Prosecution Request for Leave to Amend the Indictment) SCSL SLS-2004-16-PT 'AFRC Case' (6 May 2004) <www.sierralii.org/sl/judgment/special-court/2004/84> accessed 28 September 2017.

Prosecutor v Alex Tamba Brima, Brima Bazzy Kamara and Santigie Borbor Kanu (Prosecution Filing of Expert Report Pursuant to Rule 94(bis) and Decision of Prosecution Request for Leave to Call an Additional Expert Witness) SCSL-04-16-T 'AFRC Case' (8 August 2005) <www.rscsl.org/Documents/Decisions/AFRC/365/SCSL-04-16-T-369.pdf> accessed 28 September 2017.

Prosecutor v Alex Tamba Brima, Brima Bazzy Kamara and Santigie Borbor Kanu (Separate Concurring Opinion on the Trial Chamber's Decision on Defence Motions for Judgement of Acquittal Pursuant to Rule 98) SCSL-04-16-T 'AFRC Case' (31 March 2006).

Prosecutor v Alex Tamba Brima, Brima Bazzy Kamara and Santigie Borbor Kanu (Trial Judgment) SCSL-04-16-T 'AFRC Case' (20 June 2007) <www.legal-tools.org/doc/87ef08/> accessed 9 August 2017.

Prosecutor v Issa Hassan Sesay, Morris Kallon and Augustine Gbao (Trial Judgment) SCSL-04-15-PT 'RUF Case' (2 March 2009) <www.legal-tools.org/doc/7f05b7/> accessed 9 August 2017.

Prosecutor v Charles Taylor (Second Amended Indictment) SCSL-03-01-PT (29 May 2007).

Prosecutor v Charles Taylor (Trial Judgment) SCSL-03-01-T (18 May 2012) <www.legal-tools.org/doc/3e7be5/> accessed 9 August 2017.

United States Military Commission

Trial of General Tomoyuki Yamashita, Case No 21, IV Law Reports of Trials of War Criminals 1, United States Military Commission, Manila (8 October–7 December 1945) <www.legal-tools.org/doc/c6673f/> accessed 18 August 2017.

Interviews

Interview 9 (11 April 2014).

Interview 10 (22 April 2014).

Books

Askin, K.D., *War Crimes against Women: Prosecution in International War Crimes Tribunals* (Kluwer International Law 1997).

Barrett, F.J. and Whitehead, S.M. (eds), *The Masculinities Reader* (Polity Press 2001).
Bassiouni, M.C., *The Legislative History of the International Criminal Court* (Transnational Publishers 2005).
Bourke, J., *Rape: A History from 1860 to the Present Day* (Virago 2007).
Brouwer, A.M.L.M. de, *Supranational Criminal Prosecution of Sexual Violence: The ICC and the Practice of the ICTY and the ICTR* (Insertia 2005).
Brownmiller, S., *Against Our Will: Men, Women and Rape* (Penguin Books 1977).
Connell, R.W., *Gender and Power: Society, the Person and Sexual Politics* (Polity Press 1987).
Coulter, C., *Bush Wives and Girl Soldiers: Women's Lives through War and Peace in Sierra Leone* (Cornell University Press 2009).
Ehrenreich, B., *Blood Rites: Origins and History of the Passions of War* (Virago 1997).
Groves, J. and Jenainati, C., *Feminism: A Graphic Guide* (2nd edn, Icon Books 2013).
Haenen, I., *Force & Marriage: The Criminalisation of Forced Marriage in Dutch, English and International Criminal Law* (Intersentia 2014).
Harrell-Bond, B.E., *Modern Marriage in Sierra Leone: A Study of the Professional Group* (Mouton 1975).
Hooper, C., *Manly States: Masculinities, International Relations, and Gender Politics* (Columbia University Press 2001).
Leatherman, J.L., *Sexual Violence and Armed Conflict* (Polity Press 2011).
Quénivet, N.N.R., *Sexual Offenses in Armed Conflict and International Law* (Transnational Publishers 2005).

Chapters in edited books

Annan, J. and Blattman, C., 'On the Nature and Causes of LRA Abduction: What the Abductees Say' in Bernd Allen and Koen Vlassenroot (eds), *The Lord's Resistance Army: Myth and Reality* (Zed Books 2010).
Barrett, F.J., 'The Organizational Construction of Hegemonic Masculinity: The Case of the US Navy' in Frank J. Barrett and Stephen M. Whitehead (eds), *The Masculinities Reader* (Polity Press 2001).
Brouwer, A.M. de, 'Gacumbitsi Judgement' in Goran Sluiter and André Klip (eds), *Annotated Leading Cases of International Criminal Tribunals: The International Criminal Tribunal for Rwanda 2005–2006* (Volume 24, Intersentia 2009).
Cockburn, C., 'The Gendered Dynamics of Armed Conflict and Political Violence' in Fiona Clark and Caroline N.O. Moser (eds), *Victims, Perpetrators or Actors? Gender, Armed Conflict and Political Violence* (Zed Books 2001).
Connell, R.W., 'The Social Organization of Masculinity' in Frank J. Barrett and Stephen M. Whitehead (eds), *The Masculinities Reader* (Polity Press 2001).
Dolan, C., 'Collapsing Masculinities and Weak States: A Case Study of Northern Uganda' in Frances Cleaver (ed), *Masculinity Matters: Men, Masculinities and Gender Relations in Development* (Zed Books 2003).
Gardam, J., 'Law of Armed Conflict: A Gendered Regime?' in Dorinda G. Dallmeyer (ed), *Reconceiving Reality: Women and International Law* (American Society of International Law 1993).
Jackson, S., 'The Social Context of Rape: Sexual Scripts and Motivations' in Ronald J. Berger and Patricia Searles (eds), *Rape and Society: Readings on the Problem of Sexual Assault* (Westview Press 1995).

Kerfoot, D., 'The Organization of Intimacy: Managerialism, Masculinity and the Masculine Subject' in Frank J. Barrett and Stephen M. Whitehead (eds), *The Masculinities Reader* (Polity Press 2001).

Messner, M.A., 'Friendship, Intimacy, and Sexuality' in Frank J. Barrett and Stephen M. Whitehead (eds), *The Masculinities Reader* (Polity Press 2001).

Moser, C.O.N., 'The Gendered Continuum of Violence and Conflict: An Operational Framework' in Fiona Clark and Caroline N.O. Moser (eds), *Victims, Perpetrators or Actors? Gender, Armed Conflict and Political Violence* (Zed Books 2001).

Pankhurst, D., 'Sexual Violence in War' in Laura J. Shepherd (ed), *Gender Matters in Global Politics: A Feminist Introduction to International Relations* (Routledge 2010).

Parpart, J.L. and Zalewski, M., 'Introduction' in Jane L. Parpart and Marysia Zalewski (eds), *Rethinking the Man Question: Sex, Gender and Violence in International Relations* (Zed Books 2008).

Seifert, R., 'Krieg und Vergewaltigung: Ansätze zu einer Analyse' in Alexandra Stiglemayer (ed), *Massenvergewaltigungen: Krieg gegen die Frauen* (Fischer Taschenbuchverlag 1993).

Turshen, M., 'The Political Economy of Rape: An Analysis of Systematic Rape and Sexual Abuse of Women during Armed Conflict in Africa' in Fiona Clark and Caroline N.O. Moser (eds), *Victims, Perpetrators or Actors? Gender, Armed Conflict and Political Violence* (Zed Books 2001).

Viseur Sellers, P., 'The Context of Sexual Violence: Sexual Violence as Violations of International Humanitarian Law' in Gabrielle Kirk McDonald and Olivia Swaak (eds), *Substantive and Procedural Aspects of International Criminal Law: The Experience of International and National Courts, Volume 1, Commentary* (Kluwer Law International 2000).

Weiner, P., 'The Evolving Jurisprudence of the Crime of Rape in International Criminal Law' (2013) 54 *Boston College Law Review* 1207.

Whitworth, S., 'Militarized Masculinity and Post-Traumatic Stress Disorder' in Jane L. Parpart and Marysia Zalewski (eds), *Rethinking the Man Question: Sex, Gender and Violence in International Relations* (Zed Books 2008).

Journal articles

Amowitz, L.L. and others, 'Prevalence of War-Related Sexual Violence and Other Human Rights Abuses among Internally Displaced Persons in Sierra Leone' (2002) 287 *Journal of the American Medical Association* 513.

Annan, J. and others, 'Civil War, Reintegration, and Gender in Northern Uganda' (2011) 55 *Journal of Conflict Resolution* 877.

Askin, K.D., 'Prosecuting Wartime Rape and Other Gender-Related Crimes under International Law: Extraordinary Advances, Enduring Obstacles' (2003) 21 *Berkeley Journal of International Law* 288.

Baines, E., 'Forced Marriage as a Political Project: Sexual Rules and Relations in the Lord's Resistance Army' (2014) 51 *Journal of Peace Research* 405.

——— and Stewart, B., '"I Cannot Accept What I Have Not Done": Storytelling, Gender and Transitional Justice' (2001) 3 *Journal of Human Rights Practice* 245.

Bassiouni, M.C., 'The Perennial Conflict Between International Criminal Justice and Realpolitik' (2006) 22 *Georgia State University Law Review* 541.

Boon, K., 'Rape and Forced Pregnancy under the ICC Statute: Human Dignity, Autonomy, and Consent' (2001) 32 *Columbia Human Rights Law Review* 625.
Bunting, A., '"Forced Marriage" in Conflict Situations: Researching and Prosecuting Old Harms and New Crimes' (2012) *Canadian Journal of Human Rights* 165.
Buss, D.E., 'Rethinking "Rape as a Weapon of War"' (2009) 17 *Feminist Legal Studies* 145.
Chantler, K., 'Recognition of and Intervention in Forced Marriage as a Form of Violence and Abuse' (2012) 13 *Trauma, Violence and Abuse* 176.
Connell, R.W. and Messerschmidt, J.W., 'Hegemonic Masculinity: Rethinking the Concept' (2005) 19 *Gender and Society* 829.
Copelon, R., 'Surfacing Gender: Re-Engraving Crimes against Women in Humanitarian Law' (1994) 5 *Hastings Women's Law Journal* 243.
Dauvergne, C. and Millbank, J., 'Forced Marriage as a Harm in Domestic and International Law' (2010) 73 *Modern Law Review* 57.
Demetriou, D.Z., 'Connell's Concept of Hegemonic Masculinity: A Critique' (2001) 30 *Theory and Society* 337.
Gardam, J., 'Women and the Law of Armed Conflict: Why the Silence?' (1997) 46 *International and Comparative Law Quarterly* 55.
Haenen, I., 'The Parameters of Enslavement and the Act of Forced Marriage' (2013) 13 *International Criminal Law Review* 895.
Hall, C.K., 'The First Five Sessions of the UN Preparatory Commission for the International Criminal Court' (2000) 94 *American Journal of International Law* 773.
Halley, J., 'Rape at Rome: Feminist Interventions in the Criminalization of Sex-Related Violence in Positive International Criminal Law' (2009) 30 *Michigan Journal of International Law* 1.
Kirby, P., 'How Is Rape a Weapon of War? Feminist International Relations, Modes of Critical Explanation and the Study of Wartime Sexual Violence' (2012) 9 *European Journal of International Relations* 797.
Kramer, S., 'Forced Marriage and the Absence of Gang Rape: Explaining Sexual Violence by the Lord's Resistance Army in Northern Uganda' (2012) 23 (1) *Columbia University Journal of Politics and Society* 11.
Lutz-Priefert, M., 'A Call for a More Permanent International Definition of Rape' (2015) 6 *Creighton International Law and Comparative Law Journal* 85.
Marks, Z., 'Sexual Violence in Sierra Leone's Civil War: "Virgination", Rape, and Marriage' (2013) 112 *African Affairs* 67.
Novotna, K. and Piotrowicz, R., 'Forced Marriage in the Jungle: Time to Stop Beating about the Bush' (2007) 81 *Australian Law Journal* 302.
Nowrojee, B., 'Making the Invisible War Crime Visible: Post-Conflict Justice for Sierra Leone's Rape Victims' (2005) *Harvard Human Rights Journal* 85.
O'Brien, M., '"Don't Kill Them, Let's Choose Them as Wives": The Development of the Crime of Forced Marriage, Sexual Slavery and Enforced Prostitution in International Criminal Law' (2016) 20 *The International Journal of Human Rights* 386.
Oosterveld, V., 'Forced Marriage and the Special Court for Sierra Leone: Legal Advances and Conceptual Difficulties' (2011) 2 *Journal of International Humanitarian Legal Studies* 127.
———, 'Sexual Slavery and the International Criminal Court: Advancing International Law' (2004) 25 *Michigan Journal of International Law* 605.

——— and Marlowe, A., 'Prosecutor v Alex Tamba Brima, Brima Bazzy Kamara & Santigie Borbor Kanu. Case No SCSL-04-16-T. at <www.sc-sl.org/AFRC.html>. Special Court for Sierra Leone, Trial Chamber II, June 20, 2007 and Prosecutor v Moinina Fofana & Allieu Kondewa. Case No SCSL-04-14-T. at <www.sc-sl.org/CDF.html>. Special Court for Sierra Leone, Trial Chamber I, August 2, 2007' (2007) 101 *American Journal of International Law* 848.

Skjelsbeak, I., 'Sexual Violence and War: Mapping Out a Complex Relationship' (2001) 7 *European Journal of International Relations* 211.

Toy-Cronin, B.A., 'What Is Forced Marriage? Towards a Definition of Forced Marriage as a Crime against Humanity' (2010) 19 *Columbia Journal of Gender and Law* 539.

Wood, E.J., 'Conflict-Related Sexual Violence and the Policy Implications of Recent Research' (2015) *International Review of the Red Cross/FirstView Article* 1 <http://journals.cambridge.org/action/displayAbstract?fromPage=online&aid=9579578&fileId=S1816383115000077> accessed 6 May 2015.

(Research) reports and working papers

Allen, T. and Schomerus, M., 'A Hard Homecoming: Lessons Learned from the Reception Center Process in Northern Uganda: An Independent Study' (2006) <http://pdf.usaid.gov/pdf_docs/PNADI241.pdf> accessed 8 July 2013.

Barker, G. and Ricardo, C., 'Young Men and the Construction of Masculinity in Sub-Saharan Africa: Implications for HIV/AIDS, Conflict, and Violence' (2005) The World Bank, Social Development Papers, Conflict Prevention and Reconstruction, Paper Number 26 <www-wds.worldbank.org/external/default/WDSContentServer/WDSP/IB/2005/06/23/000012009_20050623134235/Rendered/PDF/327120rev0PAPER0AFR0young0men0WP26.pdf> accessed 16 October 2014.

Beber, B. and Blattman, C., 'The Logic of Child Soldiering and Coercion' (2011) <http://chrisblattman.com/documents/research/2011.LogicOfChildSoldiering.pdf> accessed 23 December 2012.

Carlson, K. and Mazurana, D., 'Forced Marriage within the Lord's Resistance Army, Uganda' (2008) Tufts University Feinstein International Center <https://wikis.uit.tufts.edu/confluence/download/attachments/14553676/Forced+Marriage+within+the+LRA.pdf?version=1> accessed 8 July 2013.

GBV under the Khmer Rouge, 'Forced Marriage' <http://gbvkr.org/gender-based-violence-under-khmer-rouge/facts-and-figures/forced-marriage/> accessed 8 April 2015.

The Justice and Reconciliation Project, 'Young Mothers, Marriage, and Reintegration in Northern Uganda: Considerations for the Juba Peace Talks' (2006) Liu Institute for Global Issues and the Gulu District NGO Forum, The Justice and Reconciliation Project Field Notes, No 2 <www.ligi.ubc.ca/sites/liu/files/Publications/23Oct2006_YoungMothers_JRP.pdf> accessed 8 July 2013.

Kristastout, 'What's in a Name? The Feasibility and Desirability of Naming Forced Marriage as a Separate Crime under International Humanitarian Law' (8 May 2012) <http://de.scribd.com/doc/94709906/3/III-The-Constituent-Crimes-that-Underpin-the-Crime-of-Forced-Marriage> accessed 6 December 2012.

Refugee Law Project, 'Behind the Violence: Causes, Consequences and the Search for Solutions to the War in Northern Uganda' (2004) Refugee Law Project

Working Paper No 11 <www.refugeelawproject.org/files/working_papers/RLP.WP11.pdf> accessed 8 July 2013.

United Nations Division for the Advancement of Women, 'Sexual Violence and Armed Conflict: United Nations Response' (April 1998) <www.un.org/womenwatch/daw/public/cover.htm> accessed 20 November 2014.

Conference presentations and papers

Lawry, L., 'Panel Six: Methodological Challenges and Opportunities' (The Missing Peace Symposium 2013, Washington, DC, 14–16 February 2013).

ICC advocacy papers, commentaries, recommendations, reports and working papers

Human Rights Watch, 'Commentary on the Second Preparatory Commission on Rules of Procedure and Elements of Crime' (July 1999) <www.iccnow.org/documents/HRWComment2ndPrepComJuly99.pdf> accessed 9 February 2012.

Women's Caucus for Gender Justice, 'Priority Concerns Related to the Elements Annex' (February 1999) <www.iccwomen.org/wigjdraft1/Archives/oldWCGJ/icc/iccpc/021999pc/pcconcerns.htm> accessed 22 January 2014.

———, 'Recommendations and Commentary for December 1997 PrepCom on the Establishment of an International Criminal Court' (December 1997) <www.iccnow.org/documents/5PrepComRecommWomensC.pdf> accessed 4 December 2013.

———, 'Recommendations and Commentary for the Elements Annex' (July 1999) <www.iccwomen.org/wigjdraft1/Archives/oldWCGJ/icc/iccpc/071999pc/elements.htm> accessed 22 January 2014.

Other

———, 'The Woman's Rights Movement' <http://utc.iath.virginia.edu/abolitn/wmhp.html> accessed 3 April 2015.

Centre on Law and Globalization, 'What Counts as Rape in International Crimes?' <http://clg.portalxm.com/library/keytext.cfm?keytext_id=182> accessed 27 October 2012.

National Women's History Museum, 'The Abolition Movement and Woman Suffrage' (2007) <www.nwhm.org/online-exhibits/rightsforwomen/abolitionandsuffrage.html> accessed 3 April 2015.

4 The dynamics of the ICC negotiations

Actors' identities, influences and methods

Introduction

Chapter 3 provided the broader thematic context for the assessment of the International Criminal Court's (ICC) definitions of war rape and forced marriage in times of armed conflict, and the analysis of how these definitions came about.

Moving on to the ICC negotiations themselves, Chapter 4 focuses on the identity of actors involved. Following feminist and constructivist theories, it is important to critically examine not only contexts, agendas and assumptions but also actors and their identities that shape their interests and actions. As explained in Chapter 2, actors' identities, in turn, are shaped by normative structures, by personal, national and international values, norms and rules. Since actors and structures mutually influence each other (constructivist circle), they have to be analysed together.

In the context of treaty negotiations, individuals are mainly viewed as representatives of different constituencies. They are rarely seen as individuals who can have an impact on negotiation dynamics, courses and outcomes. The second part of the chapter portrays state delegates at the ICC negotiations as individual experts who have to follow their governments' instructions. However, their instructions leave space for personal and international values, norms and rules to come into play. Therefore, in this context, an emphasis is placed on normative structures shaping actors. However, the examples given also show that actors shape normative structures, for example by influencing the content and interpretation of their instructions, which impacts on the making of international rules. In addition to these two inter-connected lenses, the third part of this chapter outlines the formation of state coalitions based on shared national norms. This way, the (power) dynamics of the ICC negotiations are highlighted. The fourth part of Chapter 4 moves away from a state-centric view on the ICC negotiations and analyses non-governmental organisations (NGOs) as a group that also played a crucial role. A focus is placed on the Coalition for the International Criminal Court (CICC), its founding, composition, motivation, general interests, sources of funding, ways of participation in, and influencing, the ICC negotiations, and its relationship with state delegations. The Women's Caucus is singled out as a specific group within the NGO Coalition. The Caucus is of great relevance for this research project as it was the main actor driving the negotiations of sexualised crimes.

Especially the last two sections of this chapter explore the methods the CICC and the Women's Caucus used to influence states' positions.

State delegates as individuals

As may be expected, government delegations at the ICC negotiations were constituted mainly of career diplomats and senior civil servants, to a lesser extent of public and private experts including legal specialists mainly of international law and domestic criminal law, and a few politicians. Delegates were not subject specialists. To a certain extent, they negotiated in a vacuum.[1] Many 'lacked experience in [...] [International Criminal Law], comparative criminal law, or comparative criminal procedure. Most delegates had no criminal practice experience of any kind.'[2] They also seldom had experience of war and military conduct.[3]

Delegates had to secure their national interests as laid out in instructions they received from their governments. These instructions included negotiation objectives; information on what a state aimed for, what it was prepared to accept and what it could not compromise on.[4] The representative of the United Kingdom of Great Britain and Northern Ireland (UK), Elizabeth Wilmshurst, stands as an example. Before a change of government in 1997, the UK was sceptical about the establishment of an international criminal court. When the Labour Party took over from the Conservatives, however, the UK's position changed. Wilmshurst represented the country before and after the 1997 elections and argued for the position of each respective government.[5]

At first glance, the relevance of governmental instructions seems to put personal and international values and norms in the backseat. When considering, however, that instructions from national governments were vague, contradictory and/or inadequate,[6] it becomes clear that they did leave room for both, personal and international normative structures to come into play. In these situations,

1 Interview 3 (25 March 2014); Interview 18 (25 June 2014); M. Cherif Bassiouni, *The Legislative History of the International Criminal Court* (Transnational Publishers 2005) 91; Fanny Benedetti and John L. Washburn, 'Drafting the International Criminal Court Treaty: Two Years to Rome and an Afterword on the Rome Diplomatic Conference' (1999) 5 *Global Governance* 1 16.

2 Bassiouni, *The Legislative History of the International Criminal Court* (n 1) 91.

3 Interview 3 (n 1).

4 Interview 1 (21 March 2014); Interview 3 (n 1); Interview 17 (17 June 2014); see also Fanny Benedetti, Karine Bonneau and John Washburn, *Negotiating the International Criminal Court: New York to Rome, 1994–1998* (Brill 2013) 65.

5 Interview 15 (27 May 2014).

6 Interview 1 (n 4); Interview 11 (23 April 2014); Interview 18 (n 1); Bassiouni, *The Legislative History of the International Criminal Court* (n 1) 87; Benedetti, Bonneau and Washburn (n 4) 65; Anna-Karin Lindblom, *Non-Governmental Organisations in International Law* (Cambridge University Press 2005) 474–475; William R. Pace and Jennifer Schense, 'Coalition for the International Criminal Court at the Preparatory Commission' in Roy S. Lee (ed), *The International Criminal Court: Elements of Crimes and Rules of Procedure and Evidence* (Transnational Publishers 2001) 706–707.

delegates had to take into account their own professional experience as negotiators, regular progress evaluations and their perception of the overall interest of the international community. Delegates can and often did have an impact on the content of their instructions through reports to, and influence on, their ministries.[7] Moreover, committed, creative and enthusiastic delegates would approach others to show them that certain proposals or positions, including those on gender and sexualised violence, were not contrary to the instructions they received from their governments.[8] This way, individual delegates influenced international normative structures. Here, personal contacts were of vital importance.[9] The example of a speech made by a member of the Colombian delegation in relation to the crime of forced pregnancy in which he voiced an opinion contrary to the previously negotiated compromise definition, however, was rebuked. This demonstrates that international norms in the wake of becoming rules trumped personal values.[10] The example of the Canadian delegation further indicates that international, national and personal values and norms mattered in the ICC negotiations. At the time the ICC negotiations took place, the Canadian Minister of Foreign Affairs championed the Human Security Agenda. This included the view that human security could not exist as long as gender inequality persists and violence against women is perpetrated. This motivated the minister and his delegation to work towards ensuring that an international criminal court would learn from past mistakes of the International Military Tribunal (IMT, Nuremberg Tribunal) and the International Military Tribunal for the Far East (IMTFE, Tokyo Tribunal) as well as the International Criminal Tribunal for the former Yugoslavia (ICTY) and the International Criminal Tribunal for Rwanda (ICTR) in not paying enough attention to gender crimes and their appropriate investigation.[11] These points of view were supported by Australia and New Zealand.[12] For New Zealand, this was in line with its support for gender equality and non-discrimination at United Nations (UN) level.[13] A similar interplay between international, national and personal values, norms and rules can be seen from the example of the Bosnian delegation. Influenced by his country's experience of the war in the 1990s, the Bosnian ambassador was keen to have sexualised violence included in the list of war crimes. Therefore, he actively supported instructions received from the Bosnian government to

7 Interview 11 (n 6); Interview 18 (n 1); Bassiouni, *The Legislative History of the International Criminal Court* (n 1) 87; Pace and Schense, 'Coalition for the International Criminal Court at the Preparatory Commission' (n 6) 706–707.

8 Interview 5 (1 April 2014); Interview 6 (2 April 2014); Interview 9 (11 April 2014); Interview 13 (n 2); Bassiouni, *The Legislative History of the International Criminal Court* (n 1) 87; see also Lindblom (n 6) 474–475.

9 Interview 1 (n 4); Interview 4 (26 March 2014); Interview 5 (n 8).

10 Interview 2 (24 March 2014).

11 Interview 17 (n 4); Interview 18 (n 1); Interview 19 (26 November 2014).

12 Interview 19 (n 11): Canada, Australia and New Zealand consulted with each other on most United Nations (UN) issues.

13 ibid.

make sure that the instruments and jurisprudence of the *ad hoc* tribunals would be considered in drafting the ICC instruments.[14]

State delegations as groups

As the paragraphs above indicated, the ICC negotiations can be characterised as political rather than technical, 'an exercise in international relations'[15] that constructed its own reality.[16] Coalitions formed by state delegations contributed to the creation of this distinct reality. Initially, state coalitions formed along geographic lines. Increasingly, however, they were based on states' positions on an international criminal court. Therefore, some of these coalitions transcended traditional divides. However, they did not completely remove boundaries as traditional power dynamics remained in place at least partly. The support for the Rome Statute of the permanent members of the United Nations Security Council (UNSC), for example, was still seen as crucial.[17]

The coalition approach facilitated equality between the global North and South. However, a low level of awareness of civil society, parliamentarians and government leaders regarding the ICC negotiations until August 1998,[18] as well as a lack of funding,[19] resulted in a low level of participation of state and NGO delegations from the global South in the first Preparatory Committee on the Establishment of an International Criminal Court (PrepCom) sessions. For example, the initial absence or low level of involvement of Arab states in the ICC negotiations was put down to practical rather than normative reasons. It was argued that they lacked training in legal reform processes and therefore did not fully participate. However, their behaviour and the attitude that others will take care of everything were also brought forward as possible explanations. Also invoking national and regional norms, it was said that Arab states did not engage because of the perceived inherent unfairness of the court as a Western institution, and concerns that it would interfere in domestic matters.[20] Practical and

14 Interview 2 (n 10); Interview 18 (n 1): The International Criminal Tribunal for the former Yugoslavia (ICTY) and *Prosecutor v Anto Furundžija* were mentioned explicitly here.

15 Interview 3 (n 1).

16 Interview 2 (n 10); Interview 3 (n 1); Interview 7 (4 April 2014); Interview 8 (11 April 2014); Bassiouni, *The Legislative History of the International Criminal Court* (n 1) 91.

17 Interview 3 (n 1); Interview 16 (10 June 2014); Benedetti and Washburn (n 1).

18 Coalition for the International Criminal Court, 'Regional Reports' *ICC Monitor* (New York, August 1997) 11, 14; Pace and Schense, 'Coalition for the International Criminal Court at the Preparatory Commission' (n 6) 705: Ghana, Lesotho, Malawi, South Africa, Tanzania, and Uganda were among the more active African delegations.

19 Christopher Keith Hall, 'The First Two Sessions of the UN Preparatory Committee on the Establishment of an International Criminal Court' (1997) 91 *American Journal of International Law* 177, 186; Amando Miclat, 'A View from the South' *ICC Monitor* (New York, January 1997) 11.

20 Interview 14 (26 May 2014).

strategic reasons were also brought forward in trying to explain the initial low level of engagement of other states in the ICC negotiations. It was argued that developing countries were concerned about the costs of (establishing) the ICC. Rather than taking the process seriously, they participated only to be seen as civilised.[21] The latter explanation resonates with the motivation of other states, for which participation meant legitimation for their national governments.[22] However, these arguments raise the question whether states from the global South did not see the advantages of having a permanent international criminal court independent of the UNSC and specific situations like many others did.[23] A low level of engagement from certain states can also be understood as resistance towards the external imposition of a legal reform process that should have been initiated by the domestic government. This imposition can be understood as a form of social engineering if main donor countries are also the main sponsors of a new international treaty that may require national implementation and therefore national law reform. Donor countries could then make continuing financial support for some states dependent upon them participating in negotiations and signing the treaty. And vice versa, if donor countries like the United States of America (USA, US) are opposed to a new treaty, continuing support, for example for some African states, could be made dependent upon them not signing the treaty. Making governments appear helpless, pushed about and out of control, this could give rise to low-level participation in international law-making processes or opposition to the outcomes.[24]

As the negotiations continued, the initial North–South divide decreased. Countering arguments that the involvement of the global South in the ICC negotiation was not genuine, African delegations from all parts of the continent participated actively from the sixth PrepCom session in March/April 1998 on. They cooperated closely on many issues on the basis of principles adopted by members of the Southern African Development Community (SADC) in September 1997, and the Dakar Declaration adopted by government and NGO representatives at a conference in Senegal in February 1998. At Rome and since, African diplomats took a lead in pushing for an international criminal court with a significant degree of independence from the UNSC and European powers. Due to the size of the group – 53 African states were involved in the negotiations – they were able to steer the debate forcefully.[25] 'Since many of

21 Interview 4 (n 9).
22 Interview 2 (n 10).
23 Interview 11 (n 6).
24 Interview 3 (n 1); Interview 4 (n 9) Interview 14 (n 20).
25 Interview 4 (n 9); 'Africa Speaks Strongly for Court' *Terra Viva* (Rome, 16 June 1998) 4; Benedetti, Bonneau and Washburn (n 4) 82–83; Richard Dicker, 'S. African Governments Adopt Common Approach to ICC Ratification' *ICC Monitor* (New York, August 1999) 3; Christopher Keith Hall, 'The Sixth Session of the UN Preparatory Committee on the Establishment of an International Criminal Court' (1998) 92 *American Journal of International Law* 548, 555; Human Rights Watch, 'World Report 1999: Special Issues and Campaigns: The ICC' <www.hrw.org/legacy/worldreport99/special/icc.html> accessed 23 January 2014.

the countries involved [had] only recently ended colonial rule [...] or set up "truth commissions" [...], many also [had] the moral authority to push for the Court to be an effective one.'[26] The assignment of this authority can be seen as another example of national and international normative structures shaping actors' identities. National experiences of colonialism and conflict highlight that norms and rules related to independence, self-determination, peace and justice were held high at national level. These national normative structures coincided with international ones. African actors were seen as allies in the struggle to end impunity for acts of genocide, war crimes and crimes against humanity. This shapes the identities of these actors in the international fora of the ICC negotiations. The example above also indicates that experiences of war and human rights abuses motivated African state delegations to participate in the ICC negotiations.[27]

Contributing to this heightened level of participation of actors from all over the world in the ICC negotiations, the CICC used the funding it received from various foundations, individuals, states and other institutions, including the

26 'Africa Speaks Strongly for Court' (n 25); see also Benedetti, Bonneau and Washburn (n 4) 3.

27 'African Leaders Plan Mass withdrawal From International Criminal Court' *The Guardian* (31 January 2017) <www.theguardian.com/law/2017/jan/31/african-leaders-plan-mass-withdrawal-from-international-criminal-court> accessed 17 July 2017; Franziska Boehme, '"We Chose Africa": South Africa and the Regional Politics of Cooperation with the International Criminal Court' (2017) 11 *International Journal of Transitional Justice* 50; Marlies Glasius, 'Expertise in the Cause of Justice: Global Civil Society Influence on the Statute for an International Criminal Court' in Helmut K. Anheier, Marlies Glasius and Mary Kaldor (eds), *Global Civil Society 2005/6* (Oxford University Press 2002) 145; Abraham Joseph, 'Why Did South Africa, Burundi and Gambia Decide to Leave the International Criminal Court?' *The Wire* (1 November 2016) <https://thewire.in/76869/why-did-south-africa-burundi-and-gambia-decide-to-leave-the-international-criminal-court/> accessed 17 July 2017; Jean-Baptiste Jeangéne Vilmer, 'The African Union and the International Criminal Court: Counteracting the Crisis' (2016) 92 (2) *International Affairs* 1319: Contrary to the initial support of African states including Botswana, Lesotho, Senegal and South Africa for an international criminal court, the African Union now encourages its member states not to cooperate with, and withdraw from, the court. South Africa, Burundi and Gambia have already withdrawn or have taken steps to leave. Kenya and Uganda might follow. Other African states including Botswana, Cape Verde, Central African Republic, the Democratic Republic of the Congo, Gabon, Ivory Coast, Mali, Nigeria, Seychelles, Senegal, Sierra Leone, Tanzania and Tunisia, however, continue to support the International Criminal Court (ICC). Officially, state withdrawal is motivated by the ICC's arguably unjustified focus on African situations and prioritisation of justice over peace, concerns about states' sovereignty, and divergent positions on immunity of heads of states and senior officials. Examining the situations of South Africa, Burundi and Gambia further, however, it becomes apparent that their withdrawal might have been motivated by the wish to protect their leaders from ICC investigation, and to maintain and/or strengthen their regional political reputation. It has to be noted that at least the ICC's Afro-centrism is a reality that is cause for concern and that has to be addressed to establish or strengthen the court's credibility and legitimacy.

European Union and some of its member states, the Ford Foundation and the MacArthur Foundation, to support NGOs and state delegations from developing countries. It assisted state delegations by providing representatives, legal experts and interns to serve (on) smaller delegations.[28] The delegations of Bosnia and Herzegovina, Burundi, Comoros, Congo, Samoa, Senegal, Sierra Leone, and Trinidad and Tobago are examples of state delegations that included NGO representatives.[29] On the one hand, this enabled state delegations as well as members of civil society to participate more actively and directly in the ICC negotiations. With more people on a state delegation, more meetings could be covered. Being present in a meeting meant knowing what was discussed and being able to participate in ongoing (informal) work. For the state delegation, this cooperation helped to develop its legal arguments.[30] For members of the civil society, serving on a state delegation meant access to, and speaking rights in, all meetings. This way, a civil society member of a state delegation was, for example, able to influence the provision covering forced pregnancy.[31] It enabled members of the civil society to continue to argue their original points in a different forum. They stayed true to their own and their organisations' views and still argued for, and on the basis of, the same views when they became members of state delegations.[32] In these situations, national norms had a low impact. In

28 Bassiouni, *The Legislative History of the International Criminal Court* (n 1) 76; Coalition for the International Criminal Court, 'Who We Are & What We Do: Global Partners' <www.iccnow.org/?mod=supporters> accessed 5 December 2013; Lindblom (n 6) 476–477; Pace and Schense, 'Coalition for the International Criminal Court at the Preparatory Commission' (n 6) 708; Zoe Pearson, 'Non-Governmental Organizations and the International Criminal Court: Changing Landscapes of International Law' (2006) 39 *Cornell International Law Journal* 243, 260, 267.

29 Interview 15 (n 5); Benedetti, Bonneau and Washburn (n 4) 80; Glasius, 'Expertise in the Cause of Justice' (n 27) 151; The Stanley Foundation, 'The New Court: Civil Society's Victory' *Common Ground Radio* (6 October 1998) <www.commongroundradio.org/shows/98/9840.html> accessed 16 February 2015; Johan D. van der Vyver, 'Civil Society and the International Criminal Court' (2003) 2 *Journal of Human Rights* 425: In addition, the delegations of Canada and Costa Rica included representatives from non-governmental organisations (NGOs) as a gesture of goodwill. Other states engaged the services of domestic (Germany, the Netherlands, the United States of America (USA, US)) or foreign (Samoa, the Solomon Islands) professors of law as delegation members. Academics who served as official delegates included M. Cherif Bassiouni, Professor of Law at De Paul University (Egypt and chair of the Drafting Committee in Rome), Theo van Boven, Professor of International Law at Maastricht University (Netherlands), Aziz Chukri, Professor of International Law at the University of Damascus (Syria), Professor Roger Clark of Rutgers University in Camden, New Jersey (Samoa), Professor Gerhard Hafner, Director of the Institute for International Law and International Relations of the University of Vienna (Austria), and Medard Rwelamira, Professor of Law at the University of the Western Cape (South Africa).

30 Glasius, 'Expertise in the Cause of Justice' (n 27) 151.

31 Interview 4 (n 9).

32 Interview 15 (n 5); Glasius, 'Expertise in the Cause of Justice' (n 27) 151; Lindblom (n 6) 477.

addition to providing civil society members to support small state delegations, some state delegations like Canada also included two civil society members not only to benefit from their expertise amongst others on gender issues, but also to have NGO's points of view reflected in the delegation.[33] On the other hand, however, CICC funding made NGOs and government delegations especially from the global South dependent on support from the global North. Donors could have exploited this power imbalance to push state or NGO delegations to take on certain issues or points in return for support, manipulating discussions and outcomes.[34]

Even though the previous paragraphs show that the coalition approach facilitated equality between state delegations, inequalities based on language existed and restricted opportunities for actors to influence international normative structures. Those who actively participated in the ICC negotiations were largely English-speaking. How crucial English language skills were becomes apparent when considering that much of the information that was circulated was in English. Moreover, the decisive working group and informal meetings took place in English only without translation (and record). Those who wanted to speak or discuss a proposal had to do so in English. This led to a situation where a delegation's advisor was sent to negotiate in these meetings because he was the only English speaker.[35] It also resulted in some states having an advantage regarding the submission of proposals and therefore they became key actors in the negotiations. This indicates that states that contributed written proposals gained more visibility than those that participated mainly verbally. This is due to the fact that if a written proposal was submitted, it had to be dealt with seriously. It could not be ignored. In situations where sceptics submitted a proposal that, if adopted, would have made the court acceptable to them, disregarding their proposal would have created the risk that these sceptics might have withdrawn their support for the court completely. Conversely, written proposals also could not be ignored as to do so might have risked alienating the court's allies.[36] Too much attention paid to sceptical proposals and the

33 Interview 3 (n 1); Interview 4 (n 9); Interview 9 (n 8); Interview 17 (n 4).

34 Interview 3 (n 1); Anne Bichsel, 'NGOs as Agents of Public Accountability and Democratization in Intergovernmental Forums' in William M. Lafferty and James Meadowcroft (eds), *Democracy and the Environment: Problems and Prospects* (Edward Elgar Publishing 1996) 237; Pearson (n 28) 260, 267.

35 Interview 2 (n 10); Interview 3 (n 1); Interview 7 (n 16); Interview 12 (15 May 2014); Interview 18 (n 1); Bassiouni, *The Legislative History of the International Criminal Court* (n 1) 76, 80; Benedetti, Bonneau and Washburn (n 4) 96; Marlies Glasius, *The International Criminal Court: A Global Civil Society Initiative* (Routledge 2006) 126; Cynthia Rothschild, *Written Out: How Sexuality Is Used to Attack Women's Organizing* (International Gay and Lesbian Human Rights Commission and Center for Women's Global Leadership 2005) 100.

36 Interview 2 (n 10); Interview 3 (n 1); Interview 7 (n 16); Interview 12 (n 35); Interview 18 (n 1).

potential result of a watered-down institution and instruments might have frustrated the court's allies, resulting in withdrawal of support.

The number of key actors in the ICC negotiations was further limited by the fact that consensus was needed. The more actors discussed a proposal, the more difficult it became to agree on it. Therefore, the informal or working group meetings, in which a lower number of delegations participated already, were further downsized into smaller groups or blocks who worked on a proposal together. Once they drafted a proposal, it was fed back into the larger groups, step by step.[37] The compromise they delivered was often so fragile that not a word could be changed.[38] The negotiations of the elements of genocide in the first session of the Preparatory Commission for the International Criminal Court (PrepCom2) stand as an example here. Disagreement about the contextual element was overcome in informal discussions between the US and Canada, supported by the UK, Germany, Australia and others. A compromise was worked out which was then put before an informal meeting chaired by Herman von Hebel, the coordinator of the working group on the elements of crimes, before it was incorporated into a rolling text.[39] A degree of secrecy was upheld about the block meetings, their participants and about what was discussed. Especially small states were seldom invited or able to participate. This indicates that the size of delegations mattered. Bigger delegations had an advantage because they could send members to simultaneous meetings.[40]

Much of the dynamism of the ICC negotiations was driven by the Like-Minded Group (LMG)[41] which was formed with encouragement of the CICC in the second PrepCom session. The LMG was first chaired by Canada, then by Australia. At the beginning of the Rome Conference, its members also included Austria, Argentina, Belgium, Chile, Croatia, Denmark, Egypt, Finland, Germany, Greece, Guatemala, Hungary, Ireland, Italy, Lesotho, the Netherlands, New Zealand, Norway, Samoa, Slovakia, South Africa, Sweden, Switzerland, Trinidad and Tobago (representing 12 Caribbean states), Uruguay, and Venezuela.[42] Based on shared goals, it developed a strong, but sometimes uneasy partnership with the CICC and other experts.[43] Like the CICC, the LMG

37 ibid; Rothschild (n 35) 100.

38 Interview 4 (n 9).

39 Elizabeth Wilmshurst, 'ICC: PrepCom. 16–26 February 1999' (1 March 1999).

40 Interview 2 (n 10); Interview 3 (n 1); Interview 7 (n 16); Interview 12 (n 35); Rothschild (n 35) 100.

41 Benedetti, Bonneau and Washburn (n 4) 97: The name goes back to a resolution negotiated by Australia, Canada, Germany, New Zealand, Norway and others, proposing revisions to the International Law Commission's (ILC) draft statute for an international criminal court.

42 Interview 11 (n 6); Bassiouni, *The Legislative History of the International Criminal Court* (n 1) 74; Benedetti, Bonneau and Washburn (n 4) 84; Farhan Haq, 'Alliances Cut through North–South Divide' *Terra Viva* (Rome, 22 June 1998) 1.

43 For more information on the relationship between the Coalition for the International Criminal Court (CICC) and state delegations at the ICC negotiations see below.

advocated the immediate creation of an independent court with an independent prosecutor, jurisdiction over all core crimes, 'and the power [...] to finally decide on the unavailability or unwillingness of national systems to proceed with a case' as well as full state cooperation.[44]

Like the LMG, the Non-Aligned Movement (NAM) made up of China, India, Israel, Pakistan, a group of Arab states and others also advocated the independence of the court from the UNSC. In general, however, they favoured a much weaker institution. The members of the Arab block, for example, spoke out for war crimes provisions covering only international armed conflicts, for the exclusion of the term 'gender' and related provisions, for a change in the provisions covering child soldiers to exclude the Palestinian intifada, and the inclusion of the death penalty. The NAM also focused on the prohibition of nuclear weapons. It saw nuclear weapons as the weapons of developed countries while chemical and biological weapons were those of developing states. Therefore, if the former would not be included in the list of prohibited weapons under the war crimes provision, neither should the latter. The Movement's influence on the ICC negotiations, however, was weakened due to historical enmities between the members of the group, preventing it from growing together. NAM's cohesion soon faded and the Movement broke apart. Its members either joined the LMG or reformed into regional groups like SADC.[45] It can be assumed that their decision which group to join was based on assessments of compatibility of a delegation's national norms and rules with those of the groups they could join.

Led by South Africa, SADC stood as a counterweight to Europe that was eventually integrated into the LMG.[46] Again, this change of identity could be based on an evaluation resulting in the perception that SADC's and the LMG's values and norms were compatible. Constructivist theory suggests for both situations, the inclusion of former NAM members into SADC and the LMG as well as the eventual incorporation of SADC into the LMG, that the change in SADC's and the LMG's composition had an effect on their identities and consequently their interests and actions.

Many Caribbean states also joined forces, advocating the inclusion of drug-related crimes in the jurisdiction of an international criminal court and the court's power to impose the death penalty.[47]

In contrast to the LMG and NAM, the five permanent members of the UNSC aimed at keeping the court under UNSC control, modelling it after the *ad hoc*

44 Benedetti and Washburn (n 1) 21.

45 Elizabeth Wilmshurst, 'Report on the Conference for the Establishment of an International Criminal Court: 15 June–17 July 1998' (23 September 1998); Benedetti, Bonneau and Washburn (n 4) 148, 150, 160; Benedetti and Washburn (n 1) 30–31; Glasius, *The International Criminal Court* (n 35) 22–26.

46 Benedetti and Washburn (n 1) 31.

47 Glasius, *The International Criminal Court* (n 35) 24.

tribunals.[48] As noted above, in 1997 however, the UK changed its position after a change of government and joined the LMG.[49] It worked towards the Western objective to succeed in establishing a permanent international criminal court and to have the maximum number of states involved.[50] Following a pragmatic approach, for the UK, as for many Western states, an international criminal court was a foreign policy issue, intended to close a gap in states' foreign policy armoury. It was envisaged as a permanent juridical process to assist peace after conflict by initiating prosecutions straight away rather than having to create a new institution on an *ad hoc* basis first. Invoking issues of national sovereignty, it was important that the court was not to (be seen to) damage Western governments who were worried that the institution might prosecute their own people. It can be argued that their concerns were unnecessary because the ICC needs states' support to be effective. Furthermore, Western armed forces enjoy a working military discipline where breaches thereof are dealt with appropriately within the military system.[51] They may have had a reason to worry, however, when considering that UN peacekeepers, including Western military personnel, have been involved in crimes like trafficking in human beings and forced prostitution.[52] Therefore, Western states could be pressured to launch investigations against their own people to avoid involvement of an international criminal court, which would be 'poison'[53] for every government. As mentioned above in relation to the UK, the example of the French delegation also shows that it was a change in national power dynamics and consequently national normative structures that led to a change in France's identity in the ICC negotiations. Initially, when the establishment of a permanent international criminal court still seemed unlikely, France was very supportive of the project. When the court began to take shape, however, France took a more cautious position. France shared the UK's concerns regarding the protection of its own people. Like the UK, after a change of government in 1997, the French policy changed again and became more constructive. This was supported by the Minister of Justice, indicating once more that in addition to national norms, personal values mattered in the ICC negotiations. The French delegation did not go as far as joining the LMG however. Rather, the French were approached by the LMG, wishing to secure

48 Benedetti and Washburn (n 1) 30–31; Glasius, *The International Criminal Court* (n 35) 22–26.

49 Interview 15 (n 5); Human Rights Watch, 'World Report 1998' <www.hrw.org/legacy/worldreport/Intro97.htm#P1_0> accessed 5 December 2013.

50 Interview 3 (n 1).

51 Interview 3 (n 1); Interview 15 (n 5); Pam Spees, 'Women's Advocacy in the Creation of the International Criminal Court: Changing the Landscape of Justice and Power' (2003) 28 *Signs* 1233.

52 Natalie Novick, 'When Those Meant to Keep the Peace Commit Sexualized Violence' (Women Under Siege, 25 May 2012) <www.womenundersiegeproject.org/blog/entry/when-those-meant-to-keep-the-peace-commit-sexualized-violence> accessed 6 November 2014.

53 Interview 3 (n 1); Interview 16 (n 17).

the ratification of the Rome Statute by some of the permanent members of the UNSC. The importance ascribed to the support of this group of states indicates that, contrary to what is argued by some, traditional power dynamics were at least partly reinforced.[54]

NGOs as groups

Traditional state-centric models are still important in forming our understanding of the international system. Traditional constructions of international law are deeply engrained and continue to restrict opportunities for NGOs to get involved in international law-making.[55] The existing structures and processes of

54 Interview 16 (n 17).

55 *Prosecutor v Alex Tamba Brima, Brima Bazzy Kamara and Santigie Borbor Kanu* (Prosecution Filing of Expert Report Pursuant to Rule 94(bis) and Decision of Prosecution Request for Leave to Call an Additional Expert Witness) SCSL-04-16-T 'AFRC Case' (8 August 2005) <www.rscsl.org/Documents/Decisions/AFRC/365/SCSL-04-16-T-369.pdf> accessed 28 September 2017; Coalition on Women's Human Rights in Conflict Situations, 'RE: The Prosecutor of the Tribunal against Jean-Paul Akayesu: Amicus Brief Respecting Amendment of the Indictment and Supplementation of the Evidence to Ensure the Prosecution of Rape and Other sexual Violence Within the Competence of the Tribunal' (27 May 1997) <www.iccwomen.org/publications/briefs/docs/Prosecutor_v_Akayesu_ICTR.pdf> accessed 13 August 2013; Patrick Cotter and others, 'Affecting the Rules for the Prosecution of Rape and other Gender-Based Violence before the International Criminal Tribunal for the Former Yugoslavia: A Feminist Proposal and Critique' (1994) 5 *Hastings Women's Law Journal* 171; Patrizia De Cesari, 'NGOs and the Activities of the Ad Hoc Criminal Tribunals for Former Yugoslavia and Rwanda' in Alessandro Fodella and others (eds), *Civil Society, International Courts and Compliance Bodies* (TMC Asser Press 2004); Mark S. Ellis, 'The Contribution of Non-Governmental Organizations to the Creation of International Criminal Tribunals' in Bartram S. Brown (ed), *Research Handbook on International Criminal Law* (Edward Elgar Publishing 2011); Janet Halley, 'Rape at Rome: Feminist Interventions in the Criminalization of Sex-Related Violence in Positive International Criminal Law' (2009) 30 *Michigan Journal of International Law* 1; International Human Rights Law Group, 'No Justice, No Peace: Accountability for Rape and Gender-Based Violence in the Former Yugoslavia' (1994) 5 *Hastings Women's Law Journal* 89; Michael O'Flaherty, 'Sierra Leone's Peace Process: The Role of the Human Rights Community' (2004) 26 *Human Rights Quarterly* 29, 40; Sarah Williams and Hannah Woolaver, 'The Role of the Amicus Curiae before International Criminal Tribunals' (2006) 6 *International Criminal Law Review* 151: Despite this, NGOs have been involved in the establishment of the ICTY, International Criminal Tribunal for Rwanda (ICTR) and the Special Court for Sierra Leone (SCSL). Human Rights Watch's report of its investigations and interviews with witnesses in the former Yugoslavia influenced the United Nations Security Council (UNSC) in its decision to establish an international tribunal. It also contributed to the Expert Commission's findings. When drafting the statutes of the *ad hoc* tribunals, the United Nations Office of Legal Affairs sought comments on the drafts from governments and NGOs. International women's organisations and activists like the Green/Copelon Group played a key role. They promoted the explicit inclusion of war rape as a war crime, a genocidal act and a grave breach of the Geneva Conventions in the ICTY statute. As stated by Cotter and others, the Green/Copelon Group advocated for an informed,

international law-making are struggling to accommodate NGOs' diversity and fluidity.[56] However, this only tells part of the story of how structures shape actors in international law-making. As is discussed further below, NGOs can contribute to international law-making processes in a number of ways. Through their participation, they can facilitate a development away from the traditional state-centric power dynamics of international relations and towards the active participation of a wider range of actors.

The ICC negotiations can be understood as evidence of new diplomacy, where large and small states, international organisations, and NGOs worked together in partnership in which all sides were interested.[57] Cooperation between governments, international organisations and civil society organisations is not a new phenomenon.[58] Especially at the UN, NGOs have played a considerable role since the drafting of its charter.

> [A] parallel NGO […] forum, has been a feature of most UN conferences and their preparatory meetings since the 1972 Stockholm Conference on the Environment. [Through] exhibitions and [other] activities […], NGOs seek to influence the governmental agenda, exploit news coverage of the event, and carry on business among themselves.[59]

In the ICC negotiations, however, no parallel NGO forum was organised. Instead, NGOs participated in all stages of the actual negotiation process. As discussed in detail below, while states still made the final decisions, NGOs

---

gender-neutral understanding of war rape as a crime in and of itself as well as potentially constituting torture. Thy defined rape as coerced and non-consensual sexual intercourse including introducing a body part of object into the victim's mouth, vagina or anus. No Peace without Justice developed a programme supporting the UN and the Sierra Leonean government in their plans to establish the SCSL. International NGOs were also involved in drafting the SCSL's statute, focusing on children's rights and childcare rehabilitation. Together with the United Nations Development Programme, the International Centre for Transitional Justice contributed to the gender-related aspects of the SCSL statute.

In addition to influencing the establishment of international courts and tribunals, NGOs and women's rights activists and advocates influenced their jurisprudence. The Coalition on Women's Human Rights in Conflict Situations, for example, submitted *amicus* briefs to the ICTR in the *Akayesu* case and to the ICTY in *Furundžija*, and Zainab H Bangura acted as expert witness on forced marriage in the *AFRC* case dealt with by the SCSL.

56 Pearson (n 28) 244.

57 Interview 17 (n 4); Farhan Haq, 'Annan Throws Down Gauntlet' *Terra Viva* (Rome, 16 June 1998) 1; William R. Pace, 'ICC Treaty Passes Half-Way Mark: Croatia, Paraguay and Andorra Bring Ratifications up to 32' *ICC Monitor* (New York, May 2001) 1, 5; Pearson (n 28) 254.

58 See for example Steve Charnovitz, 'Two Centuries of Participation: NGOs and International Governance' (1997) 18 *Michigan Journal of International Law* 183.

59 Ann Marie Clark, Elisabeth J. Friedman and Kathryn Hochstetler, 'The Sovereign Limits of Global Civil Society: A Comparison of NGO Participation in UN' (1998) 51 *World Politics* 1, 8.

became their strategic partners that influenced states' decisions in various ways.[60] The direct participation of NGOs in the ICC negotiations can be understood as a result of the positive relationship between states and NGOs that has developed during the last century. The extent and depth of cooperation and the scale of the targets that the partnership between large and small states, international organisations, and NGOs had set for itself and that it eventually achieved, establishes the ICC process as a 'vanguard approach to international diplomacy and the development of international laws and institutions'.[61]

Within the analysis of NGOs as important actors in the ICC negotiations, the following sections focus on the CICC as a particular group of NGOs, and the Women's Caucus as a particular group within the CICC. An emphasis is placed on both groups' founding, composition, motivations, general interests, funding, methods and relationships with state delegations

The NGO Coalition for the International Criminal Court (CICC)[62]

Exemplifying new diplomacy and permeating the boundaries of state-centric models of international relations and law-making, a group of particularly strong, mainly European and American Human Rights organisations participated in the establishment of an international criminal court from the early 1990s onwards. The organisations were led by the World Federalist Movement, represented by William R. Pace.[63] The CICC's founding members also included Amnesty International, represented by Christopher Keith Hall; Human Rights Watch, represented by Richard Dicker; the Lawyers' Committee for Human Rights, represented by Jelena Pejic; No Peace Without Justice/Transnational Radical Party, represented by Emma Bonino; and Parliamentarians for Global Action.[64] Some of these NGOs later became members of the self-appointed CICC

60 'Welcome' *Terra Viva* (Rome, 15 June 1998) 5; Lloyd Axworthy, 'A Court That Is Worth Having' *Terra Viva* (Rome, 15 June 1998) 6–7; Human Rights Watch, 'World Report 1999' (n 25); Lindblom (n 6) 474; Pace and Schense, 'Coalition for the International Criminal Court at the Preparatory Commission' (n 6) 706.

61 Pace and Schense, 'Coalition for the International Criminal Court at the Preparatory Commission' (n 6) 706.

62 See Appendix 2 for an organigram of the CICC.

63 Benedetti and Washburn (n 1) 8–9; Benedetti, Bonneau and Washburn (n 4) 70, 76–77: William R. Pace's interests and actions in the ICC negotiations were shaped by his career as a professional official of NGOs dedicated to world peace and the development of international organisations. Pace recognised the importance of the solidarity between members of the CICC, which he preserved and used as needed. Together with his personal strengths, he influenced the ICC discussions this way.

64 For more information on these actors see Benedetti, Bonneau and Washburn (n 4) 68–73; Mariacarmen Colini, 'The Experience of No Peace without Justice' in Alessandro Fodella and others (eds), *Civil Society, International Courts and Compliance Bodies* (TMC Asser Press 2004).

Steering Committee which provided policy and programme coherence for the Coalition's efforts and activities.[65]

The organisations that founded the CICC maintained long-standing relationships with diplomats, scholars and the United Nations Secretariat. They participated in the work of the International Law Commission (ILC) on the establishment of a permanent international criminal court from 1994 onwards.[66] When the ILC submitted its draft statute for a permanent international criminal court in 1994, the group was disappointed by the United Nations General Assembly's (UNGA) decision not to convene an international conference and shocked about the willingness of friendly states to compromise on key issues. This motivated them to found the CICC.[67]

The founding of the CICC arguably stands as an example of a 'fortunate coincidence'[68] where people with coinciding values came together; where structures shaped actors. Initially, the CICC encouraged diplomats to call for a preparatory process and a diplomatic conference for the establishment of a permanent international criminal court.[69] In cooperation with the LMG, the Coalition later pushed to realise the idea of a fair, free and independent international criminal court. It was perceived to be necessary to create a permanent institution that, unlike the *ad hoc* tribunals, was independent of the UNSC on the one hand, and specific cases and situations on the other. Like many Western governments, the CICC envisaged a fair, free and independent international criminal court to fill an impunity gap.[70]

The coalition approach facilitated equality between large and small NGOs.[71] However, it has to be noted that the NGOs that are experienced in dealing with core global governance issues are big international organisations mostly from the global North. They are well-connected to other, mainly Northern, NGOs, developing a clear core-periphery structure and therefore a hierarchy.[72] However, even though the CICC itself was founded by exactly those

65 Interview 8 (n 16); Interview 11 (n 6); Colini (n 64) 107: The Steering Committee included Amnesty International, Fédération Internationale des Ligues des Droits de l'Homme (FIDH), Human Rights Watch, the International Commission of Jurists, the Lawyers Committee for Human Rights, No Peace Without Justice, Parliamentarians for Global Action and the World Federalist Movement.

66 Interview 8 (n 16); Benedetti and Washburn (n 1) 21; Interview 11 (n 6); Alison Dickens, 'Legalese Aside, NGOs Want Independent, Effective Court' *Terra Viva* (Rome, 16 June 1998) 7.

67 Interview 8 (n 16); Interview 11 (n 6).

68 Interview 6 (n 8).

69 Interview 8 (n 16); Benedetti, Bonneau and Washburn (n 4) 79–81.

70 Interview 3 (n 1); Interview 8 (n 16); Interview 11 (n 6); Spees, 'Women's Advocacy in the Creation of the International Criminal Court' (n 51).

71 Pearson (n 28) 279.

72 Helmut Anheier and Hagai Katz, 'Global Connectedness: The Structure of Transnational NGO Networks' in Helmut Anheier, Marlies Glasius and Mary Kaldor (eds), *Global Civil Society 2005/6* (Sage Publications 2006) 255–256; Glasius, *The International Criminal Court* (n 35) 36.

international Western organisations, its membership broadened to include Latin American and African NGOs but only a few civil society groups from North Africa, Asia and the Middle East. Latin American and African NGOs were motivated to participate in the ICC negotiations by their experiences of war and human rights abuses. The example of individuals like the Senegalese Lawyer Abdul Koroma, M. Cherif Bassiouni[73] and Richard Goldstone as well as the establishment of the ICTR and Truth and Reconciliation Commissions (TRCs) further motivated African civil society groups to become involved. The low number of North African, Asian and Middle Eastern NGOs that participated in the ICC negotiations might have been related to the weakness in the development of international law, in particular of human rights, in these regions. This confirms the idea that the development of international law and civil society are co-dependent.[74]

At the request of other Coalition members, the CICC established an International Secretariat. Continuously, the International Secretariat worked towards maintaining momentum. To this end, it successfully mobilised and coordinated different NGO groups, legal experts and private organisations such as parliamentary, religious, humanitarian, and women's associations that represented every part of the world. The CICC International Secretariat supported the development of a common strategy and provided information services.[75] This way, the Secretariat contributed towards a high degree of transparency, resulting in inclusivity. It remained neutral in the negotiations so as to maintain the CICC's cohesiveness. Not taking a position enabled the International Secretariat to identify and expand areas of commonality between CICC members in the face of a plurality of ideas and objectives that existed in the negotiations. This was utilised to uphold relationships with a large number of actors and to contribute the NGOs' wide range of expertise to all parts of the negotiations. It was possible for the International Secretariat to maintain a neutral position in the ICC negotiations because it was hosted by the World Federalist Movement, whose broad and general mandate allowed the Secretariat to remain neutral on

73 Benedetti and Washburn (n 1) 9; Benedetti, Bonneau and Washburn (n 4) 101–103: M. Cherif Bassiouni's interests and behaviour in the ICC negotiations were influenced by his experiences as diplomat as well as his scholarly work and knowledge. He gave expert advice to governments who respected and trusted him because of his personal strengths, experience and commitment. This way, he made his voice heard. Furthermore, his role as vice-chair of the Preparatory Committee on the Establishment of an International Criminal Court (PrepCom) shaped his actions in the ICC negotiation.

74 Glasius, 'Expertise in the Cause of Justice' (n 27) 145–146; Glasius, *The International Criminal Court* (n 35) 36–37.

75 Interview 11 (n 6); Benedetti and Washburn (n 1) 21–33; Glasius, *The International Criminal Court* (n 35) 26–27; Pace and Schense, 'Coalition for the International Criminal Court at the Preparatory Commission' (n 6) 708; William R. Pace and Jennifer Schense, 'The Role of Non-Governmental Organizations' in Antonio Cassese, Paola Gaeta and John R.W.D. Jones (eds), *The Rome Statute of the International Criminal Court: A Commentary* (Volume 1, Oxford University Press 2002) 124–126; Pearson (n 28).

many specific issues. Here, the World Federalist Movement performed its role as convenor, offering a platform for discussion and amplifying voices from the ground through inter-governmental processes.[76] This is not to say that the World Federalist Movement did not engage in substantive work during the ICC negotiations. It was interested in the creation of an international criminal court as it would 'entrench certain rights and responsibilities, [...] putting into place a proper panoply of power and relationships where states can be held accountable'.[77] This indicates that the Coalition members followed their own mandate if compatible with the overall CICC goal to create a free, fair and independent court.[78]

The members of the CICC met in groups such as regional and thematic caucuses. Members of regional caucuses lobbied state delegations from their own region. Thematic caucuses were based on shared values and norms to develop their positions and to employ concerted efforts. They were created around issues of children, faith, gender justice, peace and victims.[79]

The Women's Caucus

Of particular relevance for this research project is the thematic caucus on gender justice, the Women's Caucus, as it played a vital role in ensuring that gender crimes were appropriately addressed as separate crimes as well as constituting other crimes such as torture. Although this was the Caucus' main goal, its areas of interest were broader and in line with the overall goal of the CICC.[80]

Before 1997, the efforts of women's rights advocates and activists were employed at the Vienna, Cairo and Beijing conferences.[81] Therefore, they did

76 Interview 6 (n 8); Interview 8 (n 16); Coalition for the International Criminal Court, 'Who We Are & What We Do' (n 28); Pace and Schense, 'Coalition for the International Criminal Court at the Preparatory Commission' (n 6) 708–711.

77 Interview 6 (n 8).

78 Interview 11 (n 6).

79 Benedetti and Washburn (n 1) 23; Glasius, 'Expertise in the Cause of Justice' (n 27) 147; Pearson (n 28) 264.

80 Interview 2 (n 10); Interview 10 (22 April 2014); Interview 11 (n 6); Rhonda Copelon, 'Gender Crimes as War Crimes: Integrating Crimes against Women into International Criminal Law' (2000) 46 *McGill Law Journal* 217, 234; Human Rights Watch, 'World Report 1999' (n 25); Spees, 'Women's Advocacy in the Creation of the International Criminal Court' (n 51) 1234.

81 Benedetti, Bonneau and Washburn (n 4) 70; Charlotte Bunch, 'Women's Rights as Human Rights: Toward a Re-Vision of Human Rights' (1990) 12 *Human Rights Quarterly* 486; Charnovitz, 'Two Centuries of Participation' (n 58) 214; Martha Alter Chen, 'Engendering World Conferences: The International Women's Movement and the UN' (1995) 16 *Third World Quarterly* 477; Diplomatic Conference for the Establishment of International Conventions for the Protection of Victims of War, 'Final Record of the Diplomatic Conference of Geneva of 1949, Vol. 2, Section A' (Federal Political Department Berne 1963) 643, 822 <www.loc.gov/rr/frd/Military_Law/pdf/Dipl-Conf-1949-Final_Vol-1.pdf> accessed 15 August 2013; Rothschild (n 35) 36. Through

not pay much attention to the ICC negotiations. When the PrepCom began, William Pace communicated with Rhonda Copelon[82] about the need to include women's organisations in the CICC as they represented an important constituency among international NGOs and had a considerable capacity for outreach. Although women's rights groups including Equality Now first participated in the third PrepCom meeting in February 1997, it was only after this session and with the influence of the MacArthur Foundation that they decided to form a

influencing the Vienna, Cairo and Beijing conferences, women's rights advocates from all over the world aimed to make women's voices heard in discussions on human rights, peace and security as well as on developmental and environmental issues. Experiences of women's rights advocates in the world conferences on women taught women's rights advocates at the ICC negotiations that concerted and deliberate effort is crucial to achieve their goals. Chen argues that women's rights advocates also learned that '[NGOs] have to master lobbying techniques, understand UN conference procedures clearly and lobby effectively during the preparatory process to make an impact on the official debates.' In addition, women's NGOs had to develop and/or strengthen their substantive and technical skills in the field of research and policy analysis, documentation and communication as well as leadership. To influence decision-makers and official documents, women's NGOs at the world conferences on women as well as in the ICC negotiations also participated in preliminary drafting work. In addition to lobbying, women's groups also influenced state delegations by influencing their composition, publishing reports, organising briefings and working with the media. In this way, they bridged NGO and official debates and generated publicity that provided a focus on women worldwide. In this way too, the Vienna, Cairo and Beijing conferences expanded the public space in which women's groups could work, network and learn.

However, it has to be noted that the UN world conferences are not the first international fora in which women's organisations became involved. The International Council of Women and the Inter-Allied Conference of Women Suffragists, for example, made presentations to the leaders of the League of Nations Commission at the Paris Peace Conference resulting in the Treaty of Versailles. Their claims focused on trafficking in women and the Versailles Treaty reflects some of their demands. In addition, at the negotiations of the Geneva conventions, the International Council of Women and the International Abolitionist Federation were actively involved in the drafting of art 27(2) of the fourth Geneva Convention and submitted the crucial proposal that was adopted without dissent.

82 Lisa Gormley, 'Rhonda Copelon Obituary' *The Guardian* (London, 24 May 2010) <www.theguardian.com/law/2010/may/24/rhonda-copelon-obituary> accessed 6 November 2014; Dennis Hevesi, 'Rhonda Copelon, Lawyer in Groundbreaking Rights Cases, Dies at 65' *The New York Times* (New York, 8 May 2010) <www.nytimes.com/2010/05/09/nyregion/09copelon.html?_r=0> accessed 6 November 2014; Women's Caucus for Gender Justice, 'About the Women's Caucus' <www.iccwomen.org/wigjdraft1/Archives/oldWCGJ/aboutcaucus.htm> accessed 6 November 2014: After having completed a degree in history and political science as well as in law, Rhonda Copelon was a professor of law and director of the International Women's Human Rights Law Clinic at the City University of New York School of Law. Working with her students, she filed ***amicus*** briefs in cases before the ICTY and ICTR. This way, she contributed to the recognition of rape as potentially constituting acts of genocide and torture under international law.

The International Women's Human Rights Law Clinic at the City University of New York School of Law functioned as the Women's Caucus' Legal Secretariat.

formal caucus to better organise their efforts and promote women's concerns.[83]

Additional staff – scholars, lawyers and activists specialised in human rights and women's rights, most of them with previous experience in international justice work – were recruited.[84] This indicates that expertise of violence against women prevailed over experience of violence. Amongst the Caucus' members of staff were Donna Axel,[85] Alda Facio[86] and Betty Murungi.[87] Another member of the Women's Caucus was María Eugenia Solís.[88] At the time of the Rome Conference, the Women's Caucus had more than 300 women's organisations and 500 individual members. Twelve to 15 people were present at Rome at any time during the conference.[89]

The Caucus received funding from a foundation headquartered in the US to bring survivors and women working on the ground with survivors in various

83 Benedetti, Bonneau and Washburn (n 4) 70; Jessica Neuwirth, 'Equality Now Calls on Women's Movement to Support the ICC' *ICC Monitor* (New York, January 1997) 8; Women's Caucus for Gender Justice, 'About the Women's Caucus' (n 82).

84 Benedetti, Bonneau and Washburn (n 4) 70; Spees, 'Women's Advocacy in the Creation of the International Criminal Court' (n 51) 1237.

85 New Jersey City University, 'Donna Axel' <http://web.njcu.edu/sites/faculty/daxel/content/bio.asp> accessed 7 November 2014; Austin Ruse, 'UNFPA's Sadik Calls for "Reproductive Freedom" at Annual UN NGO Forum' (C-FAM) <http://t.c-fam.org/en/issues/un-organizations/112-unfpas-sadik-calls-for-reproductive-freedom-at-annual-un-ngo-forum> accessed 7 November 2014: Like Rhonda Copelon, Donna Axel is a law professor and women's rights activist. Her field of expertise includes reproductive health for which she has advocated with various international organisations.

86 Association for Women's Rights in Development, 'An Interview with Alda Facio' (12 February 2008) <www.awid.org/Library/An-Interview-with-Alda-Facio> accessed 7 November 2014; Benedetti, Bonneau and Washburn (n 4) 70; Women's Human Rights Education Institute, 'Faculty Profiles' <http://learnwhr.org/about/> accessed 7 November 2014: Alda Facio is a feminist human rights activist, jurist and writer with decades of experience in both grassroots movements and more formal legal and UN contexts. She has carried out hundreds of trainings on women's human rights with an emphasis on the Convention on the Elimination of Discrimination against Women (CEDAW) for judges, the police and judicial officials throughout Latin America as well as for women's and civil society organisations throughout the world.

87 Madre, 'Women's Rights Exchange' <www.madre.org/index/press-room-4/womens-rights-exchange-15/network-of-experts-89.html> accessed 7 November 2014; Women's Caucus for Gender Justice, 'About the Women's Caucus' (n 82): Betty Murungi was the chair of the Women's Caucus' Executive Committee. She is a Kenyan lawyer and women's human rights activist. Her experiences in international human rights organisations include being a consultant and legal advisor to the International Center for Human Rights and Democratic Development on gender-related crimes at the ICTR.

88 Madre (n 87): María Eugenia Solís was the Women's Caucus' only Guatemalan member. She is a feminist professor and attorney with expertise in human rights and women's rights. She has been involved in feminist activism in the national and international arena.

89 Glasius, 'Expertise in the Cause of Justice' (n 27) 143, 147; Women's Caucus for Gender Justice, 'Recommendations and Commentary to the Elements Annex and Rules of Procedure and Evidence' (June 2000) <www.iccwomen.org/wigjdraft1/Archives/oldWCGJ/icc/iccpc/062000pc/elementsannex.htm> accessed 23 January 2014.

countries to New York and Rome. Survivors of sexualised war violence who participated in the ICC negotiations were at the same time activists. They were members of the Caucus' delegation and had direct input into its positions. Additionally, emails were sent out, outlining positions the Women's Caucus thought about adopting and asking for feedback. Contacts in different countries would then reach out to local women and organisations to collect their views and feed those back to the Caucus who would take them into account when drafting its final positions.[90]

In general, however, only a few survivors were involved in the ICC negotiations and had the opportunity to shape international rules. Amongst them were Barnes de Carlotto, Abuela, Rachel Edralin-Tigalo and Robert Green. An advert for a press conference in the second issue of *Terra Viva*, the conferences' daily newspaper, indicates that parents of victims were given the opportunity to speak about their experiences.[91] However, Hebe de Bonafini and Evel Pertini, two members of Madres de Plaza de Mayo, were forcibly led away after disrupting a speech by Argentinian Justice Minister Raul Enrique Castillo as they were not accredited participants of the Rome Conference. Security guards further prevented them from presenting their case to the press.[92]

The Women's Caucus guided the work of its members. This was necessary because of the geographic scope of its members and the wide range of activities undertaken. The Caucus provided orientation sessions before PrepCom sessions for new members, some of whom still had to be persuaded about the Women's Caucus' positions so that they could lobby governments accordingly. In regard to the Women's Caucus' drafting work and lobbying, at the ICC negotiations, in Vienna, Cairo and Beijing, the members of the Caucus discussed the language they wanted to introduce in a democratic and cooperative fashion. At this stage, only women were involved. The initiative often came from Rhonda Copelon. This indicates that the Caucus' members as individual actors shaped the Caucus' values and norms. Its positions were informed by thorough research on relevant existing treaties and case law, and based on (survivors') experiences of the Nuremberg, Tokyo, Yugoslavia and Rwanda tribunals. This indicates that personal

---

Some member organisations like the Women's Coalition against Crimes against Women in the Former Yugoslavia had already been actively involved in the establishment of the ICTY.

90 Interview 17 (n 4); Interview 19 (n 11).

Women's Caucus for Gender Justice, 'The Women's Caucus for Gender Justice Has Received Support from' <http://iccwomen.org/wigjdraft1/Archives/oldWCGJ/index.html> accessed 10 February 2015: The Women's Caucus received funding in general from the CICC, the Ford Foundation, the Global Fund for Women, the MacArthur Foundation, Rights and Democracy, the Shaler Adams Foundation, UNIFEM, the United Methodists and Urgent Action Fund as well as from the governments of Canada, Germany, the Netherlands and the United Kingdom of Great Britain and Northern Ireland (UK).

91 'Parents of Victims Take the Floor' *ICC Monitor* (New York, 16 June 1998) 4.

92 'Madres Thrown Out after Disrupting Argentina Speech' *Terra Viva* (Rome, 18 June 1998) 1.

and international values, norms and rules mattered in the Women's Caucus' discussions. Different members then approached delegates from different states, suggesting that normative structures influenced actors. Who they approached depended on evaluations of who might be empathetic towards their concerns and requests based on the general orientation of the respective state's government.[93] The Women's Caucus had good relations amongst others with Australia, Canada, Costa Rica, Mexico, European and Southern African countries.[94] Moreover, contacts were established based on shared nationality as well as through personal commonalities, trust and understanding. Here, the importance of informal contacts and personal values becomes apparent. Even though many men did not see gender issues as international crimes, members of the Women's Caucus found that most friendly delegates were men. This is to be expected considering that most delegates at the ICC negotiations were men. The impact of personal values can also be seen in the different styles of lobbying that different members of the Women's Caucus applied. In conversations with state delegates, some Caucus members went on to the next point after agreement had been reached on a certain issue. Others continued to bring forward arguments supporting a particular point the Women's Caucus raised even after agreement had been reached with a delegate. This supports the opinion voiced that NGOs provided alternative or additional lines of reasoning to a proposal rather than drafting one themselves. Some members of the Women's Caucus were very attached to their language, very definite about it and disappointed when it was changed. Others acknowledged that compromises were necessary. This raises the question whether it was more important to achieve a satisfactory overall outcome than to include certain wordings in the ICC instruments. It raises the question whether the words that are used in a definition are only interesting from a theoretical point of view but less so in practice. After all, in practice it has to be kept in mind that meanings of terms may change from one language to the other and distinctions exist in one but not the other. After having reached agreements or compromises on the Caucus' proposals, delegates would officially propose them. It has to be stressed that this did not happen out of pure empathy towards the Women's Caucus. Rather, state delegations that presented the Caucus' proposals did so based on evaluations of their own experiences and of how the Women's Caucus' positions fitted with those of the state delegation in question. Here again, personal and national values, norms and rules influenced actors.[95]

93 Interview 5 (n 8); Interview 7 (n 16); Interview 8 (n 16); Interview 9 (n 8); Interview 10 (n 80); Interview 11 (n 6); Interview 17 (n 4); Interview 19 (n 11); Chen (n 81).

94 Glasius, 'Expertise in the Cause of Justice' (n 27) 159; see also Benedetti, Bonneau and Washburn (n 4) 71.

95 Interview 4 (n 9); Interview 5 (n 8); Interview 6 (n 8); Interview 9 (n 8); Interview 10 (n 80); Interview 14 (n 20); Interview 17 (n 4); Interview 18 (n 1); Interview 19 (n 11); Copelon, 'Gender Crimes as War Crimes' (n 80) 220, 233.

Although the Women's Caucus' advocacy strategy was effective, it was also exclusive. It disregarded state delegations that were perceived to have contrary opinions or shared no common ground with the Caucus. These delegations in turn were not aware of women's rights at stake and saw other issues like the inclusion of non-core crimes and the relationship between the UNSC and the court as dominating the discussions. They perceived the negotiations to have taken place without a strong women's lobby. This illustrates the significance of penetrating an environment that is not very gender-sensitive by networking delegates.[96]

In pursuing the objective of ensuring that gender crimes were appropriately addressed, the Women's Caucus enjoyed the cooperation and support of many of CICC's members who endorsed papers the Caucus had drafted, sharing its views. This was crucial for the Caucus' overall success.[97] However, the Women's Caucus also encountered opposition from a small number of government delegations who perceived it to be in 'pursuit of a purely [feminist] political agenda rather than the contribution of legal expertise based on the real-life experience of war-affected women and survivors of sexual violence'.[98] Voicing male norms, some state actors considered attention to gender issues unnecessary as objective laws would certainly address them and advised the members of Caucus on the proper behaviour and dress code at international treaty negotiations.[99]

While some governments were hostile, others were unsupportive. Following male norms, gender issues were not a priority for the German delegation who relied on the headway made by the *ad hoc* tribunals in this regard. The German delegation accepted NGOs' active participation in the negotiations as long as it was in line with states' positions.[100]

The French delegation adopted a similar point of view. They perceived the concept of gender as Anglo-Saxon or American and exact definitions of the crimes of rape and sexual slavery and, by extension, forced marriage were of no great concern for them. Indicating that personal values mattered, their female chief of delegation still was close to the Women's Caucus. She gave her team instructions to support the group, especially in its struggle against the Holy See. However, as any delegation, the French had hard and soft points in the negotiations. Disagreement arose, for example, over the element of coercion in relation to rape. While the Women's Caucus was understood to have argued that coercive circumstances automatically negate any consent, the French delegation drew on the state's experience of the Second World War. It was argued that many French women had genuine relationships with German soldiers.

96 Interview 1 (n 4); Interview 2 (n 10); Interview 11 (n 6); Interview 14 (n 20); Alison Dickens, 'Women-Friendly Tribunal Sought' *Terra Viva* (Rome, 17 June 1998) 8.

97 Interview 11 (n 6).

98 Pace and Schense, 'Coalition for the International Criminal Court at the Preparatory Commission' (n 6) 719.

99 Rothschild (n 35) 99.

100 Interview 15 (n 5).

Therefore, not all sexual encounters between people of any background in war could be classified as rape. This illustrates that the Caucus was perceived to simplify things.[101]

In addition to hostile and unsupportive governments, the Women's Caucus also encountered opposition from different NGOs. In the early phase of the Women's Caucus' involvement in the ICC negotiations, some NGOs were concerned that the Caucus' objectives would divert interests away from, and weaken, key concepts, definitions and messages for example on jurisdiction and trigger mechanisms. 'In these cases, the Women's Caucus was often portrayed as rigid, intrusive, and uncompromising.'[102] Other NGOs considered the Caucus not to be very important, did not want to be associated with it and consequently did not support its proposals. Other NGOs like Redress shared the views of the Women's Caucus and agreed that the issues the Caucus addressed were of relevance. However, Redress had to follow its own mandate that required the organisation to focus on different concerns.[103] Other NGOs opposed the Women's Caucus because of values and norms grounded in religious objections to the gender provisions in the Rome Statute, especially the provisions relating to forced pregnancy in Article 7. Prompted by concerns raised by the Holy See in regard to the term 'gender', North American conservative Christian NGOs got more involved in the negotiations.[104] Particularly noticeable for their destructive, highly emotive, intimidating and harassing behaviour during the Rome Conference, 'pro-family' groups caused difficulties with other NGOs, especially the Women's Caucus.[105] The Caucus, in response, became more careful and

101 Interview 16 (n 17).

102 Benedetti, Bonneau and Washburn (n 4) 71.

103 Interview 17 (n 4); For more information on REDRESS and the ICC negotiations see Benedetti, Bonneau and Washburn (n 4) 72–73.

104 Interview 17 (n 4). See Glasius, *The International Criminal Court* (n 35) 32, 121; Marlies Glasius, 'Who Is the Real Civil Society? Women's Groups versus Pro-Family Groups at the International Criminal Court Negotiations' in Jude Howell and Diane Mulligan (eds), *Gender and Civil Society* (Routledge 2004); Pearson (n 28): Pro-family groups that participated in the ICC negotiations included the Canadian group Campaign Life Coalition, the Catholic Family and Human Rights Institute, Human Life International, the International Right to Life Federation and REAL (Realistic Active for Life) Women of Canada. Pro-family groups used similar lobbying tactics to the Women's Caucus and the CICC. They focused their attention on sympathetic states, circulated position papers and aimed at influencing their governments' position on the ratification of the Rome Statute this way. However, they were also accused of not playing according to the rules, making handouts without identifying themselves as the authors and destroying other delegations' documents. Even though pro-family groups made their voices heard, the cohesiveness, size and strength of the CICC as well as the relative lack of support from a majority of states made it impossible for these NGOs to effectively influence the negotiation process and outcomes. They were marginalised at the ICC negotiations.

105 Interview 11 (n 6); Glasius, *The International Criminal Court* (n 35) 32, 121; Pearson (n 28).

For more information on the pro-family groups and their relationship to the Women's Caucus see Glasius, 'Who Is the Real Civil Society?' (n 104).

secretive when discussing issues in public, falling silent when strangers joined their group.[106]

Similarly to NGOs prioritising other questions, it was argued that individuals also corrupted the debate about gender issues and sexualised violence by continuously advancing strong opinions, for example about the relationship between sexualised violence and pornography. Acting strategically and knowing how to organise enabled them to make their voices heard.[107]

Forms of participation

As mentioned above, the Women's Caucus shared some objectives and advocacy strategies with the CICC in general. In the PrepCom and at Rome, NGOs were highly visible. They closely monitored and distributed information on the status of the negotiations, co-sponsored news conferences, expert meetings, public debates, seminars, symposia and workshops, and coordinated parallel activities conducted by NGOs. In addition to very directed and sometimes aggressive lobbying, NGOs facilitated exchange, discussion and participation amongst others through meetings and communicating with UN officials and members of state delegations. Aiming at moderating and neutralising states' positions, these meetings were conducted to give states the opportunity to discuss controversial issues on a technical rather than political basis. Here, the CICC would state the facts regarding a certain issue and aim to provide a way out for disagreeing delegations.[108] The larger groups within the CICC were the intellectual leaders of the Coalition. Amongst them were Amnesty International, Human Rights Watch, the International Service for Human Rights, the Lawyers Committee for Human Rights and the International Commission for Jurists. They produced, circulated and promoted new research and expert documents including journal articles and reports, aiming to inform and influence state and non-state experts. This way, they provided the context for the decisions that were to be made by states. These forms of NGO participation in law-making negotiations were taken as a sign of NGOs' growing professionalism. Smaller groups were often more effective at disseminating information, networking and building coalitions. In addition to lobbying, producing expert documents, trying to influence the negotiating bodies' reports to the UNGA, disseminating information to the wider public and convening conferences, Amnesty International, No

106 Interview 5 (n 8).
107 Interview 9 (n 8).
108 Interview 1 (n 4); Interview 8 (n 16); Interview 11 (n 6); Interview 17 (n 4); Interview 18 (n 1); Benedetti and Washburn (n 1) 21–33; Coalition for the International Criminal Court, 'History of the ICC' <www.iccnow.org/?mod=icchistory> accessed 3 December 2013; Glasius, 'Expertise in the Cause of Justice' (n 27) 150; Glasius, *The International Criminal Court* (n 35) 31–32, 39, 43–46, 115; Human Rights Watch, 'World Report 1999' (n 25); Lindblom (n 6) 471–477; Pace and Schense, 'The Role of Non-Governmental Organizations' (n 75); Pearson (n 28).

Peace Without Justice and others also staged street actions in the form of demonstrations, signature lists, human carpets and vigils.[109]

In recognition of the CICC's role in the process to establish an international criminal court, the CICC's International Secretariat was asked by the UN to organise the accreditation of NGOs to the Rome Conference. This was a unique form of self-regulation that had not been attempted before at international conferences.[110]

Through regional and national networks and initiatives, CICC members raised awareness of the establishment of an international criminal court and developed important personal contacts at a local level. They circulated position papers and supported and coordinated inter-sessional meetings, contributing to national policy-making and therefore influencing normative structures. This way, CICC members contributed to the capacity-building and mobilised policy advocacy of local NGOs to pressure their governments at home.[111] During the PrepCom2 negotiations, the CICC joined the LMG in insisting that the PrepCom2 should protect the integrity of the Rome Statute. They wanted to avoid that the statute would be reopened for discussion and its spirit would be changed. However, the CICC decided to focus its efforts on influencing structures by addressing shortcomings of the statute at the national level through promoting the adoption of strong national implementing legislation. The Coalition gathered information about national ratification processes, discussed with delegates the obligations which would come with ratifying the Rome Statute, briefed them and NGOs on progress towards entry into force, and planned activities at national and regional level.[112] Therefore, NGOs had a mediating role between the international and national level.

The relationship between the CICC and state delegations

As mentioned before, the CICC worked in cooperation with state delegations. Especially through consultative roles with a growing number of governments, particularly from the LMG, the CICC developed into a strategic partner in the

109 Benedetti, Bonneau and Washburn (n 4) 77; Glasius, 'Expertise in the Cause of Justice' (n 27).

110 Interview 8 (n 16); Glasius, 'Expertise in the Cause of Justice' (n 27) 146–147; Glasius, 'Who Is the Real Civil Society?' (n 104); Lindblom (n 6) 459: In deciding which NGOs to accredit, coordinator William Pace tried to treat all groups on an equal footing. He only turned down a very low number of government-organised NGOs. In addition to this CICC-led accreditation, it was also made possible for NGOs who did not wish to go through this procedure to apply directly to Roy Lee, the UN official in charge of organising the conference. This way, about 16 groups were added to the list.

111 Interview 8 (n 16); Benedetti and Washburn (n 1) 21–33; Coalition for the International Criminal Court, 'History of the ICC' (n 108); Glasius, *The International Criminal Court* (n 35) 31–32, 39, 43–46; Human Rights Watch, 'World Report 1999' (n 25); Pace and Schense, 'The Role of Non-Governmental Organizations' (n 75); Pearson (n 28).

112 Pace and Schense, 'Coalition for the International Criminal Court at the Preparatory Commission' (n 6) 706, 710; Pace and Schense, 'The Role of Non-Governmental Organizations' (n 75) 140–141.

whole course of the negotiations. The growing acceptance of NGOs was facilitated by their acceptance of the culture and style of international treaty conferences as well as of the fact that national policy positions are better addressed through dialogue than by condemnation. NGOs knew that they had to win fights through their arguments, and they did. Early and open discussions prevented confrontations with written (counter-)proposals. NGOs were realistic about the kind of involvement they sought. They knew and accepted that states made the final decisions. At Rome, NGOs did not seek speaking rights or access to crucial informal meetings as it was important to keep government delegations satisfied. NGOs recognised the importance of the ICC negotiations being largely a state-based process for the ultimate success of the court. Therefore, NGOs promoted and galvanised broad state support.[113] However, many state delegations would agree that NGOs were key in the process of establishing the ICC.[114] As indicated above however, the partnership between states and NGOs was not always an easy one due to different organisational structures, presuppositions and interests influencing government delegations' and NGOs' short-term and long-term goals and working methods. CICC members, for example, were concerned about the focus of the LMG on unanimity and the disproportionate power this granted to uncompromising delegations, causing tensions.[115] States' willingness to engage with NGOs was issue-dependent.[116] Generally, a positive synergy existed between Canadian NGOs and the state's delegation. The actors had a common outlook and were supportive towards the Canada's Human Security Agenda. When minds did not meet, however, relationships worsened. This was the case in relation to the conservative Christian organisations mentioned above and the crime of forced pregnancy.[117] Similarly, when NGOs touched political raw nerves like the protection of states' soldiers, cooperation lessened.[118] However, governments did not want to oppose NGOs publicly. Therefore, before the negotiations began, members of NGOs were sometimes

113 Interview 4 (n 9); Interview 8 (n 16); Interview 11 (n 6); Interview 17 (n 4); 'Welcome' (n 60); Axworthy (n 60); Benedetti and Washburn (n 1) 21–33; Coalition for the International Criminal Court, 'History of the ICC' (n 108); Glasius, *The International Criminal Court* (n 35) 31–32, 39, 43–46; Human Rights Watch, 'World Report 1999' (n 25); Lindblom (n 6) 474; Pace and Schense, 'Coalition for the International Criminal Court at the Preparatory Commission' (n 6) 706; Pace and Schense, 'The Role of Non-Governmental Organizations' (n 75); Pearson (n 28); Rothschild (n 35) 100.

114 Reuters News Service as cited in Amnesty International, 'Introduction to the NGO Coalition for an International Criminal Court (CICC)' (2000) <www.iccnow.org/documents/AIDocumentCICC_en.pdf> accessed 24 January 2014.

115 Lindblom (n 6) 471–476; Pace and Schense, 'Coalition for the International Criminal Court at the Preparatory Commission' (n 6) 723.

116 Interview 4 (n 9); Benedetti and Washburn (n 1) 21–33; Coalition for the International Criminal Court, 'History of the ICC' (n 108); Glasius, *The International Criminal Court* (n 35) 31–32, 39, 43–46; Pace and Schense, 'The Role of Non-Governmental Organizations' (n 75); Pearson (n 28).

117 Interview 17 (n 4); Lindblom (n 6) 471.

118 Interview 16 (n 17).

taken aside by state representatives and told they would not get what they wanted, and how the negotiations were going to go.[119] Like the Canadian example above, this indicates that NGOs had to dance to states' tunes. Relationships between NGOs and state delegations were generally constructive until NGOs disagreed with states' positions. In such cases, cooperation lessened. State delegations also did not want NGOs around when they were trying to reach a compromise, wanting to avoid the NGOs' moral voice and being held morally responsible. The discussion about the inclusion or exclusion of nuclear and chemical weapons stands as an example here. As mentioned above, the NAM, especially Syria, argued for either both kinds of weapons to be included in, or excluded from, the Rome Statute. Since member states of the North Atlantic Treaty Organization would not have ratified the statute if it would have explicitly prohibited the use of nuclear weapons, a compromise was reached to exclude any reference to chemical and nuclear weapons.[120] In contrast, state delegations decided not to waste negotiation capital on something that they subjectively considered harmless or a waste of time. The inclusion of crimes against UN personnel in the war crimes provision of the Rome Statute stands as an example here. This way, states accumulated negotiation capital that they used in regard to issues they could not compromise on. Consequently, the most sensitive issues could be the least controversial ones.[121]

Conclusion

This chapter has shown that actors and normative structures mutually influenced each other in the ICC negotiations, confirming the constructivist circle. In regard to actors, it was demonstrated that individuals, states and NGOs played an important role in the negotiations. In regard to structures, it was highlighted that personal, national and international values, norms and rules mattered. The example of the Bosnian delegation referred to above draws most of these factors together. Influenced by his country's experiences (national) in the war in the 1990s, the Bosnian ambassador (personal) was keen to have sexualised violence included in the ICC list of war crimes (international). Therefore, he actively supported (personal) instructions received from the Bosnian government (national) to make sure that the instruments and jurisprudence of the ICTY (international) would be considered in drafting the ICC instruments (international). This example also shows how normative structures (values and norms based on national experiences) shape actors (the Bosnian ambassador) who again shaped normative structures (the ICC instruments). When adding to this the Women's Caucus, which was the main actor advocating the inclusion of various

119 Interview 3 (n 1).

120 Interview 15 (n 5).

121 Interview 3 (n 1); Wilmshurst, 'Report on the Conference for the Establishment of an International Criminal Court' (n 45).

sexualised crimes in the Rome Statute, the crucial role NGOs played in the negotiations becomes apparent.

Exploring state delegations as groups showed that states formed coalitions partly based on shared values, norms and rules, partly changing traditional dynamics of international negotiations. This already indicates that national norms can explain fundamental changes in states' identities as international actors. This was confirmed, using the examples of the UK and France where changes in national power dynamics, and consequently national norms, led to changes in the states' identities in the ICC negotiations. However, civil society members who became members of state delegations and maintained and argued for their original points serve as an example of a situation in which national norms and rules had no impact on the negotiations. The discussion of the level of engagement of actors from the global North and South also showed that in addition to normative reasons, actors' (in-)actions were motivated by practical and strategic considerations. Financial issues, the lack of awareness and competence, considerations related to a state's international image and nationalist arguments were brought up in this context. Nevertheless, the example of African states as actors in the ICC negotiations confirms the constructivist circle. Experience assigned African states the moral authority to push for an effective court because of their history of colonisation and establishment of TRCs. Their identity in the ICC negotiations was determined by national and international norms and rules. African states as actors also influenced international rules by signing the Rome Statute. In addition to social engineering potentially limiting the opportunities for certain actors to shape international rules, the same result was achieved by prioritising English over other languages, especially in informal meetings, as well as by insisting on consensus in decision-making.

Part four of this chapter moved away from a state-centric view on the ICC negotiations and analysed NGOs as a group that played a crucial role as well. NGOs directly and indirectly influenced the process and substance of the negotiations. The Women's Caucus played a vital role in ensuring that gender crimes were appropriately addressed as crimes in and of themselves as well as forms of other listed crimes such as torture. The Caucus also advocated the creation of an independent and fair court that would be associated with peace. While more specific views of NGOs, especially on sexualised crimes, are discussed in the following chapters, this chapter already highlighted that the Women's Caucus formed its views based on the input of survivors of sexualised violence and women working with survivors. The Women's Caucus also formed its views based on its members' personal backgrounds as well as on their research into existing values, norms and rules, especially those of the *ad hoc* tribunals and the Final Report of the UN Special Rapporteur on the Situation of Systematic Rape, Sexual Slavery and Slavery-Like Practices during Armed Conflict. It becomes apparent that the Women's Caucus' composition and strategy was based on experiences of previous international conferences. At Vienna, Cairo, Beijing and Rome, women's organisations incorporated members from all over the world. Therefore, it was crucial to build consensus through discussion. Women's organisations were active at local, national, regional and international level at all stages of the negotiation processes. To influence the negotiations effectively, they had to understand how international law-making conferences work. Women's organisations had to be well prepared, conduct research and policy analysis, document acts of violence against women, produce and distribute reports, organise briefings and lobby state delegations. Through cooperation with the media, they generated publicity for their agendas. In addition to building bridges between different women's NGOs and activists as well as between women's organisations and the media, women's organisations bridged NGOs and state delegations by influencing the latter's composition.

Chapter 4 explored some more general views held by the CICC and how it came to hold them. The CICC supported the establishment of a free, fair and independent permanent international criminal court because it was necessary to act upon lessons learned from challenges encountered in relation to the ICTY and ICTR, as well as to fill an impunity gap. At Rome, the NGO Coalition was concerned about the focus on unanimity because it ascribed disproportionate power to dissenting voices and consequently could cause tensions. After Rome, the CICC was of the opinion that strong national legislation implementing the Rome Statute was needed due to the shortcomings of the instrument. Throughout the whole negotiation process, the Coalition's International Secretariat remained neutral so as to maintain the CICC's cohesiveness, to identify and expand areas of commonality between CICC members, to uphold relationships with a large number of actors and to contribute the NGOs' wide range of expertise to all parts of the negotiations. Therefore, it was a strategic decision made possible by the World Federalist Movement's broad mandate. The World Federalist Movement itself supported the creation of an international criminal court because it would strengthen the rule of law, facilitate power sharing and hold states to account.[122]

While this chapter did not go into detail demonstrating that NGOs in the ICC negotiations taught their views to states, it addressed various ways in which NGOs influenced states. Central to this was the high visibility of NGOs during the ICC negotiations. Furthermore, networking and cooperation between NGOs at multiple levels, as well as between NGOs and states, was crucial. NGOs monitored the negotiations, furthering transparency. They distributed information, shared their research and expertise, held regular meetings and briefings and organised news conferences and parallel activities. They facilitated participation, provided a platform for discussion and exchange, mediated between different actors, facilitated compromises and participated in preliminary drafting work. Maintaining momentum, they continuously raised awareness, engaged in capacity building, provided orientation and guidance and mobilised NGO engagement and participation. A common strategy, concerted efforts and the work in caucuses was made possible by, and contributed to, the cohesiveness

122 Interview 6 (n 8).

of the group of NGOs involved. A very effective structure and organisation was extremely necessary due to the large number and diversity of the actors involved, as well as the wide range of activities undertaken. NGOs based their work on personal, national and international values, norms and rules talked about in democratic discussions. They amplified voices from the ground; voices of survivors of sexualised violence and those working with them. In their lobbying, they addressed supposedly friendly state delegations and delegations with which they expected to have common ground. Especially the latter highlights the importance of personal and informal contacts, creating trust and understanding. State delegations in turn evaluated NGOs' proposals in a similar fashion, based on experiences and the compatibility with the respective state's positions. Overall, NGOs provided the context for decisions that were to be made by states. They shaped the space and substance of the negotiations. What was noticed by state delegations as the growing professionalism of NGOs – their acceptance of the culture of international treaty-making negotiations, their realistic assessment of the kinds of involvement they sought and their recognition of the crucial role of states as final decision-makers – made it possible for NGOs to influence state actors' identities and actions.

In addition to demonstrating that NGOs played an important role in the ICC negotiations and succeeded in influencing the identities and actions of state actors, this chapter showed that survivors of sexualised war violence as well as actors from the global South were involved in the ICC negotiations of the definitions of war rape and forced marriage. This chapter mentioned that the Women's Caucus included, and worked with, survivors of sexualised violence. Therefore, survivors directly influenced and shaped the outcomes of the ICC negotiations. However, it has to be noted that, overall, the participation of survivors was an exception. In contrast, the direct involvement of actors from the global South was facilitated throughout NGO and state coalitions by providing various necessary resources like financial support, personnel and information. Civil society actors from all regions of the world were represented and actively engaged in the ICC negotiations as members of the CICC.

However, a word of caution seems necessary here. According to Adriaan Bos, the chair of the ICC negotiations until Rome, civil society actors strengthen democratic processes in international decision-making.[123] Arguably they can foster deliberation, develop alternative proposals, promote access and give a voice to those unheard, increase transparency for, and accountability to, the wider public, and diminish power distortions among states.[124] This chapter showed that NGOs in the ICC negotiations indeed developed alternative proposals and promoted access. NGOs also made the official state debates more

123 Adriaan Bos, 'The International Criminal Court: Recent Developments' in Herman A.M. von Hebel, Johan G. Lammers and Jolien Schukking (eds), *Reflections on the International Criminal Court: Essays in Honour of Adriaan Bos* (TMC Asser Press 1999) 44–45.

124 Glasius, 'Expertise in the Cause of Justice' (n 27) 162.

deliberative and less focused on narrow interests. When it comes to internal deliberation and transparency, however, it has to be noted that no thorough debate and no formal collective decision-making took place within the CICC.[125] The number of NGOs, their internal decision-making processes, the high pace of the negotiations and the importance of consensus and coherence made it impractical and potentially disadvantageous. In addition, 'the NGO Coalition lacked the kind of culture of consensus reflecting commitments to social transformation, non-violence, and representation of popular demands'.[126] The Coalition emphasised pluralism rather than internal democracy.[127] As mentioned in this chapter, big international NGOs are the most experienced and best connected. Therefore, their impact on international negotiations and their outcomes are more significant than those of smaller, less experienced and less well-connected organisations, creating inequalities and hierarchies. Even though the CICC included and represented civil society actors from all over the world, those actors found themselves under the guidance and leadership of international human rights groups.[128] When it comes to giving a voice to those unheard, it has to be noted that, even though the Women's Caucus included survivors of sexualised violence and women working with them on the ground, many civil society representatives were 'well-heeled, university-educated cosmopolitans with little direct experience of violence'.[129] The presence of grassroots representatives like the members of Madres de Plaza de Mayo appears to have served a symbolic purpose rather than actually involving them in the negotiations. This emphasises expertise rather than experience.[130]

Bibliography

Cases

Special Court for Sierra Leone

Prosecutor v Alex Tamba Brima, Brima Bazzy Kamara and Santigie Borbor Kanu (Prosecution Filing of Expert Report Pursuant to Rule 94(bis) and Decision of Prosecution Request for Leave to Call an Additional Expert Witness) SCSL-04-16-T 'AFRC Case' (08 August 2005) <www.rscsl.org/Documents/Decisions/AFRC/365/SCSL-04-16-T-369.pdf> accessed 28 September 2017.

125 ibid.
126 John Burroughs and Jacqueline Cabasso, 'Confronting the Nuclear-Armed States in International Negotiating Forums: Lessons for NGOs' (1999) 4 *International Negotiation* 474.
127 Glasius, 'Expertise in the Cause of Justice' (n 27) 162.
128 Benedetti and Washburn (n 1) 21–22; Glasius, *The International Criminal Court* (n 35) 26–27; Pace and Schense, 'Coalition for the International Criminal Court at the Preparatory Commission' (n 6) 708; Pace and Schense, 'The Role of Non-Governmental Organizations' (n 75).
129 Glasius, 'Expertise in the Cause of Justice' (n 27) 163.
130 ibid.

Interviews

Interview 1 (21 March 2014).
Interview 2 (24 March 2014).
Interview 3 (25 March 2014).
Interview 4 (26 March 2014).
Interview 5 (1 April 2014).
Interview 6 (2 April 2014).
Interview 7 (4 April 2014).
Interview 8 (11 April 2014).
Interview 9 (11 April 2014).
Interview 10 (22 April 2014).
Interview 11 (23 April 2014).
Interview 12 (15 May 2014).
Interview 14 (26 May 2014).
Interview 15 (27 May 2014).
Interview 16 (10 June 2014).
Interview 17 (17 June 2014).
Interview 18 (25 June 2014).
Interview 19 (26 November 2014).

Books

Bassiouni, M.C., *The Legislative History of the International Criminal Court* (Transnational Publishers 2005).

Benedetti, F., Bonneau, K. and Washburn, J., *Negotiating the International Criminal Court: New York to Rome, 1994–1998* (Brill 2013).

Glasius, M., *The International Criminal Court: A Global Civil Society Initiative* (Routledge 2006).

Lindblom, A.-K., *Non-Governmental Organisations in International Law* (Cambridge University Press 2005).

Rothschild, C., *Written Out: How Sexuality Is Used to Attack Women's Organizing* (International Gay and Lesbian Human Rights Commission and Center for Women's Global Leadership 2005).

Chapters in edited books

Anheier, H. and Katz, H., 'Global Connectedness: The Structure of Transnational NGO Networks' in Helmut Anheier, Marlies Glasius and Mary Kaldor (eds), *Global Civil Society 2005/6* (Sage Publications 2006).

Bichsel, A., 'NGOs as Agents of Public Accountability and Democratization in Intergovernmental Forums' in William M. Lafferty and James Meadowcroft (eds), *Democracy and the Environment: Problems and Prospects* (Edward Elgar Publishing 1996).

Bos, B., 'The International Criminal Court: Recent Developments' in Herman A.M. von Hebel, Johan G. Lammers and Jolien Schukking (eds), *Reflections on the International Criminal Court: Essays in Honour of Adriaan Bos* (TMC Asser Press 1999).

Colini, M., 'The Experience of No Peace Without Justice' in Alessandro Fodella and others (eds), *Civil Society, International Courts and Compliance Bodies* (TMC Asser Press 2004).

De Cesari, P., 'NGOs and the Activities of the Ad Hoc Criminal Tribunals for Former Yugoslavia and Rwanda' in Alessandro Fodella and others (eds), *Civil Society, International Courts and Compliance Bodies* (TMC Asser Press 2004).

Ellis, M.S., 'The Contribution of Non-Governmental Organizations to the Creation of International Criminal Tribunals' in Bartram S. Brown (ed), *Research Handbook on International Criminal Law* (Edward Elgar Publishing 2011).

Glasius, M., 'Expertise in the Cause of Justice: Global Civil Society Influence on the Statute for an International Criminal Court' in Helmut K. Anheier, Marlies Glasius and Mary Kaldor (eds), *Global Civil Society 2005/6* (Oxford University Press 2002).

———, 'Who Is the Real Civil Society? Women's Groups versus Pro-Family Groups at the International Criminal Court Negotiations' in Jude Howell and Diane Mulligan (eds), *Gender and Civil Society* (Routledge 2004).

Pace, W.R. and Schense, J., 'Coalition for the International Criminal Court at the Preparatory Commission' in Roy S. Lee (ed), *The International Criminal Court: Elements of Crimes and Rules of Procedure and Evidence* (Transnational Publishers 2001).

———, 'The Role of Non-Governmental Organizations' in Antonio Cassese, Paola Gaeta and John R.W.D. Jones (eds), *The Rome Statute of the International Criminal Court: A Commentary* (Volume 1, Oxford University Press 2002).

Journal articles

Benedetti, F. and Washburn, J.L., 'Drafting the International Criminal Court Treaty: Two Years to Rome and an Afterword on the Rome Diplomatic Conference' (1999) 5 *Global Governance* 1.

Boehme, F., '"We Chose Africa": South Africa and the Regional Politics of Cooperation with the International Criminal Court' (2017) 11 *International Journal of Transitional Justice* 50.

Bunch, C., 'Women's Rights as Human Rights: Toward a Re-Vision of Human Rights' (1990) 12 *Human Rights Quarterly* 486.

Burroughs, J. and Cabasso, J., 'Confronting the Nuclear-Armed States in International Negotiating Forums: Lessons for NGOs' (1999) 4 *International Negotiation* 474.

Charnovitz, S., 'Two Centuries of Participation: NGOs and International Governance' (1997) 18 *Michigan Journal of International Law* 183.

Chen, M.A., 'Engendering World Conferences: The International Women's Movement and the UN' (1995) 16 *Third World Quarterly* 477.

Clark, A.M., Friedman, E.J. and Hochstetler, K., 'The Sovereign Limits of Global Civil Society: A Comparison of NGO Participation in UN' (1998) 51 *World Politics* 1.

Copelon, R., 'Gender Crimes as War Crimes: Integrating Crimes against Women into International Criminal Law' (2000) 46 *McGill Law Journal* 217.

Cotter, P. and others, 'Affecting the Rules for the Prosecution of Rape and Other Gender-Based Violence before the International Criminal Tribunal for the Former Yugoslavia: A Feminist Proposal and Critique' (1994) 5 *Hastings Women's Law Journal* 171.

Hall, C.K., 'The First Two Sessions of the UN Preparatory Committee on the Establishment of an International Criminal Court' (1997) 91 *American Journal of International Law* 177.

———, 'The Sixth Session of the UN Preparatory Committee on the Establishment of an International Criminal Court' (1998) 92 *American Journal of International Law* 548.

Halley, J., 'Rape at Rome: Feminist Interventions in the Criminalization of Sex-Related Violence in Positive International Criminal Law' (2009) 30 *Michigan Journal of International Law* 1.

International Human Rights Law Group, 'No Justice, No Peace: Accountability for Rape and Gender-Based Violence in the Former Yugoslavia' (1994) 5 *Hastings Women's Law Journal* 89.

O'Flaherty, M., 'Sierra Leone's Peace Process: The Role of the Human Rights Community' (2004) 26 *Human Rights Quarterly* 29.

Pearson, Z., 'Non-Governmental Organizations and the International Criminal Court: Changing Landscapes of International Law' (2006) 39 *Cornell International Law Journal* 243.

Spees, P., 'Women's Advocacy in the Creation of the International Criminal Court: Changing the Landscape of Justice and Power' (2003) 28 *Signs* 1233.

Vilmer, J.B.J., 'The African Union and the International Criminal Court: Counteracting the Crisis' (2016) 92 (2) *International Affairs* 1319.

Vyver, J.D. van der, 'Civil Society and the International Criminal Court' (2003) 2 *Journal of Human Rights* 425.

Williams, S. and Woolaver, H., 'The Role of the Amicus Curiae before International Criminal Tribunals' (2006) 6 *International Criminal Law Review* 151.

(Research) reports and working papers

Human Rights Watch, 'World Report 1998' <www.hrw.org/legacy/worldreport/Intro97.htm#P1_0> accessed 5 December 2013.

———, 'World Report 1999: Special Issues and Campaigns: The ICC' <www.hrw.org/legacy/worldreport99/special/icc.html> accessed 23 January 2014.

ICC advocacy papers, commentaries, recommendations, reports and working papers

Wilmshurst, E., 'ICC: PrepCom. 16–26 February 1999' (1 March 1999).

———, 'Report on the Conference for the Establishment of an International Criminal Court: 15 June–17 July 1998' (23 September 1998).

Women's Caucus for Gender Justice, 'Recommendations and Commentary to the Elements Annex and Rules of Procedure and Evidence' (June 2000) <www.iccwomen.org/wigjdraft1/Archives/oldWCGJ/icc/iccpc/062000pc/elementsannex.htm> accessed 23 January 2014.

Blog entries, newspaper and magazine articles and radio broadcasts

———, 'African Leaders Plan Mass Withdrawal From International Criminal Court' *The Guardian* (31 January 2017) <www.theguardian.com/law/2017/jan/31/african-leaders-plan-mass-withdrawal-from-international-criminal-court> accessed 17 July 2017.

———, 'Africa Speaks Strongly for Court' *Terra Viva* (Rome, 16 June 1998) 4.

———, 'Madres Thrown Out after Disrupting Argentina Speech' *Terra Viva* (Rome, 18 June 1998) 1.

———, 'Parents of Victims Take the Floor' *ICC Monitor* (New York, 16 June 1998) 4.

———, 'Welcome' *Terra Viva* (Rome, 15 June 1998) 5.

Axworthy L, 'A Court That Is Worth Having' *Terra Viva* (Rome, 15 June 1998) 6–7.

Coalition for the International Criminal Court, 'Regional Reports' *ICC Monitor* (New York, August 1997) 11.

Dickens A, 'Legalese Aside, NGOs Want Independent, Effective Court' *Terra Viva* (Rome, 16 June 1998) 7.

———, 'Women-Friendly Tribunal Sought' *Terra Viva* (Rome, 17 June 1998) 8.

Dicker, R., 'S. African Governments Adopt Common Approach to ICC Ratification' *ICC Monitor* (New York, August 1999) 3.

Gormley, L., 'Rhonda Copelon Obituary' *The Guardian* (London, 24 May 2010) <www.theguardian.com/law/2010/may/24/rhonda-copelon-obituary> accessed 6 November 2014.

Haq F, 'Alliances Cut Through North-South Divide' *Terra Viva* (Rome, 22 June 1998) 1.

———, 'Annan Throws Down Gauntlet' *Terra Viva* (Rome, 16 June 1998) 1.

Hevesi, D., 'Rhonda Copelon, Lawyer in Groundbreaking Rights Cases, Dies at 65' *The New York Times* (New York, 8 May 2010) <www.nytimes.com/2010/05/09/nyregion/09copelon.html?_r=0> accessed 6 November 2014.

Joseph, A., 'Why Did South Africa, Burundi and Gambia Decide to Leave the International Criminal Court?' *The Wire* (1 November 2016) <https://thewire.in/76869/why-did-south-africa-burundi-and-gambia-decide-to-leave-the-international-criminal-court/> accessed 17 July 2017.

Miclat, A., 'A View from the South' *ICC Monitor* (New York, January 1997) 11.

Neuwirth, J., 'Equality Now Calls on Women's Movement to Support the ICC' *ICC Monitor* (New York, January 1997) 8.

Novick, N., 'When Those Meant to Keep the Peace Commit Sexualized Violence' (Women Under Siege, 25 May 2012) <www.womenundersiegeproject.org/blog/entry/when-those-meant-to-keep-the-peace-commit-sexualized-violence> accessed 6 November 2014.

Pace, W.R., 'ICC Treaty Passes Half-Way Mark: Croatia, Paraguay and Andorra Bring Ratifications up to 32' *ICC Monitor* (New York, May 2001) 1.

The Stanley Foundation, 'The New Court: Civil Society's Victory' *Common Ground Radio* (6 October 1998) <www.commongroundradio.org/shows/98/9840.html> accessed 16 February 2015.

Other

Amnesty International, 'Introduction to the NGO Coalition for an International Criminal Court (CICC)' (2000) <www.iccnow.org/documents/AIDocumentCICC_en.pdf> accessed 24 January 2014.

Association for Women's Rights in Development, 'An Interview With Alda Facio' (12 February 2008) <www.awid.org/Library/An-Interview-with-Alda-Facio> accessed 7 November 2014.

Coalition for the International Criminal Court, 'History of the ICC' <www.iccnow.org/?mod=icchistory> accessed 3 December 2013.

———, 'Who We Are & What We Do: Global Partners' <www.iccnow.org/?mod=supporters> accessed 5 December 2013.

Coalition on Women's Human Rights in Conflict Situations, 'RE: The Prosecutor of the Tribunal against Jean-Paul Akayesu: Amicus Brief Respecting Amendment of the Indictment and Supplementation of the Evidence to Ensure the Prosecution of Rape and Other sexual Violence Within the Competence of the Tribunal' (27 May 1997) <www.iccwomen.org/publications/briefs/docs/Prosecutor_v_Akayesu_ICTR.pdf> accessed 13 August 2013.

Diplomatic Conference for the Establishment of International Conventions for the Protection of Victims of War, 'Final Record of the Diplomatic Conference of Geneva of 1949, Vol. 2, Section A' (Federal Political Department Berne 1963) <www.loc.gov/rr/frd/Military_Law/pdf/Dipl-Conf-1949-Final_Vol-1.pdf> accessed 15 August 2013.

Madre, 'Women's Rights Exchange' <www.madre.org/index/press-room-4/womens-rights-exchange-15/network-of-experts-89.html> accessed 7 November 2014.

New Jersey City University, 'Donna Axel' <http://web.njcu.edu/sites/faculty/daxel/content/bio.asp> accessed 7 November 2014.

Ruse, A., 'UNFPA's Sadik Calls for 'Reproductive Freedom' at Annual UN NGO Forum' (C-FAM) <http://t.c-fam.org/en/issues/un-organizations/112-unfpas-sadik-calls-for-reproductive-freedom-at-annual-un-ngo-forum> accessed 7 November 2014.

Women's Caucus for Gender Justice, 'About the Women's Caucus' <www.iccwomen.org/wigjdraft1/Archives/oldWCGJ/aboutcaucus.htm> accessed 6 November 2014.

———, 'The Women's Caucus for Gender Justice Has Received Support from' <http://iccwomen.org/wigjdraft1/Archives/oldWCGJ/index.html> accessed 10 February 2015.

Women's Human Rights Education Institute, 'Faculty Profiles' <http://learnwhr.org/about/> accessed 7 November 2014.

5 The ICC negotiations of war rape and forced marriage

Introduction

After Chapter 4 focused on the identities of actors involved in the International Criminal Court (ICC) negotiations and on what influenced them in general as well as on ways how non-governmental organisations (NGOs) influenced states, the aim of Chapter 5 is to analyse who the key actors were that drove the negotiations of the definitions of war rape and forced marriage in times of armed conflict specifically. It also examines why these driving actors got involved in the ICC negotiations of these two crimes and which international, national or personal values, norms or rules influenced them and their positions.[1] The main goal of Chapter 5 is to examine how these actors interpreted the crimes of war rape and forced marriage.

Chapter 4 showed that international NGOs, in particular the Women's Caucus, played a role in the development of international criminal law regarding sexualised crimes in general, how it came to hold its views and how it influenced states. Chapter 5 presents a more detailed snapshot of two specific sexualised crimes, war rape and forced marriage in times of armed conflict. It demonstrates that the Women's Caucus was a driving actor regarding the criminalisation of war rape and forced marriage as a form of sexual slavery. It is emphasised that NGOs actually did teach their views to states. Regarding the Women's Caucus' opposition, it is shown that the Arab block raised concerns regarding the criminalisation of war rape and sexual slavery, based on their national laws, religious principles and cultural norms. This highlights the tension that existed in the negotiations between issues of national sovereignty and the extent of the ICC's jurisdiction. It also confirms that national normative structures matter in international relations by indicating that domestic norms explain the resistance towards more progressive definitions of war rape and forced marriage in International Criminal Law. Consequently, the crimes were at least partially interpreted as questions of honour. However, the reference to cultural norms also indicates an understanding of rape as a form of structural violence. This was also the

1 See also Chapter 4.

approach taken by the Women's Caucus in regard to both war rape and forced marriage.

Chapter 5 is divided into two parts. First, it focuses on the crime of rape, then on forced marriage. For both, developments in the PrepCom, Rome Conference and PrepCom2 are analysed in turn. Regarding the crime of rape, the discussions and outcomes of the Ad Hoc Committee and the Zutphen inter-sessional meeting are also mentioned.

Rape

The Ad Hoc Committee on the Establishment of an International Criminal Court

The Ad Hoc Committee was formed by the United Nations General Assembly (UNGA) in 1995 to review the International Law Commission (ILC) draft statute for an international criminal court and to consider arranging an international conference to continue the process of its realisation. To this purpose, the Ad Hoc Committee met twice and submitted its report to the UNGA in 1995.[2]

The following paragraphs discuss the ILC draft statute and the work of the Ad Hoc Committee on the subject of war rape. They analyse the identities and understandings of actors involved in the discussion of the crime of war rape at the early stages of the ICC negotiations.

The ILC's draft statute[3] lists the categories of crimes the ICC was to have jurisdiction over without elaborating on their content. The annex lists the fourth Geneva Convention and Protocol Additional to the Geneva Conventions of 12 August 1949, and relating to the Protection of Victims of International Armed Conflicts (Additional Protocol I) which explicitly include the crime of rape. In its commentary on Article 20, the ILC referenced Article 5 of the International Criminal Tribunal for the former Yugoslavia (ICTY) statute which also includes rape as a crime against humanity. Rape could therefore be considered to be included in the ILC draft statute by reference.

Based on this, some delegations at the 1995 Ad Hoc Committee identified sexualised war violence as an issue and called for the inclusion of rape and other similar offences as war crimes and crimes against humanity in the statute of a

2 Ad Hoc Committee on the Establishment of an International Criminal Court, 'Report of the Ad Hoc Committee on the Establishment of an International Criminal Court' (6 September 1995) UN Doc A/50/22 <www.legal-tools.org/doc/b50da8/> accessed 8 August 2017.

3 International Law Commission, 'Report of the International Law Commission on the Work of Its Forty-Sixth Session, 2 May–22 July 1994' (1994) UN Doc A/49/10 Chapter II <www.legal-tools.org/doc/f73459/> accessed 18 August 2017.

permanent international criminal court.[4] At this early stage in the negotiation process, two international NGOs supported this. Amnesty International and the International Commission of Jurists, however, did not advocate the inclusion of rape as a crime in and of itself that could constitute a war crime or a crime against humanity if the general qualifications are met. Instead, Amnesty International spoke out for the inclusion of rape as an act potentially constituting torture.[5] The International Commission of Jurists advocated the inclusion of 'outrageous assaults on personal dignity, such as sexual assault and enforced prostitution, (in both cases when used as a political weapon)'[6] as a crime against humanity. The 1996 Draft Code of Crimes includes rape as a crime against humanity[7] as well as 'outrages upon personal dignity in violation of international humanitarian law, in particular [...] rape'.[8]

Delegates were aware that rape as an outrage upon personal dignity invokes outdated, victim-centred notions of honour instead of stressing that rape is a violation of a person's integrity and (sexual) autonomy. Instead of codifying unacceptable conduct, including rape as an outrage upon personal dignity in the draft statute legitimised the view of war rape as an honour crime. Arguably, however, categorising war rape in this way can also be interpreted to have been recognition that some societies see rape as an honour crime. A compromise would have been a view of rape as a violation of honour being an aggravating factor rather than an element of the crime.[9]

The Preparatory Committee on the Establishment of an International Criminal Court (PrepCom)

Following the Ad Hoc Committee's recommendations, the UNGA created the PrepCom to 'combine further discussions [of issues] with the drafting of texts, with a view to preparing a consolidated text of a convention for an international criminal court as a next step towards consideration by a conference of

4 Ad Hoc Committee on the Establishment of an International Criminal Court (n 2) para 76.

5 Christopher Keith Hall, 'Challenges Ahead for the United Nations Preparatory Committee Drafting a Statute for a Permanent International Criminal Court' (1996) Amnesty International 13 <www.iccnow.org/documents/AIPreCommittee1996_en.pdf> accessed 5 December 2013.

6 International Commission of Jurists, 'Third ICJ Position Paper' (August 1995) <www.iccnow.org/documents/1PrepCmt3rdPositionPaperICJ.pdf> accessed 5 December 2013.

7 International Law Commission 'Draft Code of Crimes against the Peace and Security of Mankind' (17 July 1996) 51 UN GAOR Supp (No. 10) at 14, UN Doc A/CN.4/L.532, corr.1, corr.3 art 18(j) <www.legal-tools.org/doc/5e4532/> accessed 9 August 2017.

8 International Law Commission 'Draft Code of Crimes against the Peace and Security of Mankind' (n 7) art 20(d).

9 Interview 19 (26 November 2014); Valerie Oosterveld, 'Sexual Slavery and the International Criminal Court: Advancing International Law' (2004) 25 *Michigan Journal of International Law* 605, 613.

plenipotentiaries'.[10] Between March 1996 and April 1998, the PrepCom met six times at the United Nations (UN) headquarters in New York. In January 1998, the inter-sessional meeting in Zutphen, the Netherlands, took place to technically consolidate and restructure the draft articles into a draft statute.[11]

The following sections analyse the PrepCom negotiations of the crime of war rape. They cover the first, third, fifth and sixths PrepCom session as well as the Zutphen inter-sessional meeting because war rape was explicitly discussed in these sessions. Therefore, they shed light on the key actors in the negotiations of war rape, what influenced them, and how they understood the crime.

First session, March/April 1996

Following on from the Ad Hoc Committee's work, consensus existed in the first PrepCom session held in March/April 1996 that definitions of crimes need to be included in the ICC statute to make it more specific and meet the requirement of legality. International rules in the form of international conventions and statutes, as well as the *ad hoc* tribunals' definitions of crimes against humanity, were considered as precedents. However, they were seen as not clear enough and in need of further elaboration.[12] On war crimes, state delegations spoke out for the inclusion of, amongst others, the 1907 Hague rules, the grave breaches provisions of the Geneva Conventions, Common Article 3 and relevant provisions of Additional Protocol I and II as well as the ICTY and International Criminal Tribunal for Rwanda (ICTR) instruments in the statute of an international criminal court.[13]

The PrepCom's report on its proceedings during its first session can be interpreted as male, creating a hierarchy of crimes by stating that crimes like murder, extermination and enslavement, but not rape, need clarification. Therefore, the PrepCom Chairman Adriaan Bos[14] and the delegations of Japan,[15] the Netherlands,[16] New Zealand[17] and the United Kingdom of Great Britain

10 Interview 19 (n 9).
11 Coalition for the International Criminal Court, 'History of the ICC' <www.iccnow.org/?mod=icchistory> accessed 3 December 2013.
12 Elizabeth Wilmshurst, 'International Criminal Court: PrepCom 25 March–12 April 1996' (30 March 1996); Elizabeth Wilmshurst, 'International Criminal Court: PrepCom 25 March–12 April 1996' (15 April 1996).
13 Wilmshurst, 'International Criminal Court: PrepCom 25 March–12 April 1996' (n 12).
14 PrepCom, 'Chairman's Informal Text No 2: Article 20 Quarter, Crimes against Humanity' (29 March 1996) UN Doc A/AC.249/1996/WG.1/IP.2 <www.legal-tools.org/doc/32b618/> accessed 18 August 2017.
15 PrepCom, 'Crimes against Humanity (Japanese Text)' (26 March 1996) <www.legal-tools.org/doc/d21c80/> accessed 7 February 2014.
16 PrepCom, 'Crimes against Humanity (Delegation of the Netherlands)' (27 March 1996) <www.legal-tools.org/doc/63f87a/> accessed 7 February 2014.
17 PrepCom, 'Crimes against Humanity (Delegation of New Zealand)' (30 March 1996) <www.legal-tools.org/doc/10ff0d/> accessed 7 February 2014.

and Northern Ireland (UK)[18] submitted proposals to add crimes of sexualised violence, either in the text or in footnotes, without elaborating on the acts. The proposals include rape committed on national or religious grounds,[19] as part of a campaign of ethnic cleansing[20] and as an outrage upon personal dignity.[21] Resonating with Amnesty International's proposal mentioned above and Article 3 of the ICTR statute, it was also suggested in the first PrepCom session to list rape and serious sexual assault together with torture as a form of cruel treatment.[22] In an informal text, the chairman also proposed to include rape and serious sexual assault as a crime against humanity.[23] The potential inclusion of a reference to other serious assaults of a sexual nature, however, creates and perpetuates a hierarchy of acts of sexualised violence, assuming that acts falling short of a physical invasion are less serious than acts of rape. This, however, may be contrary to the experiences of survivors.[24]

The Chairman's Revised Informal Text on war crimes includes rape in square brackets as violence to life, health and physical or mental well-being of persons.[25] Comparable to the proposals of Austria,[26] Egypt[27] and New Zealand,[28] but

18 PrepCom, 'Article 20 Quater: Crimes against Humanity (Delegation of the United Kingdom)' (26 March 1996) <www.legal-tools.org/doc/d7a59c/> accessed 7 February 2014.

19 PrepCom, 'Report of the Preparatory Committee on the Establishment of an International Criminal Court, Volume I' (13 September 1996) UN Doc A/51/22 [Vol. I] para 98 <www.legal-tools.org/doc/e75432/> accessed 18 August 2017.

20 United Nations, 'Crimes against Humanity Must be Precisely Defined Say Speakers in Preparatory Committee for International Court' Press Release L/2763/Rev.1 3rd Meeting (AM) (26 March 1996) <www.un.org/press/en/1996/19960326.l2763.html> accessed 29 April 2015. For a discussion of individuals and communities as targets of war rape see Chapters 3 and 8.

21 PrepCom, 'Proposal by Austria on Crimes against Humanity' (26 March 1996) <www.legal-tools.org/doc/f6d477/> accessed 7 February 2014. For a discussion of the categorisation of rape as an outrage upon personal dignity see below.

22 PrepCom, 'Report of the Preparatory Committee on the Establishment of an International Criminal Court, Volume II' (13 September 1996) UN Doc A/51/22[Vol. II] 68 <www.legal-tools.org/doc/03b284/> accessed 9 August 2017.

23 PrepCom, 'Report of the Preparatory Committee on the Establishment of an International Criminal Court, Volume II' (n 22) 65.

24 Women's Caucus for Gender Justice, 'Priority Concerns Related to the Elements Annex' (February 1999) <www.iccwomen.org/wigjdraft1/Archives/oldWCGJ/icc/iccpc/021999pc/pcconcerns.htm> accessed 22 January 2014.

25 PrepCom, 'Report of the Preparatory Committee on the Establishment of an International Criminal Court, Volume II' (n 22) 61; see also PrepCom, 'Draft: Optional Approaches to the Definition of War Crimes (Delegation of Egypt)' (29 March 1996) <www.legal-tools.org/doc/d78835/> accessed 7 February 2014. See William A. Schabas, *An Introduction to the International Criminal Court* (Cambridge University Press 2007) 658: Square brackets indicated that the inclusion of a particular element or a particular wording was still under discussion.

26 PrepCom, 'Proposal by Austria on Serious Violations of the Laws and Customs Applicable in Armed Conflicts' (2 April 1996) <www.legal-tools.org/doc/302b0d/> accessed 7 February 2014.

27 PrepCom, 'Draft: Optional Approaches to the Definition of War Crimes (Delegation of Egypt)' (n 25).

28 PrepCom, 'War Crimes (Delegation of New Zealand)' (30 March 1996) <www.legal-tools.org/doc/af17c3/> accessed 7 February 2014.

contrary to the Chairman's Informal Text No 4,[29] the crime was also listed under 'outrages upon personal dignity, in particular humiliating and degrading treatment, rape, enforced prostitution and any form of indecent assault'[30] in international and non-international conflicts. Creating a link between rape and indecent assault as well as humiliating and degrading treatment respectively has a similar effect as categorising rape as an outrage upon personal dignity and an honour crime discussed above.[31]

Contrary to the majority of proposals that advocated adding crimes of sexualised violence but did not elaborate on the acts, the US suggested three definitions of rape. Initially, it defined the elements of the crime against humanity of rape to be '(1) [t]hat the accused committed an act of sexual intercourse or forcible sodomy with a person; (2) [t]hat the act of sexual intercourse or forcible sodomy was done unlawfully by force and without consent'.[32] 'Sexual intercourse' was understood as penetration of any part of the body with a part of the body or an object. 'Forcible' was determined to include (threat of) force against the victim or another person.[33] Disconnecting rape and sodomy but establishing a connection between rape and enforced prostitution, the US developed a second definition of rape as a forced sexual act.[34] A third definition that was also included in the PrepCom's report on its proceedings during its first session defines the crime against humanity of rape as 'causing a person to

29 PrepCom, 'Chairman's Informal Text No 4: Article 20 ter, War Crimes' (4 April 1996) UN Doc A/AC.249/1996/WG.1/IP.4 <www.legal-tools.org/doc/560c38/> accessed 18 August 2017.

30 PrepCom, 'Report of the Preparatory Committee on the Establishment of an International Criminal Court, Volume II' (n 22) 61.

31 Women's Caucus for Gender Justice, 'Recommendations and Commentary for December 1997 PrepCom on the Establishment of an International Criminal Court' (December 1997) <www.iccnow.org/documents/5PrepComRecommWomensC.pdf> accessed 4 December 2013. For further discussion on the categorisation of rape as an honour crime see Chapter 3.

32 PrepCom, 'Redraft of the ILC Article 20 on ICC Jurisdiction with Proposed Elements (Delegation of the United States)' (22 March 1996) <www.legal-tools.org/doc/efc778/> accessed 7 February 2014. See Federal Bureau of Investigation, 'Frequently Asked Questions about the Change in the UCR Definition of Rape' (11 December 2014) <www.fbi.gov/about-us/cjis/ucr/recent-program-updates/new-rape-definition-frequently-asked-questions> accessed 19 January 2015: Similarly, the US Federal Bureau of Investigation's definition of rape that was in use during the ICC negotiations defined rape in terms of coercion and absence of consent. The definition reads: 'The carnal knowledge of a female forcibly and against her will.' This definition focused on the rape of women and ignored offenses involving oral or anal invasion, the use of objects and rapes of men. The current Federal Bureau of Investigation definition of rape, however, addresses these issues and defines rape as: 'Penetration, no matter how slight, of the vagina or anus with any body part or object, or oral penetration by a sex organ of another person, without the consent of the victim.'

33 ibid.

34 PrepCom, 'For Annex to Statute: Elements Related to Article on Crimes against Humanity (Delegation of the United States)' (27 March 1996) <www.iccnow.org/documents/USCrimesAgainstHumanity.pdf> accessed 5 December 2013.

engage in or to submit to a sexual act by force or threat of force'.[35] The US' definitions of rape show a move away from an initial coercion- and consent-based definition to a purely coercion-based understanding. The definitions also show a move away from the use of the term 'penetration' to a broader and more neutral definition of rape as a forced sexual act. While the first definition explicitly includes sexual acts committed with objects, it appears to be implied in the second and third definition. The second and third definition are gender-neutral. They define rape as a forced sexual act without unnecessarily specifying the assailant, their sex/gender or the specifics of the sexual act. Mentioning force or threat of force, the US definitions can also be interpreted to be broad enough to include non-physical coercion.[36]

Third session, February 1997

The USA's advocacy for gender-neutral rape definitions was in line with awareness-raising efforts launched by women's organisations in the course of the third PrepCom session in February 1997.[37] In addition to advocating broad and gender-neutral definitions of rape, the number of state proposals indicating an honour-based, and therefore victim-centred, understanding of the crime made it crucial for women's organisations to place a focus on the crime of the perpetrator, not on the victim. It had to be stressed that the victim is not responsible for what happened to her.

Based on research by the International Committee of the Red Cross (ICRC),[38] New Zealand and Switzerland[39] submitted a proposal understanding rape as

35 PrepCom, 'For Annex to Statute: Elements Related to Article on Crimes against Humanity (Delegation of the United States)' (2 April 1996) <www.legal-tools.org/doc/4d62f1/> accessed 7 February 2014; PrepCom, 'Report of the Preparatory Committee on the Establishment of an International Criminal Court, Volume II' (n 22) 69.

36 Pam Spees, 'Women's Advocacy in the Creation of the International Criminal Court: Changing the Landscape of Justice and Power' (2003) 28 *Signs* 1233, 1241.

37 Nichole Eva Erb, 'Gender-Based Crimes under the Draft Statute of the Permanent International Criminal Court' (1998) 29 *Columbia Human Rights Law Review* 401, 425–426; Athena Gassoumis, Gail Lerner and Mary Marrow, 'Women's Caucus Brings Crimes against Women to Forefront of Debate' *ICC Monitor* (May 1997) 5.

38 International Committee of the Red Cross, 'Commentary: Definition of War Crimes: For the Preparatory Committee on the Establishment of an International Criminal Court (1–12 December 1997 Session)' (14 February 1997) <www.iccnow.org/documents/3PretCmtWarCrimesRedCross.pdf> accessed 7 May 2015.

39 PrepCom, 'Decisions Taken by the Preparatory Committee at Its Session from 11 to 21 February 1997' (12 March 1997) A/AC.249/1997/L.5 <www.legal-tools.org/doc/c0d16c/> accessed 9 August 2017; PrepCom, 'Working Paper Submitted by the Delegations of New Zealand and Switzerland' (14 February 1997) UN Doc A/AC.249/1997/WG.1/DP.2 <www.legal-tools.org/doc/7ba0b8/> accessed 18 August 2017; see also PrepCom, 'Draft Consolidated Text: War Crimes' (20 February 1997) UN Doc A/AC.249/1997/WG.1/CRP.2 <www.legal-tools.org/doc/4d5877/> accessed 18 August 2017; PrepCom, 'German Synoptical Working Paper on War Crimes' (25 June 1997)

constituting a grave breach of the Geneva Conventions by wilfully causing great suffering. This indicates that non-state actors taught their views on sexualised crimes as breaches of International Humanitarian Law to states. In the first PrepCom session, New Zealand spoke out for the inclusion of rape as an outrage upon personal dignity. As mentioned above, this view is victim-centred. Rape as wilfully causing great suffering, in contrast, focuses on the acts of the perpetrator. Even though this can be interpreted as progress, it still misrepresents the character of sexualised violence as its purpose goes beyond harming the victim.[40]

To understand the advancement of including rape as a grave breach, an understanding of the particular time in the ICC negotiation process is important. Throughout the negotiations, but especially in the early stages, actors did not want to risk losing support for the court by pushing the war crimes provisions too far or by including new crimes. Their fall-back position was to copy the grave breaches provisions of the Geneva Conventions and to adopt them one-to-one as war crimes under the jurisdiction of an international criminal court. This way, the ICC grave breaches provisions would save existing provisions and war crimes would at least be included in the new statute. They could always be amended in a review. In addition, actors aimed to illustrate crimes in the grave breaches provisions that were not itemised but indicated. Due to international law's gender-blind past where rape was treated as collateral damage of every war,[41] rape had to be exemplified, for example, as an act whereby the perpetrator wilfully causes great suffering to the victim which constitutes a grave breach of the Geneva Conventions. This way, even if actors would have fallen back on the narrow list of war crimes, only including grave breaches, rape would have been included in the ICC statute.[42] In contrast to this position advocating the one-to-one adoption of the grave breaches provisions of the Geneva Conventions, the ICRC proposed not to cut and paste from these instruments but to include as much as possible. Since an international criminal court should have jurisdiction over the most serious crimes of concern to the international

---

<www.legal-tools.org/doc/0d8997/> accessed 7 February 2014; PrepCom, 'Preliminary Text: War Crimes' (20 February 1997) UN Doc A/AC.249/1997/WG.1/IP/REV.1 <www.legal-tools.org/doc/596e8a/> accessed 18 August 2017; Cate Steains, 'Gender Issues' in Roy Lee (ed), *The International Criminal Court: The Making of the Rome Statute: Issues, Negotiations, Results* (Kluwer Law International 1999) 365.

40 Women's Caucus for Gender Justice, 'Recommendations and Commentary for December 1997 PrepCom' (n 31).

41 Kelly Dawn Askin, 'Women and International Humanitarian Law' in Kelly Dawn Askin and Dorean M. Koenig (eds), *Women and International Human Rights Law* (Transnational Publishers 1999); Susan Brownmiller, *Against our Will: Men, Women and Rape* (Penguin Books 1977); Gabriela Mischkowski, 'Sexualisierte Kriegsgewalt: Strafverfolgung und Wahrheitsfindung' in medica mondiale and Karin Griese (eds), *Sexualisierte Kriegsgewalt und ihre Folgen: Handbuch zur Unterstützung traumatisierter Frauen in verschiedenen Arbeitsfeldern* (2nd edn, Mabuse-Verlag 2006).

42 Interview 18 (25 June 2014).

community, it should cover customary law and serious violations of widely accepted treaties.[43] This position could be perceived as conservative as a focus is placed on clarifying existing law but not on developing new crimes. However, it was in line with the ICRC's role as the guardian of international humanitarian law. The outcome of this discussion was the exclusion of any direct references to rape in the grave breaches and Common Article 3 provisions of the draft statute. However, based on the Geneva Conventions and Additional Protocol I, and especially based on Protocol Additional to the Geneva Conventions of 12 August 1949, and relating to the Protection of Victims of Non-International Armed Conflicts (Additional Protocol II) and the Instructions for the Government of Armies of the United States in the Field, General Order No 100 (Lieber Code), rape was discussed as being illustrative of an outrage upon personal dignity and a violation to life and health, rather than a substantive addition to the grave breaches provisions of the Geneva Conventions.[44]

'[O]utrages upon personal dignity, in particular rape, enforced prostitution and other sexual violence of comparable gravity'[45] was listed as other serious violations of the laws and customs of war. In cases of internal conflict, different options regarding outrages upon personal dignity and wilfully causing great suffering to body or mind were proposed as violations of Common Article 3. Comparable to a working paper submitted by New Zealand and Switzerland,[46] they all establish a connection between rape and enforced prostitution.[47] These different suggestions illustrate the attempt to crystallise what was recognised by states as reflecting customary international law rather than to develop new crimes.[48] This includes the discussion regarding the relationship between the

43 Interview 13 (15 May 2014); International Committee of the Red Cross, 'Commentary: Definition of War Crimes' (n 38).

44 ibid.

45 PrepCom, 'Decisions Taken by the Preparatory Committee at Its Session from 11 to 21 February 1997' (n 39); see also PrepCom, 'Draft Consolidated Text: War Crimes' (n 39); PrepCom, 'German Synoptical Working Paper on War Crimes' (n 39); PrepCom, 'Informal Working Paper on War Crimes' (14 July 1997) UN Doc A/AC.249/1997/WG.1/IP/REV.1 <www.legal-tools.org/doc/39864b/> accessed 18 August 2017; PrepCom, 'Informal Working Paper on War Crimes' (31 October 1997) UN Doc A/AC.249/1997/WG.1/IP <www.legal-tools.org/doc/435c11/> accessed 18 August 2017; PrepCom, 'Preliminary Text: War Crimes' (n 39).

46 PrepCom, 'Working Paper Submitted by the Delegations of New Zealand and Switzerland' (n 39).

47 PrepCom, 'Decisions Taken by the Preparatory Committee at Its Session from 11 to 21 February 1997' (n 39); see also PrepCom, 'Informal Working Paper on War Crimes' (14 July 1997) (n 45); PrepCom, 'Informal Working Paper on War Crimes' (31 October 1997) (n 45).

48 Interview 13 (n 43); Wilmshurst, 'International Criminal Court: PrepCom 25 March–12 April 1996' (n 12); Knut Dörmann, 'War Crimes under the Rome Statute of the International Criminal Court, with a Special Focus on the Negotiations on the Elements of Crimes' in Armin von Bogdandy and Rüdiger Wolfrum (eds), *Max Planck Yearbook of United Nations Law* (Volume 7, Martinus Nijhoff Publishers 2003) 345.

crime of rape and grave breaches of the Geneva Conventions, Additional Protocol I and II, Common Article 3, and the Lieber Code respectively. Here, it becomes apparent that international rules matter in international relations and law-making.

While existing international rules strongly influenced actors, they were concerned about the regression of categorising acts of sexualised war violence as outrages upon personal dignity, focussing on honour and chastity.[49] Following feminist calls for the separate mention of sexualised crimes, it was suggested to list rape and other sexualised crimes in a separate category distinct from other crimes.[50] '[R]ape or other sexual abuse [of comparable gravity,] or enforced prostitution'[51] was included in the draft statute as a crime against humanity. This was supported by Amnesty International and the ICRC, which also understood rape to potentially constitute torture and inhumane treatment.[52] However, as the brackets indicate, the qualification 'of comparable gravity' could potentially be limiting and exclude sexualised abuses falling short of a physical invasion. Thus, it also creates and perpetuates a hierarchy of sexualised crimes. Based on male points of view, it constructs crimes falling short of physical invasion as lesser crimes than rape. The risk of the qualification 'of comparable gravity' limiting the acts that could be covered by this provision was aggravated by the fact that rape, unlike other listed crimes against humanity, was not defined in the third PrepCom session.

Fifth session, December 1997

The fifth PrepCom session in December 1997 saw steps forward and backward regarding the criminalisation of acts of sexualised war violence. The February 1997 progress of introducing an alternative definition of grave breaches including rape in an international criminal court's statute was not followed up so as to reflect the exact grave breaches language of the Geneva Conventions.[53] However, a reference to grave breaches was included in Article 20(B)(p bis) on sexualised war crimes.[54] The acceptance of this wording was facilitated by the

49 Oosterveld, 'Sexual Slavery and the International Criminal Court' (n 9) 612; see also Steains (n 39) 365.

50 Interview 6 (2 April 2014); Interview 13 (n 43); Women's Caucus for Gender Justice, 'Recommendations and Commentary for December 1997 PrepCom' (n 31).

51 PrepCom, 'Decisions Taken by the Preparatory Committee at its Session from 11 to 21 February 1997' (n 39).

52 Interview 6 (n 50); Amnesty International, 'Making the Right Choices – Part I – Defining the Crimes and Permissible Defences and Initiating a Prosecution' (January 1997) 29 <www.iccnow.org/documents/ALMakingRightChoises97PartI.pdf> accessed 5 December 2013; International Committee of the Red Cross, 'Commentary: Definition of War Crimes' (n 38).

53 Steains (n 39) 365.

54 PrepCom, 'Decisions Taken by the Preparatory Committee at Its Session Held from 1 to 12 December 1997' (18 December 1997) UN Doc A/AC.249/1997/L.9/Rev.1

understanding that the reference to grave breaches in Article 20(B)(p bis) would introduce a specific threshold, rather than be an element requiring acts of sexualised violence also to amount to one of the crimes mentioned in the grave breaches provisions of the Geneva Conventions, or indicating that sexualised crimes could already be prosecuted as grave breaches.[55] Article 20(D)(e bis) covering other serious violations of the laws and customs applicable in internal armed conflicts links the same list of crimes to serious violation of Common Article 3.[56] Both Article 20(B)(p bis) and (D)(e bis) again confirm that international rules, in the form of the Geneva Conventions, matter in international relations and law-making. They are upheld and used as points of reference.

Against opposition based on the male perception that acts of sexualised violence would already be recognised as other crimes like torture and genocide,[57] a proposal to further delineate the list of these crimes to include 'rape, sexual slavery, enforced prostitution, enforced pregnancy, enforced sterilization, and any other form of sexual violence'[58] as war crimes in international and internal conflicts and as crimes against humanity was widely supported.[59] This demonstrates the joint effort by state actors like the UK to consider and support the demands of the Women's Caucus.[60] It is a successful example of the Caucus

<www.legal-tools.org/doc/787a4d/> accessed 9 August 2017; see also PrepCom, 'Informal Working Paper on War Crimes' (3 December 1997) UN Doc A/AC.249/1997/WG.1/CRP.7 <www.legal-tools.org/doc/8e28b2/> accessed 18 August 2017; PrepCom, 'Informal Working Paper on War Crimes, Addendum' (4 December 1997) UN Doc A/AC.249/1997/WG.1/CRP.7/Add.1 <www.legal-tools.org/doc/d3b1e7/> accessed 18 August 2017; PrepCom, 'Informal Working Paper on War Crimes, Option B (Delegations of the United Kingdom and Germany)' (12 December 1997) <www.legal-tools.org/doc/5adc48/> accessed 7 February 2014.

55 Knut Dörmann, *Elements of War Crimes under the Rome Statute of the International Criminal Court: Sources and Commentary* (Cambridge University Press 2003) 332; Dörmann, 'War Crimes under the Rome Statute of the International Criminal Court' (n 48) 394–395.

56 PrepCom, 'Decisions Taken by the Preparatory Committee at Its Session Held from 1 to 12 December 1997' (n 54); see also PrepCom, 'Informal Working Paper on War Crimes' (n 54); PrepCom, 'Informal Working Paper on War Crimes, Option B (Delegations of the United Kingdom and Germany)' (n 54).

57 Rhonda Copelon, 'Gender Crimes as War Crimes: Integrating Crimes against Women into International Criminal Law' (2000) 46 *McGill Law Journal* 217, 217.

58 PrepCom, 'Decisions Taken by the Preparatory Committee at Its Session Held from 1 to 12 December 1997' (n 54); Elizabeth Wilmshurst, 'Annex to the ICC Report: Provisions of the Statute' (23 September 1998): The United Kingdom of Great Britain and Northern Ireland (UK) chaired an informal meeting resulting in small adjustments to the language of the list of sexualised crimes.

59 Interview 13 (n 43); Human Rights Watch, *Justice in Balance: Recommendations for an Independent and Effective International Criminal Court* (Human Rights Watch 1998); Women's Caucus for Gender Justice, 'Recommendations and Commentary for December 1997 PrepCom' (n 31).

60 Wilmshurst, 'Annex to the ICC Report' (n 58).

'educating'[61] states, even though the names of crimes that were eventually accepted differed from the ones initially proposed.[62] To some extent, the establishment of this list of sexualised war crimes and especially the drafting of their elements was a creative legislative exercise as these forms of violence had not constituted war crimes in their own right before the adoption of the Rome Statute and related international humanitarian law rules had not been very precise.[63] Only rape and forced prostitution were explicitly mentioned in the previous PrepCom negotiations. Therefore, the achievement to explicitly include this list of sexualised crimes in the Rome Statute shows that international relations and law-making are not always restricted by existing international normative structures. The extent of this achievement becomes apparent when considering the repeated mantra of the ICC negotiations being a conservative exercise, crystallising existing law but not creating new crimes. Therefore, it was not enough to argue that a form of conduct is wrong and/or a breach of international (customary) law. It had to be recognised as a crime under international (customary) law, resulting in hunts for the slightest hints to substantiate arguments.[64]

In the view of the Women's Caucus, the crimes mentioned in the list of sexualised crimes are forms of gender violence. Gender violence was understood as a form of discrimination exclusively or disproportionally against women because of their sex and gender and the attached social meaning. Therefore, gender violence is structural violence as social structures such as gender roles or power inequalities between men and women systematically harm or otherwise disadvantage women. The Caucus also demonstrated an understanding of rape as sexual violence as a form of gender violence and therefore a form of structural violence as it attacks a person's gender identity. The Women's Caucus' elaborations on gender violence as structural violence stress that socially constructed gender stereotypes or power differences between men and women underlie the perpetration of rape.[65]

61 Interview 19 (n 9).

62 Michael Cottier, 'Article 8 War Crimes para. 2 (b) (xxii) Rape and Other Forms of Sexual Violence' in Otto Triffterer (ed), *Commentary on the Rome Statute of the International Criminal Court: Observers' Notes, Article by Article* (2nd edn, CH Beck 2008) 435; Women's Caucus for Gender Justice, 'Recommendations and Commentary for December 1997 PrepCom' (n 31). For more information see for example Kristen Boon, 'Rape and Forced Pregnancy under the ICC Statute: Human Dignity, Autonomy, and Consent' (2001) 32 *Columbia Human Rights Law Review* 625; Marlies Glasius, 'Who Is the Real Civil Society? Women's Groups versus Pro-Family Groups at the International Criminal Court Negotiations' in Jude Howell and Diane Mulligan (eds), *Gender and Civil Society* (Routledge 2004).

63 Cottier (n 62) 435.

64 Interview 18 (n 42).

65 Johan Galtung, 'Violence, Peace, and Peace Research' (1969) 6 *Journal of Peace Research* 167; Women's Caucus for Gender Justice, 'Recommendations and Commentary for December 1997 PrepCom' (n 31).

The inter-sessional meeting in Zutphen, January 1998

The same list of sexualised crimes as put forward in the fifth PrepCom session was included in the Zutphen draft as war crimes in international and internal armed conflicts.[66] The draft also lists 'rape or other sexual abuse [of comparable gravity,] or enforced prostitution' as crimes against humanity.[67] It becomes apparent that the list of sexualised crimes included under the war crimes provisions is broader than the sexualised crimes recognised as potentially amounting to crimes against humanity. It includes not only rape, forced prostitution and other forms of sexualised violence (of comparable gravity), but also sexual slavery, enforced pregnancy and enforced sterilisation. This disparity in the development of sexualised crimes as war crimes and as crimes against humanity continued throughout the PrepCom2 negotiations and the conclusion of the Elements of Crimes.

Sixth session, March/April 1998

In the run-up to the Rome Conference, the US developed a fourth definition of rape that brings together the definitions the delegation developed in the first PrepCom session. In a Reference Paper, the US defined rape broadly as 'attack[ing] a person [...] through acts of a sexual nature'.[68] In a comment, however, it specified that '[r]ape is the forcible penetration, however slight, of any part of the body of another by the accused's sexual organ, or forcible penetration, however slight, of the anal or genital opening of another by any object.'[69] Focusing on body parts, the reference to the 'accused's sexual organ' suggests a male perpetrator even though the general wording is gender-neutral, as pushed for by the Women's Caucus. However, the definition also indicates a more informed understanding of the crime of rape as including oral sex and the use of objects in addition to vaginal and anal invasion. Even though oral sex is not explicitly mentioned, this recognises that women can also be perpetrators and men victims of rape.

The United Nations Conference of Plenipotentiaries on the Establishment of an International Criminal Court (Rome Conference)

Based on the PrepCom's draft, the UNGA convened the United Nations Conference of Plenipotentiaries on the Establishment of an International Criminal Court (Rome Conference) from 15 June to 17 July 1998 in Rome, Italy. The

66 PrepCom, 'Report of the Inter-Sessional Meeting from 19 to 30 January 1998 in Zutphen, The Netherlands' (4 February 1998) UN Doc A/AC249/1998/L.13 art 20(B) (p bis), art 20(D)(e bis) <www.legal-tools.org/doc/7ba9a4/> accessed 9 August 2017.
67 PrepCom, 'Report of the Inter-Sessional Meeting from 19 to 30 January 1998 in Zutphen, The Netherlands' (n 66) art 1(g).
68 PrepCom, 'Reference Paper Elements of Offenses for the International Criminal Court (Delegation of the United States)' (27 March 1998) <www.iccnow.org/documents/USElementsofOffensesMarch98.pdf> accessed 5 December 2013.
69 ibid.

purpose of the Rome Conference was to finalise and adopt a convention on the establishment of an international criminal court.[70]

At the Rome Conference, the contents of the war crimes and crimes against humanity provisions, but not their definitions, were extensively discussed primarily in informal sessions. The official records of plenary meetings show that many state delegates favoured the general inclusion of crimes of sexualised war violence in the ICC's jurisdiction as a preventive measure.[71] Mr Abdullah M Mohammed Ibrahim Al Sheikh of Saudi Arabia, for example, indicated that the inclusion of the crime of rape under the jurisdiction of the ICC was uncontroversial.[72] State delegates were supported in their position regarding the inclusion of sexualised crimes in the Rome Statute by international organisations and international and regional NGOs like Amnesty International, the Asian Centre for Women's Human Rights and the United Nations Children's Fund.[73] However, despite extensive discussions, the delegates did not come to an agreement on paragraph '(p bis) committing rape, sexual slavery, enforced prostitution, enforced pregnancy, enforced sterilization, and any other form of sexual violence also constituting a grave breach of the Geneva Conventions'[74] as war crimes. Regarding crimes against humanity, eventually, a compromise text that explicitly included the crime of rape received wide support. This compromise text created the only way out of repeating, though not resolving, arguments regarding specifications

70 Coalition for the International Criminal Court, 'History of the ICC' (n 11).

71 Diplomatic Conference of Plenipotentiaries on the Establishment of an International Criminal Court, 'Official Records of the United Nations Diplomatic Conference of Plenipotentiaries on the Establishment of an International Criminal Court, Vol. II, Rome, 15 June–17 July 1998' (2002) UN Doc A/CONR183/13 (Vol. II) 61–129 <www.legal-tools.org/doc/78fea6/> accessed 9 August 2017: The state delegates in favour included Australia, Austria, Bangladesh, Belgium, Bosnia and Herzegovina, Canada, Chile, Costa Rica, Denmark, Finland, Ghana, Israel, Kuwait, Lithuania, Luxemburg, Mexico, Norway, the Philippines, Portugal, Republic of Korea, Samoa, Slovenia, Spain, Trinidad and Tobago, and the USA. Ms Aguiar, delegate of the Dominican Republic, can be understood to support a wider range of acts of sexualised violence to be recognised under the Rome Statute. Without going into further detail, she voiced concerns 'that some types of crimes used as methods of war, for instance, sex abuse against women and children, were not contained in the document'.

72 Diplomatic Conference of Plenipotentiaries on the Establishment of an International Criminal Court, 'Official Records of the United Nations Diplomatic Conference of Plenipotentiaries on the Establishment of an International Criminal Court, Vol. II' (n 71) 293.

73 Diplomatic Conference of Plenipotentiaries on the Establishment of an International Criminal Court, 'Official Records of the United Nations Diplomatic Conference of Plenipotentiaries on the Establishment of an International Criminal Court, Vol. II' (n 71) 61–129; Lloyd Axworthy 'A Court That Is Worth Having' *Terra Viva* (Rome, 15 June 1998) 6–7.

74 Diplomatic Conference of Plenipotentiaries on the Establishment of an International Criminal Court, 'Report of the Preparatory Committee on the Establishment of an International Criminal Court: Addendum' (14 April 1998) UN Doc A/CONF.183/2/Add.1 20 <www.legal-tools.org/doc/816405/> accessed 11 August 2017.

and definitions already put forward in the PrepCom.[75] It was the only way to reach a solution in the extremely limited time period of six weeks that the Rome Conference lasted.[76]

Participants in the Rome Conference did not succeed in defining the elements of crimes. Then again, a large group of delegations considered a binding list of elements unnecessary.[77] At the insistence of the US delegation, however, Article 9 was inserted into the Rome Statute, stating that the elements of crimes would be defined and the definitions would be included at a later date. The USA and a small group of other delegations would have preferred it if binding elements would have been negotiated before the Rome Statute entered into force, especially where provisions traditionally imposed obligations on states now triggered individual criminal responsibility.[78] How important the development of elements of crimes before the Rome Conference was to the delegation is indicated by the fact that it had drafted a full set of elements of crimes against humanity already at PrepCom stage.[79] However, the US showed flexibility in the negotiations of their paper in the PrepCom2.[80]

The Preparatory Commission for the International Criminal Court (PrepCom2)

After the Rome Conference, the PrepCom2 was charged with negotiating complementary documents to the Rome Statute, setting out the ICC's structure, jurisdiction and functions. This would complete the establishment and contribute to the smooth functioning of the court. The PrepCom2 met ten times between February 1999 and July 2002. The following paragraphs, however, only cover the first five PrepCom2 sessions (February 1999 and July 2000) as the negotiations of the Elements of Crimes were completed in the fifth session.[81] The

75 Elizabeth Wilmshurst, 'Report on the Conference for the Establishment of an International Criminal Court: 15 June–17 July 1998' (23 September 1998).

76 Diplomatic Conference of Plenipotentiaries on the Establishment of an International Criminal Court, 'Official Records of the United Nations Diplomatic Conference of Plenipotentiaries on the Establishment of an International Criminal Court, Vol. II' (n 71) 268.

77 Oosterveld, 'Sexual Slavery and the International Criminal Court' (n 9) 627.

78 Wilmshurst, 'Annex to the ICC Report' (n 58); Coalition for the International Criminal Court, 'Definitions of Crimes' *ICC Monitor* (New York, November 1998) 3, 13; Oosterveld, 'Sexual Slavery and the International Criminal Court' (n 9) 627.

79 PrepCom, 'Redraft of the ILC Article 20 on ICC Jurisdiction with Proposed Elements (Delegation of the United States)' (n 32).

80 Interview 12 (15 May 2014); Interview 13 (n 43); Elizabeth Wilmshurst, 'ICC: PrepCom. 16–26 February 1999' (1 March 1999); Dörmann, 'War Crimes under the Rome Statute of the International Criminal Court' (n 48) 350.

81 M. Cherif Bassiouni, *The Legislative History of the International Criminal Court* (Transnational Publishers 2005) 36; Fanny Benedetti, Karine Bonneau and John Washburn, *Negotiating the International Criminal Court: New York to Rome, 1994–1998* (Brill 2013); Antonio Cassese, Paola Gaeta and John R.W.D. Jones (eds), *The Rome Statute of the International Criminal Court: A Commentary* (Volume 1, Oxford University Press

Elements of Crimes are of particular relevance to this research project as they include the definition of war rape which assists the ICC in the interpretation and application of Article 7(1)(g)[82] covering rape as a crime against humanity, and of Article 8(2)(b)(xxii)[83] and Article 8(2)(e)(vi)[84] covering rape as a war crime.[85] The Elements of Crimes differ from the (draft) instruments negotiated previously as the (draft) instruments listed rape as a crime in and of itself as well as constituting other crimes but did not define it. The rape definitions discussed above were proposed by state delegations but not included in the (draft) instruments.

First session, February 1999

Before the PrepCom2's first session in February 1999, the USA drafted two crucial proposals, one on the elements of crimes against humanity and another on the elements of war crimes. Comparable to wordings suggested previously by the US,[86] rape was defined as a situation where

> [t]he accused intended to attack one or more persons through acts of a sexual nature. The accused penetrated any part of the body of another person with the accused's sexual organ, or penetrated the anal or genital opening of another person with any object or other part of the accused's body. The penetration was committed by force.[87]

'Sexual nature' was understood as intentionally touching and arousing the victim, perpetrator or a third person. Linking rape to sexual slavery, the latter

2002); Coalition for the International Criminal Court, 'History of the ICC' (n 11); International Criminal Court, 'Establishment of the Court' <www.icc-cpi.int/en_menus/icc/about%20the%20court/icc%20at%20a%20glance/Pages/establishment%20of%20the%20court.aspx> accessed 28 January 2015; International Criminal Court, 'Factsheet' <www.icc-cpi.int/en_menus/icc/about%20the%20court/icc%20at%20a%20glance/fact-sheets/Pages/fact%20sheets.aspx> accessed 28 January 2015; Roy Lee (ed), *The International Criminal Court: The Making of the Rome Statute: Issues, Negotiations, Results* (Kluwer Law International 1999); Schabas (n 25).

82 Rome Statute of the International Criminal Court (17 July 1998) 2187 UNTS 3 <www.legal-tools.org/doc/7b9af9/> accessed 9 August 2017.

83 Rome Statute (n 82).

84 ibid.

85 ibid art 9(1).

86 PrepCom, 'Reference Paper Elements of Offenses for the International Criminal Court (Delegation of the United States)' (n 68).

87 PrepCom2, 'Proposal Submitted by the United States of America: Draft Elements of Crimes: Addendum' (4 February 1999) UN Doc PCINCC/1999/DP.4/Add.1 (Crimes against Humanity) art 7(1)(g)(1)(2), art 7(1)(g)(1)(3) <www.legal-tools.org/doc/f7f5cc/> accessed 10 August 2017; PrepCom2, 'Proposal Submitted by the United States of America: Draft Elements of Crimes: Addendum' (4 February 1999) UN Doc PCINCC/1999/DP.4/Add.2 (War Crimes) art 8(2)(b)(xxii)(1)(3), art 8(2)(b)(xxii)(1)(4), art 8(2)(e)(vi)(1) <www.legal-tools.org/doc/d6dfdc/> accessed 10 August 2017.

was given as an example of an act of a sexual nature.[88] 'Committed by force' meant that the sexual act was accomplished by direct or indirect coercion, force or threat of force against the victim or a third person, resulting in the victim fearing that she or a third person would be subjected to physical or psychological violence if the victim would not comply. It was also understood to include situations where the accused would take advantage of an inherently coercive environment. However, it was recognised that evidence of consent can negate the force element.[89] In addition to defining rape itself, Article 8(2)(b)(xxii)(1) of the USA's proposal is followed by a comment stating that rape can also amount to other crimes if the essential elements are met.[90] This resonates with a proposition made by the Women's Caucus. The Caucus argued that it is necessary to understand acts of sexualised war violence both as crimes in and of themselves as well as potentially constituting other crimes to avert the danger of marginalising those crimes by not including them when the charges of torture and other general violations are drawn up. This view was supported by a wealth of customary international law and examples from the ICTY and ICTR, demonstrating that international norms and rules mattered in the ICC negotiations. Furthermore, the prohibition against gender discrimination in the application and interpretation of law requires taking acts of sexualised war violence into account when considering charging and prosecuting other crimes.[91] Since the US did not include this understanding in its previous draft elements, it can be assumed that the Women's Caucus taught its views to the US delegation.

Similarly to the view of the US, rape was explicitly included in the suggested comments relating to the crime of genocide in the draft elements of crimes. Following the Women's Caucus' view, it is stated that acts of rape can cause serious bodily or mental harm and can constitute genocide if the essential elements are met.[92]

The Women's Caucus saw that state delegations were divided about how to define rape and became more open to a wording similar to how the crime was

88 PrepCom2, 'Proposal Submitted by the United States of America: Draft Elements of Crimes: Addendum' (4 February 1999) UN Doc PCINCC/1999/DP.4 4 <www.legal-tools.org/doc/423e2e/> accessed 18 August 2017.

89 PrepCom2, 'Proposal Submitted by the United States of America: Draft Elements of Crimes: Addendum' (n 88) 3.

90 PrepCom2, 'Proposal Submitted by the United States of America: Draft Elements of Crimes: Addendum' (War Crimes) (n 87).

91 Women's Caucus for Gender Justice, 'Priority Concerns Related to the Elements Annex' (n 24).

92 PrepCom2, 'Proceedings of the Preparatory Commission at its First Session (16–26 February 1999)' (2 March 1999) PCNICC/1999/L.3/Rev.1 art 6 <www.legal-tools.org/doc/aced45/> accessed 10 August 2017.

eventually defined.[93] Contrary to the US definition of rape, the Caucus[94] and Costa Rica[95] put forward a definition emphasising invasion – including but not limited to penetration – and coercion rather than penetration and force. This definition is in accordance with the Caucus' underlying working assumption that the definition of rape should not focus on body parts.[96] Taking into consideration national and international rules, the definition proposed by the Women's Caucus and Costa Rica goes beyond national and customary definitions[97] and melds the principles that underlay the decisions in *Prosecutor v Jean-Paul Akayesu* and *Prosecutor v Anto Furundžija*.[98] This way, it could have been aimed at mediating between actors who did not agree with the *ad hoc* tribunals' findings.[99]

Regarding the element of force or coercion, the Women's Caucus argued that the term 'coercion' is preferable to that of 'force' because it expresses less direct but no less threatening situations. Referring to international norms in the form of approaches taken by the ICTY and ICTR, the Caucus reasoned that this terminology recognises that in conflict situations, a perpetrator may accomplish rape without directly coercing or threatening the person. In addition to acts or threats of force and situations where the victim is disabled, the description of coercive circumstances should also include, for example, 'threats to deny or promises to provide the means of survival'.[100] This addition is critical 'if situations are to be included where women "choose" to trade sexual service in order to survive, such as forced temporary marriage and other slave-like conditions'.[101] In regard to the element of consent brought up by the USA in its explanation of 'committed by force', the Women's Caucus disagreed. It emphasised that discussions of consent to sexual intercourse in coercive situations are inappropriate as the notion of consent is based on gender stereotypes, places a focus on the victim, discourages women from participating in court proceedings, and furthers impunity.[102]

93 Interview 19 (n 9). The Women's Caucus' starting point was advocating for a gender-neutral, perpetrator-orientated, invasion- and coercion-based understandings of rape as a crime in and of itself as well as potentially amounting to other crimes.
94 Women's Caucus for Gender Justice, 'Priority Concerns Related to the Elements Annex' (n 24).
95 PrepCom2, 'Proposal Submitted by Costa Rica on Elements of Crimes' (24 February 1999) UN Doc PCNICC/1999/WGEC/DP.6 <www.legal-tools.org/doc/318088/> accessed 18 August 2017.
96 Interview 5 (1 April 2014).
97 Interview 10 (22 April 2014).
98 Interview 19 (n 9): State delegates at the ICC negotiations had heard of these cases but had not studied their gender aspects. Therefore, the Women's Caucus "educated" state delegates about them.
99 Interview 18 (n 42).
100 Women's Caucus for Gender Justice, 'Priority Concerns Related to the Elements Annex' (n 24).
101 ibid.
102 ibid.

Second session, July/August 1999

As indicated by the different proposals submitted by the US,[103] Costa Rica[104] and the Women's Caucus[105] in the first PrepCom2 session, one of the most contentious issues during the second PrepCom2 session in July/August 1999 was the definition of crimes of sexualised violence, especially of rape and the meaning of 'penetration'.[106]

The discussion was based on the very detailed text prepared by the ICRC on Article 8(2)(b), 8(2)(c) and 8(2)(e) of the ICC statute. The text was introduced at the request of the governments of Belgium, Costa Rica, Finland, Hungary, Korea, South Africa and Switzerland,[107] demonstrating that the ICRC, like the Women's Caucus, succeeded in teaching its views to states. The document contains research on, and an analysis of, international humanitarian law and human rights instruments and relevant national and international case law.[108] Drawing on international rules identified in the *Akayesu* and *Furundžija* cases and the Final Report of the UN Special Rapporteur on the Situation of Systematic Rape, Sexual Slavery and Slavery-Like Practices during Armed Conflict, the material element of rape is defined as:

> (1) The perpetrator committed an act of sexual penetration, however slight:
>
> (a) of the vagina or anus of the victim by the penis of the perpetrator or any other object used by the perpetrator; or
> (b) of the mouth of the victim by the penis of the perpetrator;
>
> (2) by coercion or force or threat of force against the victim or a third person.[109]

103 PrepCom2, 'Proposal Submitted by the United States of America: Draft Elements of Crimes: Addendum' (Crimes against Humanity) (n 87) art 7(1)(g)(1)(2), art 7(1)(g)(1)(3); PrepCom2, 'Proposal Submitted by the United States of America: Draft Elements of Crimes: Addendum' (War Crimes) (n 87) art 8(2)(b)(xxii)(1)(3), art 8(2)(b)(xxii)(1)(4), art 8(2)(e)(vi)(1).

104 PrepCom2, 'Proposal Submitted by Costa Rica on Elements of Crimes' (n 95).

105 Women's Caucus for Gender Justice, 'Priority Concerns Related to the Elements Annex' (n 24).

106 Nikola Gillhoff and Matthias Neuner, 'Some Observations on the Second Preparatory Commission: A NGO's Perspective' <www.iccnow.org/documents/ICLSObserve2ndPrepComNov99.pdf> accessed 22 January 2014.

107 PrepCom2, 'Request from the Governments of Belgium, Costa Rica, Finland, Hungary, the Republic of Korea and South Africa and the Permanent Observer Mission of Switzerland Regarding the Text Prepared by the International Committee of the Red Cross on Article 8, para 2 (b), (c) and (e) of the Rome Statute of the International Criminal Court' (17 July 1999) UN Doc PCNICC/1999/WGEC/INF.2 <www.legal-tools.org/doc/d8ff04/> accessed 10 August 2017.

108 Dörmann, 'War Crimes under the Rome Statute of the International Criminal Court' (n 48) 351.

109 PrepCom2, 'Request from the Governments' (n 107).

The same wording is brought forward in a proposal by Costa Rica, Hungary and Switzerland.[110] This was to be expected as this proposal is also based on ICRC research.[111] As the suggested wording was not gender-neutral, a majority of delegations was not satisfied with it. A proposal by Colombia commenting on the proposal by Costa Rica, Hungary and Switzerland reflects this concern by replacing the term 'penetration' with having 'sexual access to the victim', intended to lower the threshold for protection.[112] The background to this proposal highlights that delegates and lawyers relied on what they knew best and consequently the importance of national rules as well as the temporal and local contexts. However, delegates were also constantly reminded by the chair of the PrepCom2 not to simply reinstate their national positions but to define the crime for the purpose of the ICC statute.[113] The Colombian proposal was informed by Colombia's national criminal law at that time and the crime of carnal access which included, amongst others, rape. Even though there was no definition, rape was understood as penetration by the penis.[114] Colombia's proposal also contributed to the discussion of the element of force/coercion by stating that it includes intimidation and can be addressed to the victim or a third person.[115] Eventually, the discussion paper proposed by the Coordinator of the Working Group on Elements of Crimes, Herman von Hebel, defines rape as a war crime in international conflict that violates a person's autonomy[116] as

> [t]he accused invaded the body of a person by conduct resulting in penetration, however slight, of any part of the body of the victim or of the perpetrator with a sexual organ, or of the anal or genital opening of the victim with any object or any other part of the body.[117]

110 PrepCom2, 'Proposal Submitted by Costa Rica, Hungary and Switzerland on Certain Provisions of Article 8 Para. 2(b) of the Rome Statute of the International Criminal Court: (viii), (x), (xiii), (xiv), (xv), (xvi), (xxi), (xxii), (xxvi)' (19 July 1999) UN Doc PCNICC/1999/WGEC/DP.8 <www.legal-tools.org/doc/704a4b/> accessed 10 August 2017.

111 Interview 12 (n 80); Interview 13 (n 43); Interview 15 (27 May 2014).

112 PrepCom2, 'Proposal Submitted by Colombia: Comments on the Proposal by the Delegations of Costa Rica, Hungary and Switzerland Concerning Article 8, Paragraph 2(b) of the Rome Statute (PCNICC/1999/WGEC/DP.8)' (29 July 1999) UN Doc PCNICC/1999/WGEC/DP.16 <www.legal-tools.org/doc/a3f95c/> accessed 10 August 2017.

113 Interview 18 (n 42).

114 Interview 2 (24 March 2014); Interview 7 (4 April 2014); Ley No 599 de 2000 Por la cual se expide el Código Penal (24 July 2000) (Colombia) art 205 <www.alcaldiabogota.gov.co/sisjur/normas/Norma1.jsp?i=6388> accessed 8 May 2015.

115 PrepCom2, 'Proposal Submitted by Colombia: Comments on the Proposal by the Delegations of Costa Rica, Hungary and Switzerland Concerning Article 8, Paragraph 2(b) of the Rome Statute (PCNICC/1999/WGEC/DP.8)' (n 112).

116 Machteld Boot, 'Article 7 Crimes against Humanity para. 1 (g) Rape … or Any Other Form of Sexual Violence of Comparable Gravity' in Otto Triffterer (ed), *Commentary on the Rome Statute of the International Criminal Court: Observers' Notes, Article by Article* (2nd edn, CH Beck 2008) 210.

117 PrepCom2, 'Discussion Paper Proposed by the Coordinator: Article 8, paragraph 2(b) (xxii)' (10 August 1999) UN Doc PCNICC/1999/WGEC/RT.6 art 8(2)(b)(xxii)(1)(2)

A footnote indicates that the concept of invasion makes the definition gender-neutral.[118] This can also be inferred from the second part of this element. Including anal or genital invasion by any object or body part, it illustrates that men and women are recognised as victims and perpetrators of rape. Therefore, in addition to reflecting different national legislations and international jurisprudence,[119] this definition merges proposals made by state and non-state delegations. It includes the notion of 'penetration' as advanced by Colombia[120] and the US,[121] as well as Belgium and others,[122] and Costa Rica, Hungary and Switzerland[123] on behalf of the ICRC.[124] It also includes 'invasion' as advocated for by Costa Rica[125] and the Women's Caucus.[126] Also following the Women's Caucus view,[127] the definition of rape proposed in the coordinator's discussion paper is less dependent on body parts than the definition previously suggested by the ICRC.[128] It takes the *Akayesu* language and tries to fit it into the discussion of legality.[129]

<www.legal-tools.org/doc/a4a83f/> accessed 10 August 2017; PrepCom2, 'Proceedings of the Preparatory Commission at Its Second Session (26 July–13 August 1999)' (18 August 1999) UN Doc PCNICC/1999/L.4/Rev.1 art 8(2)(b)(xxii)(1)(2) <www.legal-tools.org/doc/0b6332/> accessed 10 August 2017.

118 PrepCom2, 'Discussion Paper Proposed by the Coordinator: Article 8, paragraph 2(b)(xxii)' (n 117) fn 1; PrepCom2, 'Proceedings of the Preparatory Commission at its Second Session' (n 117) fn 1.

119 Wilmshurst, 'ICC: PrepCom. 16–26 February 1999' (n 80); Eve La Haye, 'Article 8(2)(b)(xii): Rape, Sexual Slavery, Enforced Prostitution, Forced Pregnancy, Enforced Sterilization, and Sexual Violence' in Roy S. Lee (ed), *The International Criminal Court: Elements of Crimes and Rules of Procedure and Evidence* (Transnational Publishers 2001) 189.

120 PrepCom2, 'Comments by Colombia on the Elements of Crimes of Article 7 in Document PCNICC/1999/L.5/Rev.1/Add.2' (1 March 2000) UN Doc PCNICC/2000/WGEC/DP.2 art 7(1)(g)(1) <www.legal-tools.org/doc/c92bf1/> accessed 10 August 2017; PrepCom2, 'Comments by Colombia Regarding the Elements of Crimes of Article 8 (2) (b), 8 (2) (c) and 8 (2) (e) in Document PCNICC/1999/L.5/Rev.1/Add.2' (08 March 2000) UN Doc PCNICC/2000/WGEC/DP.4 art 8(2)(b)(xxii)(1), art 8(2)(e)(vi)(1) <www.legal-tools.org/doc/405370/> accessed 18 August 2017.

121 PrepCom2, 'Proposal Submitted by the United States of America: Draft Elements of Crimes: Addendum' (War Crimes) (n 87).

122 PrepCom2, 'Request from the Governments' (n 107).

123 PrepCom2, 'Proposal Submitted by Costa Rica, Hungary and Switzerland on Certain Provisions of Article 8 Para. 2(b) of the Rome Statute of the International Criminal Court: (viii), (x), (xiii), (xiv), (xv), (xvi), (xxi), (xxii), (xxvi)' (n 110).

124 Interview 12 (n 80); Interview 13 (n 43); Interview 15 (n 111); PrepCom2, 'Proposal Submitted by Costa Rica, Hungary and Switzerland on Certain Provisions of Article 8 Para. 2(b) of the Rome Statute of the International Criminal Court: (viii), (x), (xiii), (xiv), (xv), (xvi), (xxi), (xxii), (xxvi)' (n 110).

125 PrepCom2, 'Proposal Submitted by Costa Rica on Elements of Crimes' (n 95).

126 Women's Caucus for Gender Justice, 'Priority Concerns Related to the Elements Annex' (n 24).

127 Interview 5 (n 96).

128 PrepCom2, 'Request from the Governments' (n 107).

129 Interview 19 (n 9).

The coordinator's discussion paper continued to specify that

> [t]he invasion was committee by force, or by threat of force or coercion, such as that caused by fear of violence, duress, detention, psychological oppression or abuse of power, against such person or another person, or by taking advantage of a coercive environment, or the invasion was committed against a person incapable of giving genuine consent.[130]

The intention of the drafters to stress that coercive circumstances are not restricted to the use of physical force becomes clear.[131]

Focusing on the first element of the definition of rape, as indicated above, the expression of 'invasion resulting in penetration' reflects the importance of international as well as national rules. Drawing on the *Akayesu* definition of rape, a majority of delegations supported the concept of invasion which, even though it was seen as somewhat vague, was perceived to be broader than 'penetration' and intended to be gender-neutral. Most national definitions, in contrast, define rape using the concept of penetration.[132] Highlighting the relevance of both international and national rules, the wording is a compromise reached between defining rape as an act of invasion or penetration.[133] This compromise shows that while the ICC negotiations heavily relied on precedents, they were chosen and interpreted in the light of new contexts. The definition of rape as an 'invasion resulting in penetration' reflects the smallest common denominator between sometimes extremely diverging views.[134] It reflects the delegates' desire to ensure a high level of ratifications. The long and relatively complicated wording resulted out of the PrepCom2's intention to draft a gender-neutral and inclusive definition. It is argued that the ICC formulation is one of the most progressive and broad definitions of rape under international and national law. Moving beyond international precedents, it aimed and succeeded at including

130 PrepCom2, 'Discussion Paper Proposed by the Coordinator: Article 8, paragraph 2(b)(xxii)' (n 117) art 8(2)(b)(xxii)(1)(3); PrepCom2, 'Proceedings of the Preparatory Commission at its Second Session' (n 117) art 8(2)(b)(xxii)(1)(3).

131 La Haye (n 119) 189.

132 See Chapter 1 for references.

133 Interview 2 (n 114); Interview 8 (11 April 2014); Interview 9 (11 April 2014); Interview 11 (23 April 2014); Interview 12 (n 80); Interview 15 (n 111); Interview 16 (10 June 2014); Interview 19 (n 9); Cottier (n 62) 438; Dörmann, *Elements of War Crimes under the Rome Statute of the International Criminal Court* (n 55) 327; Dörmann, 'War Crimes under the Rome Statute of the International Criminal Court' (n 48) 391; La Haye (n 119) 188.

134 Roelof Haveman, 'Rape and Fair Trial on Supranational Criminal Law' (2002) 9 *Maastricht Journal of European and Comparative Law* 263. Drawing on Haveman, a difference can be noted in the law-making of the *ad hoc* tribunals compared to the ICC. The judges at the International Criminal Tribunal for Rwanda (ICTR) and the International Criminal Tribunal for the former Yugoslavia (ICTY) looked for the greatest common denominator derived from a number of countries that have shared norms. Actors at the ICC negotiations, in contrast, had to settle on the smallest common denominator to draft a rape definition everybody could agree on.

many acts such as rape with objects which no judgment had yet been passed on by the *ad hoc* tribunals. Therefore, the ICC rape definition was negotiated for the future. It set new standards, creating a normative force that promotes women's rights in international but also domestic contexts through the need for implementation.[135]

Even though this shows that the ICC definition of rape can be seen as a positive development and progress in international criminal law, it is not faultless. It simultaneously indicates progress and regression. It is argued that this definition is generic.[136] However, it still includes body parts. It is still based on, and reproduces, outdated notions of honour by including the concept of penetration, making it a conservative definition.[137] Therefore, it is not an entirely satisfactory compromise from a feminist point of view. In addition to its long and relatively complicated wording, the formulation 'invasion resulting in penetration' is somewhat awkward.[138] A point could be made that this wording did not only result out of the drafters' intention to create a gender-neutral definition, but also out of fear of misunderstandings of terms which necessitated a high degree of specification,[139] or out of fear of alienating support by being too radical by developing a fundamentally new rape definition. Furthermore, it can be argued that a gender-neutral definition could also have been included by adopting the definition developed by the ICTR in the *Akayesu* case, a definition only mentioning invasion. Even though it was argued that the formulation 'invasion resulting in penetration' broadens the ICC definition of rape, it could also be said, as mentioned above, that the *Akayesu* definition is even broader.

Third session, November/December 1999

Based on a joint proposal by Canada and Germany that aimed at reflecting the most thoughtful approaches taken by the *ad hoc* tribunals, rape as a crime against humanity and as a war crime in international and internal armed conflict was defined in the same words used in the discussion paper proposed by the coordinator in the second PrepCom2 session.[140]

135 Interview 2 (n 114); Interview 8 (n 133); Interview 12 (n 80); Interview 13 (n 43); Dörmann, *Elements of War Crimes under the Rome Statute of the International Criminal Court* (n 55) 327; Spees, 'Women's Advocacy in the Creation of the International Criminal Court' (n 36) 1238.

136 Interview 8 (n 133).

137 Interview 13 (n 43); Hall, 'The First Five Sessions of the UN Preparatory Commission for the International Criminal Court' (n 3) 778.

138 Cottier (n 62) 438; Hall, 'The First Five Sessions of the UN Preparatory Commission for the International Criminal Court' (n 3) 778.

139 Interview 11 (n 133).

140 Interview 19 (n 9); PrepCom2, 'Addendum: Annex III: Elements of Crimes' (22 December 1999) UN Doc PCNICC/1999/L.5/Rev.1/Add.2 art (7)(1)(g)(1)(4), art 8(2)(b)(xxii)(1)(3), art 8(2)(e)(vi)(1)(3) <www.legal-tools.org/doc/e51882/> accessed 18 August 2017; PrepCom2, 'Discussion Paper Proposed by the Coordinator: Article 8, paragraph 2(b)(xxii)'

Highlighting the controversy around the role of consent,[141] the Arab block submitted a proposal stating that '[n]othing in [the elements of the crime against humanity of rape] shall affect natural and legal marital sexual relations in accordance with religious principles or cultural norms in different national laws.'[142] If accepted, this would have made marital sexual intercourse consensual by definition. In contrast to national laws which at least partly view rape as an honour crime, the reference to cultural norms indicates an understanding of rape as a form of structural violence.[143] The Arab block's wish to protect cultural

(n 117) art 8(2)(b)(xxii)(1); PrepCom2, 'Proposal Submitted by Canada and Germany on Article 7' (23 November 1999) UN Doc PCNICC/1999/WGEC/DP.36 art (7)(1)(g)(1) <www.legal-tools.org/doc/2238df/> accessed 18 August 2017; Elizabeth Wilmshurst, 'ICC: PrepCom: 26 July–13 August: Second Week' (13 December 1999); Elizabeth Wilmshurst, 'ICC: Preparatory Commission: 29 November–17 December 1999' (21 December 1999).

141 Boon (n 62) 639; Women's Caucus for Gender Justice, 'Recommendations and Commentary for the Rules of Procedure and Evidence' (December 1999) <www.iccwomen.org/wigjdraft1/Archives/oldWCGJ/icc/iccpc/11> accessed 31 October 2013.

142 PrepCom2, 'Proposal Submitted by Bahrain, Iraq, Kuwait, Lebanon, the Libyan Arab Jamahiriya, Oman, Qatar, Saudi Arabia, the Sudan, the Syrian Arab Republic and United Arab Emirates Concerning the Elements of Crimes against Humanity (9 December 1999)' UN Doc PCNICC/1999/WGEC/DP.39 art 7(1)(g)(1)(4) <www.legal-tools.org/doc/33d070/> accessed 10 August 2017.

143 Bahrain Penal Code (1976) art 344, art 346 <www.bahrainrights.org/sites/default/files/Bahrain-Penal-Code.doc> accessed 17 March 2014; The Criminal Act of 1991 (Sudan) art 149(1) <www.icrc.org/applic/ihl/ihl-nat.nsf/xsp/.ibmmodres/domino/OpenAttachment/applic/ihl/ihl-nat.nsf/B9EEBA1CA8F54121C1256DC9005573F2/TEXT/Criminal%20Act%20-%20Sudan%20-%20EN.pdf> accessed 1 April 2014; Iraqi Penal Code No 111 (1969) art 21(1)(f), art 393(1) <www.iraq-lg-law.org/en/webfm_send/1350> accessed 18 March 2014; The Libyan Penal Code (1953) art 407 <https://ia600704.us.archive.org/25/items/LibyanPenalCodeenglish/LibyanPenalCode.pdf> accessed 24 March 2014; Omani Penal Code (1974) art 218(1) <www.fiu.gov.om/forms.html> accessed 24 March 2014; Qatari Penal Code (2004) art 279 <http://portal.www.gov.qa/wps/wcm/connect/8abaea8046be1deaae97ef70b3652ad8/Penal+Code.pdf?MOD=AJPERES&useDefaultText=0&useDefaultDesc=0> accessed 24 March 2014; Centre on Law and Globalization, 'What Counts as Rape in International Crimes?' <http://clg.portalxm.com/library/keytext.cfm?keytext_id=182> accessed 27 October 2012; Mona Chemali Khalaf, 'Lebanon' in Julia Breslin and Sanja Kelly (eds), *Women's Rights in the Middle East and North Africa: Progress Amid Resistance* (Freedom House/Rowman & Littlefield Publishers 2010) 6 <www.freedomhouse.org/sites/default/files/inline_images/Lebanon.pdf> accessed 21 March 2014; United Nations Commission on Human Rights, 'Final Report of the Special Rapporteur on the Situation of Systematic Rape, Sexual Slavery and Slavery-Like Practices during Armed Conflict' (22 June 1998) UN Doc E/CN.4/Sub.2/1998/13 para 24 <www.ohchr.org> accessed 28 August 2017 ©1998 United Nations. Reprinted with the Permission of the United Nations; US Department of State, Bureau of Democracy, Human Rights, and Labor, '2009 Human Rights Report: Saudi Arabia' (2010) <www.state.gov/j/drl/rls/hrrpt/2009/nea/136079.htm> accessed 1 April 2014; US Department of State: Bureau of Democracy, Human Rights, and Labor, '2009 Human Rights Report: Syria' (2010) <www.state.gov/j/drl/rls/hrrpt/2009/nea/136080.htm> accessed 1 April 2014: The Arab block's national rape definitions demonstrate a divergent understanding of rape. Some states define rape progressively as

norms that might allow marital rape makes clear that self-same norms underlie the perpetration of rape. The reference to national laws makes it clear that national norms and rules matter in international relations. Although this proposal was not supported, the Arab block's opposition resulted in footnote 13 in the ICC Elements of Crimes, linking the elements of rape to the debate about an alternative wording for the introductory text to crimes against humanity.[144] This

a form of sexual assault and recognise coercion as an element. Other states in contrast understand rape as an honour crime, define it using the term 'penetration' and stress the absence of consent of the survivor. However, the individual states constituting the Arab block do not clearly advance a more progressive or more conservative understanding of rape. Their national rape definitions combine progressive and conservative elements. Iraq, for example, defines rape as sexual intercourse without consent but also advances an element of force while still generally framing rape as an honour crime. Sudan advances a definition of rape as intercourse without consent. Similarly, Bahrain understands rape as sexual assault without consent.

144 PrepCom2, 'Addendum: Annex III: Elements of Crimes' (22 December 1999) (n 140) art 7(1)(g)(1); PrepCom2, 'Discussion Paper Proposed by the Coordinator: Article 7 (Crimes against Humanity)' (15 December 1999) UN Doc PCNICC/1999/WGEC/RT.16 <www.legal-tools.org/doc/225a2c/> accessed 10 August 2017; PrepCom2, 'Report of the Working Group on Elements of Crimes: Crimes against Humanity (Article 7): Addendum' UN Doc PCNICC/2000/WGEC/L.1/Add.1 <www.legal-tools.org/doc/2be303/> accessed 10 August 2017; Wilmshurst, 'ICC: Preparatory Commission' (n 140); Elizabeth Wilmshurst, 'ICC: PrepCom 12–30 June: Second Week' (26 June 2000); Elizabeth Wilmshurst, 'ICC: PrepCom 13–31 March 2000: Report' (4 April 2000); Wilmshurst, 'ICC: PrepCom: 26 July–13 August: Second Week' (n 140); Pam Spees, 'Many Gender Issues Remain to be Resolved at the June Prepcom' *ICC Monitor* (New York, June 2000) 4; Hall, 'The First Five Sessions of the UN Preparatory Commission for the International Criminal Court' (n 3) 779–780; William R. Pace and Jennifer Schense, 'Coalition for the International Criminal Court at the Preparatory Commission' in Roy S. Lee (ed), *The International Criminal Court: Elements of Crimes and Rules of Procedure and Evidence* (Transnational Publishers 2001) 721–723; Darryl Robinson, 'The Context of Crimes against Humanity' in Roy S. Lee (ed), *The International Criminal Court: Elements of Crimes and Rules of Procedure and Evidence* (Transnational Publishers 2001) 66–69: The Arab block indicated that they would not discuss the elements of individual crimes against humanity until their concerns regarding the inclusion or exclusion of family matters under the ICC's jurisdiction were satisfactorily addressed. According to Darryl Robinson, the Arab block refined its position to the effect that 'acquiescence in the long-standing cultural or religious norms concerning family matters' would not be sufficient to satisfy the policy element of the perpetration of crimes against humanity, seeking a more narrow exemption in the introductory text to crimes against humanity. However, this proposal still caused concerns about the appropriateness of cultural relativism. As a compromise, para 3 of the introductory text to the elements of crimes against humanity in the rolling text of December 1999, which defined an attack directed against a civilian population, specified that '[i]t is understood that a 'policy to commit such attack' requires that the State or organization actively promote or encourage such conduct as an attack against a civilian population.' Only after reaching this compromise, the working group agreed on a rolling text regarding the elements of the individual crimes. Although this compromise initially received a great degree of support, when the working group discussed the elements of crimes against humanity again in the fifth session, it became clear that a majority of delegations favoured dropping or modifying this sentence. The sentence raised concerns that including an action requirement into the introductory text could restrict the development of law, that it would exclude situations of passive encouragement and that this

underscores the fragile compromises repeatedly brokered by the Coordinator of the Working Group on the Elements of Crimes, Herman von Hebel, and Sub-Coordinator Prince Zeid Al-Hussein, as well as the German, Swiss, British and US delegations on the standards and definitions of sexualised crimes, potentially affecting the interpretation and application of these provisions.[145]

While the Arab block primarily relied on its national laws as a basic position in the ICC negotiations, Colombia was taught by NGOs and eventually diverted from its national laws in the ICC discussions. In a comment on Rolling Text No 6 proposed by the coordinator during the second PrepCom2 session, it recalled its previous proposal on the wording of the elements of the crime of rape and again suggested replacing the term 'invasion (resulting in penetration)' with 'having access to'. The proposal's reasoning was informed by discussions regarding a broadening of Colombia's national definition of rape with national and international NGOs like the Colombian Commission of Jurists and the ICRC that had more access than the Colombian delegation to international doctrines and materials of the *ad hoc* tribunals.[146] This highlights the importance of international norms and rules as well as the key role of NGOs in law-making processes. Colombia considered the definition worked out in the previous round of discussions to be too long and confusing. Moreover, Colombia was of the opinion that the definition did not adequately protect the right to sexual freedom and control over one's body.[147] Drawing on the *Furundžija* case, it understood the proposed changes as gender-neutral and open, specifying the violent means used in a general way rather than referring to any body parts. Furthermore, using the main verb 'to access' would make it possible to differentiate rape from sexual violence, the difference being that, in the latter, the conduct would consist of the violent sexual act falling short of carnal access.[148] Colombia spoke out

---

provision would be interpreted as requiring proof of state action. Additionally, culture-based concerns were still voiced. The compromise draft text retains the final sentence but suggests a strict construction of the paragraph and adds an explanatory footnote that reads: 'A policy which has a civilian population as the object of the attack would be implemented by State or organizational action. Such a policy may, in exceptional circumstances, be implemented by a deliberate failure to take action, which is consciously aimed at encouraging such attack. The existence of such a policy cannot be inferred solely from the absence of governmental or organizational action.'

145 Wilmshurst, 'ICC: Preparatory Commission' (n 140); Boon (n 62) 638–639; Hall, 'The First Five Sessions of the UN Preparatory Commission for the International Criminal Court' (n 3) 779.

146 Interview 2 (n 114); Interview 13 (n 43).

147 PrepCom2, 'Comments by Colombia on Document PCNICC/1999/WGEC/RT.6 Proposed by the Coordinator' (10 November 1999) UN Doc PCNICC/1999/WGEC/DP.30 1 <www.legal-tools.org/doc/e01ec9/> accessed 18 August 2017.

148 PrepCom2, 'Proposal Submitted by Colombia: Comments on the Documents Submitted by Egypt (PCNICC/1999/WGEC/DP.42), Germany and Canada (PCNICC/1999/WGEC/DP.36), and Bahrain, Iraq, Kuwait, Lebanon, the Libyan Arab Jamahiriya, Oman, Qatar, Saudi Arabia, the Sudan, the Syrian Arab Republic and the United Arab Emirates (PCNICC/1999 WGEC/DP.39)' (9 December 1999) UN Doc PCNICC/1999/WGEC/DP.43 2–3 <www.legal-tools.org/doc/b3fd41/> accessed 18 August 2017.

against the use of 'invasion' because of its indefinite character and difficulties from an evidentiary point of view resulting out of this.[149]

Fourth session, March 2000

In further discussions, NGOs explained to the Colombian delegation their understanding of 'penetration' as the use of any tool.[150] Based on this, Colombia reverted from its previous suggestions and stated that the main verb 'to have access to' could be replaced by 'to penetrate' in order to facilitate agreement on the elements of rape as a crime against humanity and a war crime in (non-) international armed conflicts.[151]

Fifth session, June 2000

In the fifth PrepCom2 session, however, the delegations of Bolivia, Colombia, Chile, Cuba, Ecuador and Spain submitted a proposal suggesting anew to replace the verb 'invasion' with 'to have access to'.[152]

Eventually, however, the delegations wanted to ensure consistency between the elements of rape as a crime against humanity and the largely completed elements of rape as a war crime. Therefore, the definition of war rape remained as developed in the second PrepCom2 session and was adopted as such.[153]

Conclusion on war rape

Retracing who the key actors were in the ICC negotiations of rape, it became apparent that the ICRC as well as the Women's Caucus were two international non-governmental delegations that drove the discussions of the crime of war

149 Interview 2 (n 114).
150 ibid.
151 PrepCom2, 'Comments by Colombia on the Elements of Crimes of Article 7 in Document PCNICC/1999/L.5/Rev.1/Add.2' (n 120) art 7(1)(g)(1); PrepCom2, 'Comments by Colombia Regarding the Elements of Crimes of Article 8 (2) (b), 8 (2) (c) and 8 (2) (e) in Document PCNICC/1999/L.5/Rev.1/Add.2' (n 120) art 8(2)(b)(xxii)(1), art 8(2)(e)(vi)(1).
152 PrepCom2, 'Proposals by Delegations of Bolivia, Colombia, Chile, Cuba, Ecuador, Spain . . . Regarding Crimes against Humanity in the Draft Elements of Crimes' (30 June 2000) UN Doc PCNICC/2000/1.1/Rev.1/Add.2 <www.legal-tools.org/doc/874907/> accessed 18 August 2017.
153 PrepCom2, 'Report of the Preparatory Commission for the International Criminal Court, Addendum: Part II, Finalized Draft Text of the Elements of Crimes' (2 November 2000) PCNICC/2000/1/Add.2 <www.legal-tools.org/doc/843931/> accessed 10 August 2017; Hall, 'The First Five Sessions of the UN Preparatory Commission for the International Criminal Court' (n 3) 773; Jennifer Schense, 'Draft Report on the Third Session of the Preparatory Commission, November 29–December 17, 1999, Coalition for an International Criminal Court' (24 January 2000) <www.iccnow.org/documents/3rdPrepComReportCICC.pdf> accessed 23 January 2014.

rape. Regarding state delegations, the Arab block, Colombia and the US made relevant contributions.

The ICRC papers constituted the historical background for the definition of rape. It outlined the state of law at the time of the ICC negotiations. Procedurally, the ICRC could not introduce its papers as formal proposals due to its observer status. For this to happen, the papers needed to be taken up by state delegations. Here the ICRC's identity as the guardian and expert of international humanitarian law, and the respect of state delegations that the organisation enjoyed because of its successful influence in the emergence and evolution of international humanitarian law, was crucial. The ICRC looked for a number of states from different regions that would submit its texts.[154] Of relevance to the discussion of the definition of rape are the ICRC papers that were taken up and submitted by Belgium and others[155] as well as by Costa Rica, Hungary and Switzerland.[156] The organisation also taught the Colombian delegation to broaden its national definition of rape that so far had guided Colombia's position on war rape in the ICC negotiations. Based on non-state actors' teaching of international doctrines and the *ad hoc* tribunals' judgments, Colombia advanced a different reasoning for its proposed wording of the definition of rape.[157] A proposal by New Zealand and Switzerland[158] that was based on ICRC research[159] was of relevance to the general inclusion of the crime in the ICC statute. Due to time constraints, the relationship between the ICRC and Switzerland was helpful. The Swiss government is the ICRC's main funder and, until the 1970s, the committee controlling the organisation was closely linked to the Swiss government.[160] 'Observers have alleged that the cultural, intellectual and political "symbiosis" between the Swiss government and the ICRC leaders

154 Interview 13 (n 43); International Committee of the Red Cross, 'Commentary: Definition of War Crimes' (n 38); International Committee of the Red Cross, 'Statement: Preparatory Committee on the Establishment of an International Criminal Court, New York, 1 to 12 December, 1997' (8 December 1997).

155 PrepCom2, 'Request from the Governments' (n 107).

156 PrepCom2, 'Proposal Submitted by Costa Rica, Hungary and Switzerland on Certain Provisions of Article 8 Para. 2(b) of the Rome Statute of the International Criminal Court: (viii), (x), (xiii), (xiv), (xv), (xvi), (xxi), (xxii), (xxvi)' (n 110); PrepCom2, 'Proposal Submitted by Costa Rica, Hungary and Switzerland on Certain Provisions of Article 8 Para. 2 (e) of the Rome Statute of the International Criminal Court, (v), (vi), (vii), (viii), (xi), (xii)' (29 July 1999) PCNICC/1999/WGEC/DP.11 <www.legal-tools.org/doc/26ef83/> accessed 18 August 2017.

157 PrepCom2, 'Comments by Colombia on Document PCNICC/1999/WGEC/RT.6 Proposed by the Coordinator' (n 147) 1.

158 PrepCom, 'Working Paper Submitted by the Delegations of New Zealand and Switzerland' (n 39).

159 International Committee of the Red Cross, 'Commentary: Definition of War Crimes' (n 38).

160 J.D. Armstrong, 'The International Committee of the Red Cross and Political Prisoners' (1985) 39 *International Organization* 615; David P. Forsythe, *The Humanitarians: The International Committee of the Red Cross* (Cambridge University Press 2005) 201–241.

has influenced the ICRC's positions and decisions.'[161] Switzerland's default policy in regard to the ICRC was to support the organisation if it could. New Zealand saw itself as gaining strength from being a good international actor. Thus, if a delegation looked for support, the state's default position was to give support if the proposal made sense on a principled basis.[162] Considering that the ICRC drew on existing national and international law as well as the Final Report of the UN Special Rapporteur on the Situation of Systematic Rape, Sexual Slavery and Slavery-Like Practices during Armed Conflict, Belgium and others, Colombia, and Costa Rica, Hungary and Switzerland proposed definitions of rape that used the term 'penetration'.

In addition to the ICRC, the Women's Caucus played a role in the development of the ICC definition of war rape. In contrast to the ICRC, however, the Caucus pushed for progress in the form of gender-neutral, perpetrator-orientated, invasion- and coercion-based understandings of rape as a crime in and of itself as well as potentially amounting to other crimes. Like the ICRC, the Caucus' positions were influenced by precedents from national and international laws. However, the Women's Caucus was not bound by a role as guardian of international humanitarian law like the ICRC, but was guided by its mandate to advance women's rights. Therefore, it developed a different focus and advanced different conclusions. Its positions were (partly) taken up by the US[163] and Costa Rica.[164] The US moved away from its initial consent-based definition and advanced a broad understanding of the element of coercion. In addition, it developed gender-neutral definitions. However, in line with its national laws,[165] it still used the term 'penetration' instead of 'invasion'. In contrast to the proposals it submitted together with Hungary and Switzerland, Costa Rica on its own advanced a definition of rape using the term 'invasion'. Considering that before the Women's Caucus got involved in the ICC negotiations, state delegations mainly discussed the crime of rape in a victim-centred, honour-based way as constituting other crimes, for example an outrage upon personal dignity, and that initial definitions only used the term 'penetration' and included an element of consent as well as force, it can be argued that the Women's Caucus taught its views to states.

161 Yves Beigbeder, *The Role and Statutes of International Humanitarian Volunteers and Organizations: The Rights and Duty to Humanitarian Assistance* (Martinus Nijhoff Publishers 1999) 66.

162 Interview 18 (n 42).

163 PrepCom, 'For Annex to Statute: Elements Related to Article on Crimes against Humanity (Delegation of the United States)' (n 34); PrepCom, 'For Annex to Statute: Elements Related to Article on Crimes against Humanity (Delegation of the United States)' (n 35); PrepCom2, 'Proposal Submitted by the United States of America: Draft Elements of Crimes: Addendum' (n 88).

164 PrepCom2, 'Proposal Submitted by Costa Rica on Elements of Crimes' (n 95).

165 Rape, Abuse and Incest National Network, 'The Laws in Your State' <www.rainn.org/public-policy/laws-in-your-state> accessed 21 November 2014.

Opposing these developments, the Arab block submitted a proposal[166] that retains the definition of rape as 'invasion resulting in penetration'. This went beyond its national laws which mainly use the term 'penetration'. Falling back on national laws as well as religious principles and cultural norms, however, the Arab block aimed to include an exception that, if accepted, would have made sexual intercourse in marriage automatically consensual. The Arab block's recourse to conservative national laws as well as religious principles and cultural norms to oppose progressive developments regarding the definition of rape confirmed that states with strong patriarchal structures, where religion plays a leading role in legal and social matters, opposed the development of a more progressive definition. It also shows that domestic norms explain the resistance towards progressive definitions of rape.

In addition to outlining who the driving actors were in the ICC negotiations of war rape as a specific sexualised crime listed in the Rome Statute, what influenced them in the discussion of the crime and how they defined it, the above discussion also argued that rape was understood as an honour crime as well as a form of structural violence. Initially, rape was included in the ILC draft statute as an outrage upon personal dignity. As this was perceived to be linked to notions of honour, rape was initially interpreted as an honour crime. This is also true for the Arab block's national understanding of rape that influenced its positions in the ICC negotiations. The Women's Caucus, in contrast, advocated an understanding of rape as a form of structural violence that has its roots in patriarchy.

Forced marriage

After the first part of this chapter focused on war rape, the second part focuses on forced marriage in times of armed conflict. As with the part on war rape, it analyses which key actors drove the ICC negotiations of forced marriage specifically, why they got involved in the discussion of this crime and what influenced their positions and how the driving actors interpreted forced marriage. Seeing that forced marriage was only mentioned as a form of sexual slavery and not discussed as a crime in and of itself, it is of interest and relevance to trace the ICC negotiations of the crime of sexual slavery. It is necessary to understand how actors interpreted the crime of sexual slavery to learn why they categorised forced marriage as such, rather than as a separate crime.[167]

As with the part on war rape, the part on forced marriage analyses the relevant negotiations in the PrepCom, Rome Conference and PrepCom2.

166 PrepCom2, 'Proposal Submitted by Bahrain, Iraq, Kuwait, Lebanon, the Libyan Arab Jamahiriya, Oman, Qatar, Saudi Arabia, the Sudan, the Syrian Arab Republic and United Arab Emirates Concerning the Elements of Crimes against Humanity (9 December 1999)' (n 142).

167 This will be discussed further in Chapter 6.

The Preparatory Committee on the Establishment of an International Criminal Court (PrepCom)

In the context of the PrepCom negotiations, forced marriage was only mentioned in the fifth session. Therefore, this is the only PrepCom session analysed below.

Fifth session, December 1997

Based on the Nuremberg charter,[168] Control Council Law No 10,[169] the Tokyo charter,[170] the statutes of the ICTY[171] and ICTR,[172] and the ILC Draft Code of Crimes,[173] there was general agreement that the crimes against humanity provisions of the Rome Statute should include the crime of enslavement.[174] This highlights the importance of international rules in the making of the ICC instruments. However, already in the Ad Hoc Committee, state delegations recognised the importance of crystallising one comprehensive definition of enslavement.[175] Encompassing not only slavery but also servitude and forced

168 Charter of the International Military Tribunal (8 August 1945) 82 UNTS 279, 59 Stat 1544, 3 Bevans 1238, 39 AJIL 258 (London Agreement) art 6(c) <www.legal-tools.org/doc/64ffdd/> accessed 18 August 2017.

169 Allied Control Council Law No 10 Punishment of Persons Guilty of War Crimes, Crimes against Peace and against Humanity (20 December 1945) 3 Official Gazette Control Council for Germany 50–55 (1946) art II(1)(c) <www.legal-tools.org/doc/ffda62/> accessed 18 August 2017.

170 London Agreement (n 168) art 5.

171 UNSC Resolution 827 (25 May 1993) UN Doc S/RES/827 art 5(c) <www.legal-tools.org/doc/dc079b/> accessed 18 August 2017.

172 UNSC Resolution 955 (8 November 1994) UN Doc S/RES/955 art 3(c) <www.legal-tools.org/doc/f5ef47/> accessed 18 August 2017.

173 International Law Commission, 'Draft Code of Crimes against the Peace and Security of Mankind' (n 7) art 18(d).

174 PrepCom, 'Decisions Taken by the Preparatory Committee at its Session from 11 to 21 February 1997' (n 39); PrepCom, 'Decisions Taken by the Preparatory Committee at Its Session Held from 1 to 12 December 1997' (n 54); PrepCom, 'Draft Consolidated Text: War Crimes' (n 39); PrepCom, 'Preliminary Text: War Crimes' (n 39); PrepCom, 'Redraft of the ILC Article 20 on ICC Jurisdiction with Proposed Elements (Delegation of the United States)' (n 32); PrepCom, 'Report of the Inter-Sessional Meeting from 19 to 30 January 1998 in Zutphen, the Netherlands' (n 66) art 20(D)(l) Option II; Amnesty International, 'Making the Right Choices' (n 52) 29, 44; Christopher Keith Hall, 'Article 7 Crimes against Humanity para. 1 (c) Enslavement' in Otto Triffterer (ed), *Commentary on the Rome Statute of the International Criminal Court: Observers' Notes, Article by Article* (2nd edn, CH Beck 2008); Human Rights Watch, *Justice in Balance* (n 59).

175 Ad Hoc Committee on the Establishment of an International Criminal Court (n 2) para 78; PrepCom, 'For Annex to Statute: Elements Related to Article on Crimes against Humanity (Delegation of the United States)' (n 34); PrepCom, 'Proposal by the United States of America on Elements of Offenses for the International Criminal Court' (2 April 1998) UN Doc A/AC.249/1998/DP.11 <www.legal-tools.org/doc/50fc48/> accessed 18 August 2017; PrepCom, 'Redraft of the ILC Article 20 on ICC Jurisdiction with Proposed Elements (Delegation of the United States)' (n 32); PrepCom, 'Reference Paper

labour, enslavement can be understood to be broad enough to include slavery-like practices such as 'compulsory betrothal of women [...] where the victims are not merely economically exploited, but totally dependent on others'.[176]

As outlined above, in the fifth PrepCom session in December 1997, the Women's Caucus proposed the inclusion of 'rape, sexual slavery, forced prostitution, forced pregnancy, forced sterilization and other sexual and gender violence'[177] in a sub-paragraph of the war crimes and crimes against humanity provisions.[178] This makes the Rome Statute the first international legal instrument to specify sexual slavery as a war crime and a crime against humanity.[179] This recognition drew on the legislative history of the crimes of slavery and enslavement. Even though slavery was one of the earliest human rights violations to be recognised as a crime under international law, it was only first regulated by treaty in 1926 when the Slavery Convention[180] was adopted. Based on the Slavery Convention, the Supplementary Convention on the Abolition of Slavery,

---

Elements of Offenses for the International Criminal Court (Delegation of the United States)' (n 68): In a redraft of art 20 of the International Law Commission (ILC) draft statute, the USA first defined the elements of enslavement as 'the accused [holding] a person against that person's will and for the purpose of performing labor'. In its draft elements of crimes of 27 March 1996, the US developed a definition of enslavement as 'intentionally placing or maintaining a person in a condition in which any or all of the powers attaching to the right of ownership are exercised over him'. In a reference paper dated 27 March 1998, the USA defined the elements of enslavement as exercising ownership rights over a person and subjecting them to forced labour without remuneration, or causing a person and their labour to be owned. The second wording was based on the 1926 Slavery Convention, demonstrating that international rules mattered in the ICC negotiations. It can be argued that the third definition developed by the US moves away from traditional understandings of slavery for the purpose of forced labour towards a broader definition, focusing on the acts of the perpetrator rather than on the purpose for which someone is enslaved. A similar focus is reintroduced in the USA's fourth definition of enslavement put forward in another reference paper dated 2 April 1998. As outlined in Chapter 4, forced marriage in times of armed conflict includes elements of enslavement, slavery, serfdom and forced labour. Therefore, it can be understood as being indirectly included in the USA's and other state delegations' proposals. However, the prominence of traditional notions such as enslavement, slavery, serfdom and forced labour raises doubts as to whether actors involved in the ICC negotiations were aware of, and considered, the gendered elements of these crimes.

176 Hall, 'Article 7 Crimes against Humanity para. 1 (c) Enslavement' (n 174).

177 Women's Caucus for Gender Justice, 'Recommendations and Commentary for December 1997 PrepCom' (n 31).

178 Additionally, an Informal Working Paper of 12 December 1997 (UD/A/AC-249/1997/WG.1/IP <www.legal-tools.org/doc/b6c406/> accessed 10 August 2017) included 'slavery and the slave trade in all their forms' in Option II to section D of the war crimes provision.

179 La Haye (n 119) 190.

180 Convention to Suppress the Slave Trade and Slavery (25 September 1926) 60 LNTS 253, Registered No 1414 (Slavery Convention) <www.legal-tools.org/doc/12c9d8/> accessed 18 August 2017.

the Slave Trade, and Institutions and Practices Similar to Slavery[181] was adopted in 1956. International rules evolved to address new forms of slavery including servitude and forced labour in the Universal Declaration of Human Rights (UDHR),[182] the European Convention on Human Rights,[183] the International Covenant on Civil and Political Rights (ICCPR),[184] the American Convention on Human Rights[185] and the African Charter.[186] The explicit inclusion of sexual slavery in the Rome Statute was further facilitated by international norms related to the crime as discussed previously at the Vienna and Beijing conferences and also in reports of the UN Special Rapporteur on the Situation of Systematic Rape, Sexual Slavery and Slavery-Like Practices during Armed Conflict and the UN Special Rapporteur on Violence against Women, its Causes and Consequences.[187] Reflecting customary law, the explicit inclusion of sexual slavery in the Rome Statute represents the codification of a specific kind of slavery that is increasingly recognised as a major problem worldwide. Its codification shows that the ICC negotiations heavily relied on precedents. However, precedents were chosen and interpreted taking new contexts into consideration.[188] Clearly linking the crime of sexual slavery to the well-recognised crime of enslavement, the inclusion of sexual slavery in the ICC instruments marks a shift away from an understanding of sexualised violence as an honour crime and refocused attention on the actions of the perpetrator.[189]

As the explicit inclusion of sexual slavery as a war crime and crime against humanity under the ICC instruments was based on the Women's Caucus' advocacy, it is an example of an NGO teaching its views to states. The Women's Caucus understood sexual slavery to be a form of gender violence, which is

181 Supplementary Convention on the Abolition of Slavery, the Slave Trade, and Institutions and Practices Similar to Slavery (7 September 1956) 266 UNTS 3 (Supplementary Slavery Convention) <www.legal-tools.org/doc/d038c8/> accessed 18 August 2017.

182 Universal Declaration of Human Rights (10 December 1948) UN Doc A/RES/217 A (III) (UDHR) art 4 <www.legal-tools.org/doc/de5d83/> accessed 18 August 2017.

183 Convention for the Protection of Human Rights and Fundamental Freedoms (European Convention on Human Rights, as Amended) (4 November 1950) 213 UNTS 222 (ECHR) art 4(1) <www.legal-tools.org/doc/c809a3/> accessed 18 August 2017.

184 International Covenant on Civil and Political Rights (16 December 1966) 999 UNTS 171 (ICCPR) art 8 <www.legal-tools.org/doc/2838f3/> accessed 18 August 2017.

185 American Convention on Human Rights (22 November 1969) (Pact of San Jose) art 6(1) <www.legal-tools.org/doc/1152cf/> accessed 18 August 2017.

186 African Charter on Human Rights and Peoples' Rights (27 June 1981) OAU Doc CAB/LEG/67/3 Rev 5, 21 ILM 58 (1982) (Banjul Charter) art 5 <www.legal-tools.org/doc/f0db44/> accessed 18 August 2017.

187 Oosterveld, 'Sexual Slavery and the International Criminal Court' (n 9) 615.

188 Katharine Bartlett, 'Feminist Legal Methods' (1990) 103 *Harvard Law Review* 829, 852–853.

189 Oosterveld, 'Sexual Slavery and the International Criminal Court' (n 9) 608–609; Women's Caucus for Gender Justice, 'Recommendations and Commentary for December 1997 PrepCom' (n 31).

structural violence.[190] It gave 'the enslavement of women through forced marriage or otherwise for domestic as well as sexual service'[191] as one example. Irrespective of an initial agreement or some kind of exchange,

> [s]lavery and enslavement are the exercise of control over another person as chattel. Kidnapping, deceiving or coercing a woman, under threat of death, bodily injury, starvation to herself or others, to submit to serial rape as 'comfort women' or to be 'temporary wives,' providing both sexual and domestic services is, in the terms of article 1(1) of the 1926 Slavery Convention, placing her in 'the status or condition of a person over whom any or all of the powers attaching to the right of ownership are exercised.' It may also qualify as a condition of 'serfdom' under article 1(b) of the Supplementary Convention on the Abolition of Slavery.[192]

Referring to international rules, this elaboration gives examples of how a woman might enter into slavery as well as of possible forms of coercion, of how powers attaching to the right of ownership might be exercised over her. Contrary to the Women's Caucus' later view that the term 'coercion' is preferable to 'force' as it more clearly includes less direct or threatening situations,[193] the elaboration only lists physical forms of coercion, most of them directed at the victim.

The Women's Caucus' elaboration on enslavement and slavery explicitly include forced marriage in times of armed conflict where women are abducted and made fighters' wives. Under threat of death and bodily injury they are forced to provide sexual and domestic services to their forced husbands. According to the Caucus, this way, rights of ownership are exercised over forced wives. As forced wives are bound to live and work on land that belongs to their forced husbands or the fighting group, forced to serve their husband sexually and otherwise and are not free to change their situation, forced marriage could also qualify as a condition of serfdom.[194]

The Women's Caucus proposed to include 'all forms of enslavement, including sexual or domestic enslavement and forced marriage, by sale, deception, coercion or threat'[195] in the war crimes provisions of the Rome Statute that cover grave breaches of the Geneva Conventions. In contrast to the above elaboration on sexual slavery, this definition is gender-neutral. It simultaneously broadens and limits ways a person can be obtained by leaving out any reference

190 Women's Caucus for Gender Justice, 'Recommendations and Commentary for December 1997 PrepCom' (n 31).

191 ibid.

192 ibid.

193 Women's Caucus for Gender Justice, 'Priority Concerns Related to the Elements Annex' (n 24).

194 Women's Caucus for Gender Justice, 'Recommendations and Commentary for December 1997 PrepCom' (n 31).

195 ibid.

to kidnapping but including sale and threat. Regarding the criminalisation of forced marriage under the ICC instruments, this change is rather unfortunate as most forced wives are abducted into forced marriage. Therefore, a direct reference to kidnapping in the definition of enslavement would have made the link between the crimes clearer. However, this is ensured by the direct inclusion of forced marriage into the definition of enslavement.

Contrary to these efforts led by the Women's Caucus, the Holy See[196] submitted a proposal deleting the reference to sexual slavery, enforced prostitution and enforced pregnancy from the list of sexualised crimes. It was replaced with a separate subsection listing 'enslavement or any other kind of involuntary servitude that emerges from the theatre of war or armed conflict'[197] as a war crime in international and internal conflicts. Eventually, the proposal was not adopted.[198] Nevertheless, it sparked a heated debate between delegates of the Holy See and Bosnia and Herzegovina about the crime of forced pregnancy.[199] The proposal also sparked questions regarding the difference between enslavement and sexual slavery. If sexual slavery would be a form of enslavement, the Holy See's proposal would have reduced overlap.[200] However, sexual slavery as a serious, distinctive, sufficiently established crime demands express recognition which would also increase the Rome Statute's gender-sensitivity.[201]

Even though it becomes clear that the Holy See's proposal was aimed at the crime of enforced pregnancy, at first glance, it could be viewed as being directed at the crime of sexual slavery. The retention of references to enslavement and involuntary servitude in the Holy See's proposal, however, indicates that the proposal did not target sexual slavery and, by extension, forced marriage. This

196 Cynthia Rothschild, *Written Out: How Sexuality Is Used to Attack Women's Organizing* (International Gay and Lesbian Human Rights Commission and Center for Women's Global Leadership 2005). The Holy See exercised considerable influence in international negotiations like the Beijing Conference and the ICC negotiations. It utilised its observer status with the UN to gain access to meetings, making the Holy See uniquely positioned to move resources including information and personnel across the physical and institutional divide between states and non-governmental organisations (NGOs). The Holy See formed alliances with Latin American countries and conservative North American NGOs to counter certain developments in women's rights. Like the Arab block, the Holy See's rhetoric exploited moral universalism and national particularism alike, depending on its conversation partner.

197 PrepCom2, 'Proposal Submitted by the Holy See' (9 December 1997) UN Doc A/AC.249/1997/WG.1/DP.12 <www.legal-tools.org/doc/b00a30/> accessed 10 August 2017.

198 Interview 1 (21 March 2014); Oosterveld, 'Sexual Slavery and the International Criminal Court' (n 9) 214. See PrepCom2, 'Proposal Submitted by Holy See, Article 5 [20] War Crimes, B (p bis)' (1 April 1998) UN Doc A/AC.249/1998/DP.13 <www.legal-tools.org/doc/f8ff69/> accessed 18 August 2017: Here, the list of sexualised crimes includes sexual slavery.

199 Interview 4 (n 736); Wilmshurst, 'ICC: PrepCom 13–31 March 2000' (n 144).

200 Oosterveld, 'Sexual Slavery and the International Criminal Court' (n 9) 622.

201 ibid 622–623.

also becomes apparent when considering that medieval canonists already stressed the importance of mutual free consent to marriage for it to be valid. Based on this, the Holy See would have had an interest in criminalising forced marriage. Since the emphasis on free consent to marriage is based on an understanding that it is related to a person's dignity, the Holy See might understand forced marriage to be a violation of someone's dignity[202] and, by extension, an honour crime. In contrast to the critique voiced above in regard to the categorisation of rape as an outrage upon personal dignity, however, the Holy See understood physical integrity, autonomy and self-determination to be based on someone's dignity.[203] Following this, forced marriage as a violation of someone's dignity would also be a violation of a person's integrity and (sexual) autonomy. Focusing on the language of the Holy See's proposal, it suggests a broader wording than the list of sexualised crimes which would still include forced marriage. In contrast to an understanding of forced marriage as a form of sexual slavery, it does not focus on the crime's sexual elements. However, by subsuming it under enslavement and involuntary servitude, exactly these sexual elements would be eclipsed. Just as it is misleading to overemphasise the sexual elements of forced marriage, it is misleading to downplay them. Consequently, the Holy See's proposal would not have contributed to a more informed understanding of the crime.

Outlining the discussions regarding the crime of sexual slavery in the fifth PrepCom session shows that the Women's Caucus explicitly mentioned forced marriage in times of armed conflict as a form of sexual slavery.[204] Therefore, forced marriage can be interpreted to be indirectly included in the Rome Statute. However, it was not discussed in any depth. The Caucus also did not consider forced marriage as a specific act of sexualised violence independent of sexual slavery.[205] Other questions such as the distinction between, and respective definition of, sexual slavery, enslavement, forced prostitution and human trafficking took priority over considerations of forced marriage and whether it indeed constitutes a form of sexual slavery.[206]

202 ibid.
203 ibid.
204 See Chapter 6 for a detailed discussion of the Women's Caucus' understanding of forced marriage as a form of sexual slavery.
205 Interview 17 (17 June 2014); Interview 18 (n 42); Women's Caucus for Gender Justice, 'Recommendations and Commentary for December 1997 PrepCom' (n 31).
206 See PrepCom, 'Report of the Preparatory Committee on the Establishment of an International Criminal Court, Volume II' (n 22) 69; Boot (n 116) 213; Melanie O'Brien, '"Don't Kill Them, Let's Choose Them as Wives": The Development of the Crime of Forced Marriage, Sexual Slavery and Enforced Prostitution in International Criminal Law' (2016) 20 *The International Journal of Human Rights* 386; Oosterveld, 'Sexual Slavery and the International Criminal Court' (n 9) 619–623; Women's Caucus for Gender Justice, 'Priority Concerns Related to the Elements Annex' (n 24); Women's Caucus for Gender Justice, 'Recommendations and Commentary for December 1997 PrepCom' (n 31).

The United Nations Conference of Plenipotentiaries on the Establishment of an International Criminal Court (Rome Conference)

During plenary discussions in Rome, forced marriage was not mentioned. An article published in the fifth issue of *Terra Viva*, however, cites Conse A, who was abducted by the Lord's Resistance Army (LRA), saying that 'girls were forcefully married off to men who were cruel'.[207]

The crime of sexual slavery was introduced by the United Nations Children's Fund and Ugandan delegate Mr Kirabokyamaria in relation to children. Regarding the conflicts in Rwanda, the former Yugoslavia, Sierra Leone and Uganda, both actors referred to children being abducted and subjected to deprivations of liberty, and physical and sexualised violence.[208] In an interview with *Terra Viva*, Eva Boenders, representative of the Children's Caucus, emphasised that 'child recruits may also be sexually abused and forced to live as sexual slaves to soldiers'.[209] During the discussions in the Committee of the Whole, Mr von Hebel of the Netherlands mentioned that a compromise text of crimes against humanity explicitly including sexual slavery received wide support.[210]

The official records of the Rome Conference show that the crime against humanity of enslavement was defined based on a proposal submitted by Italy[211] as an exercise of powers attaching to the right of ownership. Trafficking in women and children was given as an example.[212] In addition to being based

207 Farhan Haq, 'UNICEF Eyes Higher Recruitment Age' *Terra Viva* (Rome, 19 June 1998) 1–2.

208 Diplomatic Conference of Plenipotentiaries on the Establishment of an International Criminal Court, 'Official Records of the United Nations Diplomatic Conference of Plenipotentiaries on the Establishment of an International Criminal Court, Vol. II' (n 71) 112, 118; see also 'Kids Murdered, Forced into Rebel Armies in Uganda' *Terra Viva* (Rome, 15 June 1998) 12.

209 On the Record, 'Child Soldiering and Recruitment Attached' *Terra Viva* (Rome, 17 June 1998) 6; see also Eva Boenders, 'How to Protect Children with a Strong and Effective Court' *ICC Monitor* (New York, 19 June 1998) 2.

210 Diplomatic Conference of Plenipotentiaries on the Establishment of an International Criminal Court, 'Official Records of the United Nations Diplomatic Conference of Plenipotentiaries on the Establishment of an International Criminal Court, Vol. II' (n 71) 268.

211 Interview 19 (n 9); Oosterveld, 'Sexual Slavery and the International Criminal Court' (n 9) 614: The loose coalition of state and non-state actors that supported the inclusion of sexual slavery in the Rome Statute supported whichever Coalition member spoke first to ensure a progressive definition of, and approach to, sexual slavery. While it was difficult to coordinate who spoke first, it influenced the actor's power position in the International Criminal Court (ICC) negotiations.

212 Diplomatic Conference of Plenipotentiaries on the Establishment of an International Criminal Court, 'Official Records of the United Nations Diplomatic Conference of Plenipotentiaries on the Establishment of an International Criminal Court, Vol. III, Rome, 15 June–17 July 1998' (2002) UN Doc A/CONF.183/13 (Vol. III) 95 <www.legal-tools.org/doc/e03967/> accessed 10 August 2017.

on Article 1(1) of the Slavery Convention, this definition reflects the PrepCom debate regarding the overlapping circle of crimes and if it should be completed, linking the crimes of sexual slavery, enslavement and trafficking in persons.[213]

Some delegations at the Rome Conference were aware of academic proposals for the elements of sexual slavery.[214] M Cherif Bassiouni, for example, proposed the following elements for the crime of sexual bondage: 'an institution or practice whereby a person is forcibly transferred or held for the purpose of performing any sexual conduct whatsoever, whether for reward or not'.[215] Even though Kelly Dawn Askin did not include the crime of sexual slavery in her proposed definitions of sexualised crimes, her definition of forced prostitution was considered helpful in the discussions of the crime of sexual slavery. Askin proposed the following elements for the crime of enforced prostitution: '(a) [...] the accused unlawfully forced or coerced a certain named or described person to engage in sexual acts; and (b) [a]s a result of the force or coercion, the person's reproductive capacity was affected.'[216]

The Preparatory Commission for the International Criminal Court (PrepCom2)

Just as the PrepCom2 negotiations are crucial for an analysis of the process of defining war rape under the ICC instruments, they are of great importance when analysing the process of defining forced marriage as a form of sexual slavery as the PrepCom2 negotiations dealt with the question of how to define crimes. This sets them apart from previous discussions in the PrepCom and Rome Conference that focused on the categorisation of crimes as acts of genocide, crimes against humanity and war crimes. As in the first part of this chapter, the sections below cover the first five PrepCom2 sessions as the negotiations of the ICC Elements of Crime were completed in the fifth session.

First session, February 1999

After the Rome Conference, the elements of the crime of sexual slavery, including some of the questions raised in the December 1997 PrepCom, were discussed at every session of the PrepCom2.

The USA proposed for the elements of the crime against humanity and war crime of sexual slavery to include an attack on a person including depriving

213 Oosterveld, 'Sexual Slavery and the International Criminal Court' (n 9) 628.

214 ibid.

215 M. Cherif Bassiouni, *A Draft International Criminal Code and Draft Statute for an International Criminal Court* (Martinus Nijhoff Publishers 1987) 147.

216 Kelly Dawn Askin, *War Crimes against Women: Prosecution in International War Crimes Tribunals* (Kluwer International Law 1997) 396.

them of their liberty and causing them to engage in sexual acts.[217] A comment to the article states that 'deprivation of liberty' is to be understood broadly to include physical detention and confinement as well as severe deprivations of autonomy and freedom of movement.[218] This understanding resonates with the Women's Caucus view regarding the element of force to include non-physical coercion.[219] The USA's definition of sexual slavery could include forced marriage in times of armed conflict as in most cases women are forced to engage in sexual acts. While not all forced wives are confined, deprivation of autonomy and freedom of movement are characteristics of their everyday life.

Drawing on international normative structures in the form of statements of the UN Special Rapporteur on the Situation of Systematic Rape, Sexual Slavery and Slavery-Like Practices during Armed Conflict and the indictment in the *Foča* case as precedents, the Women's Caucus brought forward a different definition comparable to that of the crime of enslavement. Describing the act of enslavement rather than the status or condition of the victim,[220] the Caucus defined sexual slavery as '[t]he exercise of any or all of the powers attaching to the right of ownership or control when such exercise involves obtaining or imposing sexual service and/or access through rape or other forms of sexual violence.'[221] Explicitly mentioning forced marriage, the Women's Caucus distinguished between institutionalised and individualised sexual slavery. It gave the comfort women in the Second World War as an example for the former, and forced marriage is an example for the latter. Elaborating on forced marriage, the Caucus understood it to include situations where women are kidnapped or make a choiceless decision to become a fighter's wife or serve him sexually as a means of survival. Forced marriage can include physical confinement as well as situations where the woman is free to leave albeit with no place to go.[222]

Second session, July/August 1999

In the second PrepCom2 session, Costa Rica, Hungary and Switzerland[223] proposed a different set of elements for the war crime of sexual slavery that was based on ICRC research.[224] It was drafted to avoid the problem raised by the

217 PrepCom2, 'Proposal Submitted by the United States of America: Draft Elements of Crimes: Addendum' (Crimes against Humanity) (n 87) art 7(1)(g)(2)(1), art 7(1)(g)(2)(3); PrepCom2, 'Proposal Submitted by the United States of America: Draft Elements of Crimes: Addendum' (War Crimes) (n 87) art 8(2)(b)(xxii)(2), art 8(2)(e)(vi)(1)(2), art 8(2)(e)(vi)(1)(2)(3), art 8(2)(e)(vi)(1)(2)(4).

218 PrepCom2, 'Proposal Submitted by the United States of America: Draft Elements of Crimes: Addendum' (Crimes against Humanity) (n 87).

219 Spees, 'Women's Advocacy in the Creation of the International Criminal Court' (n 36) 1241.

220 Hall, 'Article 7 Crimes against Humanity para. 1 (c) Enslavement' (n 174).

221 Women's Caucus for Gender Justice, 'Priority Concerns Related to the Elements Annex' (n 24).

222 ibid.

223 Oosterveld, 'Sexual Slavery and the International Criminal Court' (n 9) 629.

224 Interview 12 (n 80); Interview 13 (n 43); Interview 15 (n 111).

US proposal in regard to the term 'attack', 'deprived' and 'deprivation' which some delegations saw as inappropriate and to set unnecessarily high threshold for the prosecutor.[225] Costa Rica, Hungary and Switzerland defined sexual slavery as '[t]he perpetrator treat[ing] a person as chattel by exercising any or all of the powers attaching to the right of ownership, including sexual access through rape or other forms of sexual violence'.[226] The last subordinate clause is comparable to the definition of sexual slavery suggested by the Women's Caucus in the previous PrepCom2 session. As illustrated before, forced marriage in times of armed conflict could come under this definition. Drawing on the international rules of the 1926 Slavery Convention and the UN Special Rapporteur on the Situation of Systematic Rape, Sexual Slavery and Slavery-Like Practices during Armed Conflict, the same wording can also be found in the request from the governments of Belgium, Costa Rica, Finland, Hungary, Korea, South Africa and Switzerland regarding the text prepared by the ICRC on Article 8(2)(b), (c) and (e).[227] The ICRC explicitly quoted the Special Rapporteur, who understood situations of forced marriage, forced labour and forced sexual activity as examples of sexual slavery.[228] Generally, the ICRC's proposal introduced by Belgium and others is closer to the Rome Statute's definition of enslavement.[229] The first element set out the concept of slavery while the second element described the sexual aspect of slavery.[230] However, many delegations felt that the reference to chattel was outdated, inappropriate and vague, linking the concept of sexual slavery to the ownership of saleable property and classic concepts of chattel slavery.[231] To overcome these criticisms, Colombia proposed to

225 Oosterveld, 'Sexual Slavery and the International Criminal Court' (n 9) 629.

226 PrepCom2, 'Proposal Submitted by Costa Rica, Hungary and Switzerland on Certain Provisions of Article 8 Para. 2(b) of the Rome Statute of the International Criminal Court: (viii), (x), (xiii), (xiv), (xv), (xvi), (xxi), (xxii), (xxvi)' (n 110).

227 PrepCom2, 'Request from the Governments' (n 107).

228 Special Rapporteur on the Situation of Systematic Rape, Sexual Slavery and Slavery-Like Practices during Armed Conflict as cited in PrepCom2, 'Request from the Governments' (n 107); United Nations Commission on Human Rights, 'Final Report of the Special Rapporteur on the Situation of Systematic Rape, Sexual Slavery and Slavery-Like Practices during Armed Conflict' (n 143).

229 Assembly of States Parties to the Rome Statute of the International Criminal Court, 'Official Records of the Assembly of States Parties to the Rome Statute of the International Criminal Court, First Session, New York, 3–10 September 2002' (9 September 2002) ICC-ASP/1/3 (Part II.B) art 7(2)(c) <www.legal-tools.org/doc/3c0e2d/> accessed 9 August 2017: 'The perpetrator exercised any or all of the powers attaching to the right of ownership over one or more persons, such as by purchasing, selling, lending or bartering such a person or persons, or by imposing on them a similar deprivation of liberty.'

230 Oosterveld, 'Sexual Slavery and the International Criminal Court' (n 9) 630.

231 Roger S. Clark, 'Crimes against Humanity and the Rome Statute of the International Criminal Court', in Guiseppe Nesi and Mauro Politi (eds), *The Rome Statute of the International Criminal Court: A Challenge to Impunity* (Ashgate Publishing Co 2001) 75, 83; La Haye (n 119) 191; Oosterveld, 'Sexual Slavery and the International Criminal Court' (n 9) 629.

define sexual slavery as situations where powers attaching to the right of ownership are exercised over a person who is also subjected to acts of sexualised violence.[232] In contrast to the proposal by the Women's Caucus[233] and the delegations of Costa Rica, Hungary and Switzerland, the reference to 'rape or other forms of sexual violence'[234] is eliminated here. This way, this definition circumvents discussions of consent.[235] Mediating between state delegations, the Women's Caucus developed a definition of sexual slavery that includes elements of the Costa Rican, Hungarian and Swiss definition as well as the definition proposed by Colombia. It covers situations where '[t]he perpetrator [...] [exercised] any or all of the powers attaching to the right of ownership, including sexual access through rape or other forms of sexual violence.'[236] This way, it is consistent with the ICC's definition of enslavement which emphasises the element of ownership. As illustrated in Chapter 5 and in the discussion above, all of the definitions referred to in this paragraph could include forced marriage in wartime.

Resonating with a previous elaboration on the crime of slavery and enslavement by the Women's Caucus,[237] the US suggested including an illustrative list of actions that qualify as the exercise of powers attaching to the right of ownership in the elements of the crime of sexual slavery. Similar to the USA's insistence on attaching a document outlining the elements of crimes to the Rome Statute, this was motivated by the opinion that more precision was needed.[238] Establishing a direct link between the accused and the purchase or sale and including a reference to labour without compensation, the USA's proposal was criticised for potentially excluding indirect perpetrators and situations of slavery with

232 PrepCom2, 'Proposal Submitted by Colombia: Comments on the Proposal by the Delegations of Costa Rica, Hungary and Switzerland Concerning Article 8, Paragraph 2(b) of the Rome Statute (PCNICC/1999/WGEC/DP.8)' (n 112).

233 Women's Caucus for Gender Justice, 'Priority Concerns Related to the Elements Annex' (n 24).

234 PrepCom2, 'Proposal Submitted by Costa Rica, Hungary and Switzerland on Certain Provisions of Article 8 Para. 2(b) of the Rome Statute of the International Criminal Court: (viii), (x), (xiii), (xiv), (xv), (xvi), (xxi), (xxii), (xxvi)' (n 110).

235 PrepCom2, 'Proposal Submitted by Colombia: Comments on the Proposal by the Delegations of Costa Rica, Hungary and Switzerland Concerning Article 8, Paragraph 2(b) of the Rome Statute (PCNICC/1999/WGEC/DP.8)' (n 112).

236 Women's Caucus for Gender Justice, 'Recommendations and Commentary for the Elements Annex' (July 1999) <www.iccwomen.org/wigjdraft1/Archives/oldWCGJ/icc/iccpc/071999pc/elements.htm> accessed 22 January 2014).

237 Women's Caucus for Gender Justice, 'Recommendations and Commentary for December 1997 PrepCom' (n 31).

238 Interview 12 (n 80); Dörmann, *Elements of War Crimes under the Rome Statute of the International Criminal Court* (n 55) 328; Hall, 'The First Five Sessions of the UN Preparatory Commission for the International Criminal Court' (n 3) 781; Oosterveld, 'Sexual Slavery and the International Criminal Court' (n 9) 631.

compensation.[239] Forced marriage in times of armed conflict, for example, is a crime where multiple perpetrators can play different roles including bringing, exposing and accepting a woman for the purpose of forced marriage. The material support a forced wife receives from her forced husband could arguably be understood as a form of compensation.

The outcome of the discussions of the elements of the crime of sexual slavery was a rolling text that eliminated the reference to chattel, kept the ICC's definition of enslavement, included an open list of examples of how the right of ownership might be exercised and established a specific connection to the sexual aspect of slavery.[240] It states that

> [t]he accused exercised a power attaching to the right of ownership over one or more persons, such as by purchasing, selling, lending or bartering such a person or persons, or by imposing on them a similar deprivation of liberty [and] [t]he accused caused such a person or persons to engage in one or more acts of a sexual nature.[241]

Other examples such as recruiting or abducting that would have been particularly relevant for the crime of forced marriage were not included because they were understood to define the means of obtaining a person and not to describe directly an exercise of ownership.[242] Nevertheless, forced marriage in wartime could fall within this definition if 'a similar deprivation of liberty' is interpreted so as to include abduction, a forced exclusive sexual and non-sexual relationship, forced pregnancy, forced childbearing and upbringing, and forced labour.

The wording of the definition of sexual slavery included in the rolling text is very different from the various proposals previously submitted. The first subordinate clause was taken from the 1926 Slavery Convention. The second subordinate clause reflects the USA's concerns regarding an illustrative list of how powers attaching to the right of ownership could be exercised. Of this list, only selling overlaps with a previous definition suggested by the Women's Caucus.[243] Similarly to the Caucus' definition, the one included in the rolling text includes pecuniary as well as non-pecuniary elements. The Women's Caucus' definition, however, focused on ways of obtaining a person while the definition

239 Hall, 'The First Five Sessions of the UN Preparatory Commission for the International Criminal Court' (n 3) 781; Oosterveld, 'Sexual Slavery and the International Criminal Court' (n 9) 631.

240 Oosterveld, 'Sexual Slavery and the International Criminal Court' (n 9) 632.

241 PrepCom2, 'Discussion Paper Proposed by the Coordinator: Article 8, paragraph 2(b)(xxii)' (n 117); PrepCom2, 'Proceedings of the Preparatory Commission at Its Second Session' (n 117) art 8(2)(b)(xxii)(2).

242 La Haye (n 119) 191.

243 Women's Caucus for Gender Justice, 'Recommendations and Commentary for December 1997 PrepCom' (n 31).

in the rolling text gives examples of the exercise of powers attaching to the right of ownership after a person has been obtained. The term 'similar deprivation of liberty' on the one hand resonates with the *Foča* indictment and the Women's Caucus' proposal to include physical and psychological forms of confinement.[244] On the other hand, it can be limiting as the discussion of the fourth PrepCom2 session below shows. The whole first element of the definition in the rolling text is the same as that of the crime of enslavement as defined in the ICC Elements of Crimes.[245]

Third session, November/December 1999

The discussions of the November/December 1999 PrepCom2 session reviewed questions regarding the illustrative list of ways in which rights of ownership might be exercised; its inclusion, exclusion, scope and (commercial) focus.[246] Colombia, Switzerland, the US and the Women's Caucus participated in these discussions and considered the Supplementary Slavery Convention and the *Foča* indictment.[247] Eventually, this debate on the elements of the crime of sexual slavery was overtaken by the wider discussions on an overall compromise package on the elements of crimes against humanity[248] and the August 1999 rolling text remained unchanged.[249]

Early in the December 1999 negotiations, the Arab block proposed that the elements of sexual slavery should stipulate that '[p]owers attaching to the right

244 Women's Caucus for Gender Justice, 'Priority Concerns Related to the Elements Annex' (n 24).

245 PrepCom2, 'Report of the Preparatory Commission' (n 153) art 7(1)(c)(1).

246 PrepCom2, 'Proposal Submitted by Colombia: Comments on the Documents Submitted by Egypt (PCNICC/1999/WGEC/DP.42), Germany and Canada (PCNICC/1999/WGEC/DP.36), and Bahrain, Iraq, Kuwait, Lebanon, the Libyan Arab Jamahiriya, Oman, Qatar, Saudi Arabia, the Sudan, the Syrian Arab Republic and the United Arab Emirates (PCNICC/1999 WGEC/DP.39)' (n 148); PrepCom2, 'Proposal Submitted by Columbia: Comments on the Proposals Submitted by Canada and Germany on Article 7 and by Japan on the "Structure" of Elements for Crimes against Humanity' (6 December 1999) UN Doc PCNICC/1999/WGEC/DP.41 <www.legal-tools.org/doc/0f89ea/> accessed 18 August 2017; Clark (n 231) 83; Oosterveld, 'Sexual Slavery and the International Criminal Court' (n 9) 632.

247 Oosterveld, 'Sexual Slavery and the International Criminal Court' (n 9) 632.

248 ibid 633–634.

249 PrepCom2, 'Addendum: Annex III: Elements of Crimes' (22 December 1999) (n 140) art 7(1)(g)(2), art 8(2)(b)(xxii)(2), art 8(2)(e)(vi)(2); PrepCom2, 'Addendum: Annex III: Elements of Crimes' (07 April 2000) UN Doc PCNICC/2000/L.1/Rev.1/Add.2 art 7(1)(g)(2), art 8(2)(b)(xxii)(2), art 8(2)(e)(vi)(2) <www.legal-tools.org/doc/5ca0b8/> accessed 10 August 2017; PrepCom2, 'Delegation of Samoa: Some Suggestions on How the Elements of Genocide and Crimes against Humanity might be Re-Worked in the Light of Paragraphs 5 and 6 of the Report of the Informal Intel-Sessional Meeting in Siracusa, 31 January–6 February 2000' (13 March 2000) <www.legal-tools.org/doc/addd3b/> accessed 7 February 2014; PrepCom2, 'Proposal Submitted by Canada and Germany on Article 7' (n 140) art 7(1)(g)(2).

of ownership do not include rights, duties and obligations incident to marriage between a man and a woman'.[250] The Arab block prioritised the protection of religious or cultural practices and traditions. As mentioned above, the reference to (patriarchal) cultural norms indicates an understanding of sexual slavery as a

250 PrepCom2, 'Proposal Submitted by Bahrain, Iraq, Kuwait, Lebanon, the Libyan Arab Jamahiriya, Oman, Qatar, Saudi Arabia, the Sudan, the Syrian Arab Republic and United Arab Emirates Concerning the Elements of Crimes against Humanity (9 December 1999)' (n 142); see Chapter 7 for a detailed discussion of the Arab block's proposal.

Rothschild (n 196); see also Valerie Oosterveld, 'The Definition of "Gender" in the Rome Statute of the International Criminal Court: A Step Forward or Back for International Criminal Justice?' (2005) *Harvard Human Rights Journal* 55: It has to be mentioned that the Arab block's opposition analysed in this chapter was not new. Striking parallels can be drawn between Cynthia Rothschild's analysis of the opposition raised at the Beijing Conference and against its Platform for Action and the ICC negotiations. At both occasions, Arab and Sub-Saharan countries as well as a Catholic alliance led by the Holy See and supported by Latin American countries portrayed women's rights advocacy and activism as a threat to country, community and family. Supporting the development of women's rights was viewed through a national and regional lens as officially approving sexual perversion including extra-marital sex. In Beijing, New York and Rome, opponents of the development of women's rights used rhetoric combining nationalism, traditionalism, moral absolutism and intolerance. National norms and rules were used as a defence against critique. They enabled states to position themselves as representing the uniting voice of the people in projecting a national (patriarchal) identity. Nationalism was used to defend the ideal identity of a state. In the name of divine moral values, local prejudices were endorsed by religion. The West was called upon to respect diverse traditions that were presented as if there is one truth to them. Those who were constructed as threatening national identity and independence were simultaneously constructed as foreign, as the 'other'. Universally binding international law was perceived as an affront to particularity, sovereignty and nationalism. On this base, opponents raised questions regarding the (im)possibility of translating terms like 'sexual orientation' and 'gender', stated their incomprehension of those terms and concepts, and invoked the defence of human dignity. Misinformation about the meaning of such terms fuelled fears raised by the development of women's rights. Syria, for example, feared that women would stop bearing children if they had equality. As Rothschild demonstrated in regard to the Beijing Platform for Action and as was shown in this chapter using the example of the discussions of the crime of sexual slavery in the ICC negotiations, opponents brought up domestic norms and rules as a tool to close down discussions of women's rights. In trying to erase ideas, they facilitated their construction. Links were invoked and simultaneously, their existence was denied as if this would change the facts. Using the ICC negotiations of the elements of sexual slavery as an example, the Arab block's proposal establishes a connection between sexual slavery and marital rights, duties and obligation. At the same time, however, the Arab block denied this connection by stating that powers attaching to the right of ownership exclude marital rights, duties and obligation. This, however, does not change the fact that some marital rights, duties and obligations could amount to powers attaching to the right of ownership and therefore to slavery. By aiming to explicitly exclude marriage rights, duties and obligations from the crime of sexual slavery and therefore connecting, and at the same time disconnecting, domestic marriage practices and the crime of sexual slavery, women's rights were rendered both a taboo and a pervasive threat. The urgency with which women's rights were circumscribed in the Beijing and ICC negotiations highlighted their potential power and use as a source of strength.

form of structural violence. The Arab block was concerned that activist judges could use the perceived ambiguous law on crimes against humanity as a tool of social engineering.[251] The Arab block was concerned that the elements might be drafted so wide as to criminalise certain domestic practices as crimes against humanity.[252] However, as crimes against humanity are intended to be universal and fall within human rights and international criminal law, most delegations could not accept such culturally specific exemptions and were concerned about setting a precedent that could have an adverse impact in the human rights field.[253] The inclusion of culturally specific exceptions, for example, might have led to the (discussion about the) inclusion of penalties recognised under Shari'a law such as the death penalty.[254] Since it would have also conflicted with values and norms regarding the separation of Church and State, a point was made by dissenting delegations that religious values should not shape the law.[255] Moreover, the inclusion of these exceptions might have appeared to be an international endorsement of such situations. Accepting the Arab block's proposal would have resulted in approving acts that violate values and norms most delegations at the ICC negotiations shared. These delegations would not allow the Arab states' proposal as it would permit people to do something immoral. Moreover, as a practical matter, the exceptions requested were hardly necessary. Although far from acceptable for some delegations, they would hardly qualify as a widespread or systematic attack against a civilian population. In a situation of widespread violence amounting to crimes against humanity, however, the blanket exclusion of all family matters would result in impunity for crimes committed against family members.[256] The Women's Caucus stressed that the proposal's content discriminates against women by trying to exclude crimes which affect women disproportionately from the ICC's jurisdiction. Therefore, the adoption of the Arab block's proposal would violate international law.[257] The Caucus drew on international norms in the form of the statements of the Convention on the Elimination of Discrimination against Women (CEDAW) and the Vienna Declaration and Programme of Action, and referred to Article 4 of the Declaration on the Elimination of Violence against Women (DEVAW) which affirms that

251 Robinson (n 144) 65.

252 Interview 18 (n 42); Interview 11 (n 133): It was also suggested by other delegates that the Arab block's proposal regarding the crime of sexual slavery targeted gay marriage rather than aiming at excluding marriage relations from powers attaching to the right of ownership.

253 Oosterveld, 'Sexual Slavery and the International Criminal Court' (n 9) 636–637; Robinson (n 144) 65–66.

254 Interview 1 (n 198); Interview 3 (25 March 2014).

255 Interview 2 (n 114).

256 Interview 14 (26 May 2014); Robinson (n 144) 66.

257 Women's Caucus for Gender Justice, 'Recommendations and Commentary to the Elements Annex and Rules of Procedure and Evidence' (June 2000) <www.iccwomen.org/wigjdraft1/Archives/oldWCGJ/icc/iccpc/062000pc/elementsannex.htm> accessed 23 January 2014.

'[s]tates should condemn violence against women and should not invoke any custom, tradition or religious consideration to avoid their obligations with respect to its elimination.'[258] Consequently, the Arab block's proposal was dismissed.

Fourth session, March 2000

The fourth PrepCom2 session continued to discuss questions regarding the illustrative list of ways in which rights of ownership might be exercised. Colombia proposed to explicitly include 'transferring [...] [and] trafficking' and to recognise the multiplicity of powers attaching to the right of ownership.[259] As mentioned above, the latter would be of relevance to the criminalisation of forced marriage in times of armed conflict. Human Rights Watch, in contrast, suggested to either delete the illustrative list completely or to expand it to include modern-day slave-like practices like debt bondage and forced labour. Without mentioning forced marriage even though it had been recognised as a form of sexual slavery before,[260] the international NGO argued that the current list would work to limit the scope of the Rome Statute due to the terminology 'such as', generally interpreted as limiting the scope of the definition to conduct of a similar nature to that specified in the list. In regard to the elements of sexual slavery, Human Rights Watch argued that deprivations of liberty would be restricted to deprivations of a similar nature to those set out in the list. Consequently, the common element to all of the examples would be a commercial exchange. Any further elaboration on the definition should be along the lines of powers of ownership that limit a person's (sexual) autonomy.[261] In an article published in the *ICC Monitor*, the journal of the Coalition for the International Criminal Court (CICC), Fanny Fontaine, Jean Carmalt and Bruce Broomhall followed a Canadian proposal and suggested to clarify the issues arising around the list by adding to sexual slavery the same footnote as to enslavement. This clarified that forced

258 UNGA, 'Declaration on the Elimination of Violence against Women' (20 December 1993) UN Doc A/RES/48/104 (DEVAW).

259 PrepCom2, 'Comments by Colombia on the Elements of Crimes of Article 7 in Document PCNICC/1999/L.5/Rev.1/Add.2' (n 120) art 7(1)(g)(2); PrepCom2, 'Comments by Colombia Regarding the Elements of Crimes of Article 8 (2) (b), 8 (2) (c) and 8 (2) (e) in Document PCNICC/1999/L.5/Rev.1/Add.2' (n 120) art 8(2)(b)(xxii)(2), art 8(2)(e)(vi)(2).

260 Human Rights Watch, 'Getting Away with Murder, Mutilation, Rape: New Testimony from Sierra Leone' (July 1999) <www.hrw.org/reports/1999/sierra/> accessed 2 December 2014; Human Rights Watch, 'Sowing Terror: Atrocities against Civilians in Sierra Leone' (July 1998) <www.hrw.org/legacy/reports98/sierra/> accessed 2 December 2014.

261 Hall, 'The First Five Sessions of the UN Preparatory Commission for the International Criminal Court' (n 3) 781; Human Rights Watch, 'Commentary to the 4th Preparatory Commission Meeting for the ICC' (March 2000) <www.iccnow.org/documents/HRWRulesofProcMarch2000.pdf> accessed 23 January 2014; Women's Caucus for Gender Justice, 'Recommendations and Commentary to the Elements Annex and Rules of Procedure and Evidence' (n 257).

labour, servile status and trafficking in persons fall within the scope of sexual slavery.[262] The footnote reads:

> It is understood that such deprivation of liberty may, in some circumstances, include exacting forced labour or otherwise reducing a person to a servile status. It is also understood that the conduct described in this element includes trafficking in persons, in particular women and children.[263]

Therefore, it would have also covered situations where

> a tenant who is by law, custom or agreement bound to live and labour on land belonging to another person and to render some determinate service to such other person, whether for reward or not, and is not free to change his status.[264]

Forced labour is an element of most forced marriages in wartime and forced wives are reduced to a servile status, forced to live with their forced husbands, work for them and see to their forced husbands' needs and wishes. However, the delegates remained reluctant to change the current language of the elements of the crime of sexual slavery as a war crime.[265]

Fifth session, July 2000

Contrary to the renewed advice of Human Rights Watch,[266] the final compromise for the elements of the crime of sexual slavery worked out in the fifth session of the PrepCom2 in July 2000 did not alter the list of examples. As suggested by Canada and the Women's Caucus, a clarifying footnote was added which links sexual slavery to the Supplementary Slavery Convention and establishes a

262 Bruce Broomhall, Jean Carmalt and Fanny Fontaine, 'June Preparatory Commission will Address Important Issues' *ICC Monitor* (New York, June 2000) 3.

263 PrepCom2, 'Addendum: Annex III: Elements of Crimes' (7 April 2000) (n 249) fn 11.

264 Supplementary Slavery Convention (n 181) art 1(b). The crime of forced labour is not specifically defined in the 1956 Supplementary Slavery Convention (n 181). However, in its preamble, the convention mentions the Convention Concerning Forced or Compulsory Labour (28 June 1930) No 29 (Forced Labour Convention) and subsequent action by the International Labour Organization in regard to forced or compulsory labour. The Forced Labour Convention defines forced labour as 'all work or service which is extracted from any person under the menace of any penalty and for which the said person has not offered himself voluntarily'.

265 Human Rights Watch, 'Commentary to the Preparatory Commission on the International Criminal Court: Elements of Crimes and Rules of Procedure and Evidence' (June 2000) <www.iccnow.org/documents/HRWElementsofCrimeJune2000.pdf> accessed 23 January 2014.

266 Human Rights Watch, 'Commentary to the Preparatory Commission on the International Criminal Court' (n 265) 15–17.

connection between deprivation of liberty, forced labour, reducing a person to a servile status and trafficking, especially in women and children.[267] Agreement on this language was facilitated by referring to international rules in the form of the Supplementary Slavery Convention, by describing the limits of 'servile status' and by repeating parts of the definition of enslavement.[268] This 'helped to ensure that the crime [...] include[s] slavery-like conditions such as [...] forced marriage'[269] and would also amount to other inhumane treatment if the essential elements are met.[270] The Women's Caucus' suggestion to include the words 'with or without pecuniary benefit'[271] was not taken up. The Caucus also raised the point that the inclusion of a reference to trafficking would not adequately address the link between slavery and commercial transactions as trafficking includes self-same.[272] A second footnote was added to the elements of sexual slavery, recognising that, '[g]iven the complex nature of this crime', its commission 'could involve more than one perpetrator as a part of a common criminal purpose'.[273] Attempts to illustrate variations, however, were rejected. It was argued that this result would be achieved by applying Article 25(3) of the Rome Statute, covering different forms of participation in the commission of a crime as well as the commission of a crime jointly with or through another person.[274] As the finalised draft text of the Elements of Crimes shows, the definition of sexual slavery remained as agreed in the second PrepCom2 session.[275]

In summary, the final text of the elements of crimes of sexual slavery reflects three main areas of debate. First, rejecting references to attack or chattel, the exercise of any or all of the powers attaching to the right of ownership was adopted as a test for determining slavery. Second, as a compromise, an open, illustrative list of examples of the exercise of powers attaching to the right of ownership was adopted. Third, a footnote was added to expand the illustrative list. This resulted out of the concerns of many delegations that the wording in the illustrative list would lead to an interpretation that the exercise of powers attaching to the right of ownership required a commercial or pecuniary aspect. The footnote makes it clear that the illustrative list is to be read broadly and in line with international law instruments such as the 1956 Supplementary

267 PrepCom2, 'Report of the Preparatory Commission' (n 153) fn 18.

268 Dörmann, *Elements of War Crimes under the Rome Statute of the International Criminal Court* (n 55) 328.

269 Women's Caucus for Gender Justice, 'Recommendations and Commentary to the Elements Annex and Rules of Procedure and Evidence' (n 257); see also Cottier (n 62) 446.

270 Hall, 'Article 7 Crimes against Humanity para. 1 (c) Enslavement' (n 174) 194.

271 Women's Caucus for Gender Justice, 'Recommendations and Commentary to the Elements Annex and Rules of Procedure and Evidence' (n 257).

272 ibid.

273 PrepCom2, 'Report of the Preparatory Commission' (n 153) fn 17.

274 Dörmann, *Elements of War Crimes under the Rome Statute of the International Criminal Court* (n 55) 329.

275 PrepCom2, 'Report of the Preparatory Commission' (n 153).

Slavery Convention. It confirms that commercial or pecuniary exchange or advantage is not necessary to demonstrate that a person exercised powers attaching to the right of ownership.[276]

Conclusion on forced marriage

Retracing who the key actors were in the ICC negotiations of forced marriage showed that the ICRC as well as the Women's Caucus were two international non-governmental delegations that drove the discussions. Regarding state delegations, the Arab block, Canada, Colombia, the Holy See and the US made relevant contributions.

Based on the Final Report of the UN Special Rapporteur on the Situation of Systematic Rape, Sexual Slavery and Slavery-Like Practices during Armed Conflict, the ICRC,[277] but first and foremost the Women's Caucus,[278] were the only delegations directly mentioning forced marriage. They understood it as a form of structural violence in the form of sexual slavery.

Taught by the Women's Caucus, states included sexual slavery in the list of sexualised crimes as a crime against humanity and a war crime. This was a creative legislative exercise because sexual slavery had not constituted an international crime in its own right before the adoption of the Rome Statute and related international rules were not very precise. The Holy See[279] opposed the explicit inclusion of sexual slavery in the ICC statute but retained a reference to enslavement and involuntary servitude which would still have covered forced marriage in times of armed conflict. The Holy See's understanding of the requirement for mutual free consent to marriage for a marriage to be valid further indicates that it would not oppose the criminalisation of forced marriage. Since the emphasis on free consent to marriage is based on an understanding that it is related to a person's dignity, the Holy See might understand forced marriage to be a violation of someone's dignity[280] and, by extension, an honour crime.

Regarding the definition of sexual slavery, the Women's Caucus proposed a wording based on Article 1(1) of the 1926 Slavery Convention,[281] where sexual slavery was defined in terms of exercising powers attaching to the right of ownership. To distinguish sexual slavery from slavery, the definition also includes the performance of sexual acts. A similar wording was proposed by Belgium and others[282] as well as

276 Oosterveld, 'Sexual Slavery and the International Criminal Court' (n 9) 640–641.
277 PrepCom2, 'Request from the Governments' (n 107).
278 For example, Women's Caucus for Gender Justice, 'Recommendations and Commentary for December 1997 PrepCom' (n 31).
279 PrepCom2, 'Proposal Submitted by the Holy See' (n 197).
280 Interview 1 (n 198).
281 Slavery Convention (n 180).
282 PrepCom2, 'Request from the Governments' (n 107).

by Costa Rica, Hungary and Switzerland.[283] Like their definition of rape, their definition of sexual slavery was influenced by ICRC research on the state of the law on (sexual) slavery. Colombia proposed a similar definition.[284] The definitions referred to here only differed in the words used to describe the sexual elements of the crime. In addition, the Women's Caucus initially introduced the explicit inclusion of 'control' in the definition. Costa Rica, Hungary and Switzerland added a reference to chattel. Neither wording was eventually adopted. The USA's reference to deprivation of liberty was adopted[285] and its suggestion to include an illustrative list of actions that qualify as the exercise of rights attaching to the powers of ownership was also taken up. In contrast to the USA's focus on direct perpetrators, however, a footnote now stresses that the commission of sexual slavery could involve more than one perpetrator as a part of a common criminal purpose.[286] The inclusion and wording of this as well as of footnote 18[287] in the definition of sexual slavery was supported by the Women's Caucus and Canada. This way, Colombia's proposal[288] to include an explicit reference to trafficking was respected.

Opposing these developments, the Arab block submitted a proposal[289] that excludes marriage rights, duties and obligations from powers attaching to the right of ownership. As with rape, the Arab block founded its opposition on national laws, religious principles and cultural norms. Furthermore, the Arab block was motivated by fear that some of their traditional cultural and family

283 PrepCom2, 'Proposal Submitted by Costa Rica, Hungary and Switzerland on Certain Provisions of Article 8 Para. 2(b) of the Rome Statute of the International Criminal Court: (viii), (x), (xiii), (xiv), (xv), (xvi), (xxi), (xxii), (xxvi)' (n 110).

284 PrepCom2, 'Proposal Submitted by Colombia: Comments on the Proposal by the Delegations of Costa Rica, Hungary and Switzerland Concerning Article 8, Paragraph 2(b) of the Rome Statute (PCNICC/1999/WGEC/DP.8)' (n 112).

285 PrepCom2, 'Proposal Submitted by the United States of America: Draft Elements of Crimes: Addendum' (Crimes against Humanity) (n 87); PrepCom2, 'Proposal Submitted by the United States of America: Draft Elements of Crimes: Addendum' (War Crimes) (n 87).

286 PrepCom2, 'Report of the Preparatory Commission' (n 153).

287 Assembly of States Parties to the Rome Statute of the International Criminal Court (n 229) art 7(1)(g)(2): 'It is understood that such deprivation of liberty may, in some circumstances, include exacting forced labour or otherwise reducing a person to a servile status as defined in the Supplementary Convention on the Abolition of Slavery, the Slave Trade, and Institutions and Practices Similar to Slavery of 1956. It is also understood that the conduct described in this element includes trafficking in persons, in particular women and children.'

288 PrepCom2, 'Comments by Colombia on the Elements of Crimes of Article 7 in Document PCNICC/1999/L.5/Rev.1/Add.2' (n 120); PrepCom2, 'Comments by Colombia Regarding the Elements of Crimes of Article 8 (2) (b), 8 (2) (c) and 8 (2) (e) in Document PCNICC/1999/L.5/Rev.1/Add.2' (n 120).

289 PrepCom2, 'Proposal Submitted by Bahrain, Iraq, Kuwait, Lebanon, the Libyan Arab Jamahiriya, Oman, Qatar, Saudi Arabia, the Sudan, the Syrian Arab Republic and United Arab Emirates Concerning the Elements of Crimes against Humanity (9 December 1999)' (n 142).

norms could fall within the reach of crimes against humanity, as well as fear of social engineering.

Conclusion

Building on the analysis of the ICC negotiations in general that was advanced in Chapter 4, Chapter 5 focused specifically on the negotiations of war rape and forced marriage in times of violent conflict. The aim of Chapter 5 was to analyse who the key actors were that drove the negotiations of the definitions of war rape and forced marriage, why they got involved in the ICC negotiations of these two crimes and what influenced their positions. Another goal was to examine how these actors interpreted the crimes of war rape and forced marriage.

The ICRC and especially the Women's Caucus as non-state actors as well as the Arab block, Colombia and the US as state actors drove the ICC negotiations of the crimes of war rape and forced marriage in times of armed conflict.

Chapter 5 confirmed that international as well as national norms and rules matter in international relations and law-making. The Arab block's, Colombia's and the US' national normative structures had an impact on the ICC negotiations. Amongst the international normative structures that influenced the negotiations were the 1907 Hague and 1949 Geneva conventions, Protocol I and II Additional to the Geneva Conventions, the 1926 Slavery Convention, and the ICTY and ICTR instruments and judgments in the *Akayesu* and *Furundžija* cases. In addition, the Final Report of the UN Special Rapporteur on the Situation of Systematic Rape, Sexual Slavery and Slavery-Like Practices during Armed Conflict as well as the Vienna and Beijing conferences and Platforms for Action were referred to. However, due to the actors' different mandates, common sources of information were interpreted and used differently.

In the negotiations of the definition of both war rape and forced marriage, the Women's Caucus taught its views to states. As a non-state and therefore outside actor in international law-making, it presented problems and solutions to states. Rather than sticking to their initial proposals and including rape as constituting other crimes like an outrage upon personal dignity, states followed the Caucus and listed sexualised crimes in the Rome Statute as separate offences as well as possibly constituting other crimes. This understanding avoids marginalising sexualised crimes and is in line with the prohibition of gender-based discrimination. The Women's Caucus was also partly successful in teaching states to construct a definition of rape using the term 'invasion' rather than 'penetration' as that would create a broader, more inclusive, gender-neutral definition that highlights rape as an assault on a person's integrity and autonomy rather than honour and dignity. A rape definition using 'invasion' emphasises that rape is an act of violence and domination. Following the Women's Caucus, Costa Rica advocated a rape definition using the term 'invasion'. The ICRC was another crucial non-governmental actor that influenced the definition of war rape. However, as the guardian of international humanitarian law, it had to take a more conservative stance. Based on ICRC research, Belgium, Colombia, Costa Rica, Finland, Hungary, Korea, South Africa and Switzerland suggested definitions using the term 'penetration'. This was also advanced by the US. Considering the importance of consensus in the ICC negotiations, the final wording of the definition of rape was a compromise that included suggestions from both sides. Another example of a situation in which the Women's Caucus taught its views to states is the move away from the initial understanding of rape as an outrage upon personal dignity and therefore a victim-centred honour crime, towards a focus on the perpetrator and an interpretation of rape as a form of structural violence that is rooted in patriarchy. A focus on the perpetrator is also achieved by constructing a broad coercion-based rather than consent-based definition. These views were adopted by the US.

Regarding forced marriage, only the Women's Caucus and the ICRC explicitly mentioned the crime in their discussions. Both understood it as a form of sexual slavery that was defined based on the 1926 Slavery Convention definition of slavery with an added sexual element. Here, again, Belgium and others, Colombia, Costa Rica together with Hungary and Switzerland, and the US submitted relevant proposals and Canada was also involved in the discussions. However, since the Caucus was the first actor to introduce the issue in the ICC negotiations, it can be said that it taught its views to states.

The Women's Caucus, however, did not always succeed in teaching its views to states. As the expression of 'invasion resulting in penetration' shows, its call not to construct a rape definition with cumbersome and unnecessarily specific wording was not followed. Indicating that the Caucus did not always follow its own advice, it suggested to include the words "with or without pecuniary benefit"[290] in the definition of sexual slavery. This, however, was not taken up. In general, the analysis of the development of the definition of rape and sexual slavery indicated that the Women's Caucus succeeded more in teaching its views on rape than its views on sexual slavery to states. In the negotiations of the definition of sexual slavery, the (Supplementary) Slavery Convention, the report of the UN Special Rapporteur on the Situation of Systematic Rape, Sexual Slavery and Slavery-Like Practices during Armed Conflict, and the *Foča* indictment appeared to have been more influential than the Caucus. Since the mere direct inclusion of sexual slavery already constituted a creative law-making exercise, delegates supposedly wanted to err on the side of caution in defining the crime so as not to jeopardise their gains and potentially even the whole ICC project. They had to keep in mind that every proposition that encountered

290 Women's Caucus for Gender Justice, 'Recommendations and Commentary to the Elements Annex and Rules of Procedure and Evidence' (n 257).

significant opposition might have been the straw to break the camel's back.[291] Therefore, they stayed away from more progressive definitions that could have explicitly included forced marriage in times of armed conflict and relied on established international rules like the (Supplementary) Slavery Convention in defining sexual slavery. A similar theory can be developed when taking into account that forced marriage was mentioned more often and directly in relation to the crime of enslavement and slavery, two established offences. This solid ground offered scope for progressive elaborations and definitions that included forced marriage in times of armed conflict.

Colombia, the ICRC, the US and the Women's Caucus faced opposition from the Arab block. Falling back on national laws, religious principles and cultural norms, it introduced a proposal that would have made marital sexual intercourse consensual by definition. It also would have excluded marriage rights, duties and obligations from powers attaching to the right of ownership. The Arab block's proposal arose out of concern that some of its traditional family and cultural norms could fall within the reach of crimes against humanity as well as out of concern about social engineering. This confirms that national norms and rules matter in international relations.

In addition to actors understanding rape as an act of invasion or penetration perpetrated under coercive circumstances and/or without the consent of the victim, the initial inclusion of war rape as an outrage upon personal dignity in the ILC draft statute as well as the Arab block's national understanding of the crime that influenced its position in the ICC negotiations demonstrate that war rape was at least partly understood as an honour crime. The Women's Caucus saw rape as a form of structural violence that is rooted in patriarchy. It advanced the same general understanding to sexual slavery and, by extension, forced marriage. The Holy See, in contrast, might have interpreted forced marriage as an honour crime as it is a violation of someone's dignity.

Comparing the process of defining war rape and forced marriage under the ICC instruments highlights that largely the same actors were involved in the negotiations of both crimes. Non-state actors, especially the Women's Caucus, played a role in both the discussions of war rape and of forced marriage. Actors from states with strong patriarchal structures, where religion plays a leading role in legal and social matters, opposed development of progressive definitions of war rape and forced marriage. This indicates that actors in the ICC negotiations of both crimes were shaping, and being shaped by, national and international norms and rules. The compromise definition of war rape that all actors could agree on defines the crime as an 'invasion resulting in penetration'. Forced marriage was understood as a form of sexual slavery and not defined as a crime in and of itself. Therefore, the actors in the ICC negotiations did not develop elements of the crime of forced marriage. Both war rape and forced marriage

291 Interview 18 (n 42).

were understood as honour crimes by some actors who participated in the ICC negotiations, and as a form of structural violence by others.

Bibliography

Conventions and statutes

African Charter on Human Rights and Peoples' Rights (27 June 1981) OAU Doc CAB/LEG/67/3 Rev 5, 21 ILM 58 (1982) (Banjul Charter) <www.legal-tools.org/doc/f0db44/> accessed 18 August 2017.

American Convention on Human Rights (22 November 1969) (Pact of San Jose) <www.legal-tools.org/doc/1152cf/> accessed 18 August 2017.

Charter of the International Military Tribunal (8 August 1945) 82 UNTS 279, 59 Stat 1544, 3 Bevans 1238, 39 AJIL 258 (London Agreement).

Convention Concerning Forced or Compulsory Labour (28 June 1930) No 29 (Forced Labour Convention).

Convention for the Protection of Human Rights and Fundamental Freedoms (European Convention on Human Rights, as amended) (4 November 1950) 213 UNTS 222 (ECHR) <www.legal-tools.org/doc/c809a3/> accessed 18 August 2017.

Convention to Suppress the Slave Trade and Slavery (25 September 1926) 60 LNTS 253, Registered No 1414 (Slavery Convention) <www.legal-tools.org/doc/12c9d8/> accessed 18 August 2017.

International Covenant on Civil and Political Rights (16 December 1966) 999 UNTS 171 (ICCPR) <www.legal-tools.org/doc/2838f3/> accessed 18 August 2017.

Rome Statute of the International Criminal Court (17 July 1998) 2187 UNTS 3 <www.legal-tools.org/doc/7b9af9/> accessed 9 August 2017.

Supplementary Convention on the Abolition of Slavery, the Slave Trade, and Institutions and Practices Similar to Slavery (7 September 1956) 266 UNTS 3 (Supplementary Slavery Convention) <www.legal-tools.org/doc/d038c8/> accessed 18 August 2017.

Universal Declaration of Human Rights (10 December 1948) UN Doc A/RES/217 A (III) (UDHR) <www.legal-tools.org/doc/de5d83/> accessed 18 August 2017.

United Nations documents

Commission on Human Rights

United Nations Commission on Human Rights, 'Final Report of the Special Rapporteur on the Situation of Systematic Rape, Sexual Slavery and Slavery-Like Practices during Armed Conflict' (22 June 1998) UN Doc E/CN.4/Sub.2/1998/13 <www.ohchr.org> accessed 28 August 2017 ©1998 United Nations. Reprinted with the Permission of the United Nations.

General Assembly

UNGA, 'Declaration on the Elimination of Violence against Women' (20 December 1993) UN Doc A/RES/48/104 (DEVAW).

Preparatory Committee on the Establishment of an International Criminal Court

PrepCom, 'Article 20 Quater: Crimes against Humanity (Delegation of the United Kingdom)' (26 March 1996) <www.legal-tools.org/doc/d7a59c/> accessed 7 February 2014.

———, 'Chairman's Informal Text No 2: Article 20 Quarter, Crimes against Humanity' (29 March 1996) UN Doc A/AC.249/1996/WG.1/IP.2 <www.legal-tools.org/doc/32b618/> accessed 18 August 2017.

———, 'Chairman's Informal Text No 4: Article 20 ter, War Crimes' (4 April 1996) UN Doc A/AC.249/1996/WG.1/IP.4 <www.legal-tools.org/doc/560c38/> accessed 18 August 2017.

———, 'Crimes against Humanity (Delegation of the Netherlands)' (27 March 1996) <www.legal-tools.org/doc/63f87a/> accessed 7 February 2014.

———, 'Crimes against Humanity (Delegation of New Zealand)' (30 March 1996) <www.legal-tools.org/doc/10ff0d/> accessed 7 February 2014.

———, 'Crimes against Humanity (Japanese Text)' (26 March 1996) <www.legal-tools.org/doc/d21c80/> accessed 7 February 2014.

———, 'Decisions Taken by the Preparatory Committee at Its Session from 11 to 21 February 1997' (12 March 1997) A/AC.249/1997/L.5 <www.legal-tools.org/doc/c0d16c/> accessed 9 August 2017.

———, 'Decisions Taken by the Preparatory Committee at Its Session Held from 1 to 12 December 1997' (18 December 1997) UN Doc A/AC.249/1997/L.9/Rev.1 <www.legal-tools.org/doc/787a4d/> accessed 9 August 2017.

———, 'Draft Consolidated Text: War Crimes' (20 February 1997) UN Doc A/AC.249/1997/WG.1/CRP.2 <www.legal-tools.org/doc/4d5877/> accessed 18 August 2017.

———, 'Draft: Optional Approaches to the Definition of War Crimes (Delegation of Egypt)' (29 March 1996) <www.legal-tools.org/doc/d78835/> accessed 7 February 2014.

———, 'For Annex to Statute: Elements Related to Article on Crimes against Humanity (Delegation of the United States)' (27 March 1996) <www.iccnow.org/documents/USCrimesAgainstHumanity.pdf> accessed 5 December 2013.

———, 'For Annex to Statute: Elements Related to Article on Crimes against Humanity (Delegation of the United States)' (2 April 1996) <www.legal-tools.org/doc/4d62f1/> accessed 7 February 2014.

———, 'German Synoptical Working Paper on War Crimes' (25 June 1997) <www.legal-tools.org/doc/0d8997/> accessed 7 February 2014.

———, 'Informal Working Paper on War Crimes' (14 July 1997) UN Doc A/AC.249/1997/WG.1/IP/REV.1 <www.legal-tools.org/doc/39864b/> accessed 18 August 2017.

———, 'Informal Working Paper on War Crimes' (31 October 1997) UN Doc A/AC.249/1997/WG.1/IP <www.legal-tools.org/doc/435c11/> accessed 18 August 2017.

———, 'Informal Working Paper on War Crimes' (3 December 1997) UN Doc A/AC.249/1997/WG.1/CRP.7 <www.legal-tools.org/doc/8e28b2/> accessed 18 August 2017.

———, 'Informal Working Paper on War Crimes, Addendum' (4 December 1997) UN Doc A/AC.249/1997/WG.1/CRP.7/Add.1 <www.legal-tools.org/doc/d3b1e7/> accessed 18 August 2017.

———, 'Informal Working Paper on War Crimes (Article 20(c))' (12 December 1997) UN Doc A/AC.249/1997/WG.1/IP <www.legal-tools.org/doc/b6c406/> accessed 10 August 2017.

———, 'Informal Working Paper on War Crimes, Option B (Delegations of the United Kingdom and Germany)' (12 December 1997) <www.legal-tools.org/doc/5adc48/> accessed 7 February 2014.

———, 'Preliminary Text: War Crimes' (20 February 1997) UN Doc A/AC.249/1997/WG.1/IP/REV.1 <www.legal-tools.org/doc/596e8a/> accessed 18 August 2017.

———, 'Proposal by Austria on Crimes against Humanity' (26 March 1996) <www.legal-tools.org/doc/f6d477/> accessed 7 February 2014.

———, 'Proposal by Austria on Serious Violations of the Laws and Customs Applicable in Armed Conflicts' (2 April 1996) <www.legal-tools.org/doc/302b0d/> accessed 7 February 2014.

———, 'Proposal by the United States of America on Elements of Offenses for the International Criminal Court' (2 April 1998) UN Doc A/AC.249/1998/DP.11 <www.legal-tools.org/doc/50fc48/> accessed 18 August 2017.

———, 'Redraft of the ILC Article 20 on ICC Jurisdiction with Proposed Elements (Delegation of the United States)' (22 March 1996) <www.legal-tools.org/doc/efc778/> accessed 7 February 2014.

———, 'Reference Paper Elements of Offenses for the International Criminal Court (Delegation of the United States)' (27 March 1998) <www.iccnow.org/documents/USElementsofOffensesMarch98.pdf> accessed 5 December 2013.

———, 'Report of the Inter-Sessional Meeting from 19 to 30 January 1998 in Zutphen, the Netherlands' (4 February 1998) UN Doc A/AC249/1998/L.13 <www.legal-tools.org/doc/7ba9a4/> accessed 9 August 2017.

———, 'Report of the Preparatory Committee on the Establishment of an International Criminal Court, Volume I' (13 September 1996) UN Doc A/51/22 [Vol. I] <www.legal-tools.org/doc/e75432/> accessed 18 August 2017.

———, 'Report of the Preparatory Committee on the Establishment of an International Criminal Court, Volume II' (13 September 1996) UN Doc A/51/22 [Vol. II] <www.legal-tools.org/doc/03b284/> accessed 9 August 2017.

———, 'War Crimes (Delegation of New Zealand)' (30 March 1996) <www.legal-tools.org/doc/af17c3/> accessed 7 February 2014.

———, 'Working Paper Submitted by the Delegations of New Zealand and Switzerland' (14 February 1997) UN Doc A/AC.249/1997/WG.1/DP.2 <www.legal-tools.org/doc/7ba0b8/> accessed 18 August 2017.

Preparatory Commission for the International Criminal Court

PrepCom2, 'Addendum: Annex III: Elements of Crimes' (22 December 1999) UN Doc PCNICC/1999/L.5/Rev.1/Add.2 <www.legal-tools.org/doc/e51882/> accessed 18 August 2017.

———, 'Comments by Colombia on Document PCNICC/1999/WGEC/RT.6 Proposed by the Coordinator' (10 November 1999) UN Doc PCNICC/1999/WGEC/DP.30 <www.legal-tools.org/doc/e01ec9/> accessed 18 August 2017.

———, 'Comments by Colombia on the Elements of Crimes of Article 7 in Document PCNICC/1999/L.5/Rev.1/Add.2' (1 March 2000) UN Doc PCNICC/2000/WGEC/DP.2 <www.legal-tools.org/doc/c92bf1/> accessed 10 August 2017.

———, 'Comments by Colombia Regarding the Elements of Crimes of Article 8 (2) (b), 8 (2) (c) and 8 (2) (e) in Document PCNICC/1999/L.5/Rev.1/Add.2' (8 March 2000) UN Doc PCNICC/2000/WGEC/DP.4 <www.legal-tools.org/doc/405370/> accessed 18 August 2017.

———, 'Delegation of Samoa: Some Suggestions on how the Elements of Genocide and Crimes against Humanity Might be Re-Worked in the Light of Paragraphs 5 and 6 of the Report of the Informal Intel-Sessional Meeting in Siracusa, 31 January–6 February 2000' (13 March 2000) <www.legal-tools.org/doc/addd3b/> accessed 7 February 2014.

———, 'Discussion Paper Proposed by the Coordinator: Article 7 (Crimes against Humanity)' (15 December 1999) UN Doc PCNICC/1999/WGEC/RT.16 <www.legal-tools.org/doc/225a2c/> accessed 10 August 2017.

———, 'Discussion Paper Proposed by the Coordinator: Article 8, Paragraph 2(b) (xxii)' (10 August 1999) UN Doc PCNICC/1999/WGEC/RT.6 <www.legal-tools.org/doc/a4a83f/> accessed 10 August 2017.

———, 'Proceedings of the Preparatory Commission at Its First Session (16–26 February 1999)' (02 March 1999) PCNICC/1999/L.3/Rev.1 <www.legal-tools.org/doc/aced45/> accessed 10 August 2017.

———, 'Proceedings of the Preparatory Commission at Its Second Session (26 July–13 August 1999)' (18 August 1999) UN Doc PCNICC/1999/L.4/Rev.1 <www.legal-tools.org/doc/0b6332/> accessed 10 August 2017.

———, 'Proposals by Delegations of Bolivia, Colombia, Chile, Cuba, Ecuador, Spain . . . Regarding Crimes against Humanity in the Draft Elements of Crimes' (30 June 2000) UN Doc PCNICC/2000/1.1/Rev.1/Add.2 <www.legal-tools.org/doc/874907/> accessed 18 August 2017.

———, 'Proposal Submitted by Bahrain, Iraq, Kuwait, Lebanon, the Libyan Arab Jamahiriya, Oman, Qatar, Saudi Arabia, the Sudan, the Syrian Arab Republic and United Arab Emirates Concerning the Elements of Crimes against Humanity (9 December 1999)' UN Doc PCNICC/1999/WGEC/DP.39 <www.legal-tools.org/doc/33d070/> accessed 10 August 2017.

———, 'Proposal Submitted by Canada and Germany on Article 7' (23 November 1999) UN Doc PCNICC/1999/WGEC/DP.36 <www.legal-tools.org/doc/2238df/> accessed 18 August 2017.

———, 'Proposal Submitted by Colombia: Comments on the Documents Submitted by Egypt (PCNICC/1999/WGEC/DP.42), Germany and Canada (PCNICC/1999/WGEC/DP.36), and Bahrain, Iraq, Kuwait, Lebanon, the Libyan Arab Jamahiriya, Oman, Qatar, Saudi Arabia, the Sudan, the Syrian Arab Republic and the United Arab Emirates (PCNICC/1999 WGEC/DP.39)' (9 December 1999) UN Doc PCNICC/1999/WGEC/DP.43 <www.legal-tools.org/doc/b3fd41/> accessed 18 August 2017.

———, 'Proposal Submitted by Colombia: Comments on the Proposal by the Delegations of Costa Rica, Hungary and Switzerland Concerning Article 8, Paragraph 2(b) of the Rome Statute (PCNICC/1999/WGEC/DP.8)' (29 July 1999) UN Doc PCNICC/1999/WGEC/DP.16 <www.legal-tools.org/doc/a3f95c/> accessed 10 August 2017.

———, 'Proposal Submitted by Columbia: Comments on the Proposals Submitted by Canada and Germany on Article 7 and by Japan on the "Structure" of Elements for Crimes against Humanity' (06 December 1999) UN Doc

PCNICC/1999/WGEC/DP.41 <www.legal-tools.org/doc/0f89ea/> accessed 18 August 2017.

———, 'Proposal Submitted by Costa Rica on Elements of Crimes' (24 February 1999) UN Doc PCNICC/1999/WGEC/DP.6 <www.legal-tools.org/doc/318088/> accessed 18 August 2017.

———, 'Proposal Submitted by Costa Rica, Hungary and Switzerland on Certain Provisions of Article 8 Para. 2(b) of the Rome Statute of the International Criminal Court: (viii), (x), (xiii), (xiv), (xv), (xvi), (xxi), (xxii), (xxvi)' (19 July 1999) UN Doc PCNICC/1999/WGEC/DP.8 <www.legal-tools.org/doc/704a4b/> accessed 10 August 2017.

———, 'Proposal Submitted by Costa Rica, Hungary and Switzerland on Certain Provisions of Article 8 Para. 2(e) of the Rome Statute of the International Criminal Court, (v), (vi), (vii), (viii), (xi), (xii)' (29 July 1999) PCNICC/1999/WGEC/DP.11 <www.legal-tools.org/doc/26ef83/> accessed 18 August 2017.

———, 'Proposal Submitted by the Holy See' (9 December 1997) UN Doc A/AC.249/1997/WG.1/DP.12 <www.legal-tools.org/doc/b00a30/> accessed 10 August 2017.

———, 'Proposal Submitted by Holy See, Article 5 [20] War Crimes, B (p bis)' (1 April 1998) UN Doc A/AC.249/1998/DP.13 <www.legal-tools.org/doc/f8ff69/> accessed 18 August 2017.

———, 'Proposal Submitted by the United States of America: Draft Elements of Crimes: Addendum' (4 February 1999) UN Doc PCINCC/1999/DP.4 <www.legal-tools.org/doc/423e2e/> accessed 18 August 2017.

———, 'Proposal Submitted by the United States of America: Draft Elements of Crimes: Addendum' (4 February 1999) UN Doc PCINCC/1999/DP.4/Add.1 <www.legal-tools.org/doc/f7f5cc/> accessed 10 August 2017.

———, 'Proposal Submitted by the United States of America: Draft Elements of Crimes: Addendum' (4 February 1999) UN Doc PCINCC/1999/DP.4/Add.2 <www.legal-tools.org/doc/d6dfdc/> accessed 10 August 2017.

———, 'Report of the Preparatory Commission for the International Criminal Court, Addendum: Part II, Finalized Draft Text of the Elements of Crimes' (2 November 2000) PCNICC/2000/1/Add.2 <www.legal-tools.org/doc/843931/> accessed 10 August 2017.

———, 'Report of the Working Group on Elements of Crimes: Crimes against Humanity (Article 7): Addendum' UN Doc PCNICC/2000/WGEC/L.1/Add.1 <www.legal-tools.org/doc/2be303/> accessed 10 August 2017.

———, 'Request from the Governments of Belgium, Costa Rica, Finland, Hungary, the Republic of Korea and South Africa and the Permanent Observer Mission of Switzerland Regarding the Text Prepared by the International Committee of the Red Cross on Article 8, Paragraph 2 (b), (c) and (e) of the Rome Statute of the International Criminal Court' (17 July 1999) UN Doc PCNICC/1999/WGEC/INF.2 <www.legal-tools.org/doc/d8ff04/> accessed 10 August 2017.

Security Council

UNSC Resolution 827 (25 May 1993) UN Doc S/RES/827 <www.legal-tools.org/doc/dc079b/> accessed 18 August 2017.

UNSC Resolution 955 (8 November 1994) UN Doc S/RES/955 <www.legal-tools.org/doc/f5ef47/> accessed 18 August 2017.

Other

Ad Hoc Committee on the Establishment of an International Criminal Court, 'Report of the Ad Hoc Committee on the Establishment of an International Criminal Court' 6 September 1995) UN Doc A/50/22 <www.legal-tools.org/doc/b50da8/> accessed 8 August 2017.

Assembly of States Parties to the Rome Statute of the International Criminal Court, 'Official Records of the Assembly of States Parties to the Rome Statute of the International Criminal Court, First Session, New York, 3–10 September 2002' (9 September 2002) ICC-ASP/1/3 (Part II.B) <www.legal-tools.org/doc/3c0e2d/> accessed 9 August 2017.

Diplomatic Conference of Plenipotentiaries on the Establishment of an International Criminal Court, 'Official Records of the United Nations Diplomatic Conference of Plenipotentiaries on the Establishment of an International Criminal Court, Vol. II, Rome, 15 June–17 July 1998' (2002) UN Doc A/CONR183/13 (Vol. 2) <www.legal-tools.org/doc/78fea6/> accessed 9 August 2017.

———, 'Official Records of the United Nations Diplomatic Conference of Plenipotentiaries on the Establishment of an International Criminal Court, Vol. III, Rome, 15 June–17 July 1998' (2002) UN Doc A/CONF.183/13 (Vol. 3) 95 <www.legal-tools.org/doc/e03967/> accessed 10 August 2017.

———, 'Report of the Preparatory Committee on the Establishment of an International Criminal Court: Addendum' (14 April 1998) UN Doc A/CONF.183/2/Add.1 20 <www.legal-tools.org/doc/816405/> accessed 11 August 2017.

International Law Commission, 'Draft Code of Crimes against the Peace and Security of Mankind' (17 July 1996) 51 UN GAOR Supp (No. 10) at 14, UN Doc A/CN.4/L.532, corr.1, corr.3 <www.legal-tools.org/doc/5e4532/> accessed 9 August 2017.

———, 'Report of the International Law Commission on the Work of Its Forty-Sixth Session, 2 May–22 July 1994' (1994) UN Doc A/49/10 <www.legal-tools.org/doc/f73459/> accessed 18 August 2017.

Other legal documents

Allied Control Council Law No 10 Punishment of Persons Guilty of War Crimes, Crimes against Peace and against Humanity (20 December 1945) 3 Official Gazette Control Council for Germany 50–55 (1946) <www.legal-tools.org/doc/ffda62/> accessed 18 August 2017.

Bahrain Penal Code (1976) <www.bahrainrights.org/sites/default/files/Bahrain-Penal-Code.doc> accessed 17 March 2014.

The Criminal Act of 1991 (Sudan) <www.icrc.org/applic/ihl/ihl-nat.nsf/xsp/.ibmmodres/domino/OpenAttachment/applic/ihl/ihl-nat.nsf/B9EEBA1CA8F54121C1256DC9005573F2/TEXT/Criminal%20Act%20-%20Sudan%20-%20EN.pdf> accessed 1 April 2014.

Iraqi Penal Code No 111 (1969) <www.iraq-lg-law.org/en/webfm_send/1350> accessed 18 March 2014.

Ley No 599 de 2000 Por la cual se expide el Código Penal (24 July 2000) (Colombia) <www.alcaldiabogota.gov.co/sisjur/normas/Norma1.jsp?i=6388> accessed 8 May 2015.

The Libyan Penal Code (1953) <https://ia600704.us.archive.org/25/items/LibyanPenalCodeenglish/LibyanPenalCode.pdf> accessed 24 March 2014.

Omani Penal Code (1974) <www.fiu.gov.om/forms.html> accessed 24 March 2014.

Qatari Penal Code (2004) <http://portal.www.gov.qa/wps/wcm/connect/8abaea8046be1deaae97ef70b3652ad8/Penal+Code.pdf?MOD=AJPERES&useDefaultText=0&useDefaultDesc=0> accessed 24 March 2014.

Interviews

Interview 1 (21 March 2014).

Interview 2 (24 March 2014).

Interview 3 (25 March 2014).

Interview 5 (1 April 2014).

Interview 6 (2 April 2014).

Interview 7 (4 April 2014).

Interview 8 (11 April 2014).

Interview 9 (11 April 2014).

Interview 10 (22 April 2014).

Interview 11 (23 April 2014).

Interview 12 (15 May 2014).

Interview 13 (15 May 2014).

Interview 14 (26 May 2014).

Interview 15 (27 May 2014).

Interview 16 (10 June 2014).

Interview 17 (17 June 2014).

Interview 18 (25 June 2014).

Interview 19 (26 November 2014).

Books

Askin, K.D., *War Crimes against Women: Prosecution in International War Crimes Tribunals* (Kluwer International Law 1997).

Bassiouni, M.C., *A Draft International Criminal Code and Draft Statute for an International Criminal Court* (Martinus Nijhoff Publishers 1987).

———, *The Legislative History of the International Criminal Court* (Transnational Publishers 2005).

Beigbeder, Y, *The Role and Statutes of International Humanitarian Volunteers and Organizations: The Rights and Duty to Humanitarian Assistance* (Martinus Nijhoff Publishers 1999).

Benedetti, F., Bonneau, K. and Washburn, J., *Negotiating the International Criminal Court: New York to Rome, 1994–1998* (Brill 2013).

Brownmiller, S., *Against Our Will: Men, Women and Rape* (Penguin Books 1977).

Cassese, A., Gaeta, P. and Jones, J.R.W.D. (eds), *The Rome Statute of the International Criminal Court: A Commentary* (Volume 1, Oxford University Press 2002).

Dörmann, K., *Elements of War Crimes under the Rome Statute of the International Criminal Court: Sources and Commentary* (Cambridge University Press 2003).

Forsythe, D.P., *The Humanitarians: The International Committee of the Red Cross* (Cambridge University Press 2005).

Human Rights Watch, *Justice in Balance: Recommendations for an Independent and Effective International Criminal Court* (Human Rights Watch 1998).

Lee, R. (ed), *The International Criminal Court: The Making of the Rome Statute: Issues, Negotiations, Results* (Kluwer Law International 1999).

Rothschild, C., *Written Out: How Sexuality Is Used to Attack Women's Organizing* (International Gay and Lesbian Human Rights Commission and Center for Women's Global Leadership 2005).

Schabas, W.A., *An Introduction to the International Criminal Court* (Cambridge University Press 2007).

Chapters in edited books

Askin, K.D., 'Women and International Humanitarian Law' in Kelly Dawn Askin and Dorean M. Koenig (eds), *Women and International Human Rights Law* (Transnational Publishers 1999).

Boot, M., 'Article 7 Crimes against Humanity Para. 1 (g) Rape … or Any Other Form of Sexual Violence of Comparable Gravity' in Otto Triffterer (ed), *Commentary on the Rome Statute of the International Criminal Court: Observers' Notes, Article by Article* (2nd edn, CH Beck 2008).

Clark, R.S., 'Crimes against Humanity and the Rome Statute of the International Criminal Court', in Guiseppe Nesi and Mauro Politi (eds), *The Rome Statute of the International Criminal Court: A Challenge to Impunity* (Ashgate Publishing Co 2001).

Cottier, M., 'Article 8 War Crimes Para. 2 (b) (xxii) Rape and Other Forms of Sexual Violence' in Otto Triffterer (ed), *Commentary on the Rome Statute of the International Criminal Court: Observers' Notes, Article by Article* (2nd edn, CH Beck 2008).

Dörmann, K., 'War Crimes under the Rome Statute of the International Criminal Court, with a Special Focus on the Negotiations on the Elements of Crimes' in Armin von Bogdandy and Rüdiger Wolfrum (eds), *Max Planck Yearbook of United Nations Law* (Volume 7, Martinus Nijhoff Publishers 2003).

Glasius, M., 'Who Is the Real Civil Society? Women's Groups versus Pro-Family Groups at the International Criminal Court Negotiations' in Jude Howell and Diane Mulligan (eds), *Gender and Civil Society* (Routledge 2004).

Hall, C.K., 'Article 7 Crimes against Humanity Para. 1 (c) Enslavement' in Otto Triffterer (ed), *Commentary on the Rome Statute of the International Criminal Court: Observers' Notes, Article by Article* (2nd edn, CH Beck 2008).

Khalaf, M.C., 'Lebanon' in Julia Breslin and Sanja Kelly (eds), *Women's Rights in the Middle East and North Africa: Progress Amid Resistance* (Freedom House/ Rowman & Littlefield Publishers 2010) 6 <www.freedomhouse.org/sites/default/files/inline_images/Lebanon.pdf> accessed 21 March 2014.

La Haye, E., 'Article 8(2)(b)(xii): Rape, Sexual Slavery, Enforced Prostitution, Forced Pregnancy, Enforced Sterilization, and Sexual Violence' in Roy S. Lee (ed), *The International Criminal Court: Elements of Crimes and Rules of Procedure and Evidence* (Transnational Publishers 2001).

Mischkowski, G., 'Sexualisierte Kriegsgewalt: Strafverfolgung und Wahrheitsfindung' in Medica Mondiale and Karin Griese (eds), *Sexualisierte Kriegsgewalt und ihre Folgen: Handbuch zur Unterstützung traumatisierter Frauen in verschiedenen Arbeitsfeldern* (2nd edn, Mabuse-Verlag 2006).

Pace, W.R. and Schense, J., 'Coalition for the International Criminal Court at the Preparatory Commission' in Roy S. Lee (ed), *The International Criminal Court: Elements of Crimes and Rules of Procedure and Evidence* (Transnational Publishers 2001).

Robinson, D., 'The Context of Crimes against Humanity' in Roy S. Lee (ed), *The International Criminal Court: Elements of Crimes and Rules of Procedure and Evidence* (Transnational Publishers 2001).

Steains, C., 'Gender Issues' in Roy Lee (ed), *The International Criminal Court: The Making of the Rome Statute: Issues, Negotiations, Results* (Kluwer Law International 1999).

Journal articles

Armstrong, J.D., 'The International Committee of the Red Cross and Political Prisoners' (1985) 39 *International Organization* 615.

Bartlett, K., 'Feminist Legal Methods' (1990) 103 *Harvard Law Review* 829.

Boon, K., 'Rape and Forced Pregnancy under the ICC Statute: Human Dignity, Autonomy, and Consent' (2001) 32 *Columbia Human Rights Law Review* 625.

Copelon, R., 'Gender Crimes as War Crimes: Integrating Crimes against Women into International Criminal Law' (2000) 46 *McGill Law Journal* 217.

Erb, N.E., 'Gender-Based Crimes under the Draft Statute of the Permanent International Criminal Court' (1998) 29 *Columbia Human Rights Law Review* 401.

Galtung, J., 'Violence, Peace, and Peace Research' (1969) 6 *Journal of Peace Research* 167.

Haveman, R., 'Rape and Fair Trial on Supranational Criminal Law' (2002) 9 *Maastricht Journal of European and Comparative Law* 263.

O'Brien, M., '"Don't Kill Them, Let's Choose Them as Wives": The Development of the Crime of Forced Marriage, Sexual Slavery and Enforced Prostitution in International Criminal Law' (2016) 20 *The International Journal of Human Rights* 386.

Oosterveld, V., 'The Definition of "Gender" in the Rome Statute of the International Criminal Court: A Step Forward or Back for International Criminal Justice?'(2005) *Harvard Human Rights Journal* 55.

———, 'Sexual Slavery and the International Criminal Court: Advancing International Law' (2004) 25 *Michigan Journal of International Law* 605.

Spees, P., 'Women's Advocacy in the Creation of the International Criminal Court: Changing the Landscape of Justice and Power' (2003) 28 *Signs* 1233.

ICC advocacy papers, commentaries, recommendations, reports and working papers

Amnesty International, 'Making the Right Choices – Part I – Defining the Crimes and Permissible Defences and Initiating a Prosecution' (January 1997) 29 <www.iccnow.org/documents/ALMakingRightChoises97PartI.pdf> accessed 5 December 2013.

Gillhoff, N. and Neuner, M., 'Some Observations on the Second Preparatory Commission: A NGO's Perspective' <www.iccnow.org/documents/ICLSObserve2ndPrepComNov99.pdf> accessed 22 January 2014.

Hall, C.K., 'Challenges Ahead for the United Nations Preparatory Committee Drafting a Statute for a Permanent International Criminal Court' (1996) Amnesty International 13 <www.iccnow.org/documents/AIPreCommittee1996_en.pdf> accessed 5 December 2013.

Human Rights Watch, 'Commentary to the 4th Preparatory Commission Meeting for the ICC' (March 2000) <www.iccnow.org/documents/HRWRulesofProcMarch2000.pdf> accessed 23 January 2014.

———, 'Commentary to the Preparatory Commission on the International Criminal Court: Elements of Crimes and Rules of Procedure and Evidence' (June 2000) <www.iccnow.org/documents/HRWElementsofCrimeJune2000.pdf> accessed 23 January 2014.

International Commission of Jurists, 'Third ICJ Position Paper' (August 1995) <www.iccnow.org/documents/1PrepCmt3rdPositionPaperICJ.pdf> accessed 5 December 2013.

International Committee of the Red Cross, 'Commentary: Definition of War Crimes: For the Preparatory Committee on the Establishment of an International Criminal Court (1–12 December 1997 Session)' (14 February 1997) <www.iccnow.org/documents/3PretCmtWarCrimesRedCross.pdf> accessed 7 May 2015.

———, 'Statement: Preparatory Committee on the Establishment of an International Criminal Court, New York, 1 to 12 December, 1997' (8 December 1997).

Schense, J., 'Draft Report on the Third Session of the Preparatory Commission, November 29–December 17, 1999, Coalition for an International Criminal Court' (24 January 2000) <www.iccnow.org/documents/3rdPrepComReportCICC.pdf> accessed 23 January 2014.

Wilmshurst, E., 'Annex to the ICC Report: Provisions of the Statute' (23 September 1998).

———, 'ICC: Preparatory Commission: 29 November–17 December 1999' (21 December 1999).

———, 'ICC: PrepCom 12–30 June: Second Week' (26 June 2000).

———, 'ICC: PrepCom 13–31 March 2000: Report' (4 April 2000).

———, 'ICC: PrepCom. 16–26 February 1999' (1 March 1999).

———, 'ICC: PrepCom: 26 July–13 August: Second Week' (13 December 1999).

———, 'International Criminal Court: PrepCom 25 March–12 April 1996' (30 March 1996).

———, 'International Criminal Court: PrepCom 25 March–12 April 1996' (15 April 1996).

———, 'Report on the Conference for the Establishment of an International Criminal Court: 15 June–17 July 1998' (23 September 1998).

Women's Caucus for Gender Justice, 'Priority Concerns Related to the Elements Annex' (February 1999) <www.iccwomen.org/wigjdraft1/Archives/oldWCGJ/icc/iccpc/021999pc/pcconcerns.htm> accessed 22 January 2014.

———, 'Recommendations and Commentary for December 1997 PrepCom on the Establishment of an International Criminal Court' (December 1997) <www.iccnow.org/documents/5PrepComRecommWomensC.pdf> accessed 4 December 2013.

———, 'Recommendations and Commentary for the Elements Annex' (July 1999) <www.iccwomen.org/wigjdraft1/Archives/oldWCGJ/icc/iccpc/071999pc/elements.htm> accessed 22 January 2014.

———, 'Recommendations and Commentary to the Elements Annex and Rules of Procedure and Evidence' (June 2000) <www.iccwomen.org/wigjdraft1/Archives/oldWCGJ/icc/iccpc/062000pc/elementsannex.htm> accessed 23 January 2014.

———, 'Recommendations and Commentary for the Rules of Procedure and Evidence' (December 1999) <www.iccwomen.org/wigjdraft1/Archives/oldWCGJ/icc/iccpc/11> accessed 31 October 2013.

(Research) reports and working papers

Human Rights Watch, 'Getting Away with Murder, Mutilation, Rape: New Testimony from Sierra Leone' (July 1999) <www.hrw.org/reports/1999/sierra/> accessed 2 December 2014.

———, 'Sowing Terror: Atrocities against Civilians in Sierra Leone' (July 1998) <www.hrw.org/legacy/reports98/sierra/> accessed 2 December 2014.

U.S. Department of State, Bureau of Democracy, Human Rights, and Labor, '2009 Human Rights Report: Saudi Arabia' (2010) <www.state.gov/j/drl/rls/hrrpt/2009/nea/136079.htm> accessed 1 April 2014.

———, '2009 Human Rights Report: Syria' (2010) <www.state.gov/j/drl/rls/hrrpt/2009/nea/136080.htm> accessed 1 April 2014.

Blog entries, newspaper and magazine articles and radio broadcasts

———, 'Kids Murdered, Forced into Rebel Armies in Uganda' *Terra Viva* (Rome, 15 June 1998) 12.

Axworthy L, 'A Court That Is Worth Having' *Terra Viva* (Rome, 15 June 1998) 6–7.

Boenders E, 'How to Protect Children with a Strong and Effective Court' *ICC Monitor* (New York, 19 June 1998) 2.

Broomhall, B., Carmalt, J. and Fontaine, F., 'June Preparatory Commission Will Address Important Issues' *ICC Monitor* (New York, June 2000) 3.

Coalition for the International Criminal Court, 'Definitions of Crimes' *ICC Monitor* (New York, November 1998) 3.

Gassoumis, A., Lerner, G. and Marrow, M., 'Women's Caucus Brings Crimes against Women to Forefront of Debate' *ICC Monitor* (May 1997) 5.

Haq F, 'UNICEF Eyes Higher Recruitment Age' *Terra Viva* (Rome, 19 June 1998) 1–2.

On the Record, 'Child Soldiering and Recruitment Attached' *Terra Viva* (Rome, 17 June 1998) 6.

Spees, P., 'Many Gender Issues Remain to be Resolved at the June Prepcom' *ICC Monitor* (New York, June 2000) 4.

United Nations, 'Crimes against Humanity Must be Precisely Defined Say Speakers in Preparatory Committee for International Court' Press Release L/2763/Rev.1 3rd Meeting (AM) (26 March 1996) <www.un.org/press/en/1996/19960326.l2763.html> accessed 29 April 2015.

Other

Centre on Law and Globalization, 'What Counts as Rape in International Crimes?' <http://clg.portalxm.com/library/keytext.cfm?keytext_id=182> accessed 27 October 2012.

Coalition for the International Criminal Court, 'History of the ICC' <www.iccnow.org/?mod=icchistory> accessed 3 December 2013.

Federal Bureau of Investigation, 'Frequently Asked Questions about the Change in the UCR Definition of Rape' (11 December 2014) <www.fbi.gov/about-us/cjis/ucr/recent-program-updates/new-rape-definition-frequently-asked-questions> accessed 19 January 2015.

International Criminal Court, 'Establishment of the Court' <www.icc-cpi.int/en_menus/icc/about%20the%20court/icc%20at%20a%20glance/Pages/establishment%20of%20the%20court.aspx> accessed 28 January 2015.

———, 'Factsheet' <www.icc-cpi.int/en_menus/icc/about%20the%20court/icc%20at%20a%20glance/factsheets/Pages/fact%20sheets.aspx> accessed 28 January 2015.

Rape, Abuse and Incest National Network, 'The Laws in Your State' <www.rainn.org/public-policy/laws-in-your-state> accessed 21 November 2014.

6 The Women's Caucus' understanding of forced marriage

Introduction

Chapters 6 and 7 present a more detailed snapshot of a specific part of the International Criminal Court (ICC) negotiations already mentioned in Chapter 5. Chapter 6 further analyses the Women's Caucus' understanding of the crime of forced marriage as a form of sexual slavery and examines why the Caucus defined forced marriage this way. Based on the recommendations and comments the Caucus submitted at different stages of the ICC negotiations, this chapter scrutinises the terminology the Women's Caucus used and the examples it gave. Chapter 6 also examines the sources of information the Women's Caucus referred to. Therefore, it studies how the Caucus as a specific non-governmental organisation (NGO) came to hold its views that it then taught to states. Chapter 6 considers whether the Caucus incorrectly viewed forced marriage as a purely sexual crime or if the sexual elements of a forced marriage were exaggerated, potentially explaining the group's understanding of the crime of forced marriage as a form of sexual slavery.

Forced marriage as a form of gender violence

Echoed by Amnesty International,[1] the Women's Caucus put forced marriage on the agenda of the Preparatory Committee on the Establishment of an International Criminal Court (PrepCom) and Preparatory Commission for the International Criminal Court (PrepCom2) discussions. In the context of a discussion about the incorporation of the principle of non-discrimination, it defined forced marriage as a form of gender violence.[2] The Caucus explicitly

1 Amnesty International, 'The International Criminal Court: Preliminary Comments Concerning the Elements of War Crimes other than Grave Breaches of the Geneva Conventions – Part I' (July 1999) <http://amnesty.org/en/library/asset/IOR40/011/1999/en/4304ad8f-e10c-11dd-b0b0-b705f60696a0/ior400111999en.html> accessed 5 March 2014.

2 Interview 10 (22 April 2014); Women's Caucus for Gender Justice, 'Recommendations and Commentary for December 1997 PrepCom on the Establishment of an International Criminal Court' (December 1997) <www.iccnow.org/documents/5PrepComRecommWomensC.pdf> accessed 4 December 2013.

stated that gender violence includes acts of sexual and non-sexual violence. Linking it to the crime of slavery, it noted that sexual gender violence serves 'to signal male ownership over [women] as property'.[3] Both the definition of gender violence and sexual gender violence can be classified as male as they create and perpetuate an understanding of women as victims and men as perpetrators. Even though a clear reference was made to the non-sexual and sexual elements of the crime, 'the enslavement of women through forced marriage or otherwise for domestic as well as sexual service'[4] was given as an example of a non-sexual act of gender violence.[5] Forced marriage was listed together with acts of psychological and physical violence of a non-sexual nature as well as violent acts that are linked to a women's sexuality, such as forced pregnancy and forced sterilisation. It becomes apparent that, in addition to bringing forward male definitions, the Women's Caucus did not establish a sharp distinction between sexual and non-sexual gender violence. Nevertheless, it clearly recognised both elements of the crime of forced marriage which it defined as a form of enslavement and slavery. It becomes obvious that the Women's Caucus did not misunderstand forced marriage as a purely sexual crime and categorised forced marriage as a form of sexual slavery as a result of this misunderstanding. An overemphasis on the sexual elements, however, could explain why the Caucus viewed forced marriage this way.

Examples of sexual slavery

In the context of recommending the mainstreaming of issues of sexualised violence, the Women's Caucus developed a definition of slavery and enslavement that clearly recognises the sexual and non-sexual elements of the crime as well as of forced marriage. Nevertheless, enslavement is understood as gendered because it exploits women's and men's traditional gender roles.[6] This can also be seen from the examples the Women's Caucus gave in written comments and recommendations to the ICC negotiations of situations of sexual slavery and forced marriage as a specific form of sexual slavery. They establish women as victims, perpetuating male stereotypes. As the United Nations (UN) Special Rapporteur on the Situation of Systematic Rape, Sexual Slavery and Slavery-Like Practices during Armed Conflict referred to the same examples in her Final Report, it can be assumed that the Women's Caucus' understanding of sexual slavery and forced marriage as a form of sexual slavery was influenced by the Final Report. The examples discuss experiences of women in Second World War Japan, Yugoslav rape camps, the Rwandan genocide and the conflicts in Myanmar

3 Women's Caucus for Gender Justice, 'Recommendations and Commentary for December 1997 PrepCom' (n 2).

4 ibid.

5 Interview 10 (n 2).

6 Interview 17 (17 June 2014); Women's Caucus for Gender Justice, 'Recommendations and Commentary for December 1997 PrepCom' (n 2).

(Burma), Liberia and Uganda. It becomes apparent that the Caucus recognised the sexual and non-sexual elements of forced marriage but emphasised the former. This could explain the groups' understanding of forced marriage as a form of sexual slavery.

Quoting the UN Special Rapporteur on Violence against Women, its Causes and Consequences and also referring to international norms in the form of the Final Report of the UN Special Rapporteur on the Situation of Systematic Rape, Sexual Slavery and Slavery-Like Practices during Armed Conflict, the Women's Caucus defined the situation of the comfort women as institutionalised sexual slavery.[7] During the Second World War, comfort women were forced to provide sexual services for members of the Japanese armed forces. This way, the Japanese Army wanted to reduce the number of rapes that occurred in occupied communities, aiming not to antagonise the local population even more. The enslavement of women also intended to decrease threats of espionage and potential leaks about military tactics and operations. Additionally, institutional scrutiny and outrage as occurred after the fall of Nanking was to be avoided. Built into this motivation was the male understanding that soldiers need to have sex to keep fighting. Their continuing ability to fight was also to be ensured by minimising sexually transmitted diseases amongst the troops through providing the opportunity to have intercourse with comfort women who underwent medical checks rather than with local women who did not.[8] In addition to the recruitment of 'willing' women who already worked as prostitutes, women were recruited by means of deception, purchase, force, coercion and/or abduction.[9] At first glance, rules and regulations for comfort women and their users seem to show concern for the women's correct treatment. Alcohol and weapons were prohibited. The hours of services were regulated and a requirement for payment imposed. This, however, stands in stark contrast to the inhumane, brutal and

7 Women's Caucus for Gender Justice, 'Priority Concerns Related to the Elements Annex' (February 1999) <www.iccwomen.org/wigjdraft1/Archives/oldWCGJ/icc/iccpc/021999pc/pcconcerns.htm> accessed 22 January 2014; Women's Caucus for Gender Justice, 'Recommendations and Commentary for December 1997 PrepCom' (n 2).

8 Carmen M. Argibay, 'Sexual Slavery and the Comfort Women of World War II' (2003) 21 *Berkeley Journal of International Law* 375, 376–377; Rhonda Copelon, 'Gender Crimes as War Crimes: Integrating Crimes against Women into International Criminal Law' (2000) 46 *McGill Law Journal* 217, 222; United Nations Commission on Human Rights 'Report of the Special Rapporteur on Violence against Women, Its Causes and Consequences, Ms. Radhika Coomaraswamy, in Accordance with Commission on Human Rights Resolution 1994/45: Report on the Mission to the Democratic People's Republic of Korea, the Republic of Korea and Japan on the Issue of Military Sexual Slavery in Wartime' (4 January 1996) UN Doc E/CN.4/1996/53/Add.1 <www.ohchr.org> accessed 28 August 2017; Patricia Viseur Sellers, 'Wartime Female Slavery: Enslavement?' (2011) 44 *Cornell International Law Journal* 115, 117.

9 Argibay (n 8) 377–379; United Nations Commission on Human Rights 'Report of the Special Rapporteur on Violence against Women, its Causes and Consequences, Ms. Radhika Coomaraswamy, in Accordance with Commission on Human Rights Resolution 1994/45' (n 8).

cruel treatment comfort women experienced. They had to endure sexual subjugation and mutilation, forced sterilisation, multiple rapes, severe physical abuse and acts of torture as well as malnutrition and poor living conditions. In addition to often being exposed to front-line threats, comfort women lived under constant fear of further abuse, of being killed, catching sexually transmitted diseases and becoming pregnant. Some were never allowed to leave the camp, others were allowed to take walks at set times and others again were allowed to go on trips. Either way, however, their freedom of movement as well as their personal freedom was restricted.[10]

Parallels can be drawn between the situation of the comfort women and forced wives and the kinds of abuses both groups were subjected to. Both had to endure sexual subjugation, rapes, physical abuse and torture. Both lived in constant fear. Some comfort women were allowed to leave the camp. Forced wives were allowed to move freely to complete their tasks. A difference between the situation of the comfort women and forced wives is that the reality of forced wives – as the Women's Caucus recognised – included providing sexual and domestic services exclusively to their forced husbands. Comfort women, in contrast, had to sexually serve many men but had no domestic tasks.[11] Therefore, by referring to these examples of different kinds of sexual and non-sexual gender violence in conjunction, the Women's Caucus created the impression that the crime of forced marriage would predominately be a sexual crime. This could explain why the Caucus understood forced marriage as a form of sexual slavery.

Making this misleading emphasis on the sexual elements of gender violence even more obvious, the Women's Caucus gave the rape camps in the former Yugoslavia as another example of institutionalised sexual slavery.[12] During the wars in the former Yugoslavia in the 1990s, the creation of rape camps was one hallmark of the terror against the civilian population aimed at humiliating them and instilling fear. In the rape camps, women were detained, tortured and brutalised repeatedly by many different assailants over long periods of time. Sometimes women were forcefully taken from a larger rape camp, brought to a particular soldier's home and brutalised there, only to be returned to the camp to suffer more sexualised violence. Women also had to perform domestic tasks for the soldiers, naked. A survivor, Mirsada, remembered that it appeared to be form of reward for soldiers.[13]

10 United Nations Commission on Human Rights, 'Report of the Special Rapporteur on Violence against Women, Its Causes and Consequences, Ms. Radhika Coomaraswamy, in Accordance with Commission on Human Rights Resolution 1994/45' (n 8) 3–16.

11 Copelon, 'Gender Crimes as War Crimes' (n 8) 222: Copelon, however, states that comfort women provided sexual as well as domestic services to Japanese troops.

12 Women's Caucus for Gender Justice, 'Priority Concerns Related to the Elements Annex' (n 7).

13 Michele Lent Hirsch, 'Conflict Profiles: Bosnia' (8 February 2012) Women under Siege <www.womenundersiegeproject.org/conflicts/profile/bosnia> accessed 12 March 2014.

Mirsada's tasks are comparable to those of forced wives. Both have to serve their captors sexually and otherwise. However, a crucial difference is that women in Yugoslav rape camps did not have to pretend to be the wives of their captors. They were not in a forced marital relationship that was marked by one-sided exclusivity. Mirsada's account highlights the sexual and non-sexual elements of the crimes committed against her. However again the focus clearly lies on the sexual elements and even non-sexual components like cooking and serving her captors are sexualised through the fact that Mirsada had to carry out these tasks naked.[14] As mentioned above, this creates the impression that forced marriage would predominately be a sexual crime and could explain why the Women's Caucus categorised it as a form of sexual violence.

In addition to establishing a link between the crime of forced marriage in times of armed conflict, the situation of the comfort women, and the rape camps established during the war in the former Yugoslavia, the Women's Caucus also linked forced marriage to women's experiences of the Rwandan genocide in 1994. Explicitly using the language of marriage, the Women's Caucus categorised 'the practice of taking women as "temporary wives" or [...] forced "temporary marriage"'[15] as sexual and gendered enslavement,[16] but also as individualised sexual slavery.[17]

The emphasis on the temporary nature of forced marriage stands in contrast to African Rights' definition of the crime. The non-governmental organisation distinguished forced marriage from sexual slavery based on the period of time intended to spend together rather than on the dominance of sexual or non-sexual elements. African Rights stressed that the men's behaviour showed that they meant to keep the women forever. This understanding was supported by stories forced wives told about their forced husbands who obtained Hutu

14 'Testimony: A Trio of Women's Voices Bears Witness to the Horror of War and Rape as Yugoslavia Disintegrates' *Los Angeles Times* (Los Angeles, 31 January 1993) <http://articles.latimes.com/1993-01-31/magazine/tm-857_1_serbian> accessed 12 March 2014; Lent Hirsch (n 13). See also *Prosecutor v Dragoljub Kunarac, Radomir Kovač and Zoran Vuković* (Indictment) IT-96-23-T 'Foča Case' (19 June 1996) <www.legal-tools.org/doc/3a081b/> accessed 18 August 2017, Mechanism for International Criminal Tribunals; *Prosecutor v Dragoljub Kunarac, Radomir Kovač and Zoran Vuković* (Third Amended Indictment (Kunarac and Kovač)) IT-96-23-PT 'Foča Case' (8 November 1999), Mechanism for International Criminal Tribunals; *Prosecutor v Dragoljub Kunarac, Radomir Kovač and Zoran Vuković* (Trial Judgment) ICTY IT-96-23-T and IT-96-23/1-T 'Foča Case' (22 February 2001) <www.legal-tools.org/doc/fd881d/> accessed 9 August 2017, Mechanism for International Criminal Tribunals.

15 Women's Caucus for Gender Justice, 'Recommendations and Commentary for December 1997 PrepCom' (n 2).

16 ibid.

17 Women's Caucus for Gender Justice, 'Priority Concerns Related to the Elements Annex' (n 7): Note that in establishing the distinction of institutionalised and individualised sexual slavery, the Women's Caucus built on, and expanded, the dualism and distinction between the public and the private sphere.

identification cards for them and made preparations to flee together.[18] Human Rights Watch also found that, in some cases, forced wives stayed with their forced husbands for socio-economic reasons after the genocide.[19]

Comparable to the findings of African Rights[20] and Human Rights Watch[21] as well as the understanding of forced marriage in times of armed conflict advanced in this book, the Women's Caucus described experiences of Rwandan women who were separated from their families, kidnapped, bought and sold, allocated, or chose to become a concubine or to submit themselves to conditions of sexual slavery and forced marriage as a means of survival.[22] Connected to looting sprees, women were seen as spoils of genocide that beautifully completed men's victory. In contrast, forcing women into marriage with undesired men served as a means of humiliation. Some forced wives were physically confined to the home. Some were free to leave only at the risk of being killed because they left the protected marriage status, emphasising their complete dependency on their forced husbands. Vestine, a survivor, remembered that she was allowed to leave the house to pick food, cook and farm.[23] Here, in addition to the dominant account of the sexual elements, the non-sexual elements of the crime of forced marriage become apparent.

18 African Rights, *Rwanda: Death, Despair and Defiance* (2nd edn, African Rights 1995) 748–797.

19 Human Rights Watch, 'Shattered Lives: Sexual Violence During the Rwandan Genocide and in the Aftermath' (1996) 28 <www.hrw.org/legacy/reports/1996/Rwanda.htm> accessed 13 August 2013. In Interview 17 (n 6), the present researcher was told that the Women's Caucus had based its awareness of the crime of forced marriage in times of armed conflict on the Human Rights Watch report 'Shattered Lives'. In the Caucus' written comments and recommendations to the ICC negotiations, however, this report is only referred to in December 1997. It provided examples from Rwanda for sexualised and gender-based violence that could be understood as constitutive of the war crimes of wilful killing and mutilation.

20 African Rights (n 18) 748–797.

21 Human Rights Watch, 'Shattered Lives' (n 19).

22 Amnesty International, 'The International Criminal Court: Preliminary Comments Concerning the Elements of War Crimes Other Than Grave Breaches of the Geneva Conventions – Part I' (n 1); Women's Caucus for Gender Justice, 'Priority Concerns Related to the Elements Annex' (n 7); Women's Caucus for Gender Justice, 'Recommendations and Commentary for December 1997 PrepCom' (n 2): In the context of a discussion of the element of coercion in the crime of rape, the Women's Caucus conveyed a similar understanding as in its recommendations and comments to the December 1997 PrepCom. It stated that the 'abuse of authority and threats to deny or promises to provide the means of survival are critical if situations are to be included where women "choose" to trade sexual service in order to survive, such as forced temporary marriage and other slave-like conditions'. This is contrasted by a later statement made in February 1999 (n 430), linking forced marriage to forced domestic labour rather than survival sex. In support, Amnesty International stated that '[s]exual slavery [...] encompasses situations where women and girls are forced into "marriage", domestic servitude or other forced labour that ultimately involves forced sexual activity.'

23 African Rights (n 18) 748–797; Women's Caucus for Gender Justice, 'Priority Concerns Related to the Elements Annex' (n 7).

Emphasising the sexual elements of forced marriage, in the Rwandan context, the notion of marriage was clearly linked to the crime of rape. Human Rights Watch's report focuses on the rape of women during the Rwandan genocide. In this framework, it discusses forced marriage as a form of individualised sexual slavery.[24] In women's testimonies collected by African Rights, the terms 'being taken' and 'being married' both appear to refer to rape. Survivor Catherine told the story of how she was discovered when hiding in a field. One of her captors, Patrice, announced that he would 'take [her]'. The other men became angry and argued that she 'should [...] be enjoyed by all of them'. Patrice replied that she 'would be killed by being "married" to all of them'.[25] During the Rwandan genocide, promises of marriage were also used as a justification for rapes. Two other survivors, Thérèse and Christine, told how two brothers who offered to hide them in their homes took advantage of the situation and raped them, promising to marry them when the fighting ended.[26] Awareness existed that these forced marriages were not 'real' marriages. Most women quoted in the report referred to their forced husband as their 'abductor[s]'[27] rather than their husbands. Vestine was the only woman quoted, stating that she and her forced husband 'began living as man and wife' and who referred to herself as the 'wife' and to the man as her 'husband'.[28] Reflecting the ethnic component of the Rwandan genocide, it has to be noted that, amongst the Hutu community, forced inter-marriages were not accepted. While forced wives were a status symbol for male fighters in Sierra Leone and Uganda, Hutu men had to bribe others into silence about their relationships and were seen as Tutsi accomplices. They were ordered to hand over their Tutsi wives to be killed. However, when men kept women as sex slaves without marrying them, they also had to face criticism and the stigma of being impotent because they did not marry the women.[29]

The Women's Caucus' comments and recommendations in the ICC negotiations also refer to the experience of women in Burma, which are very different from that of forced wives in, for example, Rwanda but also from the experiences of women in Sierra Leone and Uganda. In Burma, sexualised violence is used by the military regime to quell opposition and to maintain its power.[30] Blurring the line between rape and forced marriage as in Rwanda, some evidence indicates that 'soldiers use rape to coerce women into marriage and to impregnate them so they will bear "Burman" babies, known as a campaign of "Burmanization."'[31]

24 Human Rights Watch, 'Shattered Lives' (n 19).

25 African Rights (n 18) 772–773.

26 ibid 778.

27 ibid 754–755.

28 ibid 787.

29 ibid 778–788; Human Rights Watch, 'Shattered Lives' (n 19) 26.

30 Jovana Crncevic, 'Conflict Profiles: Burma' (17 December 2012) Women Under Siege <www.womenundersiegeproject.org/conflicts/profile/Burma> accessed 12 March 2014.

31 Betsy Apple and Veronika Martin, 'No Safe Place: Burma's Army and the Rape of Ethnic Women' (April 2003) Refugees International 24 <www.refworld.org/docid/47a6eb9a0.html> accessed 12 March 2014.

Burmese soldiers, married or unmarried, are promised certain rewards if they married women from certain ethnic groups. They are encouraged to leave their 'blood […] in the village'.[32] Similar to the situation in Uganda, many acts of sexualised violence occur in conjunction with other human rights abuses such as forced relocation, forced labour, slavery and torture. Comparable to the fate of the comfort women in Japan, women in Burma are forcibly conscripted by the military into situations of sexual slavery.[33] Even though the sexual elements of gender violence are stressed again, a Burmese survivor recalled sexual and non-sexual violations she was subjected to when she was kept as a porter, including rape as well as forced labour.[34]

Similarly to the accounts of forced marriage from Burma as well as to the understanding of forced marriage advanced in this book, women were abducted, raped, forced into survival sex or exploited as sex slaves during the civil war in Liberia.[35] The Women's Caucus in its comments and recommendations in the ICC negotiations stated that Liberian militias forced women into forced labour, including washing, cooking and looting as well as into sexual slavery and forced marriage as a way of rewarding soldiers.[36]

The Women's Caucus also referred to the situation in Uganda where fighters abduct children and subject them to forced labour, forced participation in direct combat, sexual slavery and forced marriage.[37] In addition to indicating that a forced marriage consists of sexual and non-sexual elements, here the Women's Caucus recognised the interconnection with the recruitment of child soldiers,

32 Betsy Apple, 'School for Rape: The Burmese Military and Sexual Violence' (1998) EarthRights International <www.earthrights.org/publication/school-rape-burmese-military-and-sexual-violence> accessed 12 March 2014.

33 Crncevic (n 30); Women's Caucus for Gender Justice, 'Recommendations and Commentary to the Elements Annex and Rules of Procedure and Evidence' (June 2000) <www.iccwomen.org/wigjdraft1/Archives/oldWCGJ/icc/iccpc/062000pc/elementsannex.htm> accessed 23 January 2014; see also United Nations Commission on Human Rights, 'Final Report of the Special Rapporteur on the Situation of Systematic Rape, Sexual Slavery and Slavery-Like Practices during Armed Conflict' (22 June 1998) UN Doc E/CN.4/Sub.2/1998/13 para 30, para 67 <www.ohchr.org> accessed 28 August 2017 ©1998 United Nations. Reprinted with the Permission of the United Nations.

34 Apple (n 32).

35 'Liberia: "The New War Is Rape"' IRIN (19 November 2009) <www.irinnews.org/report/87122/liberia-the-new-war-is-rape> accessed 12 March 2014.

36 Erin Bernstein, Sabrina Karim and Pamela Scully, 'Conflict Profiles: Liberia' (3 September 2013) Women Under Siege <www.womenundersiegeproject.org/conflicts/profile/liberia> accessed 12 March 2014; Liberia, Truth and Reconciliation Commission of Liberia, Volume I: Preliminary Findings and Determinations (2009) 45 <http://trcofliberia.org/reports/final-report> accessed 19 September 2017; Women's Caucus for Gender Justice, 'Recommendations and Commentary to the Elements Annex and Rules of Procedure and Evidence' (n 33); see also United Nations Commission on Human Rights, 'Final Report of the Special Rapporteur on the Situation of Systematic Rape, Sexual Slavery and Slavery-Like Practices during Armed Conflict' (n 33) para 30.

37 Women's Caucus for Gender Justice, 'Recommendations and Commentary to the Elements Annex and Rules of Procedure and Evidence' (n 33).

potentially breaking with traditional understandings of women's gender roles as wives, housewives and mothers.

As mentioned above, the Women's Caucus' examples of the Japanese comfort women and the rape camps in the former Yugoslavia place a misleading, male emphasis on the sexual elements of gender violence. In contrast, the examples the Caucus gave of Rwandan, Burmese, Liberian and Ugandan women's experiences of forced marriage show that the crime consists of sexual and non-sexual elements. Nonetheless, regarding most examples, the Women's Caucus placed an emphasis on the former. This could explain why the group saw forced marriage as a form of sexual slavery. However, the question arises whether the Women's Caucus was not taken aback by the incompatibility of the non-sexual elements of forced marriage with the crime of sexual slavery.

Possibly it was not. Instead, the Women's Caucus discussed forced marriage only in the context of sexual violence, as a form of sexual slavery, as it understood the sexual elements of forced marriage as key, making it a form of sexual slavery, which coincides with the way forced marriage was understood by the international community at the time of the ICC negotiations. Therefore, the crime was not discussed in depth and other issues like the relationship between the crimes of trafficking and sexual slavery as well as between sexual slavery, enslavement and forced prostitution took precedence. Arguably, both, the crime of sexual slavery and forced marriage were strengthened; sexual slavery by including forced marriage, and forced marriage by being clearly included in sexual slavery because, through this, it was identified as a serious crime.[38]

Contrary to this, as demonstrated above, women's advocates would have liked forced marriage to be listed as a separate crime in the ICC instruments. However, if the sacredness of the institution of marriage is stressed and if forced marriage is constructed as a social issue, subsuming forced marriage under sexual slavery arguably constituted a compromise that satisfied concerns of more conservative states.[39]

Sources of information

In contrast to the limited discussions of forced marriage in the ICC negotiations, the sources of information referred to, the terms used and examples cited in the writings of the Women's Caucus paint a more complex picture of the conduct. The Caucus' awareness of the crime of forced marriage appears to have been based especially on the Final Report of the UN Special Rapporteur on the Situation of Systematic Rape, Sexual Slavery and Slavery-Like Practices during Armed Conflict, Gay J. McDougall, conveying international norms.[40]

38 Interview 9 (11 April 2014); Interview 11 (23 April 2014); Interview 17 (n 6); Interview 18 (25 June 2014).

39 Interview 8 (11 April 2014); Interview 18 (n 39).

40 Nations Commission on Human Rights, 'Final Report of the Special Rapporteur on the Situation of Systematic Rape, Sexual Slavery and Slavery-Like Practices during Armed Conflict' (n 33); see also Interview 17 (n 6); Valerie Oosterveld, 'Sexual Slavery and

Since McDougall's Final Report precedes the relevant recommendations and comments raised by the Women's Caucus in the ICC negotiations, it can be supposed that the latter adopted the terminology used by the former in regard to 'forced, temporary marriage'.[41]

In addition, like the documents prepared by the Women's Caucus, the Final Report refers to the situation of the comfort women, rape camps established in the 1990s during the war in the former Yugoslavia, as well as the situation of women who were subjected to sexualised war violence, including forced marriage, in Rwanda, Burma, Liberia and Uganda. By listing them together, the report connects sexual slavery, the establishment of rape camps, (gang) rape, forced marriage, forced labour, sexual mutilation and torture.[42] Supported by the statement that '[s]exual slavery also encompasses situations where women and girls are forced into "marriage", domestic servitude or other forced labour that ultimately involves forced sexual activity',[43] the connections established indicate that McDougall recognised the sexual as well as non-sexual elements of the crime of forced marriage. She even went so far as to state that the link between rape and slavery is deliberate as many cases of sexualised war violence are most appropriately addressed as slavery. She stressed that (sexual) slavery constitutes a crime regardless of whether it was committed by public or private actors and that, furthermore, a pecuniary element is not necessary. Either way, the exercise of powers attaching to the right of ownership leads to limitations on autonomy, freedom of movement and sexual self-determination. Following the understanding brought forward in the indictment in the *Foča* case mentioned

the International Criminal Court: Advancing International Law' (2004) 25 *Michigan Journal of International Law* 605, 621 on the Women's Caucus and the Special Rapporteur on forced prostitution and sexual slavery.

Considering that the United Nations (UN) Special Rapporteur on Violence against Women, its Causes and Consequences referred to forced marriage in her reports from 1995 on, it initially appears odd that the Women's Caucus only referred to these reports to support its understanding of the situation of the comfort women during the Second World War as sexual slavery. However, since the Special Rapporteur on Violence against Women, its Causes and Consequences did not go into any detailed discussion of forced marriage, but the UN Special Rapporteur on the Situation of Systematic Rape, Sexual Slavery and Slavery-Like Practices during Armed Conflict did, the Women's Caucus' repeated reference to the latter's Final Report is understandable.

41 United Nations Commission on Human Rights, 'Final Report of the Special Rapporteur on the Situation of Systematic Rape, Sexual Slavery and Slavery-Like Practices during Armed Conflict' (n 33) para 8; Women's Caucus for Gender Justice, 'Recommendations and Commentary for December 1997 PrepCom' (n 2).

42 United Nations Commission on Human Rights, 'Final Report of the Special Rapporteur on the Situation of Systematic Rape, Sexual Slavery and Slavery-Like Practices during Armed Conflict' (n 33) para 8, para 10, para 22–23, para 30, para 66–67, para 81, para 114, fn 17.

43 United Nations Commission on Human Rights, 'Final Report of the Special Rapporteur on the Situation of Systematic Rape, Sexual Slavery and Slavery-Like Practices during Armed Conflict' (n 33) para 30.

in Chapter 3, McDougall clarified that sexual slavery extends to situations where a woman is technically free to leave but is prevented from doing so by the coercive circumstances she finds herself in.[44] McDougall made clear that sexual slavery is a form of slavery and therefore, 'its prohibition is a *jus cogens* norm in customary International Law'.[45] To establish this, McDougall referred to the judgment of the International Court of Justice (ICJ) in the *Case Concerning the Barcelona Traction, Light and Power Co., Limited* as precedent.[46] As a *jus cogens* crime, the prohibition of slavery represents the top of the international legal hierarchy. It protects the most essential interests of the international community as a whole. As a *jus cogens* norm, the prohibition of slavery does not allow for any derogation. States have a duty to prosecute and extradite. These obligations apply universally and states have universal jurisdiction. Statutes of limitations, immunities and the defence of superior orders are not applicable.[47] Therefore, (sexual) slavery is a valuable basis on which to address sexualised war violence against women.[48]

Against this background, it can be argued that, in addition to founding their awareness of the crime of forced marriage on the Final Report and in addition to adopting its examples and terminology, the Women's Caucus might also have adopted the strategy suggested by McDougall regarding the criminalisation of forced marriage. Rather than being founded on a misunderstanding of the crime or a misevaluation of the dominance of its sexual or non-sexual elements, the understanding of forced marriage as a form of (sexual) slavery appears to have been a strategic decision. Comparable to discussions about the criminalisation

44 United Nations Commission on Human Rights, 'Final Report of the Special Rapporteur on the Situation of Systematic Rape, Sexual Slavery and Slavery-Like Practices during Armed Conflict' (n 33); Machteld Boot, 'Article 7 Crimes against Humanity para. 1 (g) Rape . . . or Any Other form of Sexual Violence of Comparable Gravity' in Otto Triffterer (ed), *Commentary on the Rome Statute of the International Criminal Court: Observers' Notes, Article by Article* (2nd edn, CH Beck 2008) 211.

45 United Nations Commission on Human Rights, 'Final Report of the Special Rapporteur on the Situation of Systematic Rape, Sexual Slavery and Slavery-Like Practices during Armed Conflict' (n 33) para 30.

46 *Barcelona Traction, Light and Power Company, Limited* (Belgium v Spain) (New Application, 1962), Judgment, Merits, Second Phase, ICJ GL No 50, [1970] ICJ Rep 3, (1970) 9 ILM 227, ICGJ 152 (ICJ 1970) (5 February 1970) 32, para 34 <www.legal-tools.org/doc/b9dddb/> accessed 18 August 2017.

47 United Nations Commission on Human Rights, 'Final Report of the Special Rapporteur on the Situation of Systematic Rape, Sexual Slavery and Slavery-Like Practices during Armed Conflict' (n 33) para 36–37; Vienna Convention on the Law of Treaties (23 May 1969) 1155 UNTS 331 art 53 <www.legal-tools.org/doc/6bfcd4/> accessed 18 August 2017; Cherif M. Bassiouni, 'International Crimes: Jus Cogens and Obligatio Erga Omnes' (1997) 59 (4) *Law and Contemporary Problems* 63; David S. Mitchell, 'The Prohibition of Rape in International Humanitarian Law as a Norm of Jus Cogens: Clarifying the Doctrine' (2005) 15 *Duke Journal of Comparative and International Law* 219.

48 United Nations Commission on Human Rights, 'Final Report of the Special Rapporteur on the Situation of Systematic Rape, Sexual Slavery and Slavery-Like Practices during Armed Conflict' (n 33) para 112.

of rape as torture,[49] defining forced marriage as the *jus cogens* crime of slavery emphasises the seriousness of the conduct, increases the chances of prosecution and supersedes the principle of national sovereignty.[50] The latter would be of particular relevance considering the Arab block's concerns regarding the criminalisation and definition of sexualised crimes.

Therefore, based on the writings of the Women's Caucus rather than on accounts of the ICC negotiations, the Caucus' understanding of the crime of forced marriage as a form of sexual slavery can be understood as an attempt to keep slavery alive as a subject by adapting the name and definition to make room for new insights and perspectives generated by new contexts. Making use of the historical background of the struggle for the abolition of slavery, it then becomes a well-established label that signifies something that everybody opposes and no one would openly defend; something that is obviously wrong. As discussed in Chapter 5, this labelling, however, cannot be considered a fair and objective description of the situation in which victims of forced marriage find themselves.

Conclusion

Chapter 5 introduced the Women's Caucus' understanding of forced marriage as a form of sexual slavery. Based on this, Chapter 6 analysed the examples, terminology and sources of information the Caucus used in relation to forced marriage.

The categorisation of sexual slavery and, by extension, forced marriage as a form of gender violence that can include acts of sexual and non-sexual violence demonstrates that the Caucus did not see forced marriage as a purely sexual crime. However, the examples used in relation to forced marriage show that the Caucus overemphasised the sexual elements of the crime. Like the UN Special Rapporteur on Violence against Women, its Causes and Consequences, the Women's Caucus mentioned forced marriage in the same breath as the situation of the comfort women during the Second World War in Japan. Even though parallels can be drawn between the two, the crucial difference is that forced wives have to provide sexual and domestic services exclusively to their forced husbands while comfort women had to sexually serve many men. The situation of the comfort women was mentioned as an example of institutionalised sexual slavery, and so were the rape camps established during the war in the former Yugoslavia. Here, the misleading emphasis on the sexual elements of gender violence becomes even more obvious as even non-sexual components such as cooking and serving the captors were sexualised through the fact that they had to be carried out naked. In addition to the comfort women and the rape camps in the former Yugoslavia, the Women's Caucus also referred to Rwandan, Burmese, Liberian and Ugandan women's experiences of forced

49 For more information see for example Mitchell (n 47).
50 Mitchell (n 47).

marriage. These examples show that forced marriage consists of sexual and non-sexual elements. However, especially with the Rwandan and Burmese example, an emphasis was placed on the sexual ones. During the Rwandan genocide and in Burma, 'marriage' was used as a euphemism for rape. In Rwanda, promises of marriage were used as a justification for rape. In Burma, rape is used to coerce women into marriage. The examples of forced marriage in Liberia and Uganda, in contrast, balance the relevance of the sexual and non-sexual elements of forced marriage.

In addition to the examples referred to, the Women's Caucus' terminology of 'forced temporary marriage' is comparable to that brought forward in the Final Report of the UN Special Rapporteur on the Situation of Systematic Rape, Sexual Slavery and Slavery-Like Practices during Armed Conflict.

Since the examples and terminology used by the Women's Caucus' appear to be largely based on the Final Report of the Special Rapporteur, it could be assumed that the Caucus also might have adopted the strategy for the criminalisation of forced marriage suggested by the Special Rapporteur. As such, the categorisation of forced marriage as a particular form of the *jus cogens* norm of slavery appears to have been a strategic decision that highlights the seriousness of the crime and facilitates prosecution.

This, however, stands in contrast to how the international community saw forced marriage at the time of the ICC negotiations. Forced marriage was simply seen as a sexual crime and what mattered were its sexual elements that made it the crime of sexual slavery. Arguably, the Women's Caucus simply adopted this view.

Against the background of the international community's stand, few better alternatives than subsuming forced marriage under sexual slavery would have been likely to have emerged from the ICC negotiations. As discussed in Chapters 4 and 5, the mandate of the conference which restricted the creation of new crimes as well as the dynamics of the negotiations did not make a bigger step possible. The inclusion of the crime of sexual slavery in the ICC instruments is an important codification of a crime previously recognised under customary law but not yet mentioned in an international legal instrument.[51] Forced marriage, in contrast, was less visible as a crime under international law and therefore was not recognised as a crime in its own right. Additionally, the drafters wanted to avoid repetition and undue overlap.[52] Since the difference between forced marriage and sexual slavery was not highly theorised, the former could have fallen victim to the resulting process of specification. Therefore, increased theorisation of forced marriage in times of armed conflict is important to ensure sensitive interpretations of the crime by the ICC.[53] It also can be argued that the drafters

51 Oosterveld, 'Sexual Slavery and the International Criminal Court' (n 40) 623.

52 Interview 19 (26 November 2014); Oosterveld, 'Sexual Slavery and the International Criminal Court' (n 40) 623.

53 Valerie Oosterveld, 'The Definition of "Gender" in the Rome Statute of the International Criminal Court: A Step Forward or Back for International Criminal Justice?' (2005) *Harvard Human Rights Journal* 55, 58.

resorted to the use of constructive ambiguity by defining forced marriage as a form of sexual slavery. This way, they left open opportunities for a positive and precedent-setting approach as taken by the Special Court for Sierra Leone.

Bibilography

Conventions and statutes

Vienna Convention on the Law of Treaties (23 May 1969) 1155 UNTS 331 <www.legal-tools.org/doc/6bfcd4/> accessed 18 August 2017.

United Nations documents

Commission on Human Rights

Commission on Human Rights, 'Final Report of the Special Rapporteur on the Situation of Systematic Rape, Sexual Slavery and Slavery-Like Practices during Armed Conflict' (22 June 1998) UN Doc E/CN.4/Sub.2/1998/13 <www.ohchr.org> accessed 28 August 2017 ©1998 United Nations. Reprinted with the Permission of the United Nations.

———, 'Report of the Special Rapporteur on Violence against Women, its Causes and Consequences, Ms. Radhika Coomaraswamy, in Accordance with Commission on Human Rights Resolution 1994/45: Report on the Mission to the Democratic People's Republic of Korea, the Republic of Korea and Japan on the Issue of Military Sexual Slavery in Wartime' (4 January 1996) UN Doc E/CN.4/1996/53/Add.1 <www.ohchr.org> accessed 28 August 2017.

Cases

International Court of Justice

Barcelona Traction, Light and Power Company, Limited (Belgium v Spain) (New Application, 1962), Judgment, Merits, Second Phase, ICJ GL No 50, [1970] ICJ Rep 3, (1970) 9 ILM 227, ICGJ 152 (ICJ 1970) (5 February 1970) <www.legal-tools.org/doc/b9dddb/> accessed 18 August 2017.

International Criminal Court for the former Yugoslavia

Prosecutor v Dragoljub Kunarac, Radomir Kovač and Zoran Vuković (Indictment) IT-96-23-T 'Foča Case' (19 June 1996) <www.legal-tools.org/doc/3a081b/> accessed 18 August 2017, Mechanism for International Criminal Tribunals

Prosecutor v Dragoljub Kunarac, Radomir Kovač and Zoran Vuković (Third Amended Indictment (Kunarac and Kovač)) IT-96-23-PT 'Foča Case' (8 November 1999), Mechanism for International Criminal Tribunals.

Prosecutor v Dragoljub Kunarac, Radomir Kovač and Zoran Vuković (Trial Judgment) ICTY IT-96-23-T and IT-96-23/1-T 'Foča Case' (22 February 2001) <www.legal-tools.org/doc/fd881d/> accessed 9 August 2017, Mechanism for International Criminal Tribunals.

Interviews

Interview 8 (11 April 2014).
Interview 9 (11 April 2014).
Interview 10 (22 April 2014).
Interview 11 (23 April 2014).
Interview 17 (17 June 2014).
Interview 18 (25 June 2014).
Interview 19 (26 November 2014).

Books

African Rights, *Rwanda: Death, Despair and Defiance* (2nd edn, African Rights 1995).

Chapters in edited books

Boot, Machteld, 'Article 7 Crimes against Humanity para. 1 (g) Rape … or Any Other Form of Sexual Violence of Comparable Gravity' in Otto Triffterer (ed), *Commentary on the Rome Statute of the International Criminal Court: Observers' Notes, Article by Article* (2nd edn, CH Beck 2008).

Journal articles

Argibay, C.M., 'Sexual Slavery and the Comfort Women of World War II' (2003) 21 *Berkeley Journal of International Law* 375.

Bassiouni, C.M., 'International Crimes: Jus Cogens and Obligatio Erga Omnes' (1997) 59 (4) *Law and Contemporary Problems* 63.

Copelon, R., 'Gender Crimes as War Crimes: Integrating Crimes against Women into International Criminal Law' (2000) 46 *McGill Law Journal* 217.

Mitchell, D.S., 'The Prohibition of Rape in International Humanitarian Law as a Norm of Jus Cogens: Clarifying the Doctrine' (2005) 15 *Duke Journal of Comparative and International Law* 219.

Oosterveld, V., 'The Definition of "Gender" in the Rome Statute of the International Criminal Court: A Step Forward or Back for International Criminal Justice?' (2005) *Harvard Human Rights Journal* 55.

———, 'Sexual Slavery and the International Criminal Court: Advancing International Law' (2004) 25 *Michigan Journal of International Law* 605.

Viseur Sellers, P., 'Wartime Female Slavery: Enslavement?' (2011) 44 *Cornell International Law Journal* 115.

ICC advocacy papers, commentaries, recommendations, reports and working papers

Amnesty International, 'The International Criminal Court: Preliminary Comments Concerning the Elements of War Crimes other than Grave Breaches of the Geneva Conventions – Part I' (July 1999) <http://amnesty.org/en/library/asset/IOR40/011/1999/en/4304ad8f-e10c-11dd-b0b0-b705f60696a0/ior400111999en.html> accessed 5 March 2014.

Women's Caucus for Gender Justice, 'Priority Concerns Related to the Elements Annex' (February 1999) <www.iccwomen.org/wigjdraft1/Archives/oldWCGJ/icc/iccpc/021999pc/pcconcerns.htm> accessed 22 January 2014.

———, 'Recommendations and Commentary for December 1997 PrepCom on the Establishment of an International Criminal Court' (December 1997) <www.iccnow.org/documents/5PrepComRecommWomensC.pdf> accessed 4 December 2013.

———, 'Recommendations and Commentary to the Elements Annex and Rules of Procedure and Evidence' (June 2000) <www.iccwomen.org/wigjdraft1/Archives/oldWCGJ/icc/iccpc/062000pc/elementsannex.htm> accessed 23 January 2014.

(Research) reports and working papers

Apple, B., 'School for Rape: The Burmese Military and Sexual Violence' (1998) EarthRights International <www.earthrights.org/publication/school-rape-burmese-military-and-sexual-violence> accessed 12 March 2014.

——— and Martin, V., 'No Safe Place: Burma's Army and the Rape of Ethnic Women' (April 2003) Refugees International <www.refworld.org/docid/47a6eb9a0.html> accessed 12 March 2014.

Bernstein, E., Karim, S. and Scully, P., 'Conflict Profiles: Liberia' (3 September 2013) Women Under Siege <www.womenundersiegeproject.org/conflicts/profile/liberia> accessed 12 March 2014.

Crncevic, J., 'Conflict Profiles: Burma' (17 December 2012) Women Under Siege <www.womenundersiegeproject.org/conflicts/profile/Burma> accessed 12 March 2014.

Human Rights Watch, 'Shattered Lives: Sexual Violence During the Rwandan Genocide and in the Aftermath' (1996) <www.hrw.org/legacy/reports/1996/Rwanda.htm> accessed 13 August 2013.

Lent Hirsch, M., 'Conflict Profiles: Bosnia' (8 February 2012) Women Under Siege <www.womenundersiegeproject.org/conflicts/profile/bosnia> accessed 12 March 2014.

Liberia, Truth and Reconciliation Commission of Liberia, Volume I: Preliminary Findings and Determinations (2009) <http://trcofliberia.org/reports/final-report> accessed 19 September 2017.

Blog entries, newspaper and magazine articles and radio broadcasts

———, 'Liberia: "The New War Is Rape"' *IRIN* (19 November 2009) <www.irinnews.org/report/87122/liberia-the-new-war-is-rape> accessed 12 March 2014.

———, 'Testimony: A Trio of Women's Voices Bears Witness to the Horror of War and Rape as Yugoslavia Disintegrates' *Los Angeles Times* (Los Angeles, 31 January 1993) <http://articles.latimes.com/1993-01-31/magazine/tm-857_1_serbian> accessed 12 March 2014.

7 The Arab block's proposal

Introduction

Chapter 7 presents another more detailed snapshot of a specific part of the International Criminal Court (ICC) negotiations already mentioned in Chapter 5. It explores the Arab block's[1] concerns regarding the definitions of rape and sexual slavery as crimes against humanity. From its proposals discussed in Chapter 5 it becomes clear that it aimed to protect religious principles, cultural norms and national laws.[2] Chapter 7 explores which religious principles, socio-cultural norms and national laws exactly the Arab block might have wanted to protect.

After establishing that marital rape is not criminalised under the Arab block's national laws, the chapter analyses the ideal of obedient wives and the understanding of rape as an honour crime as two possible reasons for this. Linked to religious principles, socio-cultural norms and national laws related to the ideal of obedient wives are discussions about societal structure and cohesion, social engineering, external impositions of legal reform processes and negotiations of women's rights and sexualised violence as proxy debates for governments' broader geopolitical and economic concerns. Linked to religious principles, socio-cultural norms and national laws related to the understanding of rape as an honour crime are discussions about mediation and Shari'a courts as ways to address sexualised violence, social engineering, external impositions of legal reform processes and rape-marriage policies. After focusing on the crime of rape,

1 Interview 1 (21 March 2014); Interview 14 (26 May 2014): According to other states' delegates, the Arab block was led by Syria and Qatar. As mainly oil producing states, the states constituting the Arab block had the means to invest in the International Criminal Court (ICC) negotiations. Therefore, they were more organised than other states that might have held opinions contrary to that of the majority of delegations at the ICC negotiations. Consequently, the Arab block could make its voice heard.

2 PrepCom2, 'Proposal Submitted by Bahrain, Iraq, Kuwait, Lebanon, the Libyan Arab Jamahiriya, Oman, Qatar, Saudi Arabia, the Sudan, the Syrian Arab Republic and United Arab Emirates Concerning the Elements of Crimes against Humanity (9 December 1999)' UN Doc PCNICC/1999/WGEC/DP.39 <www.legal-tools.org/doc/33d070/> accessed 10 August 2017.

Chapter 7 then turns to the Arab block's concerns regarding the ICC definition of sexual slavery. It argues that the Arab block was aware that certain marriage rights, duties and obligations might be interpreted to be an exercise of powers attaching to the right of ownership and therefore the Arab block sought to exclude them from the ICC definition of sexual slavery. Marriage rights, duties and obligations that are explored in this context are the accepted language of a marriage offer, understandings of dowry and maintenance, irregular and temporary marriages and the ideal of obedient wives. Comparisons between these and forced marriages in times of armed conflict are established. As it becomes apparent that the Arab block's proposal did not target the indirect criminalisation of forced marriage as a form of sexual slavery under the ICC instruments, the chapter also analyses religious principles, socio-cultural norms and national laws that supported this step. Before concluding, Chapter 7 historically contextualises the Arab block's opposition in the ICC negotiations by drawing parallels to the Fourth World Conference on Women (Beijing Conference).

'Nothing in [the elements of the crime of rape] shall affect natural and legal marital sexual relations in accordance with religious principles or cultural norms in different national laws.'[3]

Even though the Arab block criminalised rape in general, only Article 279 of the Qatari Penal Code explicitly recognises, for example, relatives as perpetrators of rape, and imposes a harsher sentence on them than on other rapists.[4] In Bahrain, Iraq, Lebanon, Libya, Oman, Saudi Arabia, Syria and the United Arab Emirates, in contrast, there is no law covering marital rape. In fact, only marital sexual intercourse is considered lawful.[5] The non-criminalisation of marital

3 PrepCom2, 'Proposal Submitted by Bahrain, Iraq, Kuwait, Lebanon, the Libyan Arab Jamahiriya, Oman, Qatar, Saudi Arabia, the Sudan, the Syrian Arab Republic and United Arab Emirates Concerning the Elements of Crimes against Humanity (9 December 1999)' (n 2) art 7(1)(g)(1)(4).

4 Qatari Penal Code (2004) <http://portal.www.gov.qa/wps/wcm/connect/8abaea8046be1deaae97ef70b3652ad8/Penal+Code.pdf?MOD=AJPERES&useDefaultText=0&useDefaultDesc=0> accessed 24 March 2014.

5 Bahrain Penal Code (1976) art 339, art 344–348 <www.bahrainrights.org/sites/default/files/Bahrain-Penal-Code.doc> accessed 17 March 2014; The Criminal Act of 1991 (Sudan) art 149(2) <www.icrc.org/applic/ihl/ihl-nat.nsf/xsp/.ibmmodres/domino/OpenAttachment/applic/ihl/ihl-nat.nsf/B9EEBA1CA8F54121C1256DC9005573F2/TEXT/Criminal%20Act%20-%20Sudan%20-%20EN.pdf> accessed 1 April 2014; Iraqi Penal Code No 111 (1969) <www.iraq-lg-law.org/en/webfm_send/1350> accessed 18 March 2014; The Libyan Penal Code (1953) <https://ia600704.us.archive.org/25/items/LibyanPenalCodeenglish/LibyanPenalCode.pdf> accessed 24 March 2014; Omani Penal Code (1974) <www.fiu.gov.om/forms.html> accessed 24 March 2014; Mona Chemali Khalaf, 'Lebanon' in Julia Breslin and Sanja Kelly (eds), *Women's Rights in the Middle East and North Africa: Progress Amid Resistance* (Freedom House/Rowman & Littlefield Publishers 2010) 6 <www.freedomhouse.org/sites/default/files/inline_images/Lebanon.pdf> accessed 21 March 2014; Freedom House, 'Syria' in Julia Breslin and Sanja Kelly (eds), *Women's Rights in the Middle East and North Africa: Progress*

rape could explain why the Arab block submitted a proposal to the same effect under international criminal law.[6]

Obedient wives

The non-criminalisation of marital rape under the Arab block's national laws is in line with the ideal of an obedient wife who is sexually available to her husband.[7] Accordingly, 'the husband [...] has more extensive rights [in regard to marital sexual relations] than his wife'.[8] Husbands' more extensive rights, authority and power on the one hand can be understood as legal discrimination against wives supported by religious and socio-cultural values and norms. The result is wives' subordination which can include being obedient and in a servile status to their husbands. On the other hand, it is argued that hierarchies are a necessary element of any group structure to ensure cohesion rather than an indicator of men's superiority. The need for clearly identified and differentiated gender roles is justified by the wish to enhance the success, growth, strength and stability of the family[9] and, by extension, of society, for 'a family is [the nucleus of Islamic society,[10]] the prototype of the nation'.[11]

Attempts to alter the distinct gender roles within the family structure that are required by religious and socio-cultural values and norms could therefore

---

Amid Resistance (Freedom House/Rowman & Littlefield Publishers 2010) <www.freedomhouse.org/sites/default/files/inline_images/Syria.pdf> accessed 28 March 2014; Wael B. Hallaq, *An Introduction to Islamic Law* (5th edn, Cambridge University Press 2009) 133; US Department of State, Bureau of Democracy, Human Rights, and Labor, '2009 Human Rights Report: Saudi Arabia' (2010) <www.state.gov/j/drl/rls/hrrpt/2009/nea/136079.htm> accessed 1 April 2014; US Department of State: Bureau of Democracy, Human Rights, and Labor, '2009 Human Rights Report: United Arab Emirates' (2010) <www.state.gov/j/drl/rls/hrrpt/2009/nea/136082.htm> accessed 1 April 2014.

6 Interview 12 (15 May 2014).

7 Eleanor Abdella Doumato, 'Saudi Arabia' in Julia Breslin and Sanja Kelly (eds), *Women's Rights in the Middle East and North Africa: Progress Amid Resistance* (Freedom House/Rowman & Littlefield Publishers 2010) 12 <www.freedomhouse.org/sites/default/files/inline_images/Saudi%20Arabia.pdf> accessed 28 March 2014.

8 Wael B. Hallaq, *Shari'a: Theory, Practice, Transformations* (Cambridge University Press 2009) 278–279; see also Ahmed Shukri, *Muhammedan Law of Marriage and Divorce* (Colombia University Press 1917) 21.

9 Mashood A. Baderin, *International Human Rights and Islamic Law* (Oxford University Press 2003) 90; John E. Esposito, *Women in Muslim Family Law* (Syracuse University Press 1982) 15; Jamal J. Nasir, *The Status of Women Under Islamic Law and Under Modern Islamic Legislation* (Graham and Trotman 1990) 3.

10 Abdur Rahman I. Doi, *Women in Shari'ah (Islamic Law)* (2nd edn, Ta-Ha Publishers 1989) 32; see also International Covenant on Economic, Social and Cultural Rights (16 December 1966) 993 UNTS 3 (ICESCR) art 10(1) <www.legal-tools.org/doc/06b87e/> accessed 18 August 2017 which states that 'the family [...] is the natural and fundamental group unit of society'.

11 Hallaq, *An Introduction to Islamic Law* (n 5) 120.

be perceived not only as legal reform, but as social engineering and coercion to alter religious practices and beliefs on which Islamic identity is based.[12]

The Arab block's dissent from developments in international criminal law regarding sexualised crimes can also be understood as resistance towards the external imposition of a legal reform process that should have been initiated by national governments, limiting the ways through which states can exercise power in the domestic sphere. Making governments appear out of control, this could give rise to opposition.[13]

This indicates that negotiations of women's rights or sexualised violence are rarely solely about sexuality, sexual agency and gender but

> serve as proxy debates for governments' broader geopolitical and economic concerns. In many instances, strong language related to gender and women's experience is negotiated and traded off as a result of bilateral and multilateral security and terrorism alliances, foreign aid relations, global debt imbalances, and the legacies of colonialism, war, conflict and political/economic transition. Governments may support or oppose sexuality-related positions because they are being pressured by donor countries, because of regional and political allegiances or aspirations, or, in fact, to demonstrate that they can operate free of these political pressures.[14]

This also affects the space for advocacy and how organisations set their priorities, measure their goals and develop ideas to counter political realities and risks. Nevertheless, many women's rights advocates see the articulation of women's rights within the international sphere 'not only as a goal in itself, but as potentially affecting national level policies in ways that support their political agendas'.[15] Therefore, their aim is social engineering.

Honour

The non-criminalisation of marital rape is also in line with the Arab block's patriarchal understanding of rape as an honour crime.[16] Both the non-criminalisation

12 Baderin (n 9) 133–138.

13 Interview 3 (25 March 2014); Interview 18 (25 June 2014).

14 Cynthia Rothschild, *Written Out: How Sexuality Is Used to Attack Women's Organizing* (International Gay and Lesbian Human Rights Commission and Center for Women's Global Leadership 2005) 107.

15 Rothschild (n 14) 108.

16 Bahrain Penal Code (n 5) art 344, art 346; The Criminal Act of 1991 (Sudan) (n 5) art 149(1); Iraqi Penal Code No 111 (n 5) art 21(1)(f), art 393(1); The Libyan Penal Code (n 5) art 407; Omani Penal Code (n 5) art 218(1); Qatari Penal Code (n 4) art 279; United Nations Commission on Human Rights, 'Final Report of the Special Rapporteur on the Situation of Systematic Rape, Sexual Slavery and Slavery-Like Practices during Armed Conflict' (22 June 1998) UN Doc E/CN.4/Sub.2/1998/13 para 24 <www.ohchr.org> accessed 28 August 2017 ©1998 United Nations. Reprinted with the

of marital rape and the understanding of rape as an honour crime reflect and reinforce the trivialisation of rape which could explain how it is addressed legally.

Like other honour crimes, sexualised violence is considered a private matter often dealt with through mediation between the people concerned and interested, such as the perpetrator and survivor as well as their families, rather than in court. Therefore, dispute resolution depends on decisions made by the family or by religious or tribal authorities often resulting in judgments detrimental to women. A similar outcome is to be expected when cases of sexualised violence are dealt with in Shari'a courts. These patriarchal all-male religious courts arbitrarily decide related matters on a case-by-case basis. Drawing on Islamic sources, judges who are often conservative religious scholars with little or no formal legal training use their own discretion to interpret Islamic legal texts. They accord to the law's effects a character of sanctity. Consequently, even if a dispute comes before a court, the court has to apply the law which, in the examples of the Arab block, is based on patriarchal religious principles[17] which translate themselves into patriarchal court systems and socio-cultural norms that, again, feed back into law-making processes.[18]

Permission of the United Nations; Centre on Law and Globalization, 'What Counts as Rape in International Crimes?' <http://clg.portalxm.com/library/keytext.cfm?keytext_id=182> accessed 27 October 2012; Khalaf (n 5) 6; US Department of State: Bureau of Democracy, Human Rights, and Labor, '2009 Human Rights Report: Saudi Arabia' (n 5); US Department of State: Bureau of Democracy, Human Rights, and Labor, '2009 Human Rights Report: Syria' (2010) <www.state.gov/j/drl/rls/hrrpt/2009/nea/136080.htm> accessed 1 April 2014.

For a more nuanced discussion of the Arab block's national rape definitions and further elaboration on the understanding of rape as an honour crime see Chapter 3.

17 Constitution of the State of Bahrain (26 May 1973) <http://confinder.richmond.edu/admin/docs/Bahrain.pdf> accessed 17 March 2014; Khalaf (n 5) 4; see also The Constitution of the Republic of the Sudan (1998) art 4 <www.sudanembassy.ca/Docs/THE%20CONSTITUTION%20OF%20THE%20REPUBLIC%20OF%20THE%20SUDAN%201998.pdf> accessed 28 March 2014; Constitution of Saudi Arabia (1992) art 1 <www.servat.unibe.ch/icl/sa00000_.html> accessed 28 March 2014; The Constitution of the State of Kuwait (1962) art 2 <www.crsk.edu.kw/Photo/dastor.pdf> accessed 21 March 2014; Constitution of Syria (1964) art 3(2) <www.law.yale.edu/rcw/rcw/jurisdictions/asw/syrianarabrep/syria_constitution.htm> accessed 28 March 2014; Constitution of the United Arab Emirates (1996) art 7 <www.refworld.org/pdfid/48eca8132.pdf> accessed 28 March 2014; Iraqi Constitution (2005) art 2 <www.wipo.int/edocs/lexdocs/laws/en/iq/iq004en.pdf> accessed 18 March 2014; Oman's Constitution of 1996 with Amendments through 2011 art 2 <www.constituteproject.org/constitution/Oman_2011.pdf> accessed 21 March 2014; Permanent Constitution of the State of Qatar (2003) art 1 <www.law.yale.edu/rcw/rcw/jurisdictions/asw/quatar/qatar_constitution.doc> accessed 21 March 2014: In the Arab block, religious principles are the basis for national laws including personal status laws which include marriage laws. This becomes clear when considering that in most of these states' constitutions – with Lebanon being an exception – Sharia law is recognised as a main source of law. In Lebanon, international treaties take precedence over national laws.

18 Dunya Ahmed Abdulla Ahmed, 'Bahrain' in Julia Breslin and Sanja Kelly (eds), *Women's Rights in the Middle East and North Africa: Progress Amid Resistance* (Freedom House/

Since sexualised violence is often dealt with outside domestic courts, the Arab block supposedly would not want them to come before an international court. This would drag sexualised violence from the private into the public sphere. As a public matter, sexualised violence would be addressed by different actors. These may recognise sexualised violence as a wrong, resulting in law reform that could be perceived again as a form of social engineering and unwanted interference in national matters.

One outcome of the mediation that follows instances of extra-marital sexual violence is the marriage between the rapist and the rape survivor. According to Bahraini, Iraqi, Lebanese, Libyan, Sudanese and Syrian law as well as socio-cultural norms, the rapist would save the survivor's honour through marrying her as a social redress. In Bahrain and Iraq, the husband may later divorce his wife and consequently not only avoid punishment for rape but also his conjugal responsibilities such as financially supporting his wife and providing housing for her.[19]

Rape-marriage policies highlight a male, victim-centred and collective understanding of rape. It is the survivor's honour – and by extension the honour of her family – that needs to be saved rather than the perpetrator's breach of the law that needs to be prosecuted.

In summary, the above discussion showed that marital rape is not criminalised under national laws in the states constituting the Arab block. This could explain the group's proposal to make marital sexual intercourse consensual by definition in the ICC instruments. Digging deeper, it became apparent that the national non-criminalisation of marital rape is connected to religious principles, socio-cultural norms and national laws related to the ideal of obedient wives and understandings of rape as an honour crime. The ideal of obedient wives creates distinct gender roles. Attempts to alter these could be seen as social engineering

---

Rowman & Littlefield Publishers 2010) <www.freedomhouse.org/sites/default/files/inline_images/Bahrain.pdf> accessed 17 March 2014; Huda Ahmed, 'Iraq' in Julia Breslin and Sanja Kelly (eds), *Women's Rights in the Middle East and North Africa: Progress Amid Resistance* (Freedom House/Rowman & Littlefield Publishers 2010) 6, 12, 14 <www.freedomhouse.org/sites/default/files/inline_images/Iraq.pdf> accessed 18 March 2014; Bahrain Center for Human Rights, 'Family Law in Bahrain' (10 February 2014) 7 <www.bahrainrights.org/sites/default/files/BCHR%20Report%20on%20Family%20Law%20in%20Bahrain.pdf> accessed 17 March 2014; Doumato (n 7); Freedom House, 'Syria' (n 5) 2; Hallaq, *An Introduction to Islamic Law* (n 5) 133; Khalaf (n 5) 6; US Department of State: Bureau of Democracy, Human Rights, and Labor, '2009 Human Rights Report: Saudi Arabia' (n 5); US Department of State: Bureau of Democracy, Human Rights, and Labor, '2009 Human Rights Report: United Arab Emirates' (n 5).

19 Bahrain Penal Code (n 5) art 353; Interview 14 (n 1); Iraqi Penal Code No 111 (n 5); Bahrain Center for Human Rights (n 18); Khalaf (n 5) 6; Freedom House, 'Syria' (n 5) 12; Alison Pargeter, 'Libya' in Julia Breslin and Sanja Kelly (eds), *Women's Rights in the Middle East and North Africa: Progress Amid Resistance* (Freedom House/Rowman & Littlefield Publishers 2010) 13 <www.freedomhouse.org/sites/default/files/inline_images/Libya.pdf> accessed 21 March 2014; Organisation for Economic Co-operation and Development, 'Social Institutions and Gender Index: Sudan' (2012) <http://genderindex.org/country/sudan> accessed 28 March 2014.

and an imposition of a legal reform process. Therefore, these attempts could be quashed. Furthermore, they are quashed by geopolitical and economic concerns. Questions of honour are considered private and therefore are rarely dealt with in court. A court case would increase publicity and convey importance to an issue. This might lead to demand for reform which might again be perceived as attempts of social engineering and unwelcome interference in national matters. Rape-marriage policies, instead, are an easy and quiet solution to re-establish a woman's honour and that of her family.

'Powers attaching to the right of ownership do not include rights, duties and obligations incident to marriage between a man and a woman.'[20]

The following paragraphs address the Arab block's concerns regarding the ICC definition of sexual slavery. They first analyse the accepted language of a marriage offer as well as understandings of payments of dowry and maintenance before they examine irregular and temporary marriages as marriage rights, duties and obligations that might be interpreted to be an exercise of powers attaching to the right of ownership and therefore amount to sexual slavery. In a third step, the ideal of obedient wives recurs, this time in the context of the Arab block's concerns regarding the ICC definition of sexual slavery rather than rape. Comparisons are established to forced marriages in times of armed conflict. While this part of Chapter 7 first explores marriage rights, duties and obligations in the states constituting the Arab block that bear resemblance to situations of sexual slavery and forced marriage in times of armed conflict, it then discusses religious principles, socio-cultural norms and national laws of the Arab block that support the indirect criminalisation of forced marriage under the ICC instruments.

The language of marriage offers, and understandings of dowry and maintenance payments

The language of a marriage offer and understandings of payments of dowry and maintenance are rights, duties and obligations related to marriage that might be comparable to forced marriage and/or interpreted to be an exercise of powers attaching to the right of ownership and therefore amounting to sexual slavery.

The payment of dower by the groom to the bride rather than her marriage guardian can be understood as an action making her a party to the marriage contract. Based on this, the marriage contract cannot be considered a sale.[21] In contrast, the language of the offer of marriage shows that marriage is

20 PrepCom2, 'Proposal Submitted by Bahrain, Iraq, Kuwait, Lebanon, the Libyan Arab Jamahiriya, Oman, Qatar, Saudi Arabia, the Sudan, the Syrian Arab Republic and United Arab Emirates Concerning the Elements of Crimes against Humanity (9 December 1999)' (n 2).

21 Esposito (n 9) 24.

conceived at least by some schools of Islamic jurisprudence as a property transaction. Terms such as 'gifting', 'selling' and 'surrendering ownership' are accepted, invoking concepts of ownership and slavery.[22] The definition of dower as 'an exchange for the vulva'[23] makes this even more graphic. It is this ownership by the husband of the wife's vulva that makes sexual intercourse lawful. Following on from this, the payment of maintenance ensures the husband's exclusive use of his wife's vulva.[24] The use of the wife's vulva with or without the wife's consent could explain the Arab block's proposal to disconnect marital sexual intercourse from the crime of rape. The payment of maintenance can also be understood as an exchange or compensation for the husband's right to confine his wife to the house for his sexual gratification. This understanding verges closely on what constitutes the crime of sexual slavery. Moreover, it can be compared to situations of forced marriage in times of armed conflict where attaching the label 'wife' to a woman indicates her belonging to her forced husband and assures his exclusive sexual access for which he in turn supports the woman materially.

Irregular and temporary marriages

To prevent extra-marital sexual relations, irregular marriages are recognised as situations of quasi-ownership of the vulva.[25] Here, the wife has the right to payments of dower, but not to maintenance. Therefore, even though the husband owns her vulva, he has no right to exclusive use. The same holds true in temporary marriages.[26] In both situations, but especially in temporary marriages,

22 Hallaq, *Shari'a: Theory, Practice, Transformations* (n 8) 273–274; Shukri (n 8) 43–44: Others schools of Islamic jurisprudence adopt a more literal and formal approach and argue that marriage is an act through which two people are brought, fitted and paired together based on mutual suitability.

23 Colin Imber, *Ebu's-su'ud: The Islamic Legal Tradition* (Edinburgh University Press 1997) 174.

24 Imber (n 23) 183.

25 ibid 174–175, 189; Shukri (n 8) 21.

Doi, *Women in Shari'ah (Islamic Law)* (n 10) 46–53; Esposito (n 9) 13–19; Hallaq, *An Introduction to Islamic Law* (n 5) 115, 126; Hallaq, *Shari'a: Theory, Practice, Transformations* (n 8) 271; Shukri (n 8) 51–52: Irregular marriages are seen by Islamic law as good in their foundations but unlawful in their attributes. They are irregular because they lack a formality that may be corrected, for example marriages without witnesses, or because of an impediment which can be removed for example when the husband already has four wives. In the case of marriages without witnesses, prolonged and continuing cohabitation is permitted as proof of marriage. An irregular marriage has no legal effect until the marriage is consummated and even afterwards, the rights of the spouses are limited. The wife has the right to payments of dower, but not of maintenance. There are no mutual rights of inheritance. To dissolve the marriage, a single verbal declaration of divorce by one of the partners is sufficient.

26 Ahmed, 'Iraq' (n 18) 10, 12–13; Nasir (n 9) 16–17: A temporary marriage allows an unmarried woman to marry a man, whether already married or not, for a certain period

the question arises whether the payment of dower is more of a purchase price rather than a gift made by a man to his bride. Also, it could be argued that, without receiving maintenance, without mutual rights of inheritance, without rights to support if the wife becomes pregnant and without any divorce rights, the wife is in a vulnerable position that can easily be exploited by her husband.

A forced marriage in times of armed conflict can be understood as irregular due to the lack of involvement of a marriage guardian, official witnesses and proper offer and acceptance. In regard to the dissolution of irregular and forced marriages, in neither situation does the woman have extensive protection. Since forced marriages are formed informally, there are no formal divorce proceedings. Moreover, it has to be kept in mind that a split from her forced husband may be socio-economically detrimental to the forced wife as it is likely that she is excluded from her family and community and may have no other means of support. Since forced marriage in times of armed conflict can be seen as a form of irregular marriage, it would be lawful according to norms of the Arab block. By disconnecting marriage rights, duties and obligations, including irregular marriages, from sexual slavery, forced marriage as a form of irregular marriage would not be criminalised under international law either. It has to be noted, however, that irregular marriages differ from forced marriages in regard to payment of dower. While in irregular marriages, the woman has the right to payments of dower, but not of maintenance, it is the other way round in forced marriages. Women are abducted and given in marriage to a fighter in exchange for his services to a fighting group. The woman does not receive anything from the man in 'exchange for her vulva'. In marriage, however, she is materially supported by the forced husband.

Comparing forced marriage to temporary marriage, the man holds the exclusive power to dissolve the marriage in both situations. Highlighting differences, the label of marriage attached to forced marriages in situations of armed conflict and temporary marriages serves different purposes. In the case of the latter, in conformity with religious, socio-cultural and legal norms and rules, it makes sexual intercourse lawful. The fact that the woman does not have any rights to support if she becomes pregnant shows that these unions are not aimed at serving any reproductive purpose, but pure sexual gratification. In the case of forced marriages, the label 'wife' attached to an abductee manipulates the woman

---

of time in exchange for money. These temporary marriages leave the woman without protection as only the man has the right to dissolve the marriage, unless there was a prior agreement between them. Additionally, the woman has no right to support if she becomes pregnant. While Shiite clerics who encourage the practice argue that it prevents adultery and helps widows and poor women, critics see it as a form of prostitution. Understanding the aim of marriage to be the founding of a family, Sunni jurists agree that a marriage contract must not include or imply any time limit. Therefore, they do not consider temporary marriages to be proper marriages because they do not, as said above, establish maintenance and inheritance rights.

into loyalty towards her forced husband and the fighting group. As it does not only legitimise sexual intercourse but also implies non-sexual exploitation, it has broader implications than in temporary marriages. The fact that a woman's status and her position within the family and the fighting group increases after she gave birth as well as the acknowledgement of paternity from the forced husband reveals that reproduction rather than pure sexual gratification, which could be achieved through rape, is an important element in forced marriages. In addition to marriage and parenthood, forced marriages enable forced husbands to fulfil the masculine ideal of providing for, and protecting, their family.

Obedient wives

The ideal of obedient wives discussed above in relation to the Arab block's proposal on the ICC definition of rape may also have been one of the religious principles, socio-cultural norms and national laws the Arab block wanted to protect by disconnecting marriage rights, duties and obligations from the ICC definition of sexual slavery as an exercise of powers attaching to the right of ownership.

Contrary to the principles of Islam and the understanding that one should serve God alone[27] as well as to national prohibitions of slavery,[28] the ideal of obedient wives is linked to a view of women as men's property, overlooking considerations of autonomy. This could be interpreted to result in a state of ownership or servitude. Consequently, the ideal of obedient wives could be considered a breach of national prohibitions of slavery.

The ideal of obedient wives also resonates with situations of forced marriage in times of armed conflict. Forced wives have to be submissive to the authority of their forced husbands. Forced wives have to serve their forced husbands sexually and otherwise. Disobedience is severely punished.

So far, it has been shown that the language of marriage offers as well as understandings of dowry and maintenance were national normative structures that the Arab block might have wanted to protect by proposing to disconnect marriage rights, duties and obligations from the crime of sexual slavery as they can be linked to the notion of ownership and therefore constitute the first

27 Ahmed, 'Bahrain' (n 18) 11; Baderin (n 9) 87.

28 The Constitution of the Republic of the Sudan (n 17) art 20; Constitution of the United Arab Emirates (n 17) art 34(2); Iraqi Constitution (n 17) art 37(3); The Libyan Penal Code (n 5) art 425; Qatari Penal Code (n 4) art 321; Haya al-Mughni, 'Kuwait' in Julia Breslin and Sanja Kelly (eds), *Women's Rights in the Middle East and North Africa: Progress Amid Resistance* (Freedom House/Rowman & Littlefield Publishers 2010) 10 <www.freedomhouse.org/sites/default/files/inline_images/Kuwait.pdf> accessed 21 March 2014; Rafiah al-Talei, 'Oman' in Julia Breslin and Sanja Kelly (eds), *Women's Rights in the Middle East and North Africa: Progress Amid Resistance* (Freedom House/Rowman & Littlefield Publishers 2010) 8 <www.freedomhouse.org/sites/default/files/inline_images/Oman.pdf> accessed 21 March 2014; Doumato (n 7) 11; Freedom House, 'Syria' (n 5) 10.

element of the crime of sexual slavery. The same holds true for irregular and temporary marriages. In both instances, the payment of dowry could be seen as purchasing ownership of the woman's vulva. When considering that temporary marriages do not create any rights for the woman and that temporary marriages are comparable to prostitution, the link to sexual slavery becomes even more obvious. The ideal of obedient wives also puts women in a servile status to men. Therefore, it could be seen as amounting to sexual slavery.

In addition to demonstrating that irregular marriages, the ideal of obedient wives and understandings of maintenance can amount to an exercise of powers attaching to the right of ownership, a link can be established to forced marriage in times of armed conflict. Forced marriages are formed without any formality such as the presence of witnesses. Forced wives have to obey their forced husband. They are expected to have an exclusive relationship and receive material support.

Religious principles, cultural norms and national laws that support the criminalisation of forced marriage in times of armed conflict

Even though the Arab block's proposal invokes issues related to marriage and parallels can be drawn between certain rights, duties and obligations related to marriage in the states constituting the Arab block and forced marriage in times of armed conflict, the Arab block's proposal did not target the indirect criminalisation of forced marriage in times of armed conflict under the ICC. While the meanings of the payment of maintenance, irregular marriages, and the male ideal of obedient wives can be interpreted to include elements of forced marriage and therefore may give rise to opposition towards its international criminalisation, other religious principles, socio-cultural norms and national laws support this step.

According to the laws of the Arab block, a woman may not be forced into marriage and must always agree with the final decision to bring the marriage contract into effect. Coercion constitutes a ground for seeking annulment of marriage in a court.[29]

If a woman's absence of consent to marriage is understood to make the marriage bad in its foundation, forced marriages in times of armed conflict would be void.[30] However, if the spouses are unaware that their marriage is void, their sexual relationship is not classified as adultery. Based on socio-cultural norms,

29 The Great Green Charter of Human Rights of the Jamahiriyan Era (1988) art 21 <www.ilo.org/dyn/natlex/docs/SERIAL/57641/65910/F702695289/LBY57641.PDF> accessed 21 March 2014; al-Mughni (n 28) 8, 10; Hallaq, *Shari'a: Theory, Practice, Transformations* (n 8) 275.

30 Doi, *Women in Shari'ah (Islamic Law)* (n 10) 46–53; Esposito (n 9) 18–19; Shukri (n 8) 51–52: Void marriages are completely bad in their foundation for example because the partners are blood relatives, related by affinity or by fosterage as well as because of illicit sexual impropriety or religious differences. Void marriages do not award any rights or obligations to the spouses. They are null and void and therefore considered not to exist.

it would be considered as a quasi-marriage. However, since it is unrealistic to argue that a forced wife and her forced husband were not aware of the women's absence of consent to marriage, forced marriage in times of armed conflict would not fall under the category of a quasi-marriage.

In line with the potential understanding of forced marriages as void, Article 411 of the Libyan Penal Code explicitly criminalises marriage by capture. Broadening the group of potential targets and acts, Article 412 further prohibits abduction for the purpose of committing indecent acts.[31] A similar provision exists in the Omani Penal Code. Article 296 of the Qatari Penal Code penalises acts of, and connected to, sexual exploitation. Even though only Article 411 of the Libyan Penal Code explicitly connects the crime of abduction and confinement to marriage, forced marriage as committed in armed conflicts could also fall under the other provisions outlined. Without a doubt, the crime includes sexual exploitation where different perpetrators can play different roles including bringing, exposing and accepting a woman for that purpose as determined in the Qatari Penal Code. The commission of indecent acts as referred to in the Libyan and Omani penal codes is more ambivalent. If forced marriage is seen as void because of the woman's absence of consent and if extra-marital sex is seen as an indecent act because it violates religious principles, socio-cultural norms and national laws, the sexual elements of forced marriage would be an indecent act. Since women are abducted and detained for the purpose of forced marriage and since one of the purposes of forced marriage is sexual exploitation, it could be argued that forced marriage in times of armed conflict would fall under Article 412 of the Libyan Penal Code and Article 218(2) of the Omani Penal Code.

Conclusion

Chapter 7 explored the Arab block's concerns regarding the definitions of rape and sexual slavery as crimes against humanity that it voiced in a proposal submitted in the third Preparatory Commission for the International Criminal Court (PrepCom2) session in December 1999. Confirming that national norms and rules shape international actors, their interests and actions, the Arab block's proposal makes clear that the group's aim was to protect certain religious principles, socio-cultural norms and national laws that might be interpreted to amount to crimes against humanity. Chapter 7 explored what religious principles, socio-cultural norms and national laws exactly the Arab block might have wanted to protect.

In regard to the crime of rape, the chapter found that marital rape is not criminalised under national laws of the Arab block. This could explain the group's proposal to delink marital sexual intercourse and rape under the ICC instruments. The non-criminalisation of marital rape under the Arab block's

31 The Libyan Penal Code (n 5).

national laws can be explained based on religious principles, socio-cultural norms and national laws related to the ideal of obedient wives and understandings of rape as an honour crime. Obedient wives have to be sexually available to their husbands, indicating that there is no rape in marriage. The understanding of rape as an honour crime trivialises rape which leads to it being dealt with outside courts. Consequently, the Arab block would not want rape to be addressed by an international court which would give the issue a bigger stage.

Regarding the crime of sexual slavery, Chapter 7 found that the accepted language of a marriage offer, understandings of payments of dowry and maintenance, irregular and temporary marriages, and again the ideal of obedient wives are rights, duties and obligations related to marriage that can be interpreted to be an exercise of powers attaching to the right of ownership and therefore to amount to sexual slavery. To protect these marriage rights, duties and obligations, the Arab block might have wished to disconnect them from the crime of sexual slavery.

While the accepted language of a marriage offer, understandings of payments of dowry and maintenance, irregular and temporary marriages and the ideal of obedient wives bear resemblance to situations of sexual slavery and forced marriage in times of armed conflict and therefore could explain the Arab block's wish to disconnect them, other religious principles, socio-cultural norms and national laws can be interpreted to support the criminalisation of forced marriage in times of armed conflict. National marriage laws stress that the woman's consent to marriage is necessary for the marriage to be valid. An even stronger case can be made based on Articles 411 and 412 of the Libyan Penal Code and Article 296 of the Omani Penal Code. They cover abduction for the purpose of marriage and sexual exploitation and bringing, exposing or accepting a person for the purpose of sexual exploitation respectively.

In addition to exploring which religious principles, socio-cultural norms and national laws the Arab block might have wanted to protect, Chapter 7 also considered the Arab block's fear of social engineering. It became apparent that externally imposed legal reform processes such as those triggered by the national implementation of the Rome Statute might have been understood as attempts of social engineering. As this can have an impact on international treaty-making negotiations, it needs to be considered by participating delegations in developing their interests and actions so as not to disproportionately weaken, or jeopardise the conclusion of, a treaty.

The Arab block's proposal to exclude marital sexual relations from the crime of rape and marriage rights, duties and obligations from sexual slavery makes it very clear that in the states constituting the Arab block, men hold a power position over women. This is supported by the husband's more extensive rights regarding his marital sexual enjoyment. The husband's more extensive rights in the context of marriage are linked to the religious principle that a wife has to be obedient and sexually available to her husband. The ideal of obedient wives raises questions of their autonomy and invokes notions of ownership. The accepted language of a marriage offer, including terms such as 'gifting', 'selling' and 'surrendering ownership', has the same effect. The payment of dowry can be interpreted as payment in exchange for the wife's vulva. Following on from this, the payment of maintenance secures the husband's exclusive access. The payment of maintenance can also be understood as an exchange or compensation for the husband's right to confine his wife to the house for his sexual gratification. In irregular and temporary marriages, the wife has the right to the payments of dower, but not of maintenance. Therefore, even though the husband owns her vulva, he has no right to exclusive use. Especially in relation to temporary marriages, it can be questioned whether the payment of dower is more of a purchase price, rather than a gift made by a groom to his bride. Also, it could be argued that, without protective rights, the wife is in a vulnerable position that is easily exploited by her husband. The partial understanding of rape as an honour crime also indicates a view of women as men's property. Patriarchal values, norms and rules would become contested if men could not freely decide on their marital relations. Therefore, patriarchal values, norms and rules would become contested if marital rape would be criminalised under international law and if certain marriage rights, duties and obligations would amount to sexual slavery. Consequently, the wish to maintain existing power structures could have been the fundamental reason for the Arab block to dissent developments in national as well as international law in regard to sexualised crimes.

Bibliography

Conventions and statutes

International Covenant on Economic, Social and Cultural Rights (16 December 1966) 993 UNTS 3 (ICESCR) <www.legal-tools.org/doc/06b87e/> accessed 18 August 2017.

United Nations documents

Commission on Human Rights

Commission on Human Rights, 'Final Report of the Special Rapporteur on the Situation of Systematic Rape, Sexual Slavery and Slavery-Like Practices during Armed Conflict' (22 June 1998) UN Doc E/CN.4/Sub.2/1998/13 <www.ohchr.org> accessed 28 August 2017 ©1998 United Nations. Reprinted with the Permission of the United Nations.

Preparatory Commission for the International Criminal Court

PrepCom2, 'Proposal Submitted by Bahrain, Iraq, Kuwait, Lebanon, the Libyan Arab Jamahiriya, Oman, Qatar, Saudi Arabia, the Sudan, the Syrian Arab Republic and United Arab Emirates Concerning the Elements of Crimes against Humanity

(9 December 1999)' UN Doc PCNICC/1999/WGEC/DP.39 <www.legal-tools.org/doc/33d070/> accessed 10 August 2017.

Other legal documents

Bahrain Penal Code (1976) <www.bahrainrights.org/sites/default/files/Bahrain-Penal-Code.doc> accessed 17 March 2014.

Constitution of the Republic of the Sudan (1998) <www.sudanembassy.ca/Docs/THE%20CONSTITUTION%20OF%20THE%20REPUBLIC%20OF%20THE%20SUDAN%201998.pdf> accessed 28 March 2014.

Constitution of Saudi Arabia (1992) <www.servat.unibe.ch/icl/sa00000_.html> accessed 28 March 2014.

Constitution of the State of Bahrain (26 May 1973) <http://confinder.richmond.edu/admin/docs/Bahrain.pdf> accessed 17 March 2014.

Constitution of the State of Kuwait (1962) <www.crsk.edu.kw/Photo/dastor.pdf> accessed 21 March 2014.

Constitution of Syria (1964) <www.law.yale.edu/rcw/rcw/jurisdictions/asw/syrianarabrep/syria_constitution.htm> accessed 28 March 2014.

Constitution of the United Arab Emirates (1996) <www.refworld.org/pdfid/48eca8132.pdf> accessed 28 March 2014.

Criminal Act of 1991 (Sudan) <www.icrc.org/applic/ihl/ihl-nat.nsf/xsp/.ibmmodres/domino/OpenAttachment/applic/ihl/ihl-nat.nsf/B9EEBA1CA8F54121C1256DC9005573F2/TEXT/Criminal%20Act%20-%20Sudan%20-%20EN.pdf> accessed 1 April 2014.

Great Green Charter of Human Rights of the Jamahiriyan Era (1988) <www.ilo.org/dyn/natlex/docs/SERIAL/57641/65910/F702695289/LBY57641.PDF> accessed 21 March 2014.

Iraqi Constitution (2005) <www.wipo.int/edocs/lexdocs/laws/en/iq/iq004en.pdf> accessed 18 March 2014.

Iraqi Penal Code No 111 (1969) <www.iraq-lg-law.org/en/webfm_send/1350> accessed 18 March 2014.

Libyan Penal Code (1953) <https://ia600704.us.archive.org/25/items/LibyanPenalCodeenglish/LibyanPenalCode.pdf> accessed 24 March 2014.

Omani Penal Code (1974) <www.fiu.gov.om/forms.html> accessed 24 March 2014.

Oman's Constitution of 1996 with Amendments through 2011 <www.constituteproject.org/constitution/Oman_2011.pdf> accessed 21 March 2014.

Permanent Constitution of the State of Qatar (2003) <www.law.yale.edu/rcw/rcw/jurisdictions/asw/quatar/qatar_constitution.doc> accessed 21 March 2014.

Qatari Penal Code (2004) <http://portal.www.gov.qa/wps/wcm/connect/8abaea8046be1deaae97ef70b3652ad8/Penal+Code.pdf?MOD=AJPERES&useDefaultText=0&useDefaultDesc=0> accessed 24 March 2014.

Interviews

Interview 1 (21 March 2014).

Interview 3 (25 March 2014).

Interview 12 (15 May 2014).

Interview 14 (26 May 2014).

Interview 18 (25 June 2014).

Books

Baderin, M.A., *International Human Rights and Islamic Law* (Oxford University Press 2003).

Doi, A.R.I., *Women in Shari'ah (Islamic Law)* (2nd edn, Ta-Ha Publishers 1989).

Esposito, J.E., *Women in Muslim Family Law* (Syracuse University Press 1982).

Hallaq, W.B., *An Introduction to Islamic Law* (5th edn, Cambridge University Press 2009).

———, *Shari'a: Theory, Practice, Transformations* (Cambridge University Press 2009).

Imber, C., *Ebu's-su'ud: The Islamic Legal Tradition* (Edinburgh University Press 1997).

Nasir, J.J., *The Status of Women under Islamic Law and Under Modern Islamic Legislation* (Graham and Trotman 1990).

Rothschild, C., *Written Out: How Sexuality Is Used to Attack Women's Organizing* (International Gay and Lesbian Human Rights Commission and Center for Women's Global Leadership 2005).

Shukri, A., *Muhammedan Law of Marriage and Divorce* (Colombia University Press 1917).

Chapters in edited books

Ahmed, D.A.A., 'Bahrain' in Julia Breslin and Sanja Kelly (eds), *Women's Rights in the Middle East and North Africa: Progress Amid Resistance* (Freedom House/Rowman & Littlefield Publishers 2010) <www.freedomhouse.org/sites/default/files/inline_images/Bahrain.pdf> accessed 17 March 2014.

Ahmed, H., 'Iraq' in Julia Breslin and Sanja Kelly (eds), *Women's Rights in the Middle East and North Africa: Progress Amid Resistance* (Freedom House/Rowman & Littlefield Publishers 2010) <www.freedomhouse.org/sites/default/files/inline_images/Iraq.pdf> accessed 18 March 2014.

al-Mughni, H., 'Kuwait' in Julia Breslin and Sanja Kelly (eds), *Women's Rights in the Middle East and North Africa: Progress Amid Resistance* (Freedom House/Rowman & Littlefield Publishers 2010) <www.freedomhouse.org/sites/default/files/inline_images/Kuwait.pdf> accessed 21 March 2014.

al-Talei, R., 'Oman' in Julia Breslin and Sanja Kelly (eds), *Women's Rights in the Middle East and North Africa: Progress Amid Resistance* (Freedom House/Rowman & Littlefield Publishers 2010) <www.freedomhouse.org/sites/default/files/inline_images/Oman.pdf> accessed 21 March 2014.

Doumato, E.A., 'Saudi Arabia' in Julia Breslin and Sanja Kelly (eds), *Women's Rights in the Middle East and North Africa: Progress Amid Resistance* (Freedom House/Rowman & Littlefield Publishers 2010) <www.freedomhouse.org/sites/default/files/inline_images/Saudi%20Arabia.pdf> accessed 28 March 2014.

Freedom House, 'Syria' in Julia Breslin and Sanja Kelly (eds), *Women's Rights in the Middle East and North Africa: Progress Amid Resistance* (Freedom House/Rowman & Littlefield Publishers 2010) <www.freedomhouse.org/sites/default/files/inline_images/Syria.pdf> accessed 28 March 2014.

Khalaf, M.C., 'Lebanon' in Julia Breslin and Sanja Kelly (eds), *Women's Rights in the Middle East and North Africa: Progress Amid Resistance* (Freedom House/

Rowman & Littlefield Publishers 2010) <www.freedomhouse.org/sites/default/files/inline_images/Lebanon.pdf> accessed 21 March 2014.

Pargeter, A., 'Libya' in Julia Breslin and Sanja Kelly (eds), *Women's Rights in the Middle East and North Africa: Progress Amid Resistance* (Freedom House/Rowman & Littlefield Publishers 2010) <www.freedomhouse.org/sites/default/files/inline_images/Libya.pdf> accessed 21 March 2014.

(Research) reports and working papers

Bahrain Center for Human Rights, 'Family Law in Bahrain' (10 February 2014) <www.bahrainrights.org/sites/default/files/BCHR%20Report%20on%20Family%20Law%20in%20Bahrain.pdf> accessed 17 March 2014.

Organisation for Economic Co-Operation and Development, 'Social Institutions and Gender Index: Sudan' (2012) <http://genderindex.org/country/sudan> accessed 28 March 2014.

U.S. Department of State, Bureau of Democracy, Human Rights, and Labor, '2009 Human Rights Report: Saudi Arabia' (2010) <www.state.gov/j/drl/rls/hrrpt/2009/nea/136079.htm> accessed 1 April 2014.

———, '2009 Human Rights Report: Syria' (2010) <www.state.gov/j/drl/rls/hrrpt/2009/nea/136080.htm> accessed 1 April 2014.

———, '2009 Human Rights Report: United Arab Emirates' (2010) <www.state.gov/j/drl/rls/hrrpt/2009/nea/136082.htm> accessed 1 April 2014.

Other

Centre on Law and Globalization, 'What Counts as Rape in International Crimes?' <http://clg.portalxm.com/library/keytext.cfm?keytext_id=182> accessed 27 October 2012.

8 Conclusion

Introduction

This research project grew out of a critique of the International Criminal Court (ICC) definition of war rape and forced marriage. Therefore, it addressed the ongoing challenge of how to define the two crimes adequately, reflecting women's experiences and the nature of the crimes. The ICC Elements of Crimes define the first element of rape as

> [t]he accused invaded the body of a person by conduct resulting in penetration, however slight, of any part of the body of the victim or of the perpetrator with a sexual organ, or of the anal or genital opening of the victim with any object or any other part of the body.[1]

The awkward and regressive wording 'invasion resulting in penetration' is puzzling when taking into account that actors could have relied on the more progressive *Akayesu* precedent. Furthermore, actors in the ICC negotiations understood forced marriage as a form of sexual slavery and did not discuss it in depth. The perpetration of forced marriages in conflicts that were ongoing while the ICC instruments were negotiated makes this neglect problematic.

Against the background of this critique, this research project analysed how the ICC definitions of war rape and forced marriage came about. Based on a combined feminist and constructivist approach it focused on the driving actors, the normative structures that influenced their identities, interests and actions, their understandings of the two crimes, and their methods of influencing the ICC negotiations. The following paragraphs draw together the main findings of this research project and further comment on the points of critique regarding the ICC definition of war rape and forced marriage.

1 PrepCom2, 'Discussion Paper Proposed by the Coordinator: Article 8, paragraph 2(b)(xxii)' (10 August 1999) UN Doc PCNICC/1999/WGEC/RT.6 art 8(2)(b)(xxii)(1)(2) <www.legal-tools.org/doc/a4a83f/> accessed 10 August 2017; PrepCom2, 'Proceedings of the Preparatory Commission at Its Second Session (26 July–13 August 1999)' (18 August 1999) UN Doc PCNICC/1999/L.4/Rev.1 art 8(2)(b)(xxii)(1)(2) <www.legal-tools.org/doc/0b6332/> accessed 10 August 2017.

Who were the driving actors in the process of war defining rape and forced marriage?

Since the 18th century, a crucial development has taken place in international law-making regarding the identity of driving actors. Where initially it was largely male statesmen who took measures concerning sexualised war violence, from the mid-20th century on, women and non-governmental organisations (NGOs) became increasingly involved.[2]

2 Kelly Dawn Askin, *War Crimes against Women: Prosecution in International War Crimes Tribunals* (Kluwer International Law 1997); Steve Charnovitz, 'Two Centuries of Participation: NGOs and International Governance' (1997) 18 *Michigan Journal of International Law* 183; Christine Chinkin, 'Violence against Women: The International Legal Response' (1995) 3 (2) *Gender and Development* 23; Alison Cole, 'International Criminal Law and Sexual Violence: An Overview' in Clare McGlynn and Vanessa E. Munro (eds), *Rethinking Rape Law: International and Comparative Perspectives* (Routledge 2010); Commission on the Responsibility of the Authors of the War and on Enforcement of Penalties, 'Report Presented to the Preliminary Peace Conference' (1920) 14 *American Journal of International Law* 95; James T. Connolly and others (eds), *The Adams Papers: Papers of John Adams, Volume 16, February 1784–March 1785* (The Belknap Press of Harvard University Press 2012); Rhonda Copelon, 'Gender Crimes as War Crimes: Integrating Crimes against Women into International Criminal Law' (2000) 46 *McGill Law Journal* 217; Patrick Cotter and others, 'Affecting the Rules for the Prosecution of Rape and other Gender-Based Violence before the International Criminal Tribunal for the Former Yugoslavia: A Feminist Proposal and Critique' (1994) 5 *Hastings Women's Law Journal* 171; Patrizia De Cesari, 'NGOs and the Activities of the Ad Hoc Criminal Tribunals for Former Yugoslavia and Rwanda' in Alessandro Fodella and others (eds), *Civil Society, International Courts and Compliance Bodies* (TMC Asser Press 2004); Diplomatic Conference for the Establishment of International Conventions for the Protection of Victims of War, 'Final Record of the Diplomatic Conference of Geneva of 1949, Vol. 1' (Federal Political Department Berne 1963) <www.loc.gov/rr/frd/Military_Law/pdf/Dipl-Conf-1949-Final_Vol-1.pdf> accessed 15 August 2013; Diplomatic Conference for the Establishment of International Conventions for the Protection of Victims of War, 'Final Record of the Diplomatic Conference of Geneva of 1949, Vol. 2, Section A' (Federal Political Department Berne 1963) <www.loc.gov/rr/frd/Military_Law/pdf/Dipl-Conf-1949-Final_Vol-1.pdf> accessed 15 August 2013; Diplomatic Conference on the Reaffirmation and Development of International Humanitarian Law Applicable in Armed Conflicts, 'Official Records of the Diplomatic Conference on the Reaffirmation and Development of International Humanitarian Law Applicable in Armed Conflicts Geneva, 1974–1977, Vol. 15' (Federal Political Department Berne 1978) <www.loc.gov/rr/frd/Military_Law/pdf/RC-records_Vol-15.pdf> accessed 21 October 2013; Mark S. Ellis, 'The Contribution of Non-Governmental Organizations to the Creation of International Criminal Tribunals' in Bartram S. Brown (ed), *Research Handbook on International Criminal Law* (Edward Elgar Publishing 2011); Judith Gardam and Michelle J. Jarvis, *Women, Armed Conflict and International Law* (Kluwer Law International 2001); John Hagen, *Justice in the Balkans: Prosecuting War Crimes in the Hague Tribunal* (University of Chicago Press 2003); Janet Halley, 'Take a Break from Feminism?' in Karen Knop (ed), *Gender and Human Rights* (Oxford University Press 2004); Emily Haslam, 'Subjects and Objects: International Criminal Law and the Institutionalization of Civil Society' (2011) 5 *International Journal of Transitional Justice* 221; International Committee of the Red Cross, 'The Laws of War on Land: Oxford, 9 September 1880' <www.icrc.org/ihl/INTRO/140?OpenDocument> accessed 21 October 2013; International Committee of the Red Cross, 'Project of an International Declaration Concerning the Laws and Customs of War: Brussels, 27 August

In the ICC negotiations of the crimes of war rape and forced marriage in times of armed conflict, states were – as expected – the main actors, but NGOs also played a crucial role. The discussion was driven especially by the Women's Caucus but also the International Committee of the Red Cross (ICRC) as non-state actors, as well as by the Arab block, Colombia and the United States of America (USA, US) as state actors. The Women's Caucus' motivation to become active in the ICC negotiations of war rape and forced marriage was to ensure that sexualised crimes were appropriately addressed and that women's concerns

1874' <www.icrc.org/ihl/INTRO/135> accessed 13 August 2013; International Human Rights Law Group, 'No Justice, No Peace: Accountability for Rape and Gender-Based Violence in the Former Yugoslavia' (1994) 5 *Hastings Women's Law Journal* 89; Howard S. Levie (ed), *The Law of Non-International Armed Conflict: Protocol II to the 1949 Geneva Conventions* (Martinus Nijhoff Publishers 1987); Fionnuala D. Ni Aolain, 'Gendered Harms and Their Interface with International Criminal Law: Norms, Challenges and Domestication' (2013) Minnesota Legal Studies Research Paper No 13–19 <http://ssrn.com/abstract=2247623> accessed 6 May 2015; Stop Violence against Women, 'DEVAW' (14 September 2007) <www.stopvaw.org/devaw> accessed 13 August 2013; Virginia Law, 'The Tokyo War Crimes Trial: A Digital Exhibition: People' <http://lib.law.virginia.edu/imtfe/people> accessed 6 September 2013; Patricia Viseur Sellers, 'The Context of Sexual Violence: Sexual Violence as Violations of International Humanitarian Law' in Gabrielle Kirk McDonald and Olivia Swaak (eds), *Substantive and Procedural Aspects of International Criminal Law: The Experience of International and National Courts, Volume 1, Commentary* (Kluwer Law International 2000): In relation to the Treaty of Amity and Commerce, the Declaration of Brussels, the Oxford Manual, the Hague Convention, Protocol I and II Additional to the Geneva Conventions, and the War Crimes Commission established after the First World War, it was largely male statesmen who took measures concerning sexualised war violence. However, they actually took action only in a few cases like the von Hagenbach trial and the deliberations of Napoleon's fate after his defeat in the Battle of Waterloo. After the Second World War, this climate of state-centeredness and male exclusivity began to change. Women and non-governmental organisations (NGOs) participated in the drafting process of the Geneva Conventions. While male international observers testified on behalf of female survivors of sexualised war violence before the International Military Tribunal for the Far East (IMTFE, Tokyo Tribunal), female survivors themselves told their stories to the International Military Tribunal (IMT, Nuremberg Tribunal). As shown in the *Akayesu* and *Foča* cases, the personal testimony of survivors of sexualised war violence is crucial for the ICTR and ICTY to reach convictions. Today, women like Judge Navanethem Pillay of South Africa and Judge Florence Ndepele Mwachande Mumba of Zambia, Prosecutor Louise Arbour of Canada and Gender Advisor Patricia Viseur Sellers of the United States of America (USA, US)/Belgium hold influential positions in both tribunals as well as in the Special Court for Sierra Leone (SCSL). International and local NGOs and women's activists actively influenced international law-making and the work of international legal institutions like the ICTY, ICTR and SCSL. The international Coalition for Women's Human Rights in Conflict Situations, expert witness Zainab Hawa Bangura of Sierra Leone, the Green/Copelon Group, Human Rights Watch, the International Centre for Transitional Justice, the International Abolitionist Federation, the International Council of Women, and No Peace Without Justice played a vital role in drafting provisions, supporting on-site investigations and writing *amicus* briefs, letters and petitions. Female members of staff and NGOs contributed towards the informed inclusion of sexualised crimes in the investigation, prosecution and trial phase as well as gender-sensitive policies and processes in international courts and tribunals.

were considered. The ICRC's involvement was driven by its role as the guardian of and expert in international humanitarian law. The Arab block engaged in the ICC negotiations of war rape and forced marriage to protect national marriage laws and practices from falling within the reach of crimes against humanity. It also aimed to protect its norms and rules against international interference. Colombia had an interest in shaping the definitions of crimes as it was aware that it might become the focus of ICC investigations. Similarly, the USA insisted on defining the crimes under the jurisdiction of the ICC as it worried that the institution might prosecute its own nationals.

Individually, most actors in the ICC negotiations were career diplomats and senior civil servants. Public and private experts and activists including legal specialists also took part. In addition, the Women's Caucus included, and worked with, survivors of sexualised war violence who campaigned for women's rights. As members of the Caucus' delegation, survivors had direct input in its positions. Women and women's organisations in different countries were informed about positions the Women's Caucus thought about adopting and asked for their views. The Caucus would consider the feedback it received when drafting its final positions. Therefore, survivors directly and indirectly influenced and shaped the outcomes of the ICC negotiations. However, it has to be noted that overall the participation of survivors was an exception.

Will women and NGOs change the world?

The analysis of the main actors in the ICC negotiations places great hopes for progress in international law in the participation of women and NGOs. While this book highlighted their successes, it also demonstrated that women and NGOs in influential positions do not necessarily and automatically advance the law.

While the members of the Women's Caucus, for example, were largely successful in advocating a progressive understanding of sexualised crime, they experienced opposition from women based on religious grounds. Other women were perceived as corrupting the debate about gender issues and sexualised violence by continuously advancing strong opinions, for example about the relationship between sexualised violence and pornography.

Like women's advocacy, the generally high degree of activism of local and international NGOs in law-making also leads to mixed results. While NGOs were accepted and respected in the ICC negotiations as strategic partners of states and exercised considerable influence in the discussions of war rape and forced marriage, eventually states had the whip hand. Relationships between NGOs and state delegations were generally constructive until NGOs disagreed with states' positions. In such cases, cooperation lessened. State actors, for example, insisted on the inclusion of the term 'penetration' and a reference to body parts in the ICC rape definition despite the Women's Caucus' advocacy to the contrary. As the expression 'invasion resulting in penetration' shows, the Caucus' call not to construct a rape definition with cumbersome and irritatingly specific wording also was not followed. In addition, the Women's Caucus' suggestion to include the words ‘with or without pecuniary benefit’[3] in the definition of sexual slavery was not taken up.

It becomes apparent that the success of women and NGOs in progressively developing international law depends on the priorities, openness and receptiveness of those in charge. Women and NGOs still operate within male normative structures, circumscribing their opportunities and abilities to exercise influence. In the ICC negotiations, men behaved in a patronising way towards female actors, hampering their influence and success. In the ICC negotiations, precedents prevailed over adapting established rules to new contexts. This demonstrates that actors followed male reasoning processes. They were highly dependent on legal precedents that were analysed and applied using logic and abstraction. In the ICC negotiations, some actors considered attention to gender issues unnecessary, marginalising and trivialising them. They relied on the progress made by the *ad hoc* tribunals and the positive effect of neutral rules. In addition, the ICC’s understanding of acts of sexualised war violence against women such as forced marriage reflects and reinforces gender stereotypes of women as sexual beings and as housewives. This further limits the opportunities and abilities for women and women’s groups to exercise influence. They are considered out of place in the public sphere and therefore not taken seriously.

What influenced the driving actors?

International normative structures

Among the international normative structures that influenced the actors in negotiations of the definition of war rape and forced marriage were the 1907 Hague and 1949 Geneva conventions, Protocol I and II Additional to the Geneva Conventions, the 1926 Convention to Suppress the Slave Trade and Slavery (Slavery Convention) and the instruments of the International Criminal Tribunal for the former Yugoslavia (ICTY) and the International Criminal Tribunal for Rwanda (ICTR), judgments in the *Akayesu* and *Furundžija* cases and the *Foča* indictment. In addition, the Final Report of the United Nations (UN) Special Rapporteur on the Situation of Systematic Rape, Sexual Slavery and Slavery-Like Practices during Armed Conflict as well as the Fourth World Conference on Women (Beijing Conference) and the World Conference on Human Rights (Vienna Conference) and their outcomes were referred to.

The fourth Hague and Geneva conventions express a view of war rape as a violation of the honour of the family. The understanding of war rape as an honour crime emphasises the severity of the harm rape causes to survivors and communities. This makes it necessary to legally address rape. However, while

3 Women’s Caucus for Gender Justice, ‘Recommendations and Commentary to the Elements Annex and Rules of Procedure and Evidence’ (June 2000) <www.iccwomen.org/wigjdraft1/Archives/oldWCGJ/icc/iccpc/062000pc/elementsannex.htm> accessed 23 January 2014.

the emphasis on the collective harm that rape causes reflects a purpose of war rape, it is detrimental to survivors. Their individual violation is obscured by the violation of the community. Women's (sexual) autonomy is denied by advancing a relational view of women.

In the period from the mid-1970s to the mid-1990s, international agreements and instruments such as Protocol I and II Additional to the Geneva Conventions and the Vienna and Beijing declarations and Platforms for Action framed war rape as an issue of protecting women and their fundamental rights. While this stresses that women are human beings and have human rights, it also implies that women are helpless and vulnerable and require special treatment. From the mid-1970s on, rape was also seen as an issue of discrimination. This resonates with the argument that unequal relationships between men and women are at the root of sexualised violence in peace and wartime.

In this atmosphere of strengthened women's rights advocacy regarding the recognition of war rape as a crime, the ICTY and ICTR were established. The statutes of both *ad hoc* tribunals explicitly include rape as a crime against humanity. In addition, rape is also explicitly mentioned as a war crime in the ICTR statute. In their jurisprudence, the tribunals recognised rape as a crime against humanity, a war crime, a genocidal act, torture and as a grave breach of the Geneva Conventions. This highlights that war rape was seen as a crime in and of itself as well as potentially constituting other crimes.

In the *Akayesu* case, the ICTR developed the first definition of war rape under international criminal law; a definition that uses the term 'invasion' and stresses the element of coercion. A rape definition using the term 'invasion' is gender-neutral, inclusive and culturally sensitive. It illustrates the survivor's point of view. A coercion-based rape definition emphasises the inequality between the victim and the perpetrator, the violence of the situation and the surrounding contexts. This indicates that a coercion-based rape definition is based on the value of equality and the resulting norm of non-discrimination. Contrary to a coercion-based understanding of the crime of rape, a rape definition centred on the concept of consent stresses that being raped deprives the victim of her sexual self-determination and freedom. Therefore, it stresses the survivor's agency. The value of self-determination translates into the norm of non-interference in personal decisions. This indicates that a consent-based rape definition focuses on the psyche of the victim rather than on the acts of the perpetrator.

In the *Furundžija* case and *Foča* indictment, the ICTY disregarded the *Akayesu* definition of war rape and developed definitions using the male term 'penetration'. Both, definitions of rape using the term 'penetration' and 'invasion' can be understood to be founded on the norm 'don't touch'. The term 'penetration', however, is understood to be less vague than the term 'invasion'. In spite of this, a rape definition using 'penetration' links rape to questions of honour and focuses on the physical aspects of rape. This makes the *Furundžija* and *Foča* definitions narrower than the *Akayesu* definition. In addition, both definitions specify body parts which may be detrimental to survivors as testifying becomes more challenging because survivors have to give a detailed account of the physical aspects of the rape, which may also infringe upon cultural sensitivities. This critique also applies to the ICC rape definition.

While actors could draw on a relatively extensive legislative history in their discussions of a definition of war rape, forced marriage had only been defined in the Final Report of the UN Special Rapporteur on the Situation of Systematic Rape, Sexual Slavery and Slavery-Like Practices during Armed Conflict, Gay J. McDougall. The Final Report is one of the first instances where forced marriage is established as an internationally recognised wrong that needs to be addressed because it violates the value of personal self-determination and the norm to be free to choose whom, when and how to marry. However, since the crime of forced marriage had not been well-established in the mid-1990s, it was not recognised as a crime in and of itself. Drawing on Article 1(1) of the 1926 Slavery Convention and the *Foča* indictment instead, it was categorised as a form of sexual slavery. This categorisation, however, creates the false impression that forced marriage would predominantly be a sexual crime and consequently perpetuates stereotypes that women primarily experience war as victims of sexual violence. The categorisation of forced marriage as a form of sexual slavery does not capture the forced exclusivity and disregards the psychological force of acts of violence being disguised within the legitimate situation of marriage. It neglects that forced marriages cause different forms of suffering than sexual slavery and cause survivors to be discriminated against in unique ways. Contrary to these disadvantages of categorising forced marriage as a form of sexual slavery, it has to be acknowledged that the use of the label 'slavery' emphasises the seriousness of the crime of forced marriage. This critique also applies to the categorisation of forced marriage as a form of sexual slavery in the ICC negotiations.

National normative structures

The relevance of national norms and rules in the ICC negotiations becomes apparent when considering that state delegations received instructions from their governments, including negotiation objectives, that sometimes reflected national laws. Domestic definitions of rape, for example of the US and Colombia, prevented a more progressive wording that would not use the term 'penetration'. The Colombian Penal Code of 2000 includes the crime of violent carnal access, which includes rape. As rape is understood as penetration by the penis, the Colombian national definition of the crime ignores the use of other body parts and of objects. Similarly, the US Federal Bureau of Investigation's definition of rape at the time referred to '[t]he carnal knowledge of a female'[4] and defined rape in terms of coercion and lack of consent. The US definition focused on male to female rape, ignoring rapes of men and the use of objects. The Arab

4 Federal Bureau of Investigation, 'Frequently Asked Questions about the Change in the UCR Definition of Rape' (11 December 2014) <www.fbi.gov/about-us/cjis/ucr/recent-program-updates/new-rape-definition-frequently-asked-questions> accessed 19 January 2015.

block's proposals also highlight the relevance of national normative structures. With recourse to national laws, religious principles and cultural norms, the Arab block proposed changes to the definitions of rape and sexual slavery. Fundamental to the Arab block's dissent towards developments in international law in regard to sexualised crimes was the wish to maintain existing patriarchal power structures.

Personal normative structures

Personal values that played a role in the ICC negotiations had been formed through experiences of war and international justice work. The Women's Caucus' positions were informed by experiences of survivors of sexualised war violence with the ICTY and ICTR. Their participation in court proceedings indicates that survivors valued justice. The Caucus also based its identity, interests and actions on its members' experiences and expertise developed in previous caucuses formed at the Vienna and Beijing conferences and at the International Conference on Population and Development (Cairo Conference) as well as in their work as Human Rights and women's rights scholars, lawyers and activists. Human Rights and women's rights work is often very personal for actors who are driven by the value of equality. Civil society actors who became members of state delegations and maintained, and argued for, their personal views are another example that demonstrates the impact of personal values on the ICC negotiations. Moreover, when governments' instructions to delegates were inadequate, delegates had to depend on their professional experience, daily progress evaluations and their perception of the international community's general interests. This indicates that delegates valued professionalism and communality. Delegates approached others to show them that certain positions, including those on sexualised violence, were in fact consistent with their governments' instructions. In addition, delegates shaped the content of their instructions through reports to their ministries.

What was the driving actors' understanding of war rape and forced marriage?

The driving actors' understandings of war rape

Due to actors' different mandates, common sources of information were interpreted and used differently. Both the Women's Caucus and the ICRC were influenced by existing national and international rape laws. However, while the ICRC was bound by its role as guardian of international humanitarian law, the Caucus was guided by its mandate to advance women's rights. Therefore, the Women's Caucus was more at liberty to develop different foci and advance different suggestions. An example is the Women's Caucus' emphasis on the *Akayesu* case based on which it advocated a coercion-based rape definition using the term 'invasion'. The ICRC, in contrast, emphasised the *Furundžija* case and *Foča* indictment. As mentioned above, in both cases the ICTY arrived at a mechanical definition of rape using the term 'penetration'. The Women's Caucus and the ICRC agreed that rape should be recognised as a crime in its own right as well as constituting, for example, genocide and a grave breach of the Geneva Conventions.

Among the key actors in the ICC negotiations of the definition of rape, the Women's Caucus was the only one that held a more elaborate view. Considering its mandate, this was to be expected. In addition to advocating a coercion-based rape definition that used the term 'invasion', the Caucus stressed the importance of developing a broad, gender-neutral and perpetrator-centred understanding of rape as a crime in and of itself as well as potentially amounting to other crimes. This included a definition that does not rely on body parts and recognises situations that are directly and indirectly threatening to the victim. The Women's Caucus also highlighted that rape is a form of gender violence and therefore a form of structural violence that continues from peace into wartime. This approach is in accord with the prohibition of gender-based discrimination.

Colombia, followed by the US, was a key actor that went through a considerable learning process. Based on its national rules, Colombia initially proposed a rape definition using neither the term 'invasion' nor 'penetration' but 'to have sexual access to the victim'. It understood this wording to be inclusive and to better protect the right of sexual freedom and freedom to exercise control over one's body. A second proposal kept this wording but conversations with NGOs inspired the delegation to advance a different reasoning for it. They now took international legal developments and discussions, for example about the difference between rape and sexual violence, and evidential considerations into account. After further exchanges with NGOs led to a better understanding of the term 'penetration' as the use of any tool, the Colombian delegation proposed a rape definition using this term. Eventually, however, in a joint proposal of Spain and five South and Central American states including Colombia, the verb 'to have access to' was reintroduced.

Like Colombia, the US initially evoked national norms and rules in proposing a consent-based rape definition using the term 'penetration' before following the Women's Caucus and stressing the coercive circumstances under which war rapes are committed. The US also agreed with the Caucus that rape should be recognised as an independent crime as well as potentially constituting other offences. It consecutively established a connection between rape and sodomy, enforced prostitution and sexual slavery respectively.

Like Colombia and the US, the Arab block also advanced an understanding of rape – or rather of what it is not – based on national norms and rules. The states constituting the Arab block understand marriage to legitimise sexual intercourse. Consequently, marital rape is legally impossible. This is supported by the ideal of obedient wives according to which wives have to be sexually submissive to their husbands. When an unmarried woman is raped, the understanding of rape as an honour crime dictates that it should be dealt with in private rather than in court. Instead of a court trial, the rapist is encouraged to marry his victim to re-establish a woman's honour and the honour of her family. The act of rape itself is understood in different ways by different states constituting the Arab block. Generally, however, it is mostly defined as non-consensual, sometimes as forced, sexual intercourse.

The above demonstrates that actors' understandings of war rape were influenced by international, national and personal values, norms and rules. It indicated that the Women's Caucus' understanding of war rape was also shaped by the more theoretical view of war rape as based on the discrimination and violence committed against women in everyday life. Moreover, the understanding of war rape as a weapon of war appears to have been implied in the ICC negotiations; otherwise it would not have been recognised as a war crime. Actors would not have recognised rape as a crime at all would they have understood it as an expression of natural male aggressiveness as this implies that rape is an unavoidable by-product of war and legal pursuit is futile. Would actors have taken into consideration that war rape can be understood as an expression of social interactions in the military, they might have argued more strongly for it being a form of structural violence and focused predominantly on the actions and context of the perpetrator. While actors in the ICC negotiations placed a focus on individuals involved in an act of rape as well as on the effect war rapes have on survivors' communities, advancing an understanding of war rape as a tool of propaganda would have also highlighted the effect of war rapes on societies as a whole.

The driving actors' understandings of forced marriage

Regarding forced marriage, only the Women's Caucus and the ICRC explicitly mentioned the crime in their discussions. The Women's Caucus recognised forced marriage as a form of gender violence and therefore structural violence that has sexual and non-sexual aspects. This understanding is supported by the examples of Liberian and Ugandan women's experiences the Caucus referred to in its written recommendations and comments. Other examples like the situation of the Second World War comfort women, the rape camps that were established during the war in the 1990s in the former Yugoslavia and experiences of forced marriage of Burmese and Rwandan women, however, suggest an overemphasis on the sexual elements of forced marriage. This could explain why forced marriage was understood as a form of sexual slavery. The understanding of forced marriage as a form of sexual slavery is in line with the international community's view of forced marriage at the time of the ICC negotiations. The international community simply saw forced marriage as a sexual crime. Only its sexual elements that made it the crime of sexual slavery were important. Following the Women's Caucus and/or the international community's view, the ICRC also saw forced marriage as a form of sexual slavery.

While the implicit categorisation of forced marriage as a form of sexual slavery conceals the link between the two crimes, the Arab block's understanding of sexual slavery – or of what it is not – draws attention to the connection by denying it. According to the Arab block, marital rights, duties and obligations do not constitute elements of sexual slavery. This, however, does not change the fact that some of them – such as the accepted language of marriage offer and acceptance, understandings of dowry and maintenance, irregular and temporary marriages and the ideal of obedient wives – could amount to an exercise of powers attaching to the right of ownership and cause a person to be subjected to sexual acts. Contrary to the Arab block, the Holy See became indirectly involved in the negotiations of forced marriage and sexual slavery through a proposal deleting any explicit reference to both crimes. Even though the Holy See did not refer to forced marriage, it might have had an interest in criminalising it as a marriage formed without mutual free consent violates Christian norms. The Holy See may have interpreted forced marriage as an honour crime because it violates someone's self-determination and therefore someone's dignity.

The Arab block's general understanding of sexual slavery as an exercise of powers attaching to the right of ownership and causing a person to be subjected to sexual acts is in line with the understanding first advanced by the Women's Caucus and taken up by the ICRC. The actors established a link between sexual slavery and enslavement. While both are understood as an exercise of powers attaching to the right of ownership, the difference between the two is the sexual element that is only present in sexual slavery. The Women's Caucus highlighted direct and indirect threats through which women and men can be forced into slavery. A form of pecuniary exchange is possible but not necessary. Belgium and others as well as Costa Rica, Hungary and Switzerland convey a conflicting understanding of sexual slavery that is based on ICRC research. On the one hand, they also advanced the broad view that sexual slavery includes an exercise of powers attaching to the rights of ownership and recognised contemporary forms of slavery. On the other hand, however, they linked sexual slavery to traditional forms of chattel slavery.

While the Women's Caucus and the ICRC established a link between sexual slavery and enslavement, Canada and Colombia also understood sexual slavery to be linked to trafficking in human beings as a person can be trafficked for the purpose of sexual slavery. Colombia also emphasised that the sexual element in a situation of sexual slavery has to be understood more widely than equating it with non-consensual sexual acts. It can also include sexual acts to which the victim consented due to coercion or resignation. Moreover, Colombia stressed that the crime of sexual slavery can be committed by more than one perpetrator, each with a different role that does not need to constitute a direct threat to the victim.

The US agreed with the Women's Caucus and Colombia that sexual slavery includes direct and indirect threats. However, it emphasised a pecuniary element in the exercise of powers attaching to the rights of ownership. The US further disagreed with Colombia and stressed the role of direct perpetrators. This narrow understanding of sexual slavery is contrary to the US' initially broad view of sexual slavery that focused more generally on an attack against a person and the consequential deprivation of liberty.

While forced marriage had not been well-theorised at the time of the ICC negotiations, actors' understandings of the crime reflect theoretical explanations about its causes and meanings. The Women's Caucus's accounts of women's experiences during the conflicts in Burma, Liberia and Uganda indicate that forced marriages were perpetrated to exercise control over women, to reward fighters, and to gain additional workers and combatants. Indirectly, this is linked to the aim to destroy traditional interpersonal bonds while creating new dependency structures within fighting groups and recognises that the number of forced wives increases a fighter's status in the fighting group.

How did the driving actors influence the ICC negotiations of war rape and forced marriage?

In the ICC negotiations of the definition of war rape and forced marriage, actors taught other delegations by lobbying them. In their lobbying, NGOs addressed state delegations with which they expected to have a common ground. This highlights the importance of personal contacts that created shared understandings. States' delegates, in turn, evaluated NGOs' proposals in a similar way, based on the compatibility with their governments' positions. To influence other delegations as well as the ICC negotiations as a whole, networking and working in coalitions and caucuses was important. It facilitated cooperation, cohesion and the development of common strategies to reach common goals in the face of actors' diversity, and the wide range of activities undertaken and goals aspired to reach. NGOs taught other actors by continuously raising their awareness about issues, for example through news conferences and parallel activities. NGOs also provided guidance for state and non-state actors, amongst others by distributing information such as expert documents. This was facilitated, for example, by holding regular meetings and briefings. In this way, NGOs provided the context for decisions that were to be made by states. The growing professionalism of NGOs, as states perceived it, enabled NGOs to shape state actors' identities and actions. Based on the ICRC's research, for example, Belgium, Colombia, Costa Rica, Finland, Hungary, Korea, South Africa and Switzerland proposed definitions of rape using the term 'penetration'. In addition to the ICRC, the Women's Caucus as a non-state and therefore outside actor in international law-making also succeeded in teaching its views on rape as a form of structural violence rather than as an honour crime to the US delegation. The US also followed the Caucus' advocacy in focusing on the perpetrator instead of the victim. In addition, state delegations followed the ICRC's and especially the Women's Caucus' advocacy and included various sexualised crimes in the Rome Statute as separate offences as well as constituting other crimes if the relevant qualifications are met. With regard to the crime of rape, the Women's Caucus was successful in inspiring Costa Rica to develop a definition using the term 'invasion' instead of 'penetration'.

In general, the analysis of the negotiations of the definitions of rape and forced marriage suggests that the Women's Caucus was more successful in teaching its views on rape than its views on forced marriage to states. The Women's Caucus' ability to teach its views on forced marriage to states might have been limited by the fact that, at the time of the ICC negotiations, most actors did not see forced marriage as a serious issue that needed to be addressed legally. No precedents existed. Little research had been carried out. This again indicates the prevalence of male legal structures that see sexualised violence crimes committed against women from a male point of view and approach it using male legal reasoning that emphasises the important role of normative structures in shaping actors' interests.

In addition to teaching other actors what their interests and subsequent actions should be, actors also influenced other actors in the ICC negotiations by facilitating their participation and giving a voice to those unheard. Actors financially supported small state delegations and made members of NGOs civil society members of a state delegation. Especially NGOs also engaged in capacity building and provided orientation and information such as progress reports to other actors.

Actors also influenced the ICC negotiations more directly by carrying out drafting work and submitting proposals. In addition to exercising this very direct influence, actors influenced the negotiations in more indirect ways through monitoring. NGOs also provided a platform for discussion and exchange. They facilitated compromises by mediating between different actors. In general, the high visibility of NGOs during the ICC negotiations was central to their ability to influence the definitions of war rape and forced marriage. They were active at international, regional, national and local level at all stages of the negotiation process.

Could the definitions have been different?

Based on the research findings, it can be concluded that the final ICC definitions of war rape and forced marriage were inevitable. Considering the actors involved, incompatible mandates prevented the ICC definitions of war rape and forced marriage from being different. Different mandates pulled actors in opposite directions – advancing the position of women versus maintaining male privileges, preserving international normative structures versus preserving national normative structures – which made compromises necessary in light of the required unanimity. The carefully negotiated compromise was often the only possible one.

This was the case regarding the ICC rape definition. Based on international norms and rules, a majority of delegations supported a definition using the broad and gender-neutral term 'invasion'. A minority of delegations, however, stressed that most national definitions use the concept of penetration which was perceived to be narrower but less vague than that of invasion. Mediating between the two sides, the Women's Caucus and Costa Rica developed a definition using both terms. Their proposal went beyond national rape definitions like that of the US and Colombia and combined the *Akayesu* and *Furundžija* ones. This brief outline demonstrates that the wording of the ICC definition of rape is the smallest common denominator found between actors who sought to define rape as an act of invasion or penetration. The need for unanimity can also explain the categorisation of forced marriage as a form of sexual slavery. The consensus in the international community was that forced marriage was a form of sexual slavery, leaving no space for dissenting voices and consequently no space to develop a more progressive definition. This understanding was supported by the Final Report of the Special Rapporteur on the Situation of Systematic Rape, Sexual Slavery and Slavery-Like Practices during Armed Conflict.

In addition to taking into account the actors themselves, the normative structures that influenced them, and how they understood war rape and forced marriage, the methods actors used to influence the ICC negotiations made a different outcome unlikely. While consensus was furthered by the work in coalitions and caucuses, they silenced conservative but also progressive minorities. While non-state actors taught state actors what their interests and actions should be, they were unsuccessful when an issue was not already well-established. When NGOs pushed for progress, they were occasionally stopped by states with different interests.

The above discussion demonstrates that the actors' incompatible mandates made different outcomes of the ICC negotiations in regard to the definition of war rape and forced marriage unlikely. In addition, divergent precedents between national and international law as well as within international law led to conflicting understandings of the crime of rape which made any definition but the carefully negotiated compromise improbable. In the case of forced marriage, insufficient precedents led to unchallenged unanimous understandings of the crime as a form of sexual slavery. Regarding the methods actors used to influence the ICC negotiations of war rape and forced marriage, differences in standing between state and non-state actors, the work in coalitions and the importance of a sound basis for advocacy made different outcomes unlikely.

Comparing the criminalisation of war rape and forced marriage under the ICC instruments demonstrates that the difference in the actors' approach to them – clearly defining rape as a crime in and of itself as well as constituting other crimes and categorising forced marriage as form of sexual slavery without discussing the conduct any further – was not due to the actors involved in the discussions of both crimes. Neither can the different approach be attributed to the methods actors used to influence the ICC negotiations of war rape and forced marriage. Both the actors involved and their methods were largely the same. Different approaches to the criminalisation of war rape and forced marriage also cannot be explained by the type of normative structures that influenced actors' understandings of the crimes. Actors' understandings of war rape and forced marriage were influenced by relevant international, national and personal values, norms and rules.

Instead, it appears that the different approach actors took to the criminalisation of war rape and forced marriage was influenced by the unequal standing of the two crimes in international law and in the consciousness of the international community at the time of the ICC negotiations. The crime of rape was much better established than forced marriage in times of armed conflict. War rape had already been recognised as a serious issue. Research had been carried out about its causes, meanings and consequences and precedents existed on how to address and define rape legally. This influenced understandings of actors in the ICC negotiations of war rape as a crime that can be perpetrated by and against men and women, and causes them physical and psychological harm. Actors recognised the coercive context in which war rape takes place and its limiting impact on the possibility to give free consent while also stressing the survivor's agency. War rape in itself was understood as a war crime and a crime against humanity as well as potentially amounting to other crimes such as torture and genocide. Differences in actors' understanding of war rape lay in the detail. However, it has to be stressed that before international tribunals established war rape as a crime in its own right, it was first categorised as a violation of the honour and rights of the family and then it was more broadly and adequately viewed as a breach of a person's fundamental rights. Once precedents were established, discussions of war rape were facilitated. Consequently, it can be argued that forced marriage – a conduct that had not been widely researched, discussed and legally addressed when the ICC negotiations took place – had to be categorised as a form of sexual slavery first before it could be considered as another inhumane act and a crime in its own right. Categorising forced marriage as a form of sexual slavery established it as a serious issue that had to be addressed legally. It conveys an understanding of forced marriage as a state of possessing a woman that includes causing her to engage in sexual acts. After forced marriage had been recognised as a serious issue, it was picked up by the Special Court for Sierra Leone (SCSL) and the Extraordinary Chambers in the Courts of Cambodia (ECCC)[5] and discussed further.

In the early 2000s, the SCSL took up the issue of forced marriage in times of armed conflict and developed a legal definition of and approach to it, building on the *Foča* case as precedent.

In the *AFRC*, *RUF* and *Taylor* cases, the court developed a more nuanced and complete understanding of forced marriage as a situation where the status of marriage is conferred on someone by words or deeds. It could include conduct such as abduction, manipulation, enslavement, deprivation of liberty, sexualised violence, forced labour and corporal punishment. Nevertheless, some see it as a way to survive; to protect themselves from what they consider worse acts of violence and to gain socio-economic benefits. This is especially important because forced marriages destroy traditional interpersonal bonds between forced wives and their families and communities.

5 Case 002 (Closing Order) (15 September) 2010.

In addition, the SCSL debated the categorisation of forced marriage. The Trial Chamber in the *AFRC* and *Taylor* case determined that labelling a woman a fighter's wife, forcing her into an exclusive marital relationship, depriving her of her liberty, and controlling her sexuality, movements and labour amounts to sexual slavery. The *AFRC* Appeals Chamber as well as the Trial Chamber in the *RUF* case, however, understood forced marriage as an inhumane act because it does not easily fit the category of sexual slavery. Sexual slavery does not necessarily include forcing someone into marriage and to perform conjugal tasks that include sexual as well as non-sexual duties. In contrast to forced marriage, sexual slavery does not necessarily demand an exclusive relationship between two people. Forced marriage causes distinctive harm to forced wives and results in unique stigmatisation. Another inhumane act specified as forced marriage makes it easier to recognise the crime of forced marriage as an interrelated, whole conduct. It enables courts to fully address the crime and its consequences. However, categorising forced marriage as an inhumane act arguably conceals the seriousness of the crime.

In addition to discussing the categorisation of forced marriage, the SCSL questioned whether 'forced marriage' is the best way to refer to the conduct, or if 'conjugal slavery' might be a more appropriate term to use. The advantage of explicitly naming forced marriage is that it legitimises women's experiences during and after armed conflicts as they understand them. The disadvantage is that the term 'forced marriage' arguably hides the degree of coercion and exploitation that is exercised in a forced marriage. The term 'conjugal slavery' highlights that no actual marriage takes place between the spouses as well as the seriousness of the crime. However, it also carries the negative implications of the label 'slavery' discussed above.

In the *Ongwen* case, the ICC moved beyond the discussions during its establishment, probably taking the SCSL's jurisprudence into consideration. It understood forced marriage to be a distinct conduct that causes a particular form of harm.[6] The judges established the 'imposition of "marriage" on the victim, i.e. the imposition, regardless of the will of the victim, of duties that are associated with marriage, as well as of a social status of the perpetrator's "wife"'[7] as key elements of forced marriage. Other indicators of a situation of forced marriage are restrictions on freedom of movement, sexualised violence, forced pregnancy and forced labour. In themselves, however, they are insufficient to establish the crime. The judges stressed that exclusivity is a characteristic element that distinguishes forced marriage from other crimes. The fact that breach of exclusivity can have disciplinary consequences shows that forced

6 *Prosecutor v Dominic Ongwen* (Decision on the Confirmation of Charges against Dominic Ongwen) ICC-02/04-01/15 (23 March 2016) para 92 <www.legal-tools.org/doc/74fc6e/> accessed 10 August 2017.

7 *Prosecutor v Dominic Ongwen* (Decision on the Confirmation of Charges against Dominic Ongwen) (n 6) para 93.

marriage is not predominantly a sexual crime. Moreover, the judges in *Ongwen* specify that forced wives' right to consensually marry and establish a family is violated, resulting in separate and additional harm to that caused by other crimes.[8] This example of recent ICC jurisprudence shows that forced marriage transformed from being a neglected harm that men and women suffer in times of armed conflict to a serious issue that has to be legally addressed not only in the context of other established crimes such as sexual slavery, but as a crime in its own right.

As *Ongwen* remedied the shortcomings of the ICC negotiations of forced marriage, the *Bemba* case addressed shortcomings regarding the ICC's rape definition. While the judges followed the definition set out in the ICC Elements of Crimes, they emphasised coercive invasion rather than non-consensual penetration.[9] In discussing rape as a physical invasion of a person's body under circumstances which are coercive, the judges' elaborations in *Bemba* moved away from the mechanical *Furundžija* and consent-based *Foča* definition, and resemble the conceptual rape definition advanced in *Akayesu*. As mentioned above, this approach is preferable to the ICC rape definition as it broader, illustrates the survivor's point of view, connotes a physical and psychological invasion of a person's autonomy, self-determination and integrity, and is culturally more sensitive.

Significance of analysis for post-conflict justice

As the analysis of the legislative histories of war rape and forced marriage demonstrated, international criminal law is a way to address sexualised war violence. Despite international law's universality, however, it is important that post-conflict justice takes individual cultures into account.[10]

Part of being culturally sensitive is to consider what should be a crime and how it should be defined. If an international criminal definition of forced marriage, for example, centres on individual consent, an element of the local culture is criminalised where familial consent is prioritised. International law might then be perceived as cultural imperialism and an attempt at social engineering.[11] The same holds true, however, if forced marriage is criminalised as a form of sexual slavery, or if its definition includes elements such as abduction,

8 ibid para 92–94.

9 *Prosecutor v Jean-Pierre Bemba Gombo* (Judgment) ICC-01/05-01/08 (21 March 2016) para 53, 103–104 <www.legal-tools.org/doc/edb0cf/> accessed 10 August 2017.

10 Mark A. Drumbl, *Atrocity, Punishment, and International Law* (Cambridge University Press 2007); Tim Kesall, *Culture under Cross-Examination: International Justice and the Special Court for Sierra Leone* (Cambridge University Press 2009); Sarah M.H. Nouwen, *Complementarity in the Line of Fire: The Catalysing Effect of the International Criminal Court in Uganda and Sudan* (Cambridge University Press 2013).

11 Kesall (n 10).

manipulation, enslavement, deprivation of liberty, sexualised violence, forced labour and corporal punishment, and local marriage practices include physical and psychological control, forced labour, and (threats of) force or coercion. It also holds true where international law criminalises marital rape but domestic norms and rules do not. While cultural sensitivity is a desirable objective, it has to be noted here that 'dominant cultures in particular regions [that prioritise familial over individual consent to marriage and condone slavery-like marriages and marital rape are] usually constructed from male histories, traditions and experiences'.[12] Therefore, 'the notion of culture [...] must be unmasked for what it is: a falsely rigid, ahistorical, selectively chosen set of self-justificatory texts and practices whose patent partiality raises the question of exactly whose interests are being served'.[13]

Following from this, it has to be considered if national, regional or international institutions are most appropriate to deal with allegations of (sexualised) war violence. Again, cultural sensitivity as well as the principle of complementarity suggest that these allegations should be dealt with domestically where courts are able and willing. However, it has to be kept in mind that national adoption of international norms does not automatically address problems of national proceedings such as patriarchal and patronage systems. In addition, international courts are sometimes seen to administer better justice because they prosecute international crimes as such, rather than as ordinary crimes. Countering these arguments, it has to be noted that the ICC also is subject to patronage networks and dependent on state cooperation. Furthermore, while justice and accountability do not always take priority in post-conflict situation, complementarity can encourage capacity building and the creation of physical infrastructure. Contrary to the idea that international courts administer better justice, domestic proceedings could lead to quantitatively and qualitatively more justice.[14] '[D]omestic justice systems have more resources, capacity and experience than the ICC [and] the promotion of justice is meaningful for the society concerned and reflects [its] needs.'[15] Addressing violations of international criminal law at the national level can also positively impact state sovereignty and a state's international reputation.[16]

12 Arati Rao, 'The Politics of Gender and Culture in International Human Rights Discourse' in Julie Peters and Andrea Wolper (eds), *Women's Rights, Human Rights: International Feminist Perspectives* (Routledge 1995) 167, 174; see also Kathleen Barry, 'Female Sexual Slavery: Understanding the International Dimensions of Women's Oppression' (1981) 3 (2) *Human Rights Quarterly* 44; Ratna Kapur, 'The Tragedy of Victimization Rhetoric: Resurrecting the "Native" Subject in International/Post-Colonial Feminist Legal Politics' in Sari Kouvo and Zoe Pearson (eds), *Gender and International Law* (Routledge 2014).

13 Rao (n 12) 167, 174; see also Barry (n 12); Kapur (n 12).

14 Nouwen (n 10).

15 ibid 28.

16 ibid.

Following from the question of the appropriate level of jurisdiction, it is important to ask if allegations of sexualised war violence should be dealt with by courts at all or rather by other justice mechanisms such as truth commissions (TCs). Here, it has to be taken into consideration that, amongst others, feelings of fear and shame, information deficits and rumours about institutions' mandates, insensitive behaviour of officials, and understandings of appropriate spaces for women discourage survivors from participating in transitional justice processes in general. Consequently, they silence women. International courts and tribunals as well as TCs furthermore disregard conventions of social forgetting and material understandings of justice, healing and reconciliation. This is partially overcome by traditional justice mechanisms that focus on reintegration, forgiveness and compensation. Here, however, male officials operating within patriarchal structures could create a barrier for forgiveness. Furthermore, where compensation is awarded it is not always paid, disregarding survivors' need for material support. The same challenge arises regarding some restorative justice methods. In addition to compensation, they also advance non-material ways of empowerment such as apologies. This indicates a relational approach to crime and justice, offering survivors an opportunity to re-negotiate their exclusion. As these methods address a wider range of issues regarding the crime, they are particularly relevant to survivors of sexualised war violence.[17] Future post-conflict justice approaches addressing sexualised war violence, therefore, would benefit from incorporating these key advantages.[18]

The paragraph above indicates issues regarding the legal consequences of acts of sexualised war violence.[19] Here it is important to keep in mind that understandings of justice vary. Some might understand post-conflict justice as punishing those who committed crimes. Others see it as a flowing and fluid concept that includes truth, fairness and reconciliation as well as compensation and assistance to survivors. This points towards a material and psychological way of healing and reconciliation. Additionally, it indicates an understanding of justice as being restorative rather than retributive.[20]

17 Restorative Justice Online, 'What Is Restorative Justice?' <www.pfi.org/cjr/restorative-justice/introduction-to-restorative-justice-practice-and-outcomes/briefings/what-is-restorative-justice> accessed 3 February 2013; Martin Wright and Guy Masters, 'Justified Criticism, Misunderstanding, or Important Steps on the Road to Acceptance?' in Elmar G.M. Weitekamp and Hans-Jürgen Kerner (eds), *Restorative Justice: Theoretical Foundations* (Willan Publishing 2002).

18 For further discussion see Hannah Baumeister, 'Forced Wives as Victims and Perpetrators of War Violence in Transitional Justice Processes' (2013) 21 *eSharp* <www.gla.ac.uk/media/media_307343_en.pdf> accessed 7 May 2015.

19 Drumbl (n 10).

20 Clement Aapengnuo, 'Justice, Reconciliation and Peacebuilding: Seen through African Eyes' (13 November 2009) <www.restorativejustice.org/RJOB/justice-reconciliation-and-peacebuilding-seen-through-african-eyes> accessed 5 March 2013; Tim Allen and Mareike Schomerus, 'A Hard Homecoming: Lessons Learned from the Reception Center Process in Northern Uganda: An Independent Study' (2006) <http://pdf.usaid.gov/

Based on the above discussion of different understandings of what is legally wrong, of institutions and mechanisms to address what is legally wrong, and of the consequences of what is considered legally wrong for victims, witnesses and perpetrators, the question arises whether shared understandings of it exist. The above discussion negates this. What follows is that there are no true international laws and the analysis presented in this book is irrelevant. However, it can be argued that the views of war rape and forced marriage advanced here are relevant for post-conflict justice as they reflect women's experiences as well as the nature of the crimes more adequately. As argued above, a conceptual, coercion-based definition of rape that uses the term 'invasion' is gender-neutral, inclusive and culturally sensitive. It illustrates the survivor's point of view. Defining forced marriage in times of armed conflict as a crime in and of itself reflects survivors' understandings of the conduct's distinctive and multifaceted nature and avoids a too narrow categorisation that misrepresents the nature of the offence.

This understanding of war rape and forced marriage in times of armed conflict indicates the importance of a holistic post-conflict approach to sexualised war violence. Beyond international criminal law, it is important to address experiences of sexualised war violence long-term through social, economic and legal measures. Adequate health care and education have to be available to survivors and their children in urban and rural areas. Financial assistance has to be provided if it cannot be free. Health services have to include physical and psychosocial care and formal health services have to be supplemented by informal initiatives such as support groups. Education has to take survivors' physical and psychological condition as well as their other commitments into account. It has to have practical relevance and provide survivors with the skills to succeed professionally. Adequate employment opportunities have to be created or made available to provide survivors with the opportunity to use their education. Survivors' have to be adequately remunerated to be able to provide for their families. Day-care facilities have to be created or made available to survivors' children. Support has to be provided for survivors to rebuild their social and family ties. Loans have to be accessible to survivors for them to rebuild their lives. Survivors and their families have to be provided with adequate housing. Laws and legal processes have to reflect a holistic understanding of sexualised war violence. Survivors have to be able to access justice and receive continuous legal advice and support. They have to be included in decision-making processes to build a country that learned from their experiences. Support providers have to be aware of the physical, psychological, social, cultural, political and economic consequences of sexualised war violence for the individual survivor, her family

---

pdf_docs/PNADI241.pdf> accessed 8 July 2013; Veronica Eragu Bichetero, 'Panel Four: Surviving Sexual Violence' (The Missing Peace Symposium 2013, Washington, DC, 14–16 February 2013); Rocio Silva Santisteban, 'Panel Four: Surviving Sexual Violence' (The Missing Peace Symposium 2013, Washington, DC, 14–16 February 2013). For further discussion see Baumeister (n 18).

and community as well as society as a whole, and be trained and operate accordingly. Their practice has to be holistic and empowering, build trust, confidence and control, and reduce fear and stress. Support providers have to continuously reflect on their practices to prevent re-traumatisation and trigger phenomena. In addition to their expertise, they have to have basic knowledge of other relevant disciplines to facilitate cooperation, transparency and certainty.[21]

As shown in this book, NGOs can play a vital role in law-making processes. However, their influence goes far beyond the legal realm. This makes them well-placed to teach progressive views on sexualised war violence and how to address it holistically to a variety of actors. To make their voices heard, NGOs have to make a deliberate and concerted effort. They have to build consensus and coalitions to bridge differences. They have to strengthen their research, policy analysis, documentation, communication and leadership skills and master lobbying techniques. NGOs have to understand and follow procedures. To influence decision-making, NGOs have to engage in drafting work, publish reports, organise briefing and work with the media.

21 For further information on the consequences of sexualised war violence and psycho-social as well as medical ways to address it see for example Ellen Bass and Laura Davis, *Trotz allem: Wege zur Selbstheilung* (Orlanda Frauenverlag 1991); Claudia Bommert, *Körperorientierte Psychotherapie nach sexueller Gewalt* (Psychologie Verlags Union 1993); Willi Butollo, Maria Hagl and Marion Krüsmann, *Kreativität und Destruktion posttraumatischer Bewältigung: Forschungsergebnisse und Thesen zum Leben nach dem Trauma* (2nd edn, Pfeiffer Verlag 2003); Slavenka Drakulić, 'The Rape of Women in Bosnia' in Miranda Davies (ed), *Women and Violence: Realities and Responses World Wide* (Zed Books 1994); Nancy Farewell, 'War Rape: New Conceptualizations and Responses' (2004) 19 *Affilia* 389; Vera Folnegović-Šmalc, 'Psychiatrische Aspekte der Vergewaltigungen im Krieg gegen die Republiken Kroatien und Bosnien-Herzegowina' in Alexandra Stiglemayer (ed), *Massenvergewaltigungen: Krieg gegen die Frauen* (Fischer Taschenbuchverlag 1993); Judith Lewis Herman, *Die Narben der Gewalt: Traumatische Erfahrungen Verstehen und Überwinden* (Junfermannsche Verlagsbuchhandlung 2003); Michaela Huber, *Trauma und die Folgen: Trauma und Traumabehandlung Teil 1* (2nd edn, Junfermann Verlag 2005); Ingeborg Joachim, 'Sexualisierte Kriegsgewalt und ihre Folgen' in medica mondiale and Karin Griese (eds), *Sexualisierte Kriegsgewalt und ihre Folgen: Handbuch zur Unterstützung traumatisierter Frauen in verschiedenen Arbeitsfeldern* (2nd edn, Mabuse-Verlag 2006); Médecins Sans Frontières, '"I Have No Joy, No Peace of Mind": Medical, Psychosocial, and Socio-Economic Consequences of Sexual Violence in Eastern DRC' (Médecins Sans Frontières Holland 2004) <www.msf.org/article/msf-report-i-have-no-joy-no-peace-mind-sexual-violence-eastern-drc-introduction> accessed 6 September 2012; Médecins Sans Frontières, *Shattered Lives: Immediate Medical Care Vital for Sexual Violence Victims* (2nd edn, Médecins Sans Frontières 2009) <http://cdn.msf.org.uk/sites/uk/files/Shattered_lives_June_2009_200907153528.pdf> accessed 8 July 2013; Medico International, 'Psychosoziale Arbeit in Gewaltkontexten' in Medico International, *Im Inneren der Globalisierung: Psychosoziale Arbeit in Gewaltkontexten* (Mabuse-Verlag 2005) <www.medico.de/themen/psychosoziales/dokumente/psychosoziale-arbeit-in-gewaltkontexten/1092/> accessed 6 September 2012; Diana Milillo, 'Rape as a Tactic of War: Social and Psychological Perspectives' (2006) 21 *Affilia* 196; Anne Warburton, 'Warburton Mission II Report: EC Investigative Mission into the Treatment of Muslim Women in the Former Yugoslavia, Report to EC Foreign Ministers' (1993) <www.womenaid.org/press/info/humanrights/warburtonfull.htm> accessed 6 September 2012.

Potential contributions

Firstly, contrary to the generally very positive view of the ICC rape definition, this book contributed a more critical interpretation.

Building on this and deepening the understanding of the ICC negotiations of war rape and forced marriage, this research project narrowed two gaps in the existing literature on the process of defining war rape and forced marriage in the ICC negotiations. While the process of including rape in the Rome Statute and the final definition of the crime are well-researched, the process of defining rape itself, which took place after the Rome Conference in the Preparatory Commission for the International Criminal Court (PrepCom2), is seldom analysed. This research project contributed a detailed analysis of the record of the making of the ICC from the 1994 International Law Commission (ILC) draft statute to the adoption of the Elements of Crimes in 2000. A focus was placed on the PrepCom2 negotiations as they dealt with the definition of crimes including rape rather than their categorisation discussed in the Preparatory Committee on the Establishment of an International Criminal Court (PrepCom) and at Rome. In addition to describing what happened, this research project contributed an analysis of key actors and their motivations and influences. This way, developments in states' positions on war rape could be traced, potentially indicating broader shifts in attitudes towards sexualised (war) violence against women. Identifying who pursued which interests can also facilitate effective coalition-building. An understanding of how actors came to hold certain views is crucial as a starting-point for effective engagement and advocacy to influence their positions in the future.

The second gap this research project addressed is the neglect of forced marriage in the context of the ICC negotiations. While previous research mentioned forced marriage in relation to the definition process of the crime of sexual slavery, this research project contributed an analysis of the reasons why forced marriage was understood as a form of sexual slavery, providing the background for an analysis of the SCSL's elaboration on forced marriage.

By addressing forced marriage, this research project raised awareness of the crime and how it has been dealt with outside the framework of the SCSL. Awareness-raising gives a voice to (ex-)forced wives and educates people about their experiences. A greater awareness of forced marriage is needed to develop a better understanding of the crime and to increase advocacy. It is a first step to changing how people and institutions think about and address forced marriage. As part of this necessary awareness-raising, the research project contributed towards the theorisation of forced marriage. It advanced a new explanation of the causes and meanings of forced marriage that is grounded in hegemonic masculinity theory.

The analysis of the process of defining war rape, a well-theorised and well-established crime, and forced marriage in times of armed conflict, which is still undergoing definition and theorisation, contributes to debates about the nature of international law-making by highlighting relevant factors that need to be considered in the process of internationally criminalising yet unrecognised acts of sexualised war violence. First, a form of conduct has to be established as a serious problem. Then it can be internationally criminalised in its own right. Precedents facilitate further discussions. In regard to war rape and forced marriage, their legislative histories show that (women's) advocacy is crucial in developing a more progressive understanding of women's experiences with, and the nature of, sexualised crimes. However, the legislative histories also show that the process of arriving at a progressive definition is not linear and takes time.

While this research project identified using the term 'penetration' and the reference to body parts as shortcomings of the ICC rape definition, the whole definition of forced marriage as a form of sexual slavery was seen as ill-conceived. Divergent opinions on the one hand, and non-existent precedents resulting in a lack of discussion on the other hand, were established as grounds for these misconstructions. Identifying these shortcomings and how they came about highlights that law-makers have to be aware that international law is a male structure and consider the causes, meanings, purposes and consequences of crimes when attempting to construct more adequate definitions of sexualised crimes in the future. Therefore, analysing the process of defining war rape and forced marriage in the ICC negotiations cannot only help legislators to make more adequate laws but also survivors since they eventually benefit from definitions that more adequately capture their experiences as well as the nature of a crime.

Problems experienced and areas of future research

One of the key sources of information for this research project was the official record of the ICC negotiations. It includes official documents recording the negotiations, drafting and discussions. A comprehensive record was also understood to include academic research outputs, some of which were written by people who participated in the ICC negotiations. The challenge of working with these sources was that they mostly exclude important records of informal meetings and drafting work. Official documents focus on the contribution of states. They record outcomes but not what brought them about. Therefore, this research project could not identify which individual actors within state and non-state delegations played a key role in the ICC negotiation of the definition of war rape and forced marriage and why. Even balancing the information constructed from the official record of the ICC negotiations with interviews with people who participated in the negotiations did not shed much light on questions of individual contributions. Too much time had passed since the negotiations took place. Memory had faded and personal records were passed on or destroyed. The official records of the ICC negotiations also include lists of delegates. However, those lists were not available for all meetings and focused on state actors, making it difficult to ascertain which NGOs participated.

The research indicated that the coalition approach taken in the ICC negotiations crossed traditional divides between actors in international treaty negotiations. At face value, it facilitated equality between the global North and South. When analysing the ICC negotiations, however, it became apparent that equality was superficial. Participation of actors from the global South, for example, was facilitated by Western states and NGOs by providing them with access to various necessary resources like financial support and information, potentially creating dependency structures. In addition, members of NGOs from the global North became members of Southern state delegations, influencing their identities, interests and actions. Civil society members of state delegations might also have contributed the necessary English language skills and experience in international law-making. NGOs are often perceived to diminish power distortions among actors. However, even though the Coalition for the International Criminal Court (CICC) was global in its membership, it was led by human rights groups with headquarters in the global North. Their experience and network strengthened their impact on the ICC negotiations, creating inequalities with less experienced and less well-connected organisations. Based on these comments, it could be argued that the ICC negotiations were dominated by the global North, highlighting the applicability of postcolonial approaches. Furthermore, the relevance of postcolonial theories becomes apparent when considering that the ICC negotiations were understood by some actors as an imposition of a legal reform process and an attempt at social engineering. The Arab block, for example, 'feared that the law on crimes against humanity was too ambiguous and might be used by activist judges [...] as a tool of "social engineering"'.[22] It was concerned that new laws might alter the distinct gender roles within the family structure that the states constituting the Arab block understand to be required by religious principles and cultural norms. Future research could approach the ICC negotiations explicitly within a postcolonial framework and contribute towards a thicker analysis of the actors involved, and the relevance and role of national normative structures.

Focusing on the process of defining war rape and forced marriage under the ICC raised the question whether it was more important to achieve a satisfactory overall outcome than to include certain wordings in the ICC instruments. Future research could explore more generally if what words are used in a definition of a crime is only interesting from an academic point of view but less so in practice. After all, in practice, it has to be kept in mind that meanings of terms may change from one language to the other and distinctions may exist in one but not the other.

As this research project focused on how the ICC definitions of war rape and forced marriage came about, it did not focus on the impact of the definitions. On the face of it, both the definition of war rape and forced marriage serve survivors. The definition of war rape recognises various sexual acts and

22 Darryl Robinson, 'The Context of Crimes against Humanity' in Roy S. Lee (ed), *The International Criminal Court: Elements of Crimes and Rules of Procedure and Evidence* (Transnational Publishers 2001) 65.

a range of coercive situations under which they could be perpetrated. However, it also refers to body parts which could make it more challenging for survivors to testify because they have to give a detailed account of the physical aspects of the rape. Including forced marriage in the ICC instruments as a form of sexual slavery made it possible for survivors to bring a claim for the first time. Both definitions, however, have gendered effects. The use of the term 'invasion' makes the definition of war rape gender-neutral. At the same time, however, the use of the term 'penetration' makes it male. During the ICC negotiations of sexual slavery and, by extension, forced marriage, an underlying presumption existed that sexual slavery is perpetrated by men against women. This reinforced gender stereotypes of women as victims. In addition, the categorisation of forced marriage as a form of sexual slavery narrowly focuses on sexual crimes, neglecting other experiences of women in wartime. These comments indicate that what looks like progress at first sight may not be so progressive after all, and does not fully serve survivors and their experiences. Therefore, future research needs to explicitly address in detail whose interests the ICC definitions of war rape and forced marriage serve as well as their gendered effects.

In addition to the impact of the ICC definitions of war rape and forced marriage, this research did not address the court's application of these definitions. Future research could analyse if, and to what extent, the ICC is guided by the definitions that were set out in the Elements of Crimes and how that impacts on the cases before it and the people involved.

The research project analysed the SCSL's approach to forced marriage and how it identified the nature of the conduct. This, however, took place after the ICC Elements of Crimes had been adopted. Therefore, the SCSL could not have influenced the ICC negotiations of forced marriage. Building on the findings of this research project, future research could explore whether the ICC negotiations influenced the SCSL, its instruments and jurisprudence. The legislative history of the definition of war rape show that the ICC negotiations built on the experience of the *ad hoc* tribunals which were influenced by international agreements and documents of the mid-1970s to the mid-1990s which were set off against the International Military Tribunal (IMT, Nuremberg Tribunal) and the International Military Tribunal for the Far East (IMTFE, Tokyo Tribunal) as well as international agreements of the early and mid-20th century and bilateral and multilateral conventions concluded in the 18th, 19th and early 20th century. From this it can be deduced that the SCSL might have drawn on previous discussions of forced marriage that happened in the context of the ICC negotiations. Exploring continuities and discontinuities, it would be interesting to analyse in detail which actors influenced the making of the SCSL, especially its statute, as well as its jurisprudence and the impact of the ICC negotiations on the SCSL's statute and jurisprudence. In addition, the sources of information the SCSL drew on in its elaboration of forced marriage would offer a welcome addition to the theorisation of forced marriage in times of armed conflict.

In addition to the ICC's impact on the SCSL, its impact on domestic rape and marriage laws could be analysed. Where domestic laws changed, it could be explored if and how these laws are implemented. If domestic implementation is ineffective, it could be examined why, and what could be done to improve it. Where domestic laws have not changed, the reasons for this could be analysed.

Another opportunity for future research lies in a comparative study of the impact of treaty negotiations and the judicial process of courts and tribunals on definitions of sexualised crimes. It could be argued that treaty negotiations as a political process result more easily in watered-down definitions of sexualised crimes than when a court considers a definition in the context of a case. Definitions of crimes determined in court cases, however, are unpredictable, depending, for example, on the persons involved and the context in which the court considers a case. Therefore, it could be asked whether judicial processes or treaty negotiations hold more potential to move definitions of sexualised crimes forward. Should we have lower expectations on treaty negotiations?

In conclusion, by unravelling the process of how war rape and forced marriage were defined in the ICC instruments, this research project demonstrated that non-state actors facilitated de-politicised discussions. Nevertheless, concerns regarding national sovereignty and the protection of national normative structures limited the potential of the ICC negotiations to develop progressive definitions of war rape and forced marriage that adequately reflect women's experiences as well as the nature of the crimes.

Bibliography

United Nations documents

Preparatory Commission for the International Criminal Court

PrepCom2, 'Discussion Paper Proposed by the Coordinator: Article 8, Paragraph 2(b)(xxii)' (10 August 1999) UN Doc PCNICC/1999/WGEC/RT.6 <www.legal-tools.org/doc/a4a83f/> accessed 10 August 2017.

———, 'Proceedings of the Preparatory Commission at Its Second Session (26 July–13 August 1999)' (18 August 1999) UN Doc PCNICC/1999/L.4/Rev.1 <www.legal-tools.org/doc/0b6332/> accessed 10 August 2017.

Other

Diplomatic Conference for the Establishment of International Conventions for the Protection of Victims of War, 'Final Record of the Diplomatic Conference of Geneva of 1949, Vol. 1' (Federal Political Department Berne 1963) <www.loc.gov/rr/frd/Military_Law/pdf/Dipl-Conf-1949-Final_Vol-1.pdf> accessed 15 August 2013.

———, 'Final Record of the Diplomatic Conference of Geneva of 1949, Vol. 2, Section A' (Federal Political Department Berne 1963) <www.loc.gov/rr/frd/Military_Law/pdf/Dipl-Conf-1949-Final_Vol-1.pdf> accessed 15 August 2013.

Cases

Extraordinary Chambers in the Courts of Cambodia

Case 002 (Closing Order) (15 September) 2010.

International Criminal Court

Prosecutor v Jean-Pierre Bemba Gombo (Judgment) ICC-01/05-01/08 (21 March 2016) <www.legal-tools.org/doc/edb0cf/> accessed 10 August 2017.

Prosecutor v Dominic Ongwen (Decision on the Confirmation of Charges against Dominic Ongwen) ICC-02/04-01/15 (23 March 2016) <www.legal-tools.org/doc/74fc6e/> accessed 10 August 2017.

Books

Askin, K.D., *War Crimes against Women: Prosecution in International War Crimes Tribunals* (Kluwer International Law 1997).

Bass, E. and Davis, L., *Trotz allem: Wege zur Selbstheilung* (Orlanda Frauenverlag 1991).

Bommert, C., *Körperorientierte Psychotherapie nach sexueller Gewalt* (Psychologie VerlagsUnion 1993).

Butollo, W., Hagl, M. and Krüsmann, M., *Kreativität und Destruktion posttraumatischer Bewältigung: Forschungsergebnisse und Thesen zum Leben nach dem Trauma* (2nd edn, Pfeiffer Verlag 2003).

Connolly, J.T. and others (eds), *The Adams Papers: Papers of John Adams, Volume 16, February 1784–March 1785* (The Belknap Press of Harvard University Press 2012).

Drumbl, M.A., *Atrocity, Punishment, and International Law* (Cambridge University Press 2007).

Gardam, J. and Jarvis, M.J., *Women, Armed Conflict and International Law* (Kluwer Law International 2001).

Hagen, J, *Justice in the Balkans: Prosecuting War Crimes in the Hague Tribunal* (University of Chicago Press 2003).

Huber, M., *Trauma und die Folgen: Trauma und Traumabehandlung Teil 1* (2nd edn, Junfermann Verlag 2005).

Kesall, T., *Culture under Cross-Examination: International Justice and the Special Court for Sierra Leone* (Cambridge University Press 2009).

Levie, H.S. (ed), *The Law of Non-International Armed Conflict: Protocol II to the 1949 Geneva Conventions* (Martinus Nijhoff Publishers 1987).

Lewis Herman, J., *Die Narben der Gewalt: Traumatische Erfahrungen Verstehen und Überwinden* (Junfermannsche Verlagsbuchhandlung 2003).

Nouwen, S.M.H., *Complementarity in the Line of Fire: The Catalysing Effect of the International Criminal Court in Uganda and Sudan* (Cambridge University Press 2013).

Chapters in edited books

Cole, A., 'International Criminal Law and Sexual Violence: An Overview' in Clare McGlynn and Vanessa E. Munro (eds), *Rethinking Rape Law: International and Comparative Perspectives* (Routledge 2010).

De Cesari, P., 'NGOs and the Activities of the Ad Hoc Criminal Tribunals for Former Yugoslavia and Rwanda' in Alessandro Fodella and others (eds), *Civil Society, International Courts and Compliance Bodies* (TMC Asser Press 2004).

Drakulić, S., 'The Rape of Women in Bosnia' in Miranda Davies (ed), *Women and Violence: Realities and Responses World Wide* (Zed Books 1994).

Ellis, M.S., 'The Contribution of Non-Governmental Organizations to the Creation of International Criminal Tribunals' in Bartram S. Brown (ed), *Research Handbook on International Criminal Law* (Edward Elgar Publishing 2011).

Folnegović-Šmalc, V., 'Psychiatrische Aspekte der Vergewaltigungen im Krieg gegen die Republiken Kroatien und Bosnien-Herzegowina' in Alexandra Stiglemayer (ed), *Massenvergewaltigungen: Krieg gegen die Frauen* (Fischer Taschenbuchverlag 1993).

Halley, J., 'Take a Break from Feminism?' in Karen Knop (ed), *Gender and Human Rights* (Oxford University Press 2004).

Joachim, I., 'Sexualisierte Kriegsgewalt und ihre Folgen' in Medica Mondiale and Karin Griese (eds), *Sexualisierte Kriegsgewalt und ihre Folgen: Handbuch zur Unterstützung traumatisierter Frauen in verschiedenen Arbeitsfeldern* (2nd edn, Mabuse-Verlag 2006).

Kapur, R., 'The Tragedy of Victimization Rhetoric: Resurrecting the "Native" Subject in International/Post-Colonial Feminist Legal Politics' in Sari Kouvo and Zoe Pearson (eds), *Gender and International Law* (Routledge 2014).

Rao, A., 'The Politics of Gender and Culture in International Human Rights Discourse' in Julie Peters and Andrea Wolper (eds), *Women's Rights, Human Rights: International Feminist Perspectives* (Routledge 1995).

Robinson, D., 'The Context of Crimes against Humanity' in Roy S. Lee (ed), *The International Criminal Court: Elements of Crimes and Rules of Procedure and Evidence* (Transnational Publishers 2001).

Viseur Sellers, P., 'The Context of Sexual Violence: Sexual Violence as Violations of International Humanitarian Law' in Gabrielle Kirk McDonald and Olivia Swaak (eds), *Substantive and Procedural Aspects of International Criminal Law: The Experience of International and National Courts, Volume 1, Commentary* (Kluwer Law International 2000).

Wright, M. and Masters, G., 'Justified Criticism, Misunderstanding, or Important Steps on the Road to Acceptance?' in Elmar G.M. Weitekamp and Hans-Jürgen Kerner (eds), *Restorative Justice: Theoretical Foundations* (Willan Publishing 2002).

Journal articles

Barry, K., 'Female Sexual Slavery: Understanding the International Dimensions of Women's Oppression' (1981) 3 (2) *Human Rights Quarterly* 44.

Baumeister, H., 'Forced Wives as Victims and Perpetrators of War Violence in Transitional Justice Processes' (2013) 21 *eSharp* <www.gla.ac.uk/media/media_307343_en.pdf> accessed 7 May 2015.

Charnovitz, S., 'Two Centuries of Participation: NGOs and International Governance' (1997) 18 *Michigan Journal of International Law* 183.

Chinkin, C., 'Violence against Women: The International Legal Response' (1995) 3 (2) *Gender and Development* 23.

Commission on the Responsibility of the Authors of the War and on Enforcement of Penalties, 'Report Presented to the Preliminary Peace Conference' (1920) 14 *American Journal of International Law* 95.

Copelon, R., 'Gender Crimes as War Crimes: Integrating Crimes against Women into International Criminal Law' (2000) 46 *McGill Law Journal* 217.

Cotter, P. and others, 'Affecting the Rules for the Prosecution of Rape and Other Gender-Based Violence before the International Criminal Tribunal for the Former Yugoslavia: A Feminist Proposal and Critique' (1994) 5 *Hastings Women's Law Journal* 171.

Farewell, N., 'War Rape: New Conceptualizations and Responses' (2004) 19 *Affilia* 389.

Haslam, E., 'Subjects and Objects: International Criminal Law and the Institutionalization of Civil Society' (2011) 5 *International Journal of Transitional Justice* 221.

International Human Rights Law Group, 'No Justice, No Peace: Accountability for Rape and Gender-Based Violence in the Former Yugoslavia' (1994) 5 *Hastings Women's Law Journal* 89.

Milillo, D., 'Rape as a Tactic of War: Social and Psychological Perspectives' (2006) 21 *Affilia* 196.

Ni Aolain, F.D., 'Gendered Harms and Their Interface with International Criminal Law: Norms, Challenges and Domestication' (2013) *Minnesota Legal Studies Research Paper No 13–19* <http://ssrn.com/abstract=2247623> accessed 6 May 2015.

ICC advocacy papers, commentaries, recommendations, reports and working papers

Women's Caucus for Gender Justice, 'Recommendations and Commentary to the Elements Annex and Rules of Procedure and Evidence' (June 2000) <www.iccwomen.org/wigjdraft1/Archives/oldWCGJ/icc/iccpc/062000pc/elementsannex.htm> accessed 23 January 2014.

(Research) reports and working papers

Allen, T. and Schomerus, M., 'A Hard Homecoming: Lessons Learned from the Reception Center Process in Northern Uganda: An Independent Study' (2006) <http://pdf.usaid.gov/pdf_docs/PNADI241.pdf> accessed 8 July 2013.

Médecins Sans Frontières, '"I Have No Joy, No Peace of Mind": Medical, Psychosocial, and Socio-Economic Consequences of Sexual Violence in Eastern DRC' (Médecins Sans Frontières Holland 2004) <www.msf.org/article/msf-report-i-have-no-joy-no-peace-mind-sexual-violence-eastern-drc-introduction> accessed 6 September 2012.

———, 'Shattered Lives: Immediate Medical Care Vital for Sexual Violence Victims' (2nd edn, Médecins Sans Frontières 2009) <http://cdn.msf.org.uk/sites/uk/files/Shattered_lives_June_2009_200907153528.pdf> accessed 8 July 2013.

Medico International, 'Psychosoziale Arbeit in Gewaltkontexten' in Medico International, *Im Inneren der Globalisierung: Psychosoziale Arbeit in Gewaltkontexten* (Mabuse-Verlag 2005) <www.medico.de/themen/psychosoziales/dokumente/psychosoziale-arbeit-in-gewaltkontexten/1092/> accessed 6 September 2012.

Stop Violence against Women, 'DEVAW' (14 September 2007) <www.stopvaw.org/devaw> accessed 13 August 2013.

Warburton, A., 'Warburton Mission II Report: EC Investigative Mission into the Treatment of Muslim Women in the Former Yugoslavia, Report to EC Foreign Ministers' (1993) <www.womenaid.org/press/info/humanrights/warburtonfull.htm> accessed 6 September 2012.

Conference presentations and papers

Eragu Bichetero, V., 'Panel Four: Surviving Sexual Violence' (The Missing Peace Symposium 2013, Washington, DC, 14–16 February 2013).

Silva Santisteban, R., 'Panel Four: Surviving Sexual Violence' (The Missing Peace Symposium 2013, Washington, DC, 14–16 February 2013).

Other

Aapengnuo, C., 'Justice, Reconciliation and Peacebuilding: Seen through African Eyes' (13 November 2009) <www.restorativejustice.org/RJOB/justice-reconciliation-and-peacebuilding-seen-through-african-eyes> accessed 5 March 2013.

Diplomatic Conference on the Reaffirmation and Development of International Humanitarian Law Applicable in Armed Conflicts, 'Official Records of the Diplomatic Conference on the Reaffirmation and Development of International Humanitarian Law Applicable in Armed Conflicts Geneva, 1974–1977, Vol. 15' (Federal Political Department Berne 1978) <www.loc.gov/rr/frd/Military_Law/pdf/RC-records_Vol-15.pdf> accessed 21 October 2013.

Federal Bureau of Investigation, 'Frequently Asked Questions about the Change in the UCR Definition of Rape' (11 December 2014) <www.fbi.gov/about-us/cjis/ucr/recent-program-updates/new-rape-definition-frequently-asked-questions> accessed 19 January 2015.

International Committee of the Red Cross, 'The Laws of War on Land: Oxford, 9 September 1880' <www.icrc.org/ihl/INTRO/140?OpenDocument> accessed 21 October 2013.

———, 'Project of an International Declaration Concerning the Laws and Customs of War: Brussels, 27 August 1874' <www.icrc.org/ihl/INTRO/135> accessed 13 August 2013.

Restorative Justice Online, 'What Is Restorative Justice?' <www.pfi.org/cjr/restorative-justice/introduction-to-restorative-justice-practice-and-outcomes/briefings/what-is-restorative-justice> accessed 3 February 2013.

Virginia Law, 'The Tokyo War Crimes Trial: A Digital Exhibition: People' <http://lib.law.virginia.edu/imtfe/people> accessed 6 September 2013.

Appendix 1

The legislative history of war rape and forced marriage: A timeline

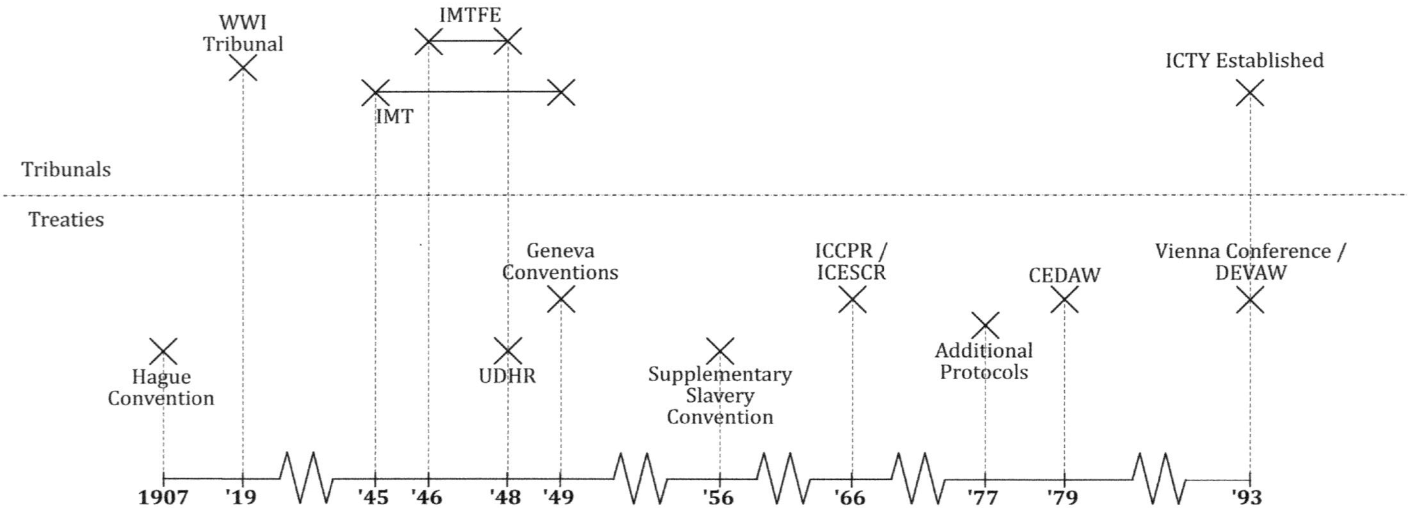

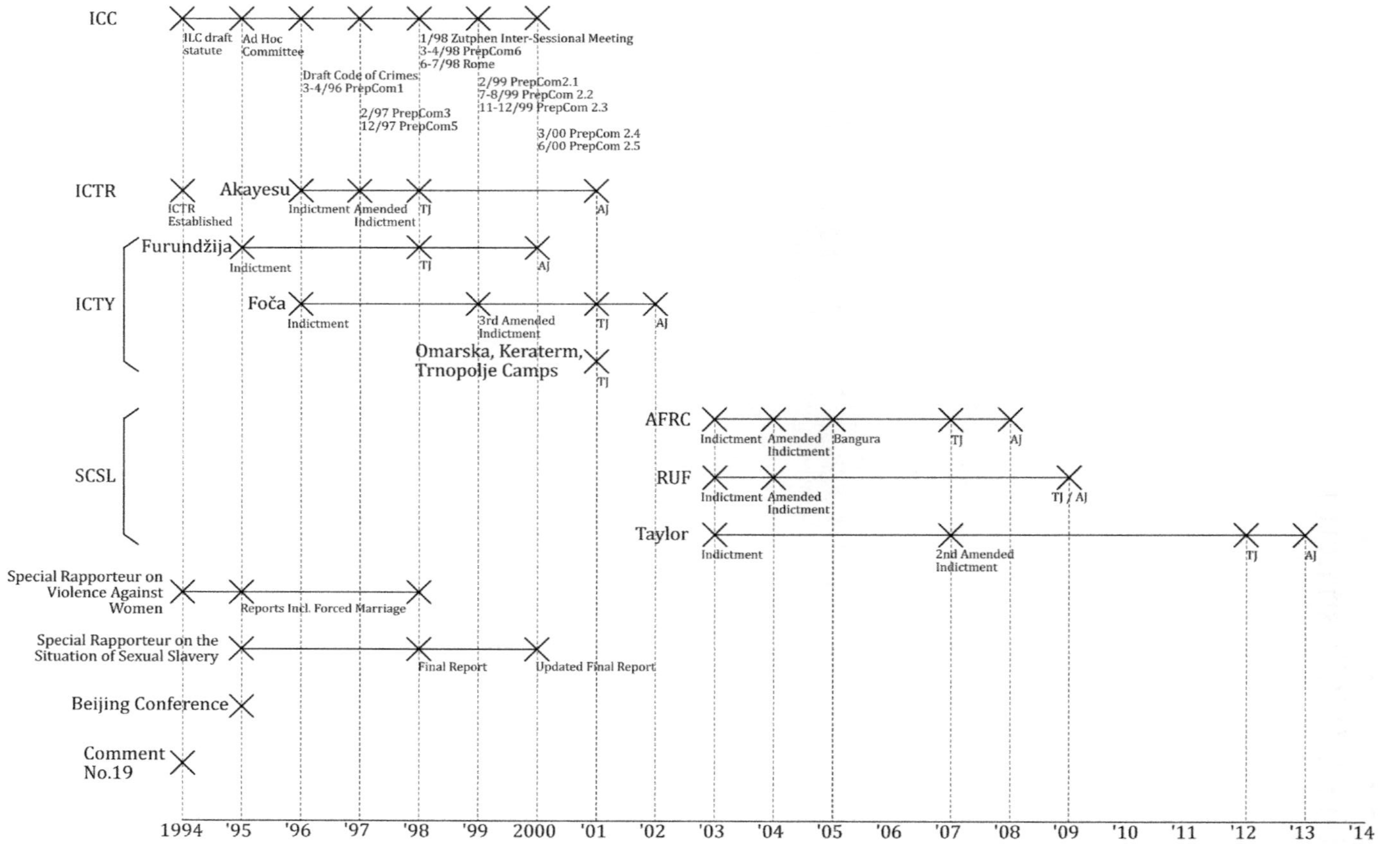
ICC
ILC draft statute
Ad Hoc Committee
Draft Code of Crimes
3-4/96 PrepCom1
2/97 PrepCom3
12/97 PrepCom5
1/98 Zutphen Inter-Sessional Meeting
3-4/98 PrepCom6
6-7/98 Rome
2/99 PrepCom2.1
7-8/99 PrepCom 2.2
11-12/99 PrepCom 2.3
3/00 PrepCom 2.4
6/00 PrepCom 2.5
ICTR
ICTR Established
Akayesu
Indictment
Amended Indictment
TJ
AJ
ICTY
Furundžija
Indictment
TJ
AJ
Foča
Indictment
3rd Amended Indictment
TJ
AJ
Omarska, Keraterm, Trnopolje Camps
TJ
SCSL
AFRC
Indictment
Amended Indictment
Bangura
TJ
AJ
RUF
Indictment
Amended Indictment
TJ / AJ
Taylor
Indictment
2nd Amended Indictment
TJ
AJ
Special Rapporteur on Violence Against Women
Reports Incl. Forced Marriage
Special Rapporteur on the Situation of Sexual Slavery
Final Report
Updated Final Report
Beijing Conference
Comment No.19
1994
'95
'96
'97
'98
'99
2000
'01
'02
'03
'04
'05
'06
'07
'08
'09
'10
'11
'12
'13
'14

Appendix 2
The CICC's structure

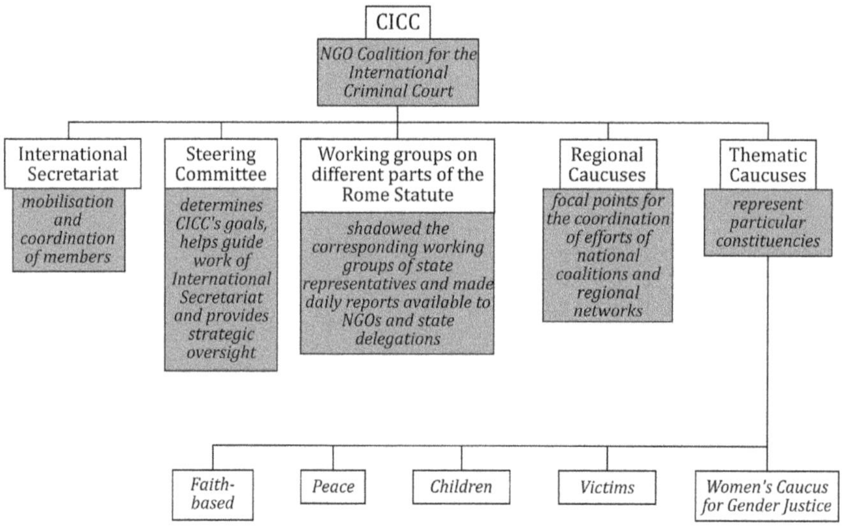

Index

www.ingramcontent.com/pod-product-compliance
Ingram Content Group UK Ltd.
Pitfield, Milton Keynes, MK11 3LW, UK
UKHW010958180926
475701UK00004B/435
9780367900267